Best Wishes
Ed Stevenson
May 2006

TEXAS OILFIELD FOLKS

(A book of Memoir)

TEXAS OILFIELD FOLKS

(A book of Memoir)

By

Ed Stevenson

To order additional copies of this book, contact:

1. Eakin Press, P.O. Drawer 90159, Austin, Texas 78709-1813

2. Your favorite bookstore

3. AUTOGRAPHED COPIES, mailed wherever, $33.00.
Mr. Ed's Texas Books, 4310 Haven Glen, Kingwood, Texas 77339
281-358-8675

FIRST EDITION
Copyright © 2005
By Ed Stevenson
Published in the United States of America
By Nortex Press
A Division of Sunbelt Media, Inc.
P.O. Drawer 90159 ✏ Austin, Texas 78709-0159
email: sales@eakinpress.com
🖥 website: www.eakinpress.com 🖥
ALL RIGHTS RESERVED.
1 2 3 4 5 6 7 8 9
ISBN 978-1-57168-050-1
ISBN 1-57168-050-0
Library of Congress Control Number 2005936786

TABLE OF CONTENTS

Acknowledgements 7
Author's Note 9

Chapter 1 : The Beginning—1904 13
             Boomtowner—1916 22
Chapter 2 : Grassburrs—1917 23
             Boomtowner—1917 30
Chapter 3 : Boomtown Cure—1917 31
Chapter 4 : Daisy—1918 37
             Boomtowner—1918 44
             Boomtowner—1919 45
Chapter 5 : Texas Bound Boomer—1920 46
Chapter 6 : Climbing Up—1920 52
Chapter 7 : Proposin'—1920 60
Chapter 8 : Nipples—1920 72
Chapter 9 : Old Straw—1921 75
Chapter 10: Pump Station—1921 83
             Boomtowner—1930 91
             Boomer's Kids—1932 92
Chapter 11: Red Devil—1932 94
Chapter 12: Health-Lax—1932 104
Chapter 13: Pusher—1932 114
Chapter 14: Jimmy—1933 119
Chapter 15: Boomtown KuKlux—1933 125
Chapter 16: The Near Miss—1933 131
             Part 1, "The Problem" 131
             Part 2, "Treatment" 139
             Part 3, "Recovery" 141

Chapter 17: Storm Cellar—1934 148
Chapter 18: Movin' Out—1935 157
Chapter 19: Boomer's Kids—1937 164
Chapter 20: Ralph—1936 167
            Boomer's Kids—1937 176
Chapter 21: Fishin' Poles—1937 178
            Boomtowner—1937 183
Chapter 22: Leaving Childhood—1937 185
Chapter 23: Saturday Morning Movies—1937 194
Chapter 24: Harvey—1940 207
            Boomtowner—1941 218
Chapter 25: Job Educaton—1ᶜ43 220
Chapter 26: Mitch—1943 228
Chapter 27: Noly—1943 245
            Boomer's Kid—1944 260
Chapter 28: Lineman—1944 262
Chapter 29: The Sweetheart—1945 276
Chapter 30: Signin' Up—1945 283
Chapter 31: Weevil School—1945 290
Chapter 32: Startin' Out—1945 297
Chapter 33: Fishin'—1945 305
Chapter 34: Runnin' Casin'—1945 314
Chapter 35: Makin' Roughneck—1945 319
Chapter 36: Movin' On—1945 329
Chapter 37: Casin' Pullin'—1947 335
Chapter 38: Doc—1952 346
Chapter 39: The Odd Couple—1954 362
Chapter 40: Trigger—1954 370
Chapter 41: Lotta Bull—1964 377
Chapter 42: The Christmas Pony—1974 398

Those Who Helped 411

ACKNOWLEDGEMENTS

THANKS TO MY wife, Marjorie, for not killing me before this book was completed and to friends as good as a man can have. These good people have read my chapters during the writing and have given repeated encouragement. I was never truly convinced, but welcomed the sentiment when they told me publishing giants were short-sighted bumblers for not snapping up this book quick as a spider grabs a fly, and spending their entire advertising budgets to sell it. Their support kept me working until the final judges, readers of books, can decide whether the writing was worthwhile.

AUTHOR'S NOTE

THIS BOOK BEGINS in 1904 at
Humble, Texas where my family merged into Texas oil. It follows
them into the Burkburnett, Texas oil boom, and the Great
American Depression of the 1930's. Continuing with my
generation, Boomtown Kids, it follows us through public school
and World War II on out into a world which had already changed far
more than any American then realized. Before and after serving in
the US Navy, I worked in the Burkburnett oilfield but, in 1945 that
former giant was only a shadow of its early robust self. Within a
few weeks I decided against the oilfield and left for college. In
1952, I was awarded a degree in Journalism from North Texas
University.

People in this book are real and their stories are true. I have set
them down on paper, not only to preserve them but because more
and more people are developing interest in the lives of early Texas
Oil pioneers. Searching through libraries and bookstores will
unearth a great amount of information about world-famous oil
millionaires and giant oil companies but little or no information is
found about the hard-working, ordinary people who made oilfield
pumpjacks go up and down. My aim in this writing has been to
preserve the ways that many early oilfield pioneers lived and to
show readers how my grandparents, my parents and my own
generation, Boomer's kids, existed and adjusted to the world which
developed around us and around Texas oil.

Old time Oil Boomers were much like their fathers and
grandfathers who farmed, ranched, fought Indians and mined for
silver and gold. They were a physical people, too busy working,
surviving and playing to sit down and write. Then, during the Great
Depression, those who might have written about their experiences

had no desire. They saw little reason to chronicle their early hardships only to add them to the misery of that horrible depression. Besides, though some of those people were God's finest creations, large numbers of them had so little education that they signed documents or checks with an "X" or painfully scribed their "mark" next to a large "X" written onto the paper.

The writing was not done to massage my ego, I am no longer that insecure. In fact, re-examining my past has been more pleasurable than I expected and pays for my trouble whether the book is successful or not. My analysis is that this book exists for three main reasons. First : To preserve stories which will die with me if they aren't recorded. Second : To share information about an earlier age with readers who are interested. Third, and most important: For reader enjoyment, without which, preservation and education seldom come about.

The stories are taken from my family's past, my own past or from the mouths of credible people who told their stories to me. I sometimes refer to them as "Memoir" but the description is not exact since I make no pretense toward being a historian and the book should not be considered as such.

Repulsive stories, describing the actions of thoroughly unsavory people, have purposefully been eliminated. Enough has already been written about them. A few names have been changed and some families have been re-structured to avoid the possibility of distressing any living person or damaging the memory of his deceased relation. My aim has been to portray the humorous, the unusual and the human qualities in lives of Texas boomtown communities and families from 1904 until the early 1980's. I have also tried to preserve the hard working and decent traits which were so typical of those people. So, except for the Great American Depression, which is hard to portray as pleasant, and the political imprint of which is still plainly visible in American life, I have omitted many unhappy parts of their lives.

Lastly, in our twenty first century, people are living much longer. So even writers like me, old as dirt, have many living contemporaries who feel honor-bound to challenge our facts and opinions. And I freely admit that many of my classmates have sharper memories, are more intelligent, and possibly more capable of describing these times than me but, so far as I know, none has yet written about it. If he has, I desperately want to buy his book and compare his memory with mine. And if our memories differ, it's likely because each of us has his own camera through which he views both past and present.

Each person's mental camera has its own unique lens, special to its owner, which portrays the image he has trained his receptors to read. We are all created differently by God and, though we see the same events, we frequently recall and nearly always interpret them differently. So I ask forgiveness of any individual who is disturbed because our recollections or conclusions differ. None of my writing is meant to aggravate, distort or to embarrass.

Where it touches my past, the book portrays things pretty much as my camera recalls them. And it was written to be enjoyed. I hope you will not only like it, but will make a place for it on your shelf. Now—START READING! Those who ignored this preface are already a chapter ahead of you!

Ed Stevenson

CHAPTER 1

THE BEGINNING—1904

"I GREW UP as a share cropper in the Tennessee hills and was 21 years old when I traveled to Humble, Texas", the old man announced. Leaning back in his chair, he grimaced because even that slight motion twisted his tender joints, prompting him to move again, seeking a less painful position. "It was back in 1904 and I'd never seen anything like an oil boom until then. That town was cranked up awfully tight and, for such a small place, it was as busy as a five-gallon hornet's nest. People also said it was 10 times as dangerous and I soon came to believe them."

He told his story in 1934, at Holliday, Texas, 30 years after it began to happen. Never a large man, he had shrunk to 120 pounds of total body weight because Rheumatoid Arthritis had attacked him two years before. He was no longer able to work at his profession, an oil well driller. Hobbling about on one, sometimes two, crutches, he had been shoved out of life's mainstream and was unable to perform any forceful physical activity except talking. Stuffing a large spoon-sized cud of Cyclone chewing tobacco into his right jaw, he talked around it, and moved only as far as necessary when spitting because any significant motion propelled acute cutting pain through his tortured bones.

Sitting gingerly in a padded rocking chair, he spat into a front yard without a single blade of grass. This was not only because his wife swept the yard daily but because their chickens ran freely over the yard, carefully plucking out each green blade which dared to emerge. While talking, he lightly stroked a self-made wooden crutch without which he could not mogate. The man's family called him "L. O.". People in Holliday called him "Louis Johnson" and I called him "Grandpa."

He thought his disease had been caused by years of working outside under severe weather conditions. And, because even doctors had only vague ideas of what caused it or how to treat it, people nodded wisely when the subject arose. Then they prescribed several folk remedies or changed the subject. Most people, including him and his family, figured he would die pretty soon anyway. But he fooled everyone by living to age eighty nine before laying down his ravaged body and moving on to a better place. His bones, along with those of his brother, Tom, lie in the cemetery at Holliday, Texas.

"I was supposed to meet my older brother in Humble," he continued. "Tom wrote saying that those people needed help in drilling up their brand-new oilfield. I had been a farmer all my life, but since 1900, we had been facing slow starvation in those Tennessee hills. Something had to be done. So, when I got Tom's letter in 1904, I sold off all my farm stuff. Leaving most of the money with relatives who agreed to care for your grandmother and my sons Tommy and Bill until I could come back for them, I struck out for Texas."

"When I got to Humble, Tom had left. The postmaster said he had gone over to Galveston and shipped out on a steamer. He wanted to investigate some oilfield down in South America, Venezuela, I think it was. And I didn't see him again for seven years."

While sitting and listening while my granddad talked, I was too young to realize the drama of what I saw. A kid of my age could only vaguely understand how hard the life of this crippled old ex-oilfield driller had become. Each and every morning, clad only in his "long johns", he crippled out of bed at five o'clock and grabbed onto a bedpost, barely managing to stand erect before his "slop jar". Finished with the first task, and accepting help from no one, he fumbled with buttons and laces, finally managing to dress his body.

Increased body movement limbered him up some, and 15 minutes after rising, he would hobble out onto his back "stoop" to select a corn cob from several which rested in an old pie tin half filled with kerosene. Back inside, he dropped the cob on top of kindling already laid in their small wood-fired kitchen stove. Placing a burning match on top, he rattled stove lids and adjusted the draw of his stove pipe. After that, he filled a battered 10 cup aluminum percolator with cold well water. Pouring in a small kitchen cup full of ground coffee, he punched up the fire a little and waited impatiently for his first cup of steaming, black Texas coffee.

Every morning he repeated this program, no matter how intense the pain, and a pot of coffee, that family's sole luxury, simmered on the stove until he went to bed at night. After eating breakfast and reading the paper, even if a Norther, a hard rain or sleet plagued Archer County, he crippled downtown to the domino hall. There he gambled seriously at dominoes, risking a quarter a "hickey" on each game of "Shoot The Moon", and normally won more quarters than he lost. I was too young to appreciate the courage with which he fought his disease and the simplicity of his direct answer to a neighbor who asked why he bothered to rise and go down town every day: "If I stay in bed just once," he responded, "I'm afraid I will never get up again."

Nobody in Holliday laughed at Louis Johnson. Most of his neighbors saved up carpentry and odd jobs for him to do. Patiently, they waited for the brief remissions in his illness that allowed him to perform the minor repair jobs they needed done. Without realizing it, I learned more from him than I thought, and when that same disease attacked me at age 42, I tried to fight as valiantly as him but didn't do as well as he did.

Because times had changed, I was lucky and Grandpa wasn't. First, I had been able to attend college and learn other ways to make a living than by hard labor. He did not have that chance. Second, in 1969 when I was stricken, medical science had learned one or two ways to limit the malady and even to slow down its crippling effect. In L. O.'s day nothing helped, except bunches of aspirin and frequent shots of Kentucky Bourbon. But, even when his wife allowed whiskey, there was seldom enough money to purchase either one.

L. O. was almost penniless when he died in 1976. But, like many of America's Oilfield Pioneers, he had shown his family the way in which a man could earn a minimal living, endure true hardship, and still die with dignity. He managed to pave the way for his children to have better life choices than he did, even though some of them didn't choose correctly. It is hard for a man to accomplish more in life.

"Humble was a fast moving place", Grandpa went on. "Those folks were just beginning to chew, and were havin' trouble swallowing, this big oil boom right in their own back yard. For me it was a case of "make-do" or starve, so I hired out to a rig-building contractor who was "throwin' up" 60 to 90-foot high oil derricks just as fast as us rig builders could nail them together. Customers were standing in line to buy those derricks because every oilwell which is drilled has to have one. We built those tall wooden structures from 3 by 12 inch "loblolly" pine timbers, some as long as 14 feet."

"Long lines of wagons hauled giant virgin logs out of the vast Big Thicket piney woods into what folks called "popgun" sawmills located here and there around the county. Rig timbers and other kinds of lumber were sold by the wagonload just as fast as logs could be milled. Humble people joked, saying the lumber was 'kiln-dried' because those logs were killed in the woods and dried on wagons on the way out to well locations."

"Rig building crews worked 12-hour days and climbing around in derricks all day long with no safety lines made workdays pretty strenuous. We had to stick to our perches like monkeys, holding on with one knee or one hand and a lot of imagination while balancing heavy timbers with the other knee or with body weight. All the time we were swinging those heavy rig axes with whichever arm was loose. Rig axes were what we used to trim and notch those heavy planks. Each one had a large hammer head fitted opposite its blade, like an Indian tomahawk, but they were twice as big and heavy as regular carpenter's hatchets. The hammer head was used to drive long "30 and 60-penny" timber spikes, some longer than the lead pencils you kids use in school. And the workers on the ground never stopped pulling timbers up, sending them a lot faster than we could fit and nail them together."

"Rigger pay was four dollars a day, a lot more than I had ever made before, and roughly a dollar more than other oilfield hands got. But those wages never went up and there was a good reason they were high. It was a punishing business that most men couldn't stand for long. Not only was it brutal and body-bruising labor, but a week seldom passed without some unlucky worker falling through the derrick, "down the hole", to be crippled or killed."

"When funerals were held, rig builders working near the church or the cemetery slowed down for 30 minutes, allowing riggers who wanted to, to visit and pay their respects. After that it was "business as usual" all over again." When I climbed down at the end of my second Saturday I told the timekeeper that if his boss had no other kind of work for me, I wanted to 'draw down my time'."

"He never answered. He just reached into his shirt pocket and pulled out his time book, showing me the hours he had written down. When I nodded my head up and down, he reached to the floorboard of his buggy, shoved aside a double-barreled ten-gauge shotgun and pulled out a money box. Laying it on the seat, he counted out my wages and handed them over. That took me out of the rig-building business forever and I have never regretted it for a single day."

"Oilfield people," he continued, "had exactly the same needs as other folks. We had to eat, dress and sleep just like Texas people but a few Humble residents, like folks in other Boom towns, didn't care whether we ate and slept or not. Most of the merchants and many original settlers loved boom-time money, but a few bad apples looked down their noses at oilfield workers, calling them nuisances and sometimes even bad people. Others who were really mouthy about it, called us oilfield trash. And that description was true just often enough to make things hard on honest and hard-working oilfield hands."

"In the early 1900's there were no government welfare agencies waiting around to pass out food stamps, beds, medical treatment and clothes to needy folks. If there had been, they would have drawn plenty of customers, but welfare back then simply didn't exist. Still, many good Americans of that time, and especially Texans, were kind and helpful to sick people who were truly unable to work. But able-bodied people who were hungry, Texans included, were expected by society to find jobs and work hard at them so they could buy their own groceries. No one was allowed to loaf without a good reason. Vagrancy, which most towns declared was being able-bodied but broke and having no job or any money, was considered a crime. So, during those early oil booms, you never saw gangs of loafers squatted around on stumps and benches spitting and whittling, or holding up signs to ask for food."

"Many people, in modern times will act pitiful and beg for a living, knowing that the good folks of Texas won't let them starve. But back in 1904 they could not have survived. Those who were polite might have gotten a free meal or a beer, along with a tip on where to find a job. And maybe, just maybe, they might have gotten two free meals but they were generally warned that having a job was the price they had to pay for hanging around. If they didn't find one, they must hit the road. Texas lawmen seldom wasted money by throwing vagrants in jail. They were much more apt to escort them to the edge of town and give them a good shellacking as a proper incentive to keep on going."

"Most lawmen back then favored shooting a guy who was caught in the act of committing a crime as the easiest way to solve that problem. It was a good lesson to other hardcases hanging around and a lot less expensive than jailing and trying them. If they didn't like the looks of a tough-looking guy and couldn't catch him committing a crime, but figured he might, they would fine him, walk him to the edge of town an' tell him so long. That way, they figured some other city or boomtown could handle the problems he might bring with him."

"After looking for three days, I found a blacksmith shop near one of the San Jacinto River crossings. The owner offered me two dollars a day plus bed and board for dressing oilwell bits. I learned the business in a hurry and after two months could heat, point up and temper any kind of a drill bit those old cable tool drillers needed.

My new boss and I got along, understanding each other very well, so I located a small house over near Moonshine Hill. Renting it, I sent back to Tennessee for my family."

Several months later, after my Grandmother and my Uncles, Tommy and Bill had arrived in Humble, Grandpa took a new job as bit dresser on a cable-tool drilling rig. This boss set up a forge near the rig and wanted him to keep a fire burning day and night so he could heat and dress bits for an entire drilling company, which kept several rigs running in that part of the field. He also dressed bits for several of his friends who were always drilling "Wildcat" wells. After heating those tools on his forge Grandpa hammered them back into proper cutting shape. After they were dressed and re-tempered, each one was ready to go back down in the hole.

He also helped out with cable-splicing crews. Always skillful with his hands, he soon learned how to wield their heavy steel marlin spikes and within three weeks was splicing, binding and tying off all sizes of steel cable. Cables, or 'wirelines' were plentiful in every oilfield, and are just as important there today. Rigging-up those heavy derrick "traveling blocks" and connecting them to the crown blocks, or "sheaves", on the top of the derricks at new well-sites was a never-ending task. Owners whose employees weren't well educated in such things, hired Grandpa to do them and he was able to earn extra money at splicing and rigging as long as he worked in the "oilpatch".

Within 18 months, L. O. quit dressing bits and moved up onto a derrick floor where he began learning to be a floor hand, or "roughneck." A roughneck was, and still is, the name given to any driller's helper. A year later he was shifted over to be a boiler fireman, and eight months after that he finally graduated. His boss promoted him to be driller on a Cabletool rig after a regular driller showed up too drunk for work. But it was only five or six more years before the Cabletool drilling method began losing ground to a new method called "rotary" drilling. Rotary drilling used heavy steel drillpipe to turn an oil well's drillbit.

Recognizing that Rotary drilling was the future of all drilling, Grandpa switched over to one of those rigs as soon as possible, and quickly became proficient in the most modern drilling procedures. Six years later, in 1916, he traveled North to a new boom, right on the bank of Red River at Burkburnett, Texas near Wichita Falls. This boom quickly became the subject of every wildcatter's speculation, and boomers swore it was the biggest and wildest boom since Spindletop, near Beaumont.

"I'd heard about Burkburnett being a promising oilfield, and decided I ought to come up here to check it out for myself," L. O. said. "The Humble field was tailing off and Burk promised plenty of work for a long time, so I came on up. When I got here it was already bigger than Humble ever was and was growing by the week. Two years later it was the most active field anywhere and twice the size. It also had twice the crime rate of any other oil boom except maybe Spindletop or Batson in Southeast Texas. This fast growth, along with an equally fast crime increase, kept on until the field peaked out in 1922."

A few cable tool rigs were still operating in Burk when he got there but rotaries were vastly preferred and L. O. was able to start out on one. As soon as he had learned the normal completion techniques for wells in North Texas geological formations, he was promoted to driller. Between wells and shifts, he spliced cable and helped drilling companies rig up at new well sites. There was always a shortage of people who knew how to spot rigs properly on their pads and who could properly thread steel cable onto the massive steel traveling blocks used to lift the millions and millions of pounds of oilfield drillpipe necessary to drill each well.

Occasional cable tool rigs were still being used in Burk when World War II broke out. This was because a "poreboy" operator could drill a shallow well cheaply with fewer hands if no one was in a giant rush. But time was money in the 1917 Burkburnett oil boom, just as it is today. If a man didn't quickly drill on his lease back then, competitors would place wells on every lease line he had, trying their best to suck all his oil out of the ground. Experienced wildcatters learned to reverse this process by drilling along their lease lines in a hurry. By doing so, they could give other Wildcatters the privilege of worrying about whose oil was filling the ever-growing number of storage tanks and lengthening pipelines which pointed toward the nearest refinery or railroad.

In 1945, just before joining the US Navy, I saw my last cable tool rig in operation. It was drilling in the Southwest Burkburnett field. By then, most oilfield workers laughed at cabletoolers, calling them "rope-chokers" and "jarr-heads". This was because of the old cable tool driller's habit of standing by his wellhead, one hand on the cable, so he could feel the bit action as the heavy "jarrs" rose up and dropped ponderously down onto the bit at the bottom of his well.

L. O. lived and worked in Burk throughout the first world war. Occasionally, he would accept a choice drilling job in one of the other hot oilfield boomtowns, but his family remained in Burk. He kept on drilling wells until 1933 when oil "got real cheap" and drilling slacked off. Then he hired out on a lease-pumping job offered by an independent well owner named Perry Boyd. That lease was located near Dad's Corner, six miles southeast of Holliday in Archer County. I asked him once how many wells he had drilled. He said he had lost the count but that it was "way less than a 1000."

He had been pumping for a year when arthritis struck him down as brutally as if he'd been run over by a truckload of oilfield pipe. He told me that, one morning, as he walked across the "prairie", he took a simple step forward and his right hip quit working, suddenly giving away. Arthritis had moved in and he was never able to earn significant money again. The loathsome disease didn't kill him but he died with it.

BOOMTOWNER—1916

"IT HAPPENED HERE in Burk when I was nearly twelve. The year was 1916 or 1917. We were walking home from school and that oil well was a quarter mile away, but the explosion when its boiler blew up, was loud enough to scare us. We felt the concussion through the air."

"I looked toward the sound and saw the large iron apron that had blown off the end of the boiler's firebox. It was spinning round and round as it rose upward and it kept on spinning until it went out of sight."

"The blast killed one worker and badly scalded several others. The fireman, closest to the boiler, was blown to bits. My father worked the daylight tour (pronounced "tower" in the oilfield), and his well was near there. He and several other drillers shut down their wells, taking their crews over to help perform any necessary rescue work. That night he came home late, and when they thought I couldn't hear, I heard him tell my mother some of the details they considered too upsetting for a young girl to hear.

For whatever reason, the fireman on that well had allowed too much steam pressure to build up in his boiler. The blowout plug hadn't worked right, and when pressure built up high enough, the boiler exploded. Dad told my mother that his crewmen had carried grocery market baskets on their arms and walked the complete area around that well for a hundred yards on all sides, carefully searching the ground for body parts, and carrying back everything they found so it could be turned over to an undertaker."

Ruby Stevenson,
Author's Mother

CHAPTER 2

GRASSBURRS—1917

"WE HAD ONLY lived in Burkburnett a few months. I was eight and Charley was ten. This was back in 1917 and America had just entered the war against Germany. The main topics we heard people talking about were the oil business and how long it would take American Doughboys to whip the Kaiser after getting a few decent shots at his German soldiers."

"I was the youngest of seven kids and our mother had worked awfully hard at trying to keep us alive long enough to grow into decent citizens. It was a difficult and mostly thankless job and Mom was a harried woman, nervous and half sick most of the time, always needing more rest than she got."

"One day, desperation weighed her down and she decided to risk letting me out of her sight for two hours while Charley looked after me. The problem was, this plan sounded better to her than anyone who knew how Charley could be when he got away from home. He was older and stouter than me. But he also found trouble five times as often as mom ever heard about because he was good at hiding stuff from her. If she had asked someone who really knew him, they would have told her to put me looking after him."

"We hadn't lived in Burkburnett long enough to settle the problems of fighting and mixing well with local boys. Normally, we either fought, threatened to fight, or took off running when we met them, depending on the numbers involved. Mom knew about some of this, but what she didn't know was that Charley was awfully bad to start fights. He knew as well as me that he wasn't that much of a fighter but he counted on me to join in and help in case he started to lose. Even when I did, both of us sometimes got whipped."

"Mom decided to send us out into that bright sunshiny Burkburnett morning while she laid down for a much-needed nap. Her idea was that we could play while she rested, secure in the knowledge that Charlie would watch me. As it turned out, all three of us were luckier that day than we might have been. The weather was nice and crisp; dry, but not extra hot. Charlie and I walked out into a nice early-fall day of North Texas weather but our Mom was lucky. She was asleep and had no idea what was happening until later."

"After leaving the house, Charley and I walked several blocks, out to the end of our street. At the corner where it tied into West Main, we walked down Main, past the railroad station to the edge of town, watching with interest as heavy traffic moved from the railroad tracks out into the Northwest Burkburnett field. Since we didn't meet any other kids, there were no fights and we had plenty of time to watch everything closely."

"West Main was the biggest street running from Burk out into the field and it was loaded to the brim with wagons and trucks. There were also many large boiler and machinery floats being pulled by long double-teamed mule spans, big high-wheeled wagons full of heavy rig timbers and countless loads of oilfield pipe. Horsebackers, buggies, cars, hacks and trucks filled up any open space on the road. Large numbers of men walked along, some of them resembling tramps because they carried bedrolls and wore long heavy coats. They ambled slowly along the road, often sticking up their thumbs at passing vehicles. When a driver nodded permission, they chucked their bedrolls up on the load, climbed on behind and, leaned back to rest, letting their feet swing."

"Heavy traffic had wallowed out great holes in the road and everything moved slowly. Car and truck horns honked continuously and men yelled constantly. Heavy draft horses grunted and dug in with their feet, trying hard to keep those heavy loads moving. Mule skinners swore, shouted and whistled at their animals, popping those long blacksnakes near their ears. Sometimes, forgetting the animals, the skinners and truck drivers shouted and swore at each other. It amazed both of us that all these grown men had worked themselves up into such a state of excitement."

"They rushed hard and when a breakdown happened, the four or five nearest drivers and teamsters would stop and climb off their rigs, working hard to help the disabled rig start up. If they couldn't get it going in a hurry, they shoved it, no matter whether loaded or empty, over into the bar ditch, out of traffic so others could move on. All these Boomers ran hard and fast at performing their jobs, whether it was leasing land, drilling for oil, setting tanks and laying pipeline, or selling oil after it was pumped up out of the ground. After I was older, I read about the gold rush days in California and I figure those men in Burk were traveling at about the same pace as those gold miners."

"After tiring of the traffic, we turned back toward town and Charley discovered a big patch of healthy grassburrs growing around a depression in the bar ditch where a pool of water had nourished them through a long summer dry spell. Most of those sticker heads held eight or more burrs apiece and were well cured out, just beginning to fall off. They were at the exact stage for us to throw at each and would stick like glue onto any clothing or skin they touched.

We picked about two dozen heads apiece and entertained ourselves by throwing them back and forth at each other. This furnished us with 10 minutes of fun before we tired, and before walking back toward town, we laid in an extra big supply, in case we met some kids we needed to fight or pester."

"We walked all the way down to the middle of Burk's Main Street and still didn't have a single fight. Mom would have been proud of us, but the reason we stayed out of trouble wasn't because we planned it that way, it was because we had met no other kids. So, walking, watching traffic and listening, we threaded slowly through heavy foot traffic along the few strips of wooden sidewalk which had been built along Main Street and finally stopped in front of the Burk Cafe.

This was a crowded restaurant whose owner had thrown away

the keys when he bought it. A business that never closed had no use for locks and keys. Half the Boomers in town had left their families when heading to the oilfields. They had no homes in Burk where women would cook for them. A few ate in boarding houses but they mostly ate in cafes, or cooked over campfires like hoboes. Just before leaving for work, the men who could afford it would stop in at the Burk Cafe to buy a sack lunch to carry out to work. If they weren't too broke, they would also order whatever special the restaurant served up that day and this would probably be their only hot meal."

"Without taking off their hats or caps they sat at homemade wooden tables that had never seen linens and paid for whatever they ordered when the waitress brought it over. Stowing the lunch sacks on the floor between their feet, they ate those hot meals with relish, and when finished, they grabbed their lunches then shouldered their way out the front door onto the sidewalk into whatever kind of Texas weather lay in wait. Then they would walk or ride out to their oilfield jobs. After working a 10 or 12 hour shift, the majority came straight home to grab a bite to eat, and take a hot bath if possible, then they climbed into bed for a sound sleep. Next day, they repeated the same routine."

"We stood in front of the restaurant for five minutes, enjoying the rich smell of greasy hamburgers blended with onions and steaming black Texas coffee. As we watched, the restaurant's screen door slammed loudly behind every patron who went in or came out. After several minutes, Charley decided it might be fun to slap a grassburr head onto the seat of one of those crude oil stained fannies just before the door slammed shut behind it. He tagged the very next one and we grinned delightedly at each other, enjoying a grand moment. Then, like those Frito-Lay potato chips advertised on TV, he couldn't stop with just one. With practiced motion, he tagged another patron and we snickered again as that one also walked inside without noticing the difference."

"It was my turn next and I copied his style precisely, tacking a big stickerhead stem five inches below a wide black leather belt just as it disappeared into the cafe. Then we decided to stick them all, but even at our young ages, we realized that time was quickly running out. So Charley motioned for me to hold the door open for everybody, and moving carefully so they wouldn't catch on, he tagged those men until we ran out of grassburrs."

"We worked quickly, me smiling to attract the men's attention and beckoning them inside. Most of them thanked me and not one ever looked back to see Charley who smirked and snickered as he tacked the stickers on and we were finished within a minute. Men who passed by on the sidewalk saw us, then grinned and poked each other. Shaking their heads, they kept on walking. None of them wanted to get stuck but they liked the idea of what we were doing."

"After finishing, Charley and I trotted down the sidewalk, laughing back and forth together. We had traveled a half block from the cafe when a large work-hardened hand grabbed each of our collars from behind. Lifting us off the ground, those big hands turned us around to face their owner. Then the large head which owned those ham-sized hands began yelling forcefully enough to throw sprays of spit into our faces."

"Charley had no defense. No kid can act or look innocent with several burrs sticking to the front of his shirt. But my case was even worse. When the guy pointed his chin at my chest, after denying my guilt, I looked down and found an entire burrhead, still with its six-inch tail, hanging off my front."

"The big guy yelled and complained until he ran out of breath then announced he was going to turn us over to the law. Dragging us each down the sidewalk by an arm, he yelled all over for the Chief of Police. And I was glad when he finally found him because he wasn't pulling us gently. Soon as the Chief crossed over Main Street to us, that big guy began to yell at him, and in no time at all, 20 or 30 grown men had stopped to watch the show."

"Burk's Police Chief was a tall man, with intense blue eyes and a gray Western hat. He listened in silence until the big guy was finished. Then he asked him to turn us loose. But that big slob objected, swearing we would run off if he did. And we might have, but that lawman reached down and took me by my free arm then looked straight into my eyes. I couldn't read his expression but he didn't seem to be a bad person, and if he was mad at us, it didn't show."

"'Son, If I turn you loose, will you run away?'"

"No, sir," I said, because I trusted him more than the big loudmouth who had caught us."

"What about this other boy, the Chief continued, 'I expect he's your brother. Will he run away?'"

"No, sir," I answered, knowing Charley wouldn't leave without me."

"The lawman then stood up and looked that big man straight in his eyeballs. Poking at his chest with a large forefinger, he ordered in a flat tone, 'You turn these boys a-loose'."

"The grip on our arms dropped away and the big man stopped talking. That lawman reached out, and as he turned me to face him I noticed that he wore a gold ring just like my dad's which had a Masonic square and compass on its top. He grinned a little, and bending lower, asked our names. I told him and he asked who our father was. I told him it was L. O. Johnson and he grinned a little more."

"Then he asked if we had tacked stickerburrs on any men's seats when they entered the cafe. We said we had, but wouldn't do it any more. He smiled then, and straightening up, told us we had better go on home and be certain to tell our dad exactly everything that had happened."

"When the big guy heard this, he began to gripe all over again and kept at it until the lawman asked what he thought should be done. That big ugly browbeater wanted him to put us in jail. The Chief's blue eyes narrowed, then turned flat and his lips tightened. 'I expect', he said in rebuke, 'that if I did put them in jail, they would just slip out between the bars and I'm not a-goin' to do it."

"Then he pointed his long forefinger at the big guy again but wagged it under his nose this time. 'Now, I have handled this problem and you have tended to all the business here that you need to see about. I suggest you go on your way, an' look after something else, because if I hear anything more about this, you are the one that I'll throw in the can.'"   Austin Johnson, Author's Uncle.

Artist Pat Conroy, Atascocita, Texas

BOOMTOWNER—1917

"I CAME TO Burk in 1917, shortly before America entered World War I. The boom was going full blast and newcomers had a hard time finding houses to live in. Hotels rented rooms on eight-hour shifts, and most Boomtowners slept in bedrolls, lived in tents, or built themselves a temporary shelter. I was single, planning to hang around, so I came prepared and bought a tent.

Reaching tent city I strung up my tent and was attaching a brand new stovepipe ell through the back vent hole. Needing a pair of pliers, I left my pipe hanging in its metal collar and walked around front to get my tool. When I got back, the stovepipe was gone.

"Well, it wasn't hard to find. Just two spaces up from me I saw a big guy takin' a rotted-out stovepipe off his tent wall and my new ell was laying on the ground at his feet. He was some bigger and older than me, but I didn't see anything around that he could use for a weapon, an' figured I could take him anyhow. Just in case, I picked up my claw hammer and walked over to where he was tearin' up his old burned out stove pipe while tryin' to pull it off."

"I told him he'd best try to save it because if he tried putting my new pipe up on his tent wall that I was going to knock it off with my hammer, an' if he got in the way, he might get hurt. He stepped back an' watched, but never said a word as I picked up my pipe an' took it home. I never had a minute's worth of trouble out of him afterward, so I guess he believed me."—Les Tuel, Boomer

NOTE: Les Tuel was a 6' 1" 210 pounder when I last saw him in 1950. He was the father of my schoolmate, Rex, who died in 1986. Les was a quiet man, widely known as an honest person who always kept his word. I never heard him curse.

CHAPTER 3

BOOMTOWN CURE—1917

CLOYCE TOLD HIS driller he had to go in because he just couldn't hack it anymore. In the last three days he'd swallowed three and a half large flat tin boxes of aspirin and the pain was worse than ever. His right cheek had swelled so much that people looked back after passing by, and his head felt as if it might snap off.

Saying he'd be back when he could, Cloyce walked carefully out to the road to stick up his thumb at the first passing vehicle. It was an empty pipe truck headed toward town and slowed just enough for him to hop on the running board when its driver motioned. With his right hand Cloyce held tightly to the metal headache bar behind the truck's cab. With his left he cradled the swollen jaw.

Many people would have taken the late train to Wichita Falls when the truck dropped him off in town, but it wouldn't run for 30 more minutes and he didn't feel up to fighting for a place on the train. It was normally so loaded that people hung all over the sides and sat on top, even during bad weather. It was also a rough ride, lasting an hour, with 50 or 60 stops. Then, after getting to Wichita, he would have to walk around in an unfamiliar city asking for directions. He was hurting too bad to put up with all that and decided to kill his pain an hour sooner by using available medical treatment in Boomtown.

The year was 1918. The time was late in a hot dry summer and the place was Burkburnett, Texas, a small farming and ranching community which, overnight, had turned into an oilfield town seething with almost 40,000 people. Most of those who walked its streets were strangers who cared a lot more for their own interests than those of anyone else. After the truck dropped him off in town, Cloyce continued to shelter his swelled cheek with his left hand while picking a careful path in as straight a line as possible through the dense crowd milling up and down West Main Street. He traveled carefully because pain washed completely over him whenever he stepped into a depression or bumped against anything. Making haste slowly, he looked a block ahead, farther East on Main, and finally saw his destination.

The shop sat on the South side of the street, a block past of the railroad. He first recognized it by its standard horseshoe-shaped sign, then by a smaller wooden sign, painted white and shaped like a tooth, which hung directly underneath. Walking through the open door, he first heard, then, as his eyes adjusted to inside light was able to see his Dentist. He was a large man, methodically swinging a 10 pound sledge down onto a red hot oilfield drill bit.

Moving carefully toward the forge, Cloyce saw that his Blacksmith wore an old-timey leather apron. He also wore knee-high laceboots and trousers fashioned of rough material, but no shirt. Sweat dripped steadily from his nose and he deftly swung the hammer as quickly as his helper, using long handled metal tongs, re-positioned the bit for another blow. The forge cast weird shadows on the wall as Smith and helper moved in strangely syncopated rhythm, attentively "dressing" the rapidly cooling bit.

Cloyce saw the Smith glance toward him but the hammer never stopped swinging and he didn't expect it to. Early in life he had learned that blacksmiths never quit until the job was finished or the metal had cooled to a point that it must be placed back in the forge. They always struck as long as the iron was hot.

Nine more hammer blows resonated against Cloyce' sore jaw before the Smith motioned his helper to roll the finished bit over with others laying in a corner. Placing the hammer in its rack, he reached for and pulled the tin cap off a double-walled water cooling can. Filling the lid half full of icy water, he slowly drank it down.

Then he moved to a wooden half-barrel used for quenching hot metal and bent down to face it. Reaching in with both hands, he splashed double handfuls of water over his face and chest, then he stood up, shaking his head rapidly like a dog. Rubbing briskly with a towel he looked straight into Cloyce's eyes

"Which tooth?"

Wordlessly, Cloyce used his protective hand and touched the next to last molar in his upper right jaw. The Smith nodded, motioned him to follow and led him up to an ancient medical treatment chair which had been placed near the front window for better light. Its seat, arms and headrest were somewhat clean but the rest was so covered with black shop dust that no one could have guessed the original color.

Cloyce sat where the Smith pointed and slowly opened his mouth for the large thumb and forefinger which clasped, then twisted only once before making him howl. Pulling out his fingers and turning Cloyce' head toward the light he pried open a reluctant jaw and peered in. Then he wasted no words. "It needs to come out. I charge 15 silver dollars! In advance! You wanta pull it?"

Pathetically, Cloyce focused on the Smith's face, nodded his head "yes" and reached for his money. Turning to a homemade wooden cabinet standing against the nearest wall, the Smith pulled out a drawer extracting an almost full quart of rye whiskey and a half pint tin cup. Pulling the bottle cork, he poured the cup half full and handed it to Cloyce, motioning him to "bottoms up." Watching closely, he reclaimed the vessel after Cloyce had finished. Expertly pouring a smaller shot for himself, he tossed it down with no change of facial expression and placed both items back in the cabinet.

"How much do you drink?"

"Not much. Why?"

"Then you have drunk enough. It'll start workin' in 10 or 15 minutes. Keep your seat an' I'll get things ready."

Dominated by pain, Cloyce continued to pet his jaw, watching miserably as the Dentismith swapped the heavy leather apron for a once white butcher's apron. Even though it was spotted here and there with spots colored from red to brown to absolute black, the cloth apron had a more sanitary appearance than the other. Back at his cabinet, the Smith pulled out a metal basin into which he placed several types of hand forged probes and pliers and poured a cup of rubbing alcohol over them. His movements were swift and sure and this meager attempt at sanitation, plus the fact that he had begun to wash his hands with soap, reassured Cloyce who, right then, needed all the support he could get.

Finishing his preparations the Smith walked out onto the worn and uneven wooden sidewalk for a smoke. Taking his time, he rolled a homemade, smoked it down almost to his fingers, tossed down the butt when finished and smashed it with his heel. Then he stopped a pair of passing roughnecks. After a brief conversation, he walked back in, trailing them behind. Cloyce heard them repeating their agreement as they neared his chair.

"We get a dollar apiece, and a drink of rye?"

"That's the deal. Just do what I tell you. I pay when we're finished an' I pour the whiskey." Then he looked at Cloyce, "You feelin' the rye any?"

Cloyce nodded his head "yes" then leaned his head back against the iron head rest atop the chairback when the Smith instructed. Picking up a long towel, he wrapped it securely around Cloyce' forehead, tying it snugly behind the rest.

"We're ready now. I'm goin' to have these fellers hold onto your arms. Don't fight any more than you can help an' we'll be through in a minute."

Cloyce hesitated, summoning up will, then widened his mouth when requested. First he felt, then tasted bitter alcohol and iron, as the puller, which the Smith had re-shaped from a pair of small hoof trimmers, probed along his upper jaw. Strangely gentle, the instrument eased back until reaching and fastening over the rotten tooth. Cloyce immediately felt, and was horrified to learn that his dentist had fastened the instrument too high up, latching onto the gum and jawbone above the bad tooth. Then it locked tight and twisted.

Artist Devon Helenschmidt, Burkburnett, Texas

Terrorized, Cloyce tried to raise an arm. He also tried to yell, stopping the procedure, but it was useless. The roughnecks tightened their holds and leaned heavily against him. The last thing he remembered before slipping into unconsciousness was his Dentist giving orders.

"I've got a good hold now and we're just about through. Hold on tight! This guy's stout as a bull!"

CHAPTER 4

DAISY—1918

"IN BOOM TOWNS people saw so many unusual things that weird happenings sort of became natural," Cecil began. Then he paused. The year was 1980 and he looked up and over my head while fishing back through sixty years of his past. Making certain of his markers, he continued, "So, on that day over there in Burkburnett, this oil company clerk didn't know what he needed to do when Harley came in and handed him a check for twice what their company's stolen drilling rig was worth."

"In 1918," he explained, "Burkburnett was not only the biggest oil boom in Texas, it claimed to be the biggest one in the world. That part of Wichita County was stuffed full of new people. They included oilfield workers, non-workers, gamblers, madams, bootleggers, preachers, stock-peddlers an' lease promoters. There were also absolute con artists, jack-leg lawyers, real lawyers, cowboys, fake doctors, farmers and a big disorganized gang of old-fashioned hold-up men. We called 'em hi-jackers and suspected that a lot of them worked in concert with the hack and cab drivers we used so often but no one ever proved it. All those people, about 45 thousand folks by that year, were in addition to the original settlers. There were preachers who called Burk a "Cesspool of Hell', and most families didn't allow their women out alone at night."

"Normal women, the ones people called "decent", disliked going downtown alone even during the day. Their men folks were all working, so for mutual protection, they went downtown and marketed together in bunches, like bananas. One lady would stay at home to supervise all the kids as well as she was able, while the other mamas shopped for her and for their own families. Next trip another lady would baby sit and the others shop for that one."

"Occasionally, when oil companies drained a large earthen oil pit, their crews would find dead men on the bottom. Somebody would have killed them and sunk the body in there. Your dad once told me that he knew a farmer whose hands were harvesting a field of oats out near Newtown in the Northwest Burkburnett Oilfield sometime in 1918. While gathering and throwing those bundles onto wagons at harvest time, his crew pulled down an extra large shock of oats and found a dead man sittin' straight up, right in the middle. The guy had been shot and robbed, then drug out into that oat field. The killer had torn down a shock or two of oats and propped the body up straight then re-shocked bundles all round him, hiding the crime very nicely."

"The guy was young, awfully ripe and had no identification on him. He really didn't look prosperous enough to rob, and the farmer said that no one ever found out who he was or where he had come from. Law officers in Burk back then didn't have a lot of time to waste on dead strangers. The Police, Sheriff and Texas Rangers all had their hands full chasin' down and lookin' after live people."

"But, back to Harley. That clerk, not knowin' what to do, refused to take the check, but Harley wasn't going to waste a visit and made him round up his boss. Introducing himself to the owner, he shook hands and advised him that he had stolen a drilling rig, plus a boiler, all the gauges and a string of drillpipe from him. "And," he added proudly, "a few days later, I drilled myself a gusher." Now he was diggin' well number two, and because he was no longer a thief but an upright and solvent oilman, he had come to pay off his honest debt."

"The rig owner was flabbergasted, mainly because his rig had been stacked and he hadn't even missed it. Looking at the check, he could tell it was for more money than it took to buy a brand new outfit good as the one he had lost, so he was definitely ahead of the game. Absently, he folded and stuffed the check in his pocket, while pondering this strange event. He was busy that month at buying up a block of leases and wouldn't begin drilling again for six more weeks and had plenty of time to buy another outfit, so that was no problem. Harley was the subject which puzzled him most right then, and he kept lookin' at him, tryin' to place him an' couldn't. Wanting to know, he finally asked outright why Harley had picked his rig and if they had known each other from sometime in the past."

"The questions made Harley mad. He answered that the rig he stole was the nearest one that would do the job he wanted done, and that, of course they hadn't known one another. He followed up his answer by asking if he looked like the kind of person who would steal from a friend. Later, he told a friend of mine that he had intended to ask the rig owner to walk down the street with him to a nearby "Blind Tiger" so they could "throw down" a social drink or two, but the man's question made him so angry that he just turned round and stomped off."

"Nowadays Harley would end up in jail, properly so. But, after the rig owner had told his story several times, and his audiences got a big kick out of it, he delayed filing any charges with the law. After two weeks, he decided to forget all about the theft. Harley's check was good and he figured that Burkburnett lawmen had plenty of work looking for crooked crooks rather than puttin' honest ones like Harley in jail. Besides, he had plenty of work to do himself. And it didn't take a genius to know that he would lose bunches of time by talking with law officers, producing records, appearing before grand juries and testifying over at the Wichita County Courthouse. Calling the Sheriff and turning Harley in was a lose-lose proposition for him."

"Time was precious to all those boomers. Every one of them worked at high speed, real hard, for the same reason that modern businessmen do. It was competition. There was only a certain amount of oil under the ground. And if one wildcatter didn't drill a well to find it, some other harder-working or luckier boomer would beat him to the draw. So everybody rushed. But, hard as they worked, they played ever' bit as hard and all of them loved a good oilfield story. That rig owner told Harley's tale all over Texas and every boomer loved hearing it. In fact, both of them became famous throughout the oilfields because of it."

"Harley turned out to be a lucky Boomtowner. He drilled several more good wells and filled up his sock with money. Then he moved over to Wichita Falls and either bought or built a big two-story house there. He also bought his wife a new Buick and hired a guy to drive her around any time she wanted to go somewhere. They lived a rich life style, high on the hog, but it wasn't long before they learned that problems plagued rich people just as they had visited when Harley was poor. Like many another Texas Boomer who made a quick pile of money, Harley figured he could throw 7's and 11's whenever he wanted to, but if he had it to do over, would probably have made better future plans than he did."

"Harley's wife was a church-going woman and liked for him to attend services with her but he wasn't what most preachers would call a "regular". In fact, he had turned his oil business over to a pair of managers so he could play more efficiently and began to spend most of his time high-rollin'. On an average day he an' his buddies drove over to Fort Worth to gamble and, ever once in a while, those trips turned into three-day outings. They also took train trips to distant locations like Chicago and Kansas City. Occasionally they took their families along, but most of those 'business trips' were for stags."

"Some folks said Harley tried to drink up half the whiskey in Wichita plus one or two surrounding counties. Others whispered that he might enjoy chasing women as much as he did gambling and drinking, but I'm not certain about any of those things. I do know that after Harley paid for that drilling rig, he changed any dishonest ways he might once have practiced and became a square-shooting businessman. Professional oil men respected him because he always kept his word on any business promise."

"I never saw Harley drunk and never knew anybody who would swear he chased women if he got a chance, but in case he did do some of those things, or even a lot of them, he had plenty of company during that boom. Lots of people will talk a mouthful of gossip, but over the years I have noticed that most of them are just talkin'. Generally, if you set one of them on a witness stand in the courthouse, they will back water in a big hurry."

"Only a month or two before that black and dismal day when Harley threw down all the money he could beg, borrow or steal and bet it all on a dry wildcat lease, his wife stepped out their front door on Sunday morning to bring in the paper and almost tripped over a market basket laying on the doorstep. Inside the basket, sleeping quietly, was a tiny baby girl."

"Wrapped in a delicately hand-worked blanket and dressed in a beautiful dress edged with expensive lace, she rested untroubled inside. She was no more than a week old, but every woman who saw her pronounced her to be beautiful. Men didn't brag so much about her beauty, but I never heard any of them call her ugly, either, as some men will when commenting about infants."

"Harley's wife loved that girl from the moment she first looked at her and immediately wanted to adopt her. Harley was the kind of man who liked most kids and had no problem with adopting. So he and his wife did exactly that, paying no mind to gossip mongers who rumored that the infant's mother probably knew the exact doorstep on which it should be left."

"Harley had all the money he needed, and like most men of his day, he placed little blame on an unfortunate mother who, for whatever reason, had brought the child to his house. Women back then were almost universal in finding fault with such a mother but Harley's wife was a good woman who loved the infant on sight and wanted to keep her. They named her "Daisy" after an old American love song about a bicycle-built-for-two, which was very popular about 1900 and had recently become popular again."

Cecil and I were seated on recliners in his living room, partly talking and partially watching a baseball game on TV. Suddenly, the pitcher struck out his final batter and Cecil cackled with delight. Nolan Ryan, the great Texas Ranger pitcher, had just finished his Seventh No-hitter. No major league pitcher had ever done this and it may never happen again. For thirty minutes we talked about the game and Nolan's wonderful record. Then Cecil began telling another story.

"You remember the old Southwest Field out from Burk, near Cashion, along the road toward Wichita Falls?" I nodded my head "yes" and he said: "Well, when your uncles, Jay and Charley, were about 10 and 12, I used to take them downtown occasionally, early on Sunday mornings, and buy 'em breakfast at the Burk Cafe."

"After breakfast, I would take them over to Harris's newsstand and buy them about 10 papers apiece. Then we would drive out into the Southwest field where I'd turn them out and they would begin sellin' papers to the oilfield workers. They trotted over those leases like a pair of hounds, chargin' around tank batteries and slushpits, and jumpin' over pipelines and rodlines until they were sold out."

"Generally, we weren't out in the field for over 30 minutes and they had a great time. They would make two or three dollars apiece an' I always enjoyed smoking a cigar while watching them run."

Then he took another pull on his cigar and I could read from his face as his mind traveled farther back in time, re-visiting well-remembered places. But he didn't start another story. Even though he tried hard, it was getting harder to properly explain the old days to new generations, most of whom, were more interested in modern things and the world that evolved after World War ll.

Young Texans had little interest in the old times any more. They were of a different age, too late to make a good connection with him. In addition to this generation gap, most of the old timers, and his oilfield associates with them, were dead. Those who still lived were past 80 and he was now past 90, and barely able to drive his automobile because of poor eyesight.

Not only had death moved between him and the past, but fewer and fewer of the friends he had left, when he called them on the telephone, remembered the old times any more. "They're all gettin' crazy," Cecil would say, his voice colored by sadness and a tinge of dread. This was because his own memory, which had once been considered infallible, was growing hazy. Blowing a large smoke ring from his mouth, Cecil turned to face me. "I don't know, Ed, whether it's life or death closing in on me, but it doesn't matter which. Either way it's going to come out just the same."

His tale about newspapers and those old Burk times reminded me again of Harley and the baby girl. In order to move his mind elsewhere, I asked, "What about Harley and that baby girl they named Daisy. Did they move away or stay in Wichita Falls? And if they stayed in Burk, would I have known them?"

Cecil removed his cigar, exhaled another cloud of smoke and peered at me though a thin spot: "Yes, you knew 'em. In fact, Daisy's little brother, Harley, Jr., was close to your grade in school at Burk. Harley, Sr. ended up running a candy store a short distance from the school ground. Daisy grew into a beautiful young girl who was loved by all who knew her. She used to trot from high school across your school yard every day to work in her dad's store at lunch time. In the store she "flipped burgers" until time for her class to start and she ate her own burger while hot-footing it back."

Then it became clear to me. Of course I had known Harley. He was the man who patiently served whatever they wanted to the many kids who had money to spend in his tiny candy store during lunch hour, recess or after school. Located just down the block and across the street from the elementary school ground, Harley, with quiet dignity, had operated this store during my early school years. He was never pushy and was always kind to us.

I also knew the baby girl and her brother. She had enchanted me as much as everyone else who knew her. She was an "A" student, with a lovely face, a strong healthy body and a bright personality. All the boys, all the teachers and most of the girls loved her. I knew her brother, but I remembered him under the name of George rather than Harley, Jr. Cecil had gotten his name wrong. But the girl's name was right. Everyone in town knew her by the same name as me. She was DAISY FLOWERS. I heard that she later married well, raised a respectable family and enjoyed a rich full life.

BOOMTOWNER—1918

"HE GOT HIS arm caught up in the Calf Wheel's belt, and mashed it almost off. They got the rig stopped but couldn't get him loose. He was hanging by some shoulder tendons and yellin' like crazy. I couldn't stand his yelling and pain, so I grabbed up a rig axe, wanting to cut his arm off but they wouldn't let me. I walked off that rig and never went back. I heard that they finally got him loose, but he lost the arm anyway."

Bill Johnson, Author's Uncle

BOOMTOWNER—1919

"ROBBERIES HAPPENED ALL the time during this boom, and Bill Johnson, along with most other young men in town, often bragged about how tough he was and what all he would do to any thug dumb enough to try hi-jacking him. Then, one night as he was walking home from the theater, he was crossing the alley that ran behind the bank and a thug stuck a gun in his back, telling him to "Stick 'em up."

"When talking about it later, Bill said he'd never had a gun shoved in his back before and, instead of fighting, he made no fuss at all. Happy to be alive, he gave the thug whatever he wanted. And the high-jacker, happy with Bill's cooperation, took everything he had, even his pocket comb and handkerchief."

Ed Stevenson, Sr.,
Author's Father

CHAPTER 5

Texas Bound Boomer—1920

"I WAS BORN near Oblong, Illinois in 1903 and my dad died when I was eleven. At 15 I was roustabouting in a small but shallow and active oilfield near Stoy, Illinois. This was while the US was fighting Germany in World War I. By age 17 I had worked a year and a half for a pipeline contractor in Stoy and all his hands were paid $2.00 a day."

"My boss was named Sam Coyne and he made me, the youngest, do the hardest and dirtiest work on every job. One day after lunch, Old Sam left us laying some 6-inch pipeline and drove into Stoy to talk with a farmer on whose land we would soon be digging. He had only been gone about 30 minutes before a black storm blew up and rain poured down on us. We ran into a nearby pumphouse to get out of the rain and lightning."

"I was the only hand who brought his shovel in with him, and when Sam came back to find us ganged up in that building, it made him mad. He was mad because we had quit working without permission, but he didn't want the whole crew mad at him so he centered on me, yelling me out for not bringing all the other workmen's shovels in out of the rain."

"He had been making me stay an hour late each afternoon to sharpen up the other worker's shovels and replace the broken handles in his hand tools. This included axes, hatchets, hammers and picks. I worked an hour longer each day than everyone else, but he never paid me an extra cent. I don't think that was because he disliked me. It was because I was only 17 years old and the other hands were grown men, most of them with wives and children."

"Illinois people in those days figured it was poor practice for a young kid to earn as much as a grown man supporting a family. They also thought he should perform the worst jobs because he was younger and should pay his dues at whatever trade he worked in before he could expect to be treated like an adult with a family. I was still a boy to those folks and a fairly young one at that."

"None of the other men noticed, or cared, that Old Sam worked me harder than he did them. So, I made two trips out in the rain to round up all their shovels and not one of those grown men offered to help. I heard one or two of them snicker behind my back, but they turned their faces away when I looked at them."

"I did exactly as Old Sam had told me, and just as I finished, it quit raining. The sun suddenly broke past the clouds, making a real pretty rainbow shine all the way across the sky. I took that as a good sign. I'd saved up $123.00 and our crew was only two miles away from Stoy, making an easy walk."

"I was already angry, feeling Sam had been treating me badly, so right then, without thinking about it any further, I decided to quit that job. I marched up with my last load of shovels, just as all the others came out of the pumphouse, and walked straight up to Old Sam. Throwing my load down in front of him, I told him to "take 'em and shove 'em. Then I asked for my pay."

"Old Sam looked puzzled but didn't rear up at me or try to fuss. He just reached into his purse, pulled out $6.50 and shoved the money over. This included full payment for that day even though it was just 2:30 in the afternoon at the time. I stuffed the money in my pocket, nodded at all of them and turned away toward Stoy, walking straight up, like I thought a soldier ought to march."

"None of those men even told me "so long". But in thinking back, I figure this was because they were surprised I had quit so suddenly. After I had walked a few steps, Old Sam hollered out, asking me what I would do. His voice wasn't angry, just curious. I had been waiting for that question and shouted back over my shoulder, without even turning around, because I had already figured out what I would say if anybody asked."

"I'm headed for Burkburnett, Texas 'cause I hear that down in their boom, a pipeliner might have to clean and sharpen his own shovel but they'll loan him a file and pay him $5.00 a day to work."

"Well, later on that evening, I was still mad about Sam's treatment and the low wage scale oilfield workers had in Illinois. Since I couldn't see much of a way to get ahead at home, I decided it really was time for me to leave. I would just make my word good and leave. After dinner that night I told Mother and my Uncle I was heading for Burkburnett, Texas to check out the oilfield there. Next morning, I visited around with friends and relatives, told them all goodbye and bought a suitcase over in Stoy. Late that evening, I packed it up."

"Early on the second morning I kissed and hugged my Mother, shook hands with my Uncle and caught a ride to Stoy with a delivery truck driver. At the railroad station I bought a ticket to St. Louis on the Pennsylvania to St. Louis railroad. I also bought one to carry me on South from there, down through Kansas and Oklahoma to Dennison, and Wichita Falls, Texas. I didn't know it would be so permanent when leaving home but I never went back to Illinois except for visits. I have lived no place other than Texas since then except for a year in Kansas and one in Oklahoma. All of my relatives are buried up in Illinois but I have owned a family plot in the cemetery over in Holliday, Texas since 1950. My wife was buried there in 1986, and it won't be much longer until I move over there to sleep beside her."

"From Dennison, it was only a three-hour train ride to Wichita Falls. But, after that, it took another hour to make the 13 miles on over to Burkburnett. That train stopped about every hundred yards. It was a stand-up-all-the-way ride unless you were one of those who liked to ride on top or hang onto the sides of the passenger car. Once in Burk, most newcomers needed to start lookin' hard for a job, but findin' a spot to sleep was harder than findin' a job."

"After several weeks of staying in Wichita Falls with an Uncle, and workin' at part-time jobs, I located a good roustaboutin' job at The Paragon Company in the Northwest Burkburnett field. They had a bunk house an' fed us breakfast and supper. Their cook also fixed up sandwiches so the hands could carry them out to the field for lunch. We only worked six days a week, so one Sunday afternoon, two months after I had gone to work at The Paragon, I was walkin' down Main Street in Burk, enjoyin' a sack of popcorn and watchin' the commotion of Boomtown people bustlin' about, when I met two of the guys who had worked for Old Sam with me back in Illinois."

"Now this wasn't unusual because oilfield hands were already a different breed of people. Some of them had been following booms since early in 1901, when the Spindletop discovery well blew in near Beaumont. A big bunch of oilfield workers, like me, had started to learn the oilfield business in Illinois, then got disgusted with working conditions there, and traveled on down to Texas."

"Some Boomers had already worked in four or five boom towns by the time I got to Burk. In fact, I had three uncles who'd been in Burk a year before I got there. Two were big strapping fellows and my family in Illinois was kind of proud of them. The third, a shorter man like me, ran a cafe over here in Wichita Falls. One of the big ones was a gambler and he ran a cafe and gambling hall out in the Northwest Field near Newtown. He also made a lot of money selling lemon extract to Indians across Red River in Oklahoma. In those days it was illegal to sell them any drinking whiskey, wine or beer."

"I didn't even know that uncle ran a gambling place before I got to Texas, but was as proud of him as I was the rest. I had this pride because he offered me money and help just like the others had. But I was even more proud to be able to thank all three of them for offering me money and be able to say I had saved up enough money on my own to get by."

"Several weeks later, on a Sunday afternoon in downtown Burkburnett, I saw a pair of familiar faces. One of them yelled at me to stop and talk for a minute. They were the ones closest to my age in old Sam's crew. Even so, they were still three years older than me and had just gotten off the Wichita Falls train. They seemed glad to see a person they knew and both of them stuck their hands out for a shake. They said that they had quit old Sam too, deciding to come down South and find a pair of those $5.00-a-day pipeline jobs I had hollered back to them about."

Artist Jessica Boatwright, Augusta, Georgia

"Now, each of these guys was twice as big as me so I didn't have the desire or nerve to tell them the truth. I decided to wait and let them find it out for themselves. The truth was that I inflated Burk's pipeline wage rates on the day when I quit Old Sam.

I stood for 30 more minutes, laughing and joking with that brand-new pair of Boomers, passing the time of day until they decided to hunt up a place to sleep for the night. When they finally walked away, I wished them luck and walked across Main to the duckpin alley, to bowl a line or two. You see, I didn't know it, on the day I had quit old Sam, but it had gotten fairly hard to locate good jobs in Burk that year. What I did know, but had intentionally lied to them about when quitting, was that no company in the Burkburnett field had ever paid pipeliners over $3.50 a day."

CHAPTER 6

CLIMBING UP—1920

"I WAS BARELY 17 when I came to realize I would have to leave home if I ever wanted to earn a decent living. So, on the second morning after quittin' Old Sam, I boarded a passenger train at a little Illinois whistle-stop named Stoy. The year was 1920 and I rode away on the Pennsylvania-St. Louis Railroad. At St. Louis we swapped trains to head South. I'm not really certain of the name of that railroad but I think it was the Missouri, Kansas and Texas, that people used to call the Katy."

"I do remember that our car was loaded up to the brim with people when we pulled out of St. Louis, and when we got to the Missouri and Kansas state line, it stopped dead still. Right after that the black people on that train all began to complain. They stood up, a lot of 'em cussin' and most of them were pitching their sacks and boxes around. Every one of them was mouthing, and while collecting their bags and rolling up their sacks, they got louder and louder."

"At first, I had no idea what was wrong. Then I understood that they were mad because they had all been told to leave our car and move into another one which was used by the railroad to carry only Black people. And that train was going to stay stopped until every one of them had changed to the black car. Kansas laws didn't allow black and white people to ride in the same cars. Now a lot of those folks had been living up North for a long time. Some hadn't been down South for years and some, like me, had never been South and this was their first experience with Jim Crow laws. Even the ones who had been visiting up North from the South had come to appreciate ridin' wherever they wanted an' sittin' in any part of a car they liked. They complained even louder than the rest. Every black person on that train was mumbling, shoutin', cussin' and waggin' his head when they stomped out of that car. I didn't really blame them."

"After the train started up again, I worked up an acquaintance with a Texas boy of my age who'd been visiting relatives in St. Louis. He was headed back down to Fort Worth but he called it "Cowtown." And when our train got to Oklahoma City, it laid over long enough for us to eat dinner. So he and I grabbed our suitcases an' got off, walking down the street until we found a good restaurant. The place we found served up some mighty good roast beef, with creamed new potatoes and green beans. They also had good hot rolls with butter plus cold milk to drink and a scalding hot bowl of tasty peach cobbler."

"Full as ticks, we hauled our bags back down to the train 10 minutes before it was time to pull out. As we walked alongside our train we saw an empty passenger car and climbed in. We had it all to ourselves. Promptly picking out two seats we liked, and leaning way back, we decided to nap most of the way on down to Texas. I was asleep before we left the station and had been napping for maybe 15 minutes when a heavy billy club whacked across the soles of my shoes. And it hurt. Real bad!"

"I jumped straight up to find a big railroad detective standin' in front of me. He said my friend and I were to haul our butts off that car in a hurry because the railroad had set it apart for use of black folks only. We pointed out that no one else was riding there and we didn't mind if it was a black folks car. He said what we minded or didn't mind cut absolutely no ice with him. The law was the law and we had to move."

"So, my friend I and grumbled just like all those black folks had and slowly picked up our bags while trying to accommodate this dose of segregation in reverse. We had located ourselves a nice quiet railroad car, where we wouldn't bother anyone and no one would bother us. It was a place where we could take a restful snooze and settle our lunch, but because we were white, the law wouldn't let us use it. We walked several cars down without finding a seat, finally stopping in a car which was way over-crowded. It was so noisy an' jammed up so tight that we might as well have been cattle."

"My friend and I stood shoulder to shoulder in the crowded aisle. Our choices were holding onto and swinging from a leather strap, or trying to stay balanced while sittin' on our bags. Neither way worked well. An hour later, when the train stopped and let off two large families, we got a seat. On curves, I could see out the window an' I watched that empty black folks car roll all the way down South to Dennison, Texas, where I swapped onto a train going up to Wichita Falls. Far as I could tell, it was still as empty when it left Dennison going on to Fort Worth as it was when they threw us off of it in Kansas."

"You could almost throw a rock from the old railroad station in Wichita Falls and hit the front window of my Uncle Walter Wallace's cafe located at 511 Indiana Street. He and a much younger wife, a real good-lookin' and high-steppin' woman, ran this cafe together, but when I got there, they were mad as a pair of wildcats an' yelling loud at one another. Far as I could tell, he was fussin' because he thought she'd been acting too friendly with some of their men customers. She wasn't a bit afraid an' yelled back as loud as him. They were too mad to notice me, so I figured I would leave and walk around in Wichita for a while, giving them some time to settle their fuss."

"Two hours later they had cooled off pretty good an' I introduced myself. Each one seemed glad to see me and they treated me nice, inviting me to sleep in their garage loft for a few days until I could locate a job. They also said I could wash dishes and mop up some in the cafe for my meals. I was glad to have this help because it allowed me to save my money until I could find a steady job. But, some people, especially young ones like I was at that time, have a hard time handlin' prosperity an' it only took me two weeks to mess up my new accommodations."

"My Uncle's wife had a 14-year-old son from an earlier marriage, and he was spoiled rotten. He never did what they asked him to and he sassed them back whenever he wanted. He also took an early dislike to me, always accusing me of lying when I told him about how things and places and people were back in Illinois. That boy never once missed a chance to give me a hard time."

"On my second Sunday afternoon in Texas, that step-son and his buddies staged what they called a "play" in my Uncle's garage. It had once been a barn and was a fair-sized building. Deciding to play a trick on him and his buddies, I hooked up an old water hose and ran it through a side window. When they had their show moving along pretty good, I watered down their performance with a few gallons from the hose."

"Now this was a time when most folks didn't think that a few drops of water would cause a kid to melt. Some figured it might even noticeably improve his smell. There were also many grownup Texas women back then who didn't run to get the undertaker if a few drops of rain water fell on their hairdo, so I didn't think I did anything very bad. Actually, I didn't get those boys very wet at all. But they were mad as a nest of yellowjackets and were convinced that I'd ruined their performance, which was mostly what I had in mind. It didn't help their opinion of me a bit when I answered back that I hadn't damaged much."

"After they dried out some, that cousin-in-law of mine began to throw rocks at me. I didn't get mad right off because I figured he was entitled to throw a few. I just watched closely and dodged when it was necessary. But he wouldn't quit when I figured it was time, so I warned him about it. You see, he was close to my size and he actually thought he was tougher than me, but he wasn't. I had already lost patience with him the day before because he had hidden my shoes and wouldn't tell me where they were."

"I had to grab an' shake him hard as I could to get the shoes back. And now, since he wouldn't quit throwin' rocks, I rounded a corner when he wasn't payin' enough attention, an' slipped up on him, grabbing him from behind. I didn't hit him, but I did slap him twice, fairly hard, and promised to kick his fanny all around the block if he threw any more rocks at me."

"You might already have decided, that this wasn't a real bright thing for me to do, an' you would be right. Thirty minutes afterward my Uncle Walter was talkin' serious to me, tellin' me I should have kicked his step-son around the block while I was at it, because now I wasn't going to get another chance. He also explained that he sometimes regretted the fact that he had picked out this boy's mother to marry, but he had gone ahead and done it and she was madder that day than he had ever seen her."

"This Aunt-in-law believed everything her son told her, and she not only decided I'd been mean to him, but had laid down the law to Uncle Walter by tellin' him if I stayed, she was movin'. And it was real obvious, if you first looked at her an' then at me, which one of us was leaving. In fact, when I looked at her, mad at me as she was right then, that woman was still a mighty pretty brunette with a fine figure. I didn't blame my Uncle a bit. I would have done exactly what he did, so I shook his hand, packed my suitcase and checked into a new hotel called The Antlers, three blocks down the street."

"Uncle Walter offered to loan me some money but I thanked him, explaining that, because of him lettin' me work for him that I had plenty to get by on, and everything worked out good anyway. The very next morning, my gamblin' an' lemon extract sellin' uncle, Earl Wallace, came over to Wichita an' looked me up."

Uncle Earl ran a sort of a restaurant too, over in Newtown, which was a community right in the middle of the busy Northwest Burkburnett oilfield. He asked if I needed any money and I explained to him that I didn't. Then he told me about a job I might land at the Magnolia Boiler Works over on West Main street in Burk, near the Bradford Pipe and Supply Company. Soon as he left I caught the first train over an' hired out."

"Uncle Earl's cafe had a card gamblin' room upstairs. And, the only way you could get up in it was to climb a ladder, which they pulled up while they were playin' cards. This helped him to keep the Texas Rangers out, he said. That an' the fact that he ran an honest game, with few customer complaints. He didn't gamble or deal, for himself. In fact, the dealers he hired didn't gamble either. They just dealt whatever game the players asked for and took a small cut out of every other pot for the house. My Uncle and the dealers split the pot cuts."

"Uncle Earl made most of his money sellin' lemon extract to the Indians over in Oklahoma. It was against the law for them to buy whiskey and beer, but the Federal Government and the State of Oklahoma hadn't made up their minds yet about lemon extract an' those Indians loved drinkin' it. Between the cafe, his card game and sellin' that lemon extract, he loaded up his sock pretty quick. Two years later, he moved over to Wichita Falls an' bought out his brother's cafe. Uncle Walter's wife had gotten homesick an' he was movin' back to Illinois with her and that rock-throwin' kid."

"The Boiler Works job paid me well and I liked it except for two things. First, you had to show up at 7:00 every morning and occasionally, every third or fourth day, they had no work for us. When that happened we had to wait around, in case something came in, but they didn't pay us for waiting time. The other thing was that in their business you worked inside the boiler fireboxes as well as on the outsides of the boilers an' you got awful dirty. Black-soot dirty. Even though they treated their help good, I got sick of ridin' that train twice a day an' goin' back to the hotel all sooty black, with people backing away from me so I started lookin' around for another job."

"Two or three days after I decided, Herb Beedameyer, a family friend from up in Illinois, looked me up. He had checked with the lady at the post office in Oblong and she had read enough off of postcards to tell him I was working at some Boiler Works in the Burkburnett oilfield. Herb was the brother-in-law of a man named Harpes who was field boss out at the Paragon Oil Company in Burk. He had just got back from Illinois an' already had a job with them. He said I ought to go and talk with Mr. Harpes because they were hiring some roustabouts."

"Six days later I came over to work at the Boiler Works and they had nothing for me to do so I took Herb's advice an' drew down my time. Thumbin' along the road, I caught a ride out to Paragon's office and hired out to them. That turned out to be a great job. They paid as good as most companies, and the money was always on time. Besides that, they had a bunkhouse for hands who wanted to sleep there, with showers, washracks and clotheslines. Better still, they fed their men breakfast and supper an' packed lunches which they could carry out in the field. A man could work for them and save almost every dollar of his pay. I liked that a whole lot."

"After I'd been with the Paragon about two days, Herb and all the rest of that bunch, jumped up an' quit. They'd heard about some outfit across Red River in Oklahoma that was payin' a dollar or two a day more than The Paragon paid us, so they lit out for the Indian Territory. They wanted me to go with them but I really liked the food that cook was turnin' out and not having to pay any hotel bills, so I decided to hang around."

"Back then, when oil companies had a lay-off, most of them cut loose the newest hands and kept the ones who had been working for them longest to fill the jobs that were left. This was the "seniority system" and many companies still use it today. It takes only a few months of working in the oilfield to learn that it's only a matter of time before a big-time "rainy" day comes along. Your company can be bought out, go broke or lay-off people for many different reasons. Most oilfield hands counted on company seniority to help them when lay-offs happened. If it didn't save their jobs, they were normally paid a few extra days of salary to help out while they looked for other work."

"Sometimes, because of the seniority system, companies laid off better hands than they kept. But most of them still continued the practice even though they often kept hands they would rather have done without and fired some they shouldn't. And, to head off any bad problems, when a man was fired out of his regular seniority turn, they would add in a day or two of wages so's he would feel better about leaving. Even after that, a few bosses had to fight when they let a hand go. That's why oilfield gang foremen were generally big and well-seasoned men."

"When Herb and those others asked me to leave with them, I thought to myself, 'Ceece', ole' boy, two weeks ago you didn't have a nickel's worth of seniority with Paragon. But now, with all these guys leaving and you staying, you'll have more seniority than anybody in Paragon's gang.'"

"So, I stayed in Burkburnett and it was more than 30 years before I finally moved out of Texas, up into Oklahoma. When I did, it was just for a year because the Sinclair Oil Company had transferred me to Shawnee as their District Gauger. By then Sinclair had bought out the Prairie Pipeline Company, which had bought out what was left of the Paragon while I was still working there many years before."

"Paragon had no problem with replacing Herb and those guys who had quit. In fact, it was less than a week before two of them drug back from Oklahoma, asking for their old jobs back. Paragon didn't hire them but it kept me on. They didn't make a gang pusher or straw boss out of me because I was too young and unseasoned. Also, they didn't know me very well yet and I wasn't large enough to suit some companies as a supervisor or strawboss. Still, I had a good job and liked it. I was working in a good gang with a good company which regularly paid my salary out right on top of the drumhead every week. And I had more seniority than anyone else in my crew."

"I was also saving a lot of money and liked that because I could send some back home to my mother and sisters. What I didn't know, yet, was that, pretty soon, my circumstances were about to improve. But, before we get to that, I need to tell you about the famous bunkhouse wedding. It was great, so don't quit out on me."

CHAPTER 7

PROPOSIN'—1920

"I WATCHED FROM my bunk as Jake pulled his suit out from between the mattress and springs of his cot," Cecil said. "He had stored it there, folded up real nice, ever since the day he walked into our bunkhouse. The company hadn't built us any closets and the only storage space we had for boxes, sacks, and worn out suitcases was under our beds."

My Uncle told me this wedding story on my next visit. We had just come back to his house after taking dinner at the Red Lobster Restaurant in Wichita Falls. Even though he was 92, 'goin' on 93', he relished the Steak and Lobster plate they brought him. Methodically, he swallowed every bite. Then, wiping his plate clean with a roll, he ate that too. Finally, after slowly sipping a third cup of hot, black Texas coffee, he decided it was okay for us to drive on home.

At his house, we nested down in side-by-side recliners, and he tuned in the Texas Ranger baseball game on TV. He was very hard of hearing and turned his TV up so loud that we had to yell at each other, but that didn't stop him from starting one of his favorite stories. Besides eating, story-telling was his most favorite thing. The stock market came next and baseball was right behind.

"We slept in rows," he continued, "like in an army barracks, all crowded up together. These metal cots weren't a real nice bed, but they were better than army cots because they had flat steel springs. Besides, we were young, and hard as we worked back then, we could sleep on the floor and rest as well as if we slept on mattresses."

"I watched Jake look at his coat with disgust and pop it a time or two, trying to shake out the wrinkles, but it was wasted work.

They wouldn't go away. The rest of his clothes looked really good, though. He'd found a lady to launder his white shirt and had bought a paper collar to wear with it. I heard later that he had postponed buying a tie, deciding to see how things worked out before investing any more money."

"He was a tall Texan, two inches over six feet and weighed about 230. I figured his age at about 21. His speech revealed little formal education, but everyone who worked with Jake knew that he was no dummy. With his wavy dark hair, bluish gray eyes, and that fresh shirt and shave, though he wore a wrinkled suit, Jake looked awfully good for a North Texas oilfield hand after finishin' his dressing."

"It was a Saturday morning, and we were off from work. I'd been watching the others loaf around the bunkhouse and had watched most of what Jake was doing from the corner of my eye. I didn't stare openly because I was barely 17, and had problems enough without making a guy big as him mad at me. Folks figured he could be awfully mean if you rattled his cage."

"Besides, I could tell he didn't enjoy being the center of attention and was doing his best to ignore the others. The older guys stared at him with open interest. He'd already shaved, was almost finished with his clean up, and was pullin' on his britches when a couple of the older men started razzin' him. They had him over a barrel by then 'cause they knew he wouldn't risk a fight for fear of tearing up his good clothes."

"He acted like he didn't hear them, and paid full attention to lacing up his fresh-shined, high-topped dress shoes. You see, Jake had important matters on his mind. Behind all this seriousness was the age-old problem of young men everywhere. He was deeply caught up in love and was dressing for the trip to meet his girl's father and ask for her hand in marriage."

"Now, the year I'm telling about was 1920. The place was in the Paragon Oil Company bunkhouse, out in the oilfields near Burkburnett. Jake's girl was a young German maiden, about 17, very pretty, black-haired and trim. Some of the guys had heard about it and told me the story about how they met at a pie supper in the First Baptist Church at Burk."

"Pie suppers were fun back then. All the young ladies taking part would cook up their very fanciest and tastiest dishes. They also cooked the best pie recipe they knew and boxed all of it up together. Each maiden wrote her name on a note and slipped it in the box before tying it up in as neat and pretty a package as she could devise. Then, on the night of the supper, she proudly carried it to church."

"No one was supposed to know whose box the auctioneer held up for bids, but security leaks often developed. Most of those girls had younger brothers who could be bribed, or girl friends who might be persuaded to disclose certain names in the furtherance of money, romance or match-making."

"Most young stags present would bid on more than one box. But a few would only bid on one, and if they didn't buy it, would leave. But most of the guys were just having fun, shopping around rather than playing for keeps, and would keep on bidding until they pulled a winner. "Proper" women were hard for oilfield workers to meet, and buying a box at a pie supper was one of the best ways. When a Boomer did that, he earned the right to sit down for a real home cooked meal and a leisurely visit with a decent girl."

"Oilfield hands and cowboys mixed in with farmers as well as young town hopefuls and all of them bid against the world that night for boxes they had picked out. When winning, they might be sitting and eating with the cutest and most popular girl there. Or they could have bought the box prepared by Burk's plainest wallflower. But, even if their pie baker turned out to be plain and maybe the youngest attending female, the high bidder who, at our age was always hungry enough to eat his shoelaces, minded his manners, acting as if she were the prettiest girl in town. After all, his evening wasn't ruined. He had bought the right to sit and talk with a nice girl from a nice family, whose age was not very far from his own."

"Custom insisted that both parties, men and girls, be polite and generous. Each put on a happy face, whether the dinner was tasty or bad, even though he bought a different box than he wanted. And, that particular night, an average box was selling for $1.50. But they said Jake had found out which one belonged to the girl he liked and had bid it up to $7.75 before winning. Old timers couldn't remember anyone paying that much for a pie supper box before."

"As was normal with pretty young girls, Jake's lady already had a boyfriend, one of her exact age. He went through all the motions of defending his territory, even offering to fight for his love. But, Jake, being older and more sensible, exercised diplomacy. He kept the discussion quiet, talking the younger guy out of a fight by insisting that neither of them could actually win, no matter who came out on top. Nursing his pride and embarrassed by his loss, the younger fellow backed off and watched while Jake and his girl ate an hour-long dinner together. Then they kept close company for the rest of the evening."

"After that Jake took to Baptisting on Sundays. He didn't join up because it turned out that his lady wasn't a Baptist. Her family was Lutheran, but the nearest church of that faith was in Wichita Falls. She often attended the Baptist church in Burk because many of her school friends attended services there. But she liked Jake right off, and this feeling quickly turned to love. And the younger boy, no longer receiving encouragement, began looking for love in other places."

"But Jake's problems weren't solved. As can happen in any part of life, problems popped up. He would have gladly "run off" to get married. Folks called it "eloping", but his girl flatly refused to marry any man unless her father gave permission. That was where his trouble lay."

"Her dairy-farming father, who still mostly spoke German at home, had no love for boomtowners. His often-stated opinion was: 'Dose peeples are nutting but oilfiel' trash'. Sixty years later, during another oil boom, Texas oil workers proudly placed stickers on their car bumpers reading, 'I'm Oilfield Trash And Proud Of It.' But in 1920, during the Burkburnett boom, few people bragged about working in the oilfield unless they had just hit a gusher."

"Burk residents were proud of their boom though not of its workers. They claimed it was the biggest since Spindletop, halfway across the state, down near Beaumont. They also swore that 40,000 or more people were moving around in the Burk oilfields, with 7,000 to 10,000 milling around in town for 24 hours every day.

About 2,000 people, maybe less, lived there before oil was discovered. I was a young guy from Oblong, Illinois who had seen one oil boom already but the Burk boom was bigger and tougher than anything I had imagined."

"Downtown Burk was a madhouse. its main roads were filled with all types of vehicles and no road was paved. Sidewalks, where they existed, were made of rough lumber. Dust blew everywhere, constantly stirred up by heavy traffic and gusty North Texas winds. But people said it could rain as little as 10 drops of water and those roads would develop mud holes 6 feet deep, paralyzing vehicle transportation. There were always hundreds of cars and trucks, plus mule, horse, and occasional ox teams passing through. Traffic never stopped and you could always see lots of jitneys and hacks plus people on horseback. People rode in wagons too, and those who were afoot, mixed up with all that traffic."

"As I first climbed off the train from Wichita Falls, I was thinking of all the stories I'd heard about mule teams bogging down and drowning in the muddy streets plus the murders and robberies that happened every day. I didn't see any drownings or robberies then, but I did see more people swarming the streets in Burk than I'd seen in St. Louis, and for three more years, the traffic always seemed the same, night or day."

"In the daytime you would see madams who ran houses for loose women, stomping around through the mud in high rubber boots. Wrapped in kimonos, they did their shopping during the day, then marched back home clutching cigarettes in one hand and carrying wicker baskets holding purchases in the other."

"Burk's main streets were covered thick as ants with lease hounds, oil company stock peddlers, jackleg lawyers and bootleggers. There were also drummers, cowboys, farmers, lots of oilfield workers, a few Indians and, once in a while, a black man. Normal people, the ones who lived in Burk before the boom, only came to town when they had to do business. Many city lots had one or more oil wells pumping on them. Derricks were always being built in every direction you looked. Schools and churches, having larger lots, sometimes sported more than one well."

"Strangers lived or slept any place they could find if no one ran them off. This might be in tents, shacks, tarpaper and boxwood houses, or in bedrolls scattered up and down the Red River bottom. Some men slept at their jobs, resting easily on the "soft side of a board" and luckier ones found rooms to rent."

"Some people paid to sleep in restaurant chairs when business was slack and some paid a dollar a night to sleep on a pool table or somebody's front porch. Others slept on stacks of boards in lumber yards while more snored in church pews when services weren't being held. Occasionally men dropped their bedrolls and napped wherever they could find a spot far enough out of traffic to keep from being run over. That was often hard to do."

"Burkburnett was an "Independent Oilman's Paradise" because wildcatters could make shallow wells almost anywhere they drilled. Few wells were deeper than 2,500 feet and some recovered oil at less than 600. People who called Burk "Boomtown" used to brag that a man could "kick a well down" with his boot heel, which wasn't far from the truth. Ranchers, drilling for water wells over near Electra had accidentally started the whole thing. They were mad about it—at first. But later, after selling some leases and cashing a few royalty checks, they liked oil better. After cashing a few royalty checks they quickly noticed that few things fattened up a skinny herd of cattle quick as a couple of oil wells."

"Drillers, job seekers, equipment salesmen, blacksmiths and other boomers, soon drifted in. Lucky wildcatters earned quick riches and, just as quickly, began selling out. That was the wrong thing to do. They didn't understand how really lucky they were, and, even though they earned a rich return on their investments, they should have held on. Those early sales opened the gates for large companies to move in and reap huge fortunes which the wildcatters could have kept."

"Jake and me and all those other men worked for the Paragon Oil Company. It later sold out to Tidal Western. Tidal sold to Prairie and was later bought by Sinclair. Later, it was named Sinclair-Prairie and was the pipeline division of their company. I was working for Sinclair when I retired in 1965. Later they changed their name to the Atlantic-Richfield Company, or Arco."

"Paragon paid its men well. They also gave them a bed. But, best of all, they had a cook shack and a kitchen where a man could eat two free meals a day. I felt lucky to be working there because I saved most of the money I made, but few oilfield workers were savers. They were Boomers. Besides working hard on long, tortuous days, they were better at throwing money away than at anything else."

"Jake finished brushing his hair in front of a small cracked mirror placed above our wash basin. Then he dried his hands and face with a sort of clean bunkroom towel hanging on a nearby nail. Pulling his hat down tight, he dragged a clean "tow sack" out from under his bed as he walked past and we followed him out the back door. He continued to ignore us as he walked out behind the bunkhouse where, just across a barbed wire fence, I saw a large, well-fed sorrel mule tied close enough so's he could drink from a 55 gallon metal drum which they used for a water barrel."

"Jake pushed down on the top fence wire with one hand and straddled the fence with ease. Walking up to the mule he fished an ear of hard corn out of his sack and gave it to the animal which deftly worked with its tongue and lower jaw to grind everything up, shuck and all, then swallow it without dropping a single grain on the ground. Watching carefully until his muleship had finished, Jake fished back in his sack and pulled out an old bridle which had been fitted to the mule's long head. None of us had ever seen Jake ride a horse or a mule, and I thought we might end up watching a live rodeo, but we didn't."

"Moving quickly and competently, Jake carefully slipped the bridle over his mule's popping ears and fastened the throat latch. After that he loosened the hackamore and leadline then looped them loosely round the mule's neck. Doubling up his tow sack, he laid it across the mule's back and, using the bridle reins, began to lead it around in a tight circle, while gradually pulling the mule's nose back toward him. Suddenly, he jumped aboard then quickly and smoothly tightened up the reins, first to pull in all the slack he could, and second to point the mule's head toward a gate up the road, so it would see and have something besides mischief to think about."

"Most of these unpolished roustabouts and pipeliners had been raised on farms, and Jake's demonstration of 'horse sense' impressed them. Instead of poking fun, or maybe sailing a hat under the mule's belly as one later admitted he had thought about, several wished him 'good luck'. Jake solemnly nodded his chin downward to show he'd heard but kept his eyes glued to the mule's ears. Anything could still happen, and we all knew it."

"The animal had obviously been trained as a road mule, the kind people called a saddler. But Jake had convinced him as well as us that he knew what he was doing so the animal made no fuss when Jake steered him through the gate and out onto the freshly-graded dirt road. Moving along without objection, the long-eared animal settled into a brisk half-sidling, half-trotting gait that rapidly carried them out of sight."

"Our sun shone brightly when Jake rode off, but, within 30 minutes, a heavy black cloud moved in, blocking it out. Fifteen minutes later a violent, quick-moving prairie storm was raining 'pitchforks and hayrakes'. Jake didn't take a slicker and was facing a two-hour ride. We knew without talking about it that he was going to get wet because he was riding straight toward that cloud when he left."

"Now a mule doesn't much care if he gets wet unless it's really cold weather, but I told them that Jake, with his best clothes on, was prob'ly mad as a wet hen by now. They all looked at each other, talked about it for a minute and nodded their heads in agreement."

"We had a new cook an' that guy wasn't much to look at, but I'm here to tell you that skimpy looks don't mean a cook cain't cook. He had fixed us up three big beef roasts for our Sunday dinner. You could cut any of them with a fork. He had baked 10 large pans of yeast rolls that melted in a man's mouth and had also worked up all the gravy an' vegetable fixins a man could want plus half a barrel of iced tea. For dessert there was a steaming cinnamon-flavored dried apple cobbler, big enough that anyone who wanted could eat two big helpings. An' I did."

"Between eatin', nappin', an' playin' a hand or two of match poker, I forgot about Jake 'til he walked through the front door right after 4:00. He had his tow sack with him but the bridle wasn't in it. I knew from this that he had taken the mule back to wherever it came from."

"Jake looked pretty rank. His clothes had gotten soaked and were only half dry. Mud was splashed all over them. His shoes were also slathered in mud with a generous overlay of damp cow plop. None of us was a stranger to that smell, and a large number of us had either walked or run off from farms to leave it behind forever. I didn't feel that strongly about it, but some of those guys would've taken a bad lickin' before agreeing to milk just one more cow."

"You have already seen that Jake was a loner with no close friends in the bunkhouse. He knew that we had all noticed and smelled him when he came in, but no emotion showed on his face. Looking neither right or left, he walked straight to his cot and stripped off his filthy clothes, dropping them onto the floor. Dragging his old suitcase out from underneath, he pulled out a suit of underwear, socks and work clothes, then dressed all over again, even changing into his work boots. When finished, he went out back to hang his wet stuff on the clothes line."

"People back then respected each other's privacy because strenuous and effective preventive measures were often used by people who decided their privacy had been invaded. I had never seen Jake unwind on anyone, but most of our guys were convinced he would hit a man hard if provoked. So nobody felt lucky enough to ask if he had gotten the girl or was given the boot by her dairy-farming daddy. Jake told us nothing. After cleaning up his filthy dress shoes, rubbing them as clean and dry as he could, he laid down on his cot and slept 'til supper time."

"Nobody was more surprised than me when, two Saturdays later, Jake started cleaning up again. This time, he was going into town. Just before leaving he stood up on the end of his cot and hollered for attention. Then he announced that he was gettin' married next afternoon out at his girlfriend's home. His future father-in-law, he announced with a grin, had especially asked him to invite all of us who would like to come and see this wedding.

Further, Jake had arranged with our boss for a gang truck to carry and bring back anyone who would like to attend. But no one who was already drinking would be allowed on the truck and no one, under threat of "serious" trouble, was to have more than two glasses of the host's home-brewed German beer after the wedding."

"'I am,' Jake finished with one of his rare smiles, 'on my way into town to buy me a tie and get my future wife a wedding ring!' Then he hopped off the cot, walked outside and jumped into a parked flivver driven by one of his future brothers-in-law."

"Well, now we knew that Jake had gotten the girl and not the gate. We also figured that both the mother and her daughter had been working on that old German, or this bunch of oilfield trash wouldn't have been invited anywhere near the wedding. So, remembering the good cooking of our German neighbors back home, I spruced up nicely and climbed aboard the gang truck when it rolled up next afternoon."

"We watched and listened as Jake and his girl experienced a much fancier wedding than most boomtowners ever had. Then we all went out back to sip some good German beer. But good as the beer was, those ladies' cooking was even better."

"Jake hadn't given any warnings about eating like those he issued about drinking, so I was looking for a new place to sit and eat my third piece of cake, when I saw the bride's father squatting under a big elm tree with three of his neighbors. They were all on the other side, and since no one seemed to care, I hunkered down behind them, leaning back against the tree trunk to eat. I hadn't intended to eavesdrop but couldn't help hearing what they said."

"'Dot young man,' the bride's father said, 'he proved that he loved my Kirsten. I was mad like nobodee's bizness 'cause I wasn't ready for her to marry with ennybody. But anyway I told she and her mudder that they shoot ask him over for me so I koot hear him say woteffer it was he had to tell me'."

"I continued to listen as the farmer talked about a hard rain shower catching him out in his dairy lot treating a sick cow. Shortly after the storm blew over, Jake, wet as a drowned rat, had trotted a wet mule up to their front yard gate. The farmer nodded grudging

approval as the young Texan alighted and tied his animal two fence
posts down from the gate so that mule droppings would not litter
the pathway. Jake walked up to the house and knocked at the door,
but the farmer didn't stop working. He had told his women to send
Jake up to the cow lot for this conversation. Any big Texan who
wanted to marry his daughter was going to have to earn the right
and ask properly."

"He guessed they'd had two inches of rain in less than an hour,
and his cow lot was so full of mud and droppings that he was wearing
rubber boots to work in. Placing his cow in a low spot in the middle
of the lot, he squatted down while doctoring her, watching under
her belly as Jake, getting taller and more determined the higher up
that hill he climbed, layered more and more mud over his once
shiny shoes."

"'He didn't like it, not much,' the farmer told his friends, 'because
he is a proud person. An' pride, to me, is one sign of a real man'."

"'I woot'nt hear him 'wen he talked at me and 'wen he climbed
the fence to get closer, I walked all over, getting more tools and
medicines, always goin' thru the deepest mud and droppings, but
he followed me ever step, just a-walkin' an' a-talkin.' Then, the old
guys all slapped their knees, laughed loudly and took long swigs
from their mugs."

"All four of them continued to squat on their hunkers because
the benches and chairs had all been claimed by women. Then they
fell silent for a time and gazed around, apparently relieved that my
boomtown bunk mates were on their best behavior. The pipeliners
had drunk lightly from their glasses of cool German beer and had
guarded their tongues better than I thought they would. Maybe
some of them were oilfield trash, as the old man had said, but they
behaved well that day anyway. Then, the old farmer finished his
story."

"'I kep' on a-workin',' he continued, 'walking all the time, and
finally he quit talking, but kept right on walkin' behind me. I knew
he figgered he was waitin' for me to tell if he could marry with my
daughter, but he wass not. I wass already whipped dere an' knew it.
He wass waiting only on me'."

"'Finally I stopped and faced him. He is a big one, dat, and I know he love my daughter or he wouldn't do dese 'tings he was doin'.'"

"'I tell him 'den dat I know he love my Kirsten, but not love her like me. He had not walk floor with her having colic or help her learn to walk, like me. Nor had he sit up with her at night when she wake up scared, and watch with her 'til she slip back to sleep'.'"

"'If my Kirsten want to marry wit you,' I tell him, 'dere isn't nothing I can do bout it, but I 'tink she is making big mistake. Our family are farming persons, not oil persons and we have different kinds of life and values'.'"

"His friends didn't laugh. Most of them had daughters and, if they hadn't already faced this problem, would soon be walking in his shoes. They nodded their heads, fully understanding and agreeing with the old gentleman's action as well as his principle."

"I didn't think it was funny either because I was remembering Jake's expression when he came back to the bunkhouse that day. We thought his face showed no expression, but now it seemed to me that there had been a trace of fear. Both these men loved the girl named Kirsten. One was afraid to lose her and the other was petrified with fear that he wouldn't get her. Leaning back and finishing my cake, I learned how the loser felt and have always remembered what he told his neighbors."

"'Dis big Texas man say he love my Kirsten jus like me an' will all her life, jus like me, an' take goot care of her un dere chilrenn, just as goot as I have did in my famly. Den we sit an talk an' I learn he knows lots about cows, but beef cows, not milk cows like me. But he can understan me an' I can understan him too. My wife, Gerta, she like him. My sons, dey like him, und me, myself: I don' tink he iss 'Oilfield Trash.' I can like him, too'.'"

"Then, his eyes watered. Barely controlling himself, the old fellow paused. His friends, embarrassed, looked at each other but I could read the sympathy in their eyes. Looking West into a brilliant and purpling sunset, the old gentleman fought hard to maintain a positive mind-set on what was one of the sadder days of his life. Finally looking back at his guests, he struggled hard, trying to convince himself as well as his friends. 'Some day I can'.'"

CHAPTER 8

NIPPLES—1920

"ON MY THIRD week after moving to Burkburnett," Cecil told me, "I hired out to the Paragon Oil Company. They paid us fair wages, always on time, and life was pretty good. That kind of job was rare in the oilfield. The company had put me to work in a field maintenance crew, working at different kinds of oilfield lease work called 'roustabouting'. My foreman was a man named Denny. Also in the crew were a man named Jake Johnson and a heavy guy we called 'Fatboy'. I don't remember the other three men's names."

"This fat feller was always talking with Denny and shinin' up to him. An' I guess Denny liked that a lot 'cause he often took the fat guy along when he was driving out to inspect and plan our next field job. The rest of us didn't get to loaf while this was goin' on. We had to keep on throwin' our shovels into the ground. Each mornin' when we rode out to the job, Fatboy would puff hisself up and tell us what kind of work we were goin' to do that day. Usually, he was right."

I had been workin' there about two weeks when, early one morning, the gang truck carried us way over to the far edge of the Southwest field, over those rutted out oilfield roads about 40 minutes away from the warehouse. We were to tie in a battery of oil tanks to a fresh dug well so the company could sell more oil. Sellin' oil was the only reason anybody did anything at all in an oilfield but a large number of those workers never figured it out. They actually didn't know that if their company didn't keep on sellin' oil an' makin' money that their jobs would dry up in a week.

Soon as we got there, Denny started all of us except Fatboy to digging a pipe ditch. He told Fatboy to cut off and thread up four three inch nipples 30 inches long so we could use them on that job. Fatboy said he would, but when he reached into the bib of his overalls to pull out his measuring rule, it wasn't there. He cussed an' blurted out that he had left it back at the bunkhouse.

Well, if it had been me, I wouldn't have left my rule at all. Even if I had, I wouldn't have blurted the news out in front of God and everybody. I would have figured out another way to do my job. But old Fatboy wasn't thinkin' fast, if at all. An' Denny got mad at him in a flash because ever since they had made him a strawboss, he had quit carryin' a rule. Later on, when I was promoted, I carried a small steel rule everywhere I went. And when I retired in 1966 as District Superintendent with Sinclair Oil Company, I still carried one in my shirt pocket, along with a notepad, a pen and a pipe thread gauge.

Denny was mad because there we were, stuck out in the middle of that big cow pasture, with no rule to measure with. He was going to have to drive all the way back to our warehouse and pick up a rule or steel tape because he hadn't figured he should carry one, at least somewhere in the gang truck. But mainly he was mad because, after we finished this little ditch, there was nothing else for us to do until those nipples were cut and threaded. And Fatboy, when he forgot that rule, had killed two hours of work time for our crew. Our farm boss wouldn't be mad at Fatboy. Instead, he would ream out Denny's sitter so deep that he would be sittin' on a thick drivin' cushion for three weeks."

"Unable to solve the problem, Denny cranked up the truck and threw in the clutch, headin' back for the warehouse. That was when I remembered we had a tow sack in the truck with a couple of 10-inch nipples in it. Along with some other spare parts we generally carried around a few short nipples, plus a bunch of miscellaneous pipe fittings commonly needed in the field, but there wasn't a steel tape. Not even a carpenter's rule."

"I hollered and waved at Denny to stop him then said we could measure out 30 inches pretty easy by marking one of those 10-inch nipples three times along a pipe joint and cutting off a 30-inch piece. He looked at me for a second, then still half mad, shut down his truck and told Fatboy to do what I said."

"While Fatboy was cutting and threadin' out his nipples, Denny came over to watch us dig the short ditch needed for layin' pipe out to the tank battery. After getting us pointed out, he walked over to watch Fatboy do his cutting and threading. Soon as Denny left, Jake Johnson, half-serious an' half kidding, called me a 'smart little so an' so'."

"Then he said that if I hadn't stopped Denny, we could have loafed around for an hour and a half while waitin' for him to get back with a rule. I was the youngest man in the crew, an' didn't need any fights with these older men, so I didn't answer back. I just kept on diggin'. About then Denny walked back over. Fatboy was trailing along behind him with an armload of 30 inch nipples."

"'Jake,' Denny told our newly married man, 'you and the rest of the gang finish diggin' out this ditch and, Fatboy, you tie in these nipples. Don't forget to dope the threads real good.' Then, lookin' at me, he said, 'Shorty, you come ride with me. I want to drive over and eyeball our next job to see if we can cut down some on our diggin' time.'"

CHAPTER 9

OLD STRAW—1921

"WE CALLED HIM Big Boss," Cecil said, and I watched as his mind journeyed back to the past, checking and arranging his facts. "That was because he was the guy who came out from the head office each week and handed our paychecks over to the lease boss. Our boss would then give them to his new strawboss who strutted around and handed them out to us, along with a lot of unnecessary criticism."

"We called that strawboss 'Old Straw' behind his back, 'cause he loved to strut and throw his voice around. He also liked for us to call him 'Boss' when the lease boss was gone. During the time he was handing out our checks and fussing at us, he was always tellin' us to keep our 'heads down and our tails up.' That's oilfield language for 'keep on workin'—hard!'"

"Now, our lease boss always did anything he thought was necessary to keep the Big Boss, over in Wichita Falls, happy. But on that particular Monday morning he had no advance warning and was completely unprepared. Big Boss showed up at the warehouse before 8:00, like a regular hand. An' he was mad as a wet hen."

"You see, our company, Paragon Oil Company, owned quite a few leases, oil wells, and gathering lines around Burkburnett, Texas, during the boom. And, in the year I am tellin' about, 1920, they sold most of their oil through a pipeline. But, like most of the other companies, they also kept a bunch of oil storage tanks filled up on their leases so's to sell as much oil to truckers as they would buy. The company made more money on truck sales because they didn't have to pay out any pipeline fees. But nothing in the oilfield is perfect, and oil storage tanks have a list of special problems all their own."

"Our home office was mad because they'd just learned that Paragon had been losing money off one of our leases by selling long oil measurements out of one of the storage tanks. No oil company, then or now, likes to lose oil, and Paragon was no exception. Smart lease bosses and superintendents plug up oil leaks awfully quick allowing very few short measurements to show up. But our lease boss had overlooked this tank and the loss had gone on so long that the home office had noticed it by comparing the tank's low production figures with others on the same lease."

"Everybody in the company, from the district office in Wichita, on up to the home office, hated this kind of problem. An' anybody who has worked in the oilfield as long as six months has learned that all the rocks and BS that pile up will always roll straight downhill. Lease bosses who are ambitious about future promotion learn to keep this kind of tank problem from happening. Our boss was better than most but even good lease bosses can get unlucky."

"Now, for people who have no idea at all what I'm talkin' about, I will explain that BS is a mixture of fine dirt and other types of sedimentation which, over many months of producing, slowly settles to the bottom of any oil field storage tank. Field hands still call it by its oilfield name, which is the same as the smelly discharge coming out from the tail end of a bull, rather than the slightly more delicate initials I've used here. Modern oil company reports call it 'sedimentation' or 'waste product' and in the old days it was trucked out of the way to be burned or mixed up with sand and gravel so it could be spread on top of oilfield lease roads. It mixes well and lasts a long time when you use it that way but the road won't hold up extra heavy weights in real hot or real wet weather. Today BS is handled differently. Companies have to dispose of it with great care, because those misguided environmentalists in Austin and Washington think it's more dangerous than raw atomic waste. But it isn't dangerous today and it wasn't then unless you maybe decided to pour it on your breakfast cereal ever' day for a week."

"Lease tanks are supposed to be cleaned out regularly, but this one had got lost in the shuffle and nobody could offer a good reason why. You see, BS often settles unevenly on tank bottoms, and if a gauger happens to place his measuring rod on a high spot, more oil will be pumped into a buyer's truck than he is charged for. An' the selling company can gripe, but after their buyer has already swallowed that extra oil, he is never goin' to spit it back up."

"And, because losin' oil is the same as losin' money, a situation like this really makes waves. My guess is that the Big Boss had already been chewed out, before visiting us so, soon as he got there, he chewed out our boss. Then, when his time came to chew, our lease boss roasted Old Straw hotly for not having that tank cleaned out before now."

"There are lots of reasons for not cleaning BS out of a tank and one or two of them is occasionally acceptable. But most of those reasons just mask the main one, which is that it's a messy and dirty job. Nobody likes to do it, and many a good foreman has put off a tank cleanout longer than he ought to."

"Big Boss led our gang truck as we drove out to the lease where that offending tank was located. He stayed just ahead of us and goosed his big Buick every time he thought about it, throwing up a good-sized cloud of road dirt and gravel. Our pumper had been called out earlier and instructed to 'pump down' the dirty tank and Big Boss intended to stay and watch this cleanout performed 'right'. We knew the situation was serious as we watched Old Straw and our lease boss through the rear glass of Big Boss's Buick. They were waving their arms and talking over each other in their efforts to keep from rubbing his fur in the wrong direction any more than it already had been."

"Now, to say that we had never liked Old Straw would have been a giant understatement. In fact, I took a considerable amount of trouble to stay out of his way. He was responsible for us losing several good hands in the short time I had worked there and was so sorry that he would slip up behind a bunch of bushes or a small rise in the prairie to watch a crew while it worked. He was always hoping to catch some unlucky roustabout sitting down and smoking or 'leaning' on his shovel."

"Whenever he caught somebody, he always chewed 'em out good, and he'd already fired two hands for very little reason. One of them was really good help. An' we had two other hands who had simply quit tolerating him and walked off the job."

"Besides all that, we had found out that Old Straw had broken company rules by wangling his cousin's son from over around Duncan, Oklahoma, a job as our truck driver. Now hiring relatives was completely against the rules of any oil company I've ever heard about and, even though we all resented it, none of us would turn him in. Still, he was lording it over us way too hard and leanin' far too much against the wrong side of trouble every time he gave us a long lecture while handing out our hard-earned pay checks."

"Everybody in the oilfield knew that roustabouts were close to the bottom of the stack. They earned less money than most other crafts and were generally 'first to be fired and last to be hired' when oil price and production dropped off."

"Any Big Boss with just one eye and a lick of sense would automatically know that no roustabout was at fault when a tank hadn't been cleaned out, and our Big Boss was no dummy. Yet, when we walked past our bosses to start cleanin' out this tank, I could hear Old Straw shamelessly trying to lay our dirty tank bottom off onto a hand he had fired several days back. I could see that Big Boss wasn't paying him any mind, but he kept right on yappin', trottin' half a step behind, like a puppy dog, just waggin' his head and giving Big Boss an earache about how sorry roustabouts are."

"Well, Big Boss drove his car right up close to that tank, stopping about 20 feet from the cleanout valve. He opened the front door, threw his feet over on the ground an' sat, elbow on knee, chin on hand, watching while we dug out a three-foot hole, four-feet wide, right under the tank's big gate valve. The idea was to drain the last few inches of crud and gunk out of the tank bottom and catch it in that hole so it could be trucked off for burning. The small amount of oil it held was so full of dirt and BS that the company didn't want it dumped into the pipeline and any customer who got it pumped into his truck tank would scream like a drunk Madam on Saturday night."

"Now, pipeliners and roustabouts dug holes with their long-handled 'idiot spoons', better than they do anything else because digging has always been the biggest part of their job. We had that hole finished up nice and clean as a grave in less than 10 minutes. A couple of 2" X 6" boards were laid across the top of the hole and, when the big gate valve was opened, a gob of thick oily sludge began to flow. But, after running freely for five minutes, it stopped. Something inside the tank had settled over the drain hole and blocked off the valve. Our hole was only half full, and we needed to get a lot more BS out of the tank so the inspection plates could be removed and our clean-out job finished up."

"Old Straw, trying to make a good impression, strutted onto the boards over the hole and began to hammer on the tank valve with a pick head, hoping to break up whatever obstruction had moved against it from the inside. But whatever was in the tank wouldn't budge. Besides that, what he was doing was dangerous. A spark generated by his pick hammering could blow up the tank and us with it!"

"Big Boss stood up and walked over. Watching for only a second he told the strawboss to stop hammering and stick his hand up into the mouth of that valve to see if he could tell what was wrong. We watched happily as that loudmouthed tinhorn squatted down to reach gingerly inside with one finger, actin' like he was stickin' his hand into a bear's mouth. He quickly pulled it back an' swore he couldn't find anything. Then he pulled a big red and white bandanna handkerchief from his hip pocket to wipe off his dirty finger."

"His attitude clearly showed that he thought he was way past the point in his career where he ought to be getting oil on his hands. Too late, he also remembered that this attitude made it look as if he was rebuking Big Boss for treating him like a real oilfield hand. But his biggest mistake, up to then, was raising his pick to strike again."

"Don't hit that valve any more, Big Boss ordered crisply."

"Looking around, the big guy saw me, the youngest person there. He asked me to bring him a heavy ball peen hammer from the gang truck. And when I handed it to him, he gave it to the strawboss, telling him to push up into the valve throat with its wooden handle, because the wood couldn't strike any sparks, and try to shove that obstruction away from the opening."

"Old Straw stepped lightly onto the boards and squatted down again, real careful, 'cause he didn't want to get any BS on his clothes. His entire crew was enjoying this show and he knew it. Half-heartedly, he reached up into the valve opening with the hammer handle and hit some sort of object but either couldn't or wouldn't apply enough pressure to move it out of the way. Then he told Big Boss it was stuck and stood up again, reaching once more for his bandanna. And that was more than Big Boss would tolerate. He had swallowed a gutfull, and decided right then was a perfect time for him to belch."

"Jump in there, he told Old Straw loudly, and see if you can push up hard enough from the bottom to move the obstruction over."

"Are you serious?"

"Sure am. Hop in!"

"I'm not gonna do that. It'll ruin my boots."

"Big Boss looked steadily into the strawboss's eyes for at least 20 seconds and said nothing else. Then, he reached over and took the hammer back. Holding it by the head, he used its handle to brace on one of the boards, and, placing his other hand on the ground, he slipped both feet easily into that stinking hole which was half full of BS. Punching upward into the valve mouth with the end of the hammer handle he poked and pried around. After several hard shoves, whatever was on the other side began to move. And, after two more twisting, sideways thrusts we saw BS once more oozing freely through the valve."

"Pulling his body up onto one of the 2 X 6's, Big Boss shoved one foot over on the ground. Then, pushing down with one arm on the ground and bracing once more with the hammer handle, he got a knee up on the board and slowly stood erect. He was a really big mess."

"A fine pair of perforated wing tipped dress shoes, freshly shined only minutes before, were ruined for good. His dress pants were also trashed. They were stained well above the knees with stinking greenish black crude oil which slowly began to seep groundward.

His straw sailor hat, white shirt and belt were still perfectly clean, but the tie had gotten a good dip and was trying hard to ruin both his belt and shirt. Big Boss paid his clothes no attention. Instead, he looked around and, finding me again, handed me the hammer."

"Kid, will you watch this valve, and if it quits flowing again, crawl into the hole and free it up?"

"Well, listen man, I needed to work and there was only one sensible answer for me to give. 'Yes sir,' I said, quickly grabbing the tool."

"But nobody walked off. Ever'body stood hitched, to watch and listen. Even the youngest hand on that lease, me, knew that this incident wasn't over with. And we were right. Big Boss was about to give us a lesson in oilfield management. After he was certain everyone was looking, he turned round to face Old Straw who suddenly developed a giant problem with looking him straight in the eye. Waiting patiently until solid eye contact was established, Big Boss looked straight into Straw's flushed face and finished him off."

"As for you—you're fired! I want you off of this lease. Far as I'm concerned, you can hitch-hike into town. Tell 'em at the office I said for you to drag down your time."

"Then he looked carefully round to make certain he hadn't lost his audience, but there was no need. You couldn't have pulled anybody away from there without tying them to a bulldozer. While scanning us, the big guy also prudently watched Straw to be certain what he would do. He'd been in the oilfield a long time and knew that bosses sometimes had to fight or run before making a firing stick. We could also tell by the way he held his body that our Big Boss wasn't about to run. But it didn't matter. Old Straw was a natural coward an' didn't even puff up. He wilted like a daisy."

"But Big Boss still wasn't finished. His lesson had two parts. The first was most obvious. It underlined to every one of us that any man who disobeyed company management, especially Big Boss's part of it, was in deep doo-doo. The second part was intended to show that good things could happen when workers followed his instructions. Locating Old Straw again, and fixing him with a pitiless gaze, Big Boss launched his final blast."

"It's all right with me if you want to wait 'til quitting time and ride in on the gang truck. That is, you can if the truck driver will carry you. It all depends on the Kid here, because he is our new truck driver."

Now finished, Big Boss turned and walked slowly over to his Buick. Opening the trunk, he pulled out a slicker. Spreading it carefully over his front seat, he walked back and cranked it up, then crawled in and started off. It took most of us that long to realize he had known about Old Straw's nephew all along, but was trying to be kind and had allowed the man to keep his job."

"I watched carefully but the tank drained properly until it was empty and I didn't have to climb into the sump hole. But I would have if necessary. And it wouldn't just have been because I needed my job any more. It would also have been because Big Boss had asked me to do it. He had not only earned the respect of his youngest employee that day but had been given the respect of every man in that crew."

"When our tank was finished I looked around for Old Straw. Even though I didn't have to take him, I decided he was entitled to a ride back to the warehouse whether I liked him or not. But he and his Oklahoma relative had disappeared. In two days the crew had forgotten them both but none of them ever forgot the Big Boss."

CHAPTER 10

PUMP STATION—1921

"WITHIN THREE WEEKS after Big Boss gave me the truck driver's job, I had learned the exact location of every pump station, well and pipeline connection that Paragon Oil Company owned. I also got acquainted with the gang bosses, the lease foremen and with Big Boss, too. I hadn't been expecting that, but I ended up talking with him every week, sometimes two or three times."

"At least once a week, when I hauled machinery or supplies from an oilfield supply store, the railroad station in Burk, or from anywhere else we got our stores, he would leave orders for me to drive by his office because he wanted to inspect my load. While checking, he would tell me why he had ordered the different brands of supplies and equipment I was carrying and insisted that I never take any substitutions."

"I was not to deliver any brands of tools or equipment for company use which the Big Boss had not ordered. He explained that he had tested all of them and knew which kind would do the best job and earn the most money for Paragon. He also explained that some manufacturers would pay supply house salesmen under-the-table money to push their brands off onto truck drivers like me. He preferred that our competition, not Paragon, lose money on those sub-standard brands. At first I thought he was too picky, but the more I learned about the oilfield, the smarter he got."

"Most of the time, my job was to carry roustabouts out to the field and drop them off with tools and water and lunches, to perform lease work. After that I hauled stuff around for the company and returned that afternoon to bring the men in. If they had only a short job to do, I would stay until they were finished so I could haul them to some other job location."

"On those short stops, most drivers would loaf around or nap in the shade of their truck while the gang worked. I'd never been a daytime sleeper and had been taught that a man, when he hired out, ought to work and not sleep. So, unless I needed to do something on my truck, I would grab a shovel and help the gang dig."

"If the job was so small that I would be in the way, I kept back and carried water for the men. They appreciated that. Those guys were all older than me but they were still young men, and awfully wild. Only three in our bunkhouse were married men with families. They were staying in the bunkhouse because their families were back in places they had left, mostly on family farms."

"Most oilfield workers had little ambition, if any at all. In fact, if they noticed another man working harder than necessary or doing anything he hadn't been told, they would rag him, callin' him a "company" man. Those Boomers often thought a whole lot more about five o'clock and pay day than about their job. And most of them looked forward to eating a big meal in town then maybe heading out to a roadhouse or dancehall where they could find whiskey and women and get into fights. They loved to fight, and if they couldn't find a good one, they sometimes chose up sides and fought each other."

"I was different from them because I'd been working and planning like a man ever since my dad died. And I had learned to save a little money but saving never occurred to most oilfield hands. I had outgrown their attitudes, and developed ambition, but had to hide it so the others wouldn't make my life miserable. During each work day they mostly planned about big eatin', big drinkin' and chasin' after women. I thought of some of those things too, but I also planned to move as high up with Paragon as I could get. So I always worked hard and looked forward to promotion."

"Six weeks later, at quitting time, I dropped a tired, dirty and hungry bunch of roustabouts off at the bunkhouse. By the time I'd finished gassing up my truck and cleaning off some of its dirt, then rubbing on the paint and checking out the oil, water an' tires, so it would be ready to go next morning, it was supper time. I walked over to the bunkhouse and took my place in the wash line, to clean up for supper. That was when I heard two field hands just ahead of me talking about a Paragon pump station operator."

"They paid me no attention and talked in normal tones, not seeming to care if anyone heard them. One was tellin' the other about a pump station operator who had said he was going to quit Paragon. The man's father had died and he was going back to Oklahoma to run the family farm. The talkative guy was telling his buddy that, in a day or two, he intended to go over and ask Mr. Harpes for that pumper's job."

"Well, I knew that Paragon's pump station operators made more money than truck drivers, but I wasn't certain whether I knew enough to do that work. Yet, when I thought about the guy doing all his talking, I figured I could do it if he could. Probably better. I also figured, that if Mr. Harpes could give the job to someone in a day in a day or two, he could do it that afternoon if he took the notion. So, I left the wash line and walked straight over to the other side of camp, where there were two company houses. Mr. Harpes an' his family lived in the biggest."

"I stood on that tiny front porch, barely large enough to hold a big metal boot scraper someone had nailed on the edge of its floor and waited for somebody to answer my knock. When the door opened, Mr. Harpes stood there, gnawing on a big chicken drumstick. Pulling it loose and chewing while he talked, he asked, 'What do you need, Shorty?'"

"I didn't much enjoy this nickname but figured it was okay for my boss to use it if he decided to and didn't bother correcting him. Instead, I spoke up quickly, telling him I'd heard that his pumphouse operator was quitting. I also said, that if he thought I could handle the job, and hadn't promised it to somebody else, that I sure would like to have it."

"Well, he didn't smile or frown or say anything for at least a full minute. He just leaned on his door frame, chewin' the chicken leg,

and watching me. I was nervous, but couldn't do anything other
than stand there and wait. Hat in hand, grinning tightly, I looked
him in the face, while he decided to say something. An' finally, he
did."

"What's your intentions, Shorty?"

"I didn't understand his question and said so."

"I mean, what are you gonna' do? Do you want to work here as
a permanent sort of hand or will you quit out on me and take off
the very first time somebody says he'll pay you a nickel an hour
more?"

"Without missing a beat, I said, 'Mr. Harpes, my intentions are
to keep workin' here long as you let me.'"

"He looked at me a while longer, never takin' his eyes off my
face, and finished up his chicken leg. Then, flipping the bone out
into the front yard, he jerked his head and said that sounded OK to
him. He also said he would 'sorta look out for me' and would get
back in touch with me about the pump-station job. Then he went
back in and closed the door."

"Two weeks later, a week before the month ended, Mr. Harpes
sent word for me to pick up my bedroll an' clothes. The new truck
driver, Fatboy, was to drive by an' haul me an' my junk over to the
pump station where I would get a week of training from the old
operator before he left."

"That pump station operator didn't impress me much. He slept
on a cot inside the pumphouse but the place was so filthy and
littered up with trash that I spread my quilts outside and slept on a
pile of lumber. He worked a ten hour shift from 8:00 at night 'til
6:00 in the morning. While looking around, I could see he didn't
believe in performing one more minute of work than he had to."

"His instructions were simple. All an operator had to do, he
said, was shut everything down if the pump died and call in for help.
Otherwise, he just filled up the those three bright and pretty glass
lubricator bowls on the compressor every time he thought about
it. During that entire week he taught me nothing else except how
to switch lines into and out of the oil tanks that were set up near
the station."

"Soon as he headed for Oklahoma I started cleanin' up that station. The windows came first because they were so black you couldn't see through 'em. Then I talked Fatboy into bringing me a wheelbarrow, a lot of hand tools and a large jack. After that I gathered up all the trash, piling it on the barrow and burying it. Next, I raked up four wheel barrow loads of dead bugs, mostly grasshoppers and crickets, along with a lot of oily dirt off the pumphouse floor. I dumped all of them in a little draw below the station. Following that I cut all the grass round the building so's a driver who visited could see all the big holes and not run off into them. After cutting, I used the wheel barrow and filled up all the holes so a truck could drive and maneuver round the building anywhere it needed to."

"Continuing my cleanup I jacked up a drooping corner of the pumphouse and shoved several large flat sandstones underneath to hold it up where it was supposed to be. Then I hauled 10 or 15 loads of dirt inside and spread them on the floor, grading the surface and ramming the dirt tight, so that any loose fluid would drain out properly. After that I filled up one or two large holes in the road leading to my station and covered them with dirt and gravel to keep them from wallowing out again."

"Last of all, I got Fatboy to bring me some company paint from the warehouse. Their colors were red and black, so to finish the cleanup, I scraped and painted that pumphouse inside and out. After that I figured the building was clean enough to sleep in during bad weather. I had already seen every one of Paragon's pumphouses and lease buildings and mine was now cleaner and shinier than any of them, so I called my cleanup done."

"My work schedule was easy. I started each shift by looking everywhere for any sign of trouble. The pump and compressor were good machines and there was seldom any trouble to find. After that I worked at cleaning up the station and doing odd jobs until it was too dark to work outside. Then I filled up all the compressor's lubricator bowls and, throwing my quilts down on the softest board in my lumber pile, slept outside because it was quieter and much cooler during that hot Texas summer."

"About midnight, I got up, filled the bowls again, and looked for any trouble signs. Then I slept 'til daylight. Getting up, I filled the lubricators once more and performed whatever cleaning there was until my relief showed up. Afterward, I walked two miles over to the bunkhouse for breakfast."

"At the end of my third week on the pump station job, while I was polishing off a breakfast of fried pork chops, pancakes, syrup, biscuits and coffee over at the cookshack, the cook told me that Mr. Harpes, the boss who had made absolutely certain that I would be a permanent and long-time hand, had up and quit the company. He had gotten mad about something, pulled down his time an' headed back home to Kentucky. Our new boss was named Mr. Abrams."

"I had finished up my shift but had slept most of the night and didn't need a nap, so I went over for a visit in the warehouse, which had our field office in one corner. Mr. Abrams was talking on the phone when I came in and telling somebody that all his hands were out working and he had no one to help them. When he got off the phone, I said I would help them if he wanted me to."

"He looked at me and asked who I was. After I told him, he wanted to know if I was the one they said had been doin' all the cleanup work over at the pump station. I admitted that this was so, and after looking at me a minute, he pulled down the telephone and cranked on its generator. Talking again to the guy he had just finished with, he told him to send somebody over to pick me up."

"In those days all our leases were busy. Lease foremen were continually calling or coming by, to ask for help. And that new boss was always having to tell them they'd have to wait because he didn't have anybody to send. But, after I had hung around a week, and kept volunteering, he began to point at me and tell them to 'just take Cecil'."

"That, I guess, was when Mr. Abrams really began to notice me. Because, about a week afterward, Big Boss called the warehouse and wanted to talk with me. He asked how I liked my new job. After I told him, he said the company really appreciated it that I was makin' them a good hand.

"This kept on for about three months 'til a day when I was talking with Wilbur Schofley, a Paragon gauger. Wilbur said he was going to retire at the end of the week. Now I didn't know how to gauge tanks, but I knew gaugers made more money than me, so I asked if he thought I could handle his kind of work. He said he thought I could. In fact, he figured I could learn everything I needed to know about it in a couple of weeks.

"Then, I asked if he minded me asking for his job. He told me he didn't. In fact, he figured it might be a good idea to tell Mr. Abrams he was quitting. He had notified Mr. Harpes but didn't know if he had told anybody else before he got mad and quit. He figured it didn't matter a whole lot because it wouldn't be hard to find a replacement for him, so he thought I should go ahead and ask Mr. Abrams. Later in the day, he would call in and formally quit. Then he finished up by saying that, if Mr. Abrams gave me the job, he would stay two weeks longer and teach me how things worked in Paragon's gauging business."

"It was about one o'clock that afternoon when I finished a delivery and started over to the Paragon camp and, luckily, Mr. Abrams pulled up to park at his regular spot near the warehouse door. I walked straight over and told him about Wilbur quitting, then asked if he would consider giving me his job. Mr. Abrams was a large man, like Big Boss, and had a heavy voice, but he was generally polite and thoughtful before saying what he did or didn't want. I also told him that Wilbur offered to stay around and teach me if they wanted him to."

"After listening quietly to what I told him and thinking about it for a little bit he said, 'Well, I didn't know Wilbur was going to quit, but I'm not surprised. He's pretty old and heavy to be breaking out eight or ten times a day and climbing up and down tanks on those rickety wooden ladders. If he quits me, you can have the job.'"

"Just as he finished, the telephone horn, which was mounted on the warehouse wall, blasted off and it was the correct number of honks for our lease. He went inside to answer and I walked over to wash up for anything I could pry out of the cook for a lunch. After drying off, I walked back to the road, and turned toward the messhall. Mr. Abrams drove past, and when he saw me, he stopped and backed up to talk. Sticking his head out the window, he spoke only two sentences."

"Cecil, you're a gauger now. Meet me in the warehouse at 7:45 in the morning."

"This was a real break for me. I had gotten a job which could actually lead to a management position with Paragon. My new pay would be $205.00 a month and I would have a company car. Within five months after coming to Burk I had opened up a bank account, bought myself two new suits and could afford to smoke a cigar whenever I wanted one."

BOOMTOWNER—1930

"TWO MEN WERE unconscious and, when I went down to pull them out, the gas got me too. Two other men were on top of the tank, but were afraid to come down to help us. We would all have died if a 16-year-old boy, a large farm type kid, hadn't walked by. They told him what was happening and he climbed down into that stinking tank three times, bringing us out, one at a time.

"When I got over being gassed, I tried to find the boy and thank him but couldn't. In all the excitement no one had bothered to get his name and no one knew how to locate him. He must have been passing through and kept on going. We never learned who he was.

Ray Mills

Note: Mr. Mills was a small man, weighing about 145 pounds and was lease foreman for Magnolia Oil Company.

BOOMER'S KIDS—1932

IT WAS A bright August morning in Burkburnett, Texas. The year was 1932. I would be five years old in four more months but there were lots of things I wanted to learn that my father hadn't yet taken time to teach me. So out on our front porch, I was down on both knees, trying hard to learn from my dad's youngest brother how to spin a top. That was when we heard it, and the noise was as loud as a nearby lightning strike, crackling with power, but different from any sound I had ever heard. It wasn't quite as loud as close lightning but it resonated with inbred force. Alarmed, I jumped straight up and grabbed onto my Uncle's nearest leg when I came down. Then we heard the first strong ululant scream, like the noise of a large, badly wounded animal. I clung tighter.

Searching for guidance, I saw that my uncle's face had bleached to white. But he was nine years older than me and a little less afraid. Turning, he jumped for our front yard, to see what had happened but made little real progress because I stuck to him like a gob of tar. By the time we reached a place where we could see, the only visible sign was a cloud of rapidly thinning whitish smoke, big as a Shetland pony, which rose slowly in the quiet air above our neighbor's roof. We could still hear the anguished howls, but not as loud as before. Now they were coming from inside the Parson's home, three doors West of us on Eighth Street.

Finally peeling me loose, my uncle legged straight down to the neighbor's home, jumped onto their front porch and vanished inside. Afraid to follow, I turned back to look for my mother. She was only three steps away and the color moved rapidly back into her face when she saw I was standing up, apparently unhurt. She grabbed and hugged me, then asked what happened.

"Shotgun?" I suggested.

"No, Son, the noise was way too loud.

Then she missed my uncle. "Where's J. B. ?"

Before I could answer, she heard the less strident but still earnest wailing from inside our neighbor's home. "Who's crying at the Parson's house?"

"I don't know." Then pulling on her hand, "Let's go in. I'm scared."

Mom turned toward the Parsons. "You go on. "I need to see about J. B."

Then we saw him returning. Jumping off the Parson's porch, he ran hard toward us, but before he arrived, their old Chevrolet had backed speedily from its driveway. Driven by Mrs. Parsons, accompanied by a neighbor lady, it passed us before he arrived. The car's rear wheels threw spatters of gravel back toward us as it skidded full speed round the corner of Avenue C, toward Doc Russell's office downtown. Rising above the engine noise, we could still hear those lusty cries until the vehicle was half a block away.

Mom questioned sharply. "J. B. What happened?"

Something exploded and Bobby Parsons got hurt! Blood was all over his face and everything else!"

"What blew up?"

"They don't know an' were too busy to find out." Then he added what even I already knew. "They just took him to the doctor!"

That evening after dark, my dad saw Mr. Parsons drive slowly back into their drive and walked down to talk. Mr. Parsons said that, on the day before, Bobby and some of his 10-year-old buddies had been playing near an abandoned oil well site, located down in Red River bottom, half a mile from where we lived. While rooting around the derrick, they pried up an old timber and discovered a half-rotted, box of dynamite caps. Not realizing the danger involved, Bobby had brought them home. In their back yard next morning, he decided to hammer one on a brick to explode it, as boys often did with the caps fired in their toy pistols.

Both Bobby's eyes were gone and our neighbors had decided to move to Austin, as soon as their affairs could be settled in Burkburnett. There was no other place in Texas where blind people could learn to perform the pitifully small number of jobs which were offered them in the 1930's.

CHAPTER 11

RED DEVIL—1932

BECAUSE HE WAS mean and scared me witless, I always hated him. I was too young then to know that people hate most the things they fear most. My grandfather had a fair-sized mean streak and he liked that horrible bird because it was as mean as a snake. My grandmother took up for him because her hens loved him more and laid more eggs for him than for any rooster she ever owned. No one bothered to ask how I felt because they already knew.

In 1932, a year before I started public school, my mother gave birth to a second child, my sister Gwynda. The pair of us added up to a giant sized work week, and mother quickly felt the need of some tender loving care for herself. So she packed up, and struggling to haul both of us around, took a one week visit to her own parents. It was a tough year for her and we made two more of those visits before my sister reached her first birthday.

Granddad was an old-time oilfield driller who once told me he didn't know how many wells he had shoved into the ground but the number was "not nearly a thousand". He had been forced out of the oilfield because he had "come down" with a disease which, in the year 2004, medical science calls "rheumatoid arthritis". Back then people called it "rheumatism", and because of it, my grandpa never worked on a derrick floor again. But, for several years before the disease crippled him permanently, he worked at occasional light jobs and the year my sis was born, he was pumping a lease in Archer County, Texas for a small independent oil operator, named Perry Boyd.

In 1932, America had sunk downward into the deepest and longest lasting depression we have ever known. The thing seemed willing to go on forever, and a growing number of American families found it harder to store up or can enough home grown vegetables and other supplies to last through our hard North Texas winters. And if Texans and Oklahomans had known this depression was going to hang on long as it did, many would have started for California a lot sooner.

Granddad lived seven or eight miles Southeast of Holliday, Texas near Dad's Corner, on a small oilfield lease, right in the middle of Willason's Cattle Ranch. Mr. Boyd, had built a small "shotgun" house on this lease for his pumpers to live in. Shotgun houses were single-walled and wooden framed, with a covering of boards nailed on the outside to make walls. There was no insulation inside and this one had a corrugated tin roof. Inside, when you looked up, you could follow the rise of every rafter all the way up to where it was nailed to the ridge row.

This house was some better than a pioneer's cabin or dugout, mainly because it was above ground. Its main plus was that it had four small rooms and the roof didn't leak, but you still had to trot 75 feet from the back door to use their two-hole toilet. The house floor was made of pine boards which my grandmother scoured with home-made lye soap once every week, and when winter winds gusted, the house moaned in time with the gusts. Anybody who moved over six feet away from the stove in cold weather might as well go on out.

Mr. Boyd had fenced in a two-acre plot of dirt with a four-strand barbed wire fence. This allowed plenty of room for a garden, a hen house and granddad's smokehouse. It also kept out the wild prairie cattle that ranged all over the Willason ranch. But the fence had no effect whatsoever on an ever-present supply of spiders, scorpions and red wasps plus an occasional rattlesnake which crawled into the yard for shade.

My mother's younger brothers, Jay and Austin, were still at home. Jay, the oldest had just graduated from a small rural school named Geraldine and had hired out at the ranch to help with summer fencing.

Austin was still a student and had developed a local reputation as a tennis player. The seven of us filled Mr. Boyd's house to the brim, but this was a time when people didn't mind being crowded up with smelly bodies as much as they disliked being wet and hungry. And while the house had absolutely no extra room, there was plenty to eat and it kept out most Texas storms fairly well.

Money had virtually stopped moving from one person to another and, if anyone had told us that people would someday use credit cards to buy food and clothing we would have thought they were crazy. Every merchant knew about credit in those days, but none of them would have been dumb enough to honor a credit card. Every Texan we knew bought things on credit, but lenders and borrowers each hated the system.

Neither ordinary citizens or business people who came into a few extra dollars would mention it to anyone. Banks with money acted as if the government was never going to make any more and might run out. So, they stopped making loans and their money was locked in the vaults. People often told each other that the last place in the world a man ought to go, if he really needed a loan, was to a bank. No banker, they said, wanted to loan a man a dollar unless he could mortgage up 10 or 20 more to secure that loan.

Granddad kept a cow and grandmother kept her laying hens, hatching hundreds of eggs in order to raise healthy fryers for house meat. If they were lucky, the cow would bring a calf every year, which could be sold when he was large enough to butcher. Grandmother constantly stuck her choicest red-brown eggs under her chicken "brooders" bringing off a hatch every other week so the chicks could grow up to be fryers.

We considered chicks to be fryers at six to eight weeks. When she needed meat, grandmother had one of her sons to wring a pair of chicken necks. This would provide meat for the next meal. It took 20 or more hens, laying hard, to furnish their household, and its visitors, with enough meat and eggs.

As a boy in the Tennessee hills, granddad had learned from his father how to smoke beef and hams in a home-built smokehouse. He had also learned how to kill wild game and had taught his Texas sons to do the same. Most mornings, at daylight, while he hunted up the cow and led her back home to be milked, one of my uncles would hike down toward Holliday creek, shouldering the family's double-barreled 12-gauge shotgun. They killed rabbits, squirrels and quail, normally shooting two or three animals or birds, sometimes even four or five, on each trip. All game was brought home and carefully cleaned, then cut up, dipped in brine water and dumped straight into a hot skillet where grandmother fried it up for breakfast.

No matter how little game was killed, none was thrown away. My grandparents taught that waste was a sin, whether of food, money or life. A determined person, they said, could replace wasted money or food, but life, after being taken, could never be replaced. "All life", they said, "is precious to its owner, and no living thing should ever be killed for fun or curiosity." To them death was a serious matter, requiring a serious reason.

Fresh game, after being fried brown, was stripped from the bones and crumbled into a giant skilletful of rich cream gravy which the family spooned out over plates of grandmother's big, brown-topped breakfast biscuits. The menfolk drank cups of steaming black coffee, and unless sick, would eat at least one plate of biscuits, meat and gravy. Normally they topped that off with smaller servings of biscuits and butter, laid flat in their plates and covered all over with thick, sulphury-tasting blackstrap molasses. On lucky days there could be a jar of home-canned plum, or Mustang grape or peach preserves. Our women ate as heartily as the men, but like me, only half as much.

If no game was available, grandma diced up small cubes of salt pork, frying it brown to make grease for the gravy. When it was finished, she cooked her gravy and scattered the pork cubes into it because nothing edible could be wasted. Sometimes the boys sniffed their noses at the near-rancid pork smell but they seldom complained. I loved fried salt pork, or squirrel with dumplings or any other dish my grandmother cooked and always filled up big-time when we visited her.

Grownups allowed me to play anywhere outside as long as I stayed within the barbed wire fence. If I crawled through, they constantly reminded, the cows would get me. That was true. Untamed range cattle occasionally chased oilfield crews, many of whom were ex-cowboys, back onto the beds of their gang trucks.

My worst problem at my grandparents' house was their gigantic Rhode Island Red Rooster. Whenever he caught me outside he crowed gleefully, quickly ran over, and tried his hardest to flop onto my back. If he made it, he slashed viciously with his filthy spurs and beat me repeatedly with his bony and smelly old wings.

I always looked carefully before going out, and if the old sinner was in sight, would wait until his business called him elsewhere before playing in the yard. But the problem was, I was a little kid. I became interested in my games, often forgetting about the old dry-gulcher. When that happened, my first indication of danger would be when I heard his scaly feet scratching on the yard's surface as he stormed up from behind at full speed.

I could run almost as fast as him and always took off without looking when I heard him coming. But, more than once, I barely made it into the kitchen before hearing his heavy old body flop against the back door screen just as it slammed shut. Once, he actually got inside but dropped a few feathers on his way out. Grandmother, forgetting for the moment how much her hens loved him, whacked him several times with her broom. Nothing was allowed in her kitchen that didn't belong there. Except maybe me.

The rooster problem developed because, when the old bird was hatched, he was larger than the other chicks. Grandmother needed a new rooster and he was the one grandpa decided would be best to be lord and master of all her hens. When young, he was petted, humored, carried about and fed extra grain. He was a spoiled pet that had lost all fear of humans, and quickly developed into a natural tyrant.

As a young hotspur, he fought anything that walked and my uncles delighted in teasing him. He enjoyed their games, flopping high in the air when they came around, engaging in mock chicken battles with them. Everybody was amused at first, but after aging he grew stronger and more arrogant. A year later, when almost a grown chicken, he decided to adopt his regal duties. They included protection of his loving harem from anything at all, and he became a definite nuisance. Then he began to fly up into the faces of curious prairie cattle who nosed round the yard fence, scaring them away. This increased his self-importance to the point that even grownups needed to watch him closely.

My first memory of the old reprobate was watching him, jump straight up in the air to flog my mother on the arm. She screamed and kicked at him but missed. She fussed at my grandfather, but her anger only made him chuckle. I grinned a little myself, but next time I met him, the old pirate jumped onto my back, flogging and spurring me, and I never grinned about him again. After he learned I wouldn't fight back, he took advantage of any chance that happened to make my life miserable.

If grownups were near, he ignored me, pretending not to see, because he knew very well they would kick his deserving fanny if he molested me. But, soon as they left, he crowed loudly and charged, running me back into the house. My uncles, after spoiling him completely, would punish him heavily enough for fighting them that he had learned not to pick on most adults. But he loved chasing children and would normally test a visiting stranger. Grandpa always chuckled when this happened. As I said, he had a wide mean streak himself.

None of the grownups was really concerned about my rooster problem. I figured this was because they were bigger than us kids and he was no real threat to them. Even though he had left a half dozen spur marks on my back, they simply advised me to stop running and he would quit chasing me. But I had seen pictures of large birds named ostriches and wondered how they would act if this old outlaw was six feet tall. I also fantasized about what I was going to do to him when I was a few inches taller but the old vandal's time expired before that happened.

My grandmother was a regular "church-going" Baptist. Grandpa, who believed in God and argued the bible as well as anybody, told everyone he was a "Campbellite." Most folks figured Campbellites were about the same as Church of Christ folks and there was a whole church full of those worshippers in Holliday, but granddad insisted there was a lot of difference between the two denominations. Besides that, he didn't like the Church of

Christ preacher and wouldn't go to his church anyway. Neither would he visit in the Baptist Church with the rest of his family.

So, on the first Sunday morning of our second visit to my grandparents that year, grandpa stayed home to work on his smokehouse and the rest of us went to church. I shared his opinion of the Baptist Church, or any other church for that matter, but had my own reasons. At age four and a half, I considered all churches to be boring and confining. One brand was like the rest to me, so I happily volunteered to stay home and keep grandpa company. But I only wasted my breath. Mother scrubbed and curried me, then stuffed me into the kind of clothes she wanted me to wear and hauled me off to church anyway.

The four of us, Mother, grandmother, Gwyn and me, rode to the Holliday church with one of grandmother's Baptist friends who lived on a neighboring ranch and had a big car. My uncles had spent the night with friends and were trotline fishing on the Brazos river, so they didn't have to go. It was just me and Gwyn, who was so little that her opinion didn't count, our women and those neighbors.

As soon as we were dropped back at home after church, the women relaxed. Changing out of their Sunday clothes, they began putting our dinner on the table. Too busy to amuse themselves by bossing me around, they allowed me to play outside until eating time.

Before venturing outside I looked carefully for the old red skalawag. He wasn't around so I went on out. I picked the front yard because I knew the old stalker preferred to roost in his shady mesquite tree out back when the weather was hot, like now. I had been playing intently for 10 minutes before hearing grandmother's voice, sudden and loud, talking straight to grandfather. This was a woman who seldom lifted her voice against her husband and when I heard that tone, it captured my interest. "L. O.", she asked forcefully, "What have you done to my rooster?"

I didn't hear his answer, but on the off-chance that something bad had happened to the old Hellion, I trotted around back to see what was going on. Today, when looking back from the safety of adulthood and 70 years, I can muster a small amount of pity, but on that day I was highly gratified to see the hated old vulture hanging by his feet from the clothesline—minus his head. Grandpa worked intently, head down and saying nothing, as grandmother "blessed him out."

What had happened was a catastrophic case of mis-judgment on the part of that disgraceful old chicken. While working outside in the sun, grandpa had worked up a little sweat. Removing his shirt to be cooler, he had squatted down to effect improvements in the chimney of his smokehouse. He was a small man and the old corsair, after waking from his nap, apparently decided grandpa was an invader. Not only that, he was small enough to be easy prey and there was no doubt whatsoever in his perverted mind that he was the best rooster in the world to rid the chicken yard of this trespasser.

Granddad saw him slipping up from behind, then chuckled and forgot about it. He assumed the old ambusher was simply practicing and wouldn't dare attack him, from the front, the rear or even from above. But he was wrong.

Sneaking along carefully, and using surprise to full effect, when the distance suited him, that old rebel cackled triumphantly. Flouncing straight up into the air, he landed hard on grandpa's bare back. Then, screeching with sheer delight, he spurred again and again with those long untrimmed spurs and flogged repeatedly with that pair of broad, bony wings. It was his most triumphant moment, which was good, because it was also his last battle. That dumb chicken committed suicide because, without caring who he was attacking, he had viciously molested his own creator, the very human who had picked him out to be the boss of all my grandma's hens.

Because of arthritis, granddad couldn't move as fast as he once had. So the attack was more effective than it should have been. The old driller's back was streaming blood by the time he struggled erect and penned that sorry specimen of roosterhood under his mesquite tree in a fence corner. Even then the old Demon almost survived by jumping straight up. But he lost his nerve at the last second and his jump was short. Grandpa grabbed his loud, profane neck and never stopped wringing. After the headless villain stopped flopping, grandpa tied his feet to the clothesline so he could properly drain.

I'm guessing that the only thing which kept my grandpa from having to visit relatives for a week were those long streaks of fast-clotting blood which ran down his back. Also, maybe me. Grandmother looked at the blood for a moment, reflected a second, then glanced over at me. Remembering the old scoundrel's sinful past, she finally decided that he had violated the law one time too often.

There was no question about cooking him. He was old and tough, but he was also meat and throwing meat away would have been sinful waste. So, at noon next day, grandmother served up a large kettle of chicken and dumplings for our dinner.

She refused to eat, explaining that she had been too fond of him. The others complained that he was too tough but ate very well. I had always my loved grandmother's chicken and dumplings so, though I chewed a little more than normal, I thought our dinner was great!

Artist Lisa Weidner, Conroe, Texas

CHAPTER 12

HEALTH-LAX—1932

IN THE FALL of 1932 I was nearly five and trying hard to remember important happenings in my life so I could keep them in proper order. Remembering impressive events was pretty easy but I simplified the system even more by leaving out the bad stuff I didn't like. Like many kids before and since, I concentrated on the good stuff and did my best to forget the bad. But there was this problem; after two or three days, I couldn't always remember which event happened first. Like most kids under five, I was a born dictator and placed small value on the feelings of others. All my energy was directed toward eating what I liked and getting my own way.

We lived in a North Texas oilfield and farming town called Burkburnett, in Wichita County, Texas. By 1932 the nation had dragged itself through three years of the Great American Depression, and God was merciful in not letting us know that we still had 10 more years to go. The following decade bruised us way too hard and I have never heard anyone say he would like to do it again.

Few Texas men in 1932 acted as baby sitters or helped very much with women's housework. Our society insisted that men work hard at providing food, shelter and clothes for their families and most were pretty good at it when they could find a job.

Most Texas ladies gracefully performed the roles our society imposed on them, and scored as high as, often higher than, their men. Dutifully, seldom enjoying complete rest, they wived, mothered and ordered their homes in the way our culture had decided those duties should be done. Their jobs included washing without machines, ironing with "sad" irons heated on the lids of wood burning stoves, cooking without microwave ovens and trying to keep food from spoiling when there wasn't enough money to buy ice for the box. Then, after catching up on the basic stuff, they planted vegetable and flower gardens, washed and dressed their families, took them to church, and worked hard to decorate flower beds and create more attractive homes from the graceless oilfield shacks in which we lived.

Our society insisted so greatly that a father be the complete breadwinner that it sometimes punished husbands whose wives took jobs, implying that he might be a poor provider. Sometimes it was necessary for him to bluster or fight when idle gossipers insulted his manhood after his woman took a job. At our house, dad worked hard to provide a living but mother worked even harder at being a housewife. And like most kids, I received most of my supervision from her rather than him.

My father worked five and a half days each week in a small, out-dated machine shop that specialized in oilfield repairs. He never took vacation because he couldn't afford to lose a week of work. Burk's oil boom had died, and when the Great Depression began to grow faster than malignant cancer, he hired out in the last machine shop in town. It was owned by a good man, named P. A. Wiggins.

Dad earned $18.00 a week and was on 24-hour call. The only overtime pay he received was an occasional meal, generally a hamburger, munched somewhere out in the oilfield, as he repaired a large piece of oilfield machinery too heavy to haul into Wiggins' Machine shop for repair. But he was glad to have his job and the burger. Half of America's men weren't working and many had no idea when they would next see a $10 bill.

Grown men all over the nation were getting out of bed each morning with no place to go. This was before people had radios, and without a job they had nothing to do except visit the combination domino-pool hall or lay around the house swigging coffee. Many would have drunk beer but we lived in a dry precinct. Young men were graduating from high school with no job in sight, and many teen-agers, barely existing in hungry families, dropped out of school when any kind of job turned up. Most never returned.

On Christmas dad's boss gave his employees a small sack of oranges and a $10 bonus. We bragged to the neighbors about these gifts because few employers gave bonuses back then. Most employers felt workers had it too easy after President Roosevelt's recent declaration that a 40-hour work week was America's new goal. A short time before, oilfield people had worked 10 hour days, six days a week. Ten years before that, the same men had labored on 12-hour shifts, seven days a week. Their only days off came between tearing down drilling rigs from the last well and rigging up to drill a new one.

It was a time when North Texans with regular jobs tended to show up on time, wore big smiles and worked hard because they wanted to keep working. Idle workers were always near, ready to pick up the shovel of any man who quit, got sick or was fired. Frequently, a worker's boss would go broke and his employees got nothing when payday came. Times were lean.

I was the oldest of what ultimately became a four-kid family. Since dad was working steadily, mother held the oilfield title of "Chief Cook and Bottlewasher" at our house. Her word was final on anything happening during the daytime. But this finality never stopped the war she and I fought almost from the day I was born. Our fight was always to see who was the real boss. She won, hands down, in those days because she was bigger than me. When she wanted to get my attention, she spanked me hard enough that I remembered it next time I considered breaking her rules. And, tough as she often had to be, I sometimes needed more punishment than she gave.

Grown folks used to tell each other I was smart, but they stopped mentioning it around me when I began to nod my head wisely and grin confidently when the subject arose. Yet, I must have been fairly bright because I quickly memorized all my mother's good places to hide stuff from me. In fact, I was convinced that the worst thing about living in our house was that I was too short to reach her best hiding spots. I would also guess she figured the worst thing about living there was putting up with me because my ability to climb was improving daily and she was running out of hidey-holes.

To re-balance a deteriorating situation, she began spanking me more often. "Impressing" me, she explained. This worked so well that I transferred my attention to the outdoors and developed a vast new interest—world travel.

Overnight, geography became my biggest hobby and my quick-moving feet soon turned me into the youngest long-distance explorer and irritating visitor in our end of town. It embarrassed mom to be thanking neighbors she barely knew after they had walked me back home from wearing out my welcome. So, she spanked me more often, a little harder, but I was growing larger and getting harder to catch. Spanking soon lost its effect so she turned to negotiation. And negotiate we did, with varying levels of success, until, at age 87, she left Texas for a better place.

Dad was the oldest of a five-kid family. The one just under him, my Aunt Hazel, also lived in Burk. Hazel normally moved in with us after each big fuss with her husband. This happened fairly often and her visits lasted from overnight to as long as a month, because like mom and me, they also experienced varying levels of success when negotiating.

Hazel had no children of her own and loved me more than was good for either of us. She invested more time with me than most aunts would, often bringing me candy and small toys on her visits. She also taught me to read before I entered first grade. I wasn't wholly ungrateful and returned her love as much as a miniature Napoleon could love anyone but I also watched her closely. She was a "bottom-line", no-nonsense, sort of school teacher who promptly swatted my behind when I did something she figured I shouldn't.

Aunt Hazel taught me more times in school than a relative should. First it was a kindergarten, which she organized and operated either from our house or hers, depending on how her married life was working that month. She had started her kindergarten because the Fairview Public School, where she had been teaching, closed. When it merged into the Burkburnett system, her first grade teacher's job became history.

Working women back then were just like their husbands. They worked because they needed money. People in Burk knew Hazel's husband, B. O. Willis, as a likable and handsome ex-preacher who was a somewhat irregular provider, though not by choice. Half his earnings supported four children from a first marriage who lived in Lawton, Oklahoma with their mother. He seldom owned a car in those days and, when visiting his kids, normally rode the Greyhound to Lawton. Always short on funds, he occasionally found it necessary to stay overnight. When this happened, he slept on a pallet in his ex-wife's living room. But all his explanations fell on deaf ears when he returned and those visits to Lawton always increased the level of difficulty in their negotiating sessions.

After Hazel hired out in the Burkburnett school, she closed her kindergarten but often taught my class in school. First, she was a substitute, and could turn up to boss me on any day at all. Later, she was hired full-time and I would see her twenty times a day. She was always more strict on me than other kids and I didn't enjoy the arrangement.

She taught much of my fifth grade. Then, when I figured I was out from under her thumb, she turned up again, moving up to sixth grade with me, where I learned Civics and Texas History from her. Then she showed up again in high school, never teaching me regularly, but for much of World War II, she substituted as my home room teacher.

Everyone in school knew Hazel was my aunt and always squealed to her about anything I did that they didn't like. I did more stuff than I should, and normally took double heat when I did. First it was from Hazel, then again at home. I liked, probably even loved my industrious and conscientious aunt, but never quit hoping she would get a better job, in some other town.

One Sunday afternoon, exactly when my mother was running out of hiding places, Aunt Hazel, turned her old green Packard coupe into our driveway. Alighting, she dragged out two suitcases and a cosmetic bag which was crowded out of shape with all her medications.

Pressing a tissue to her face, she gave me a drippy hug and charged inside to recite a long list of complaints to my parents about B. O.'s most recent transgressions. I was too young to know, but a two-bag visit meant there'd been a big fuss and she'd be around for a while.

Next morning, as was her custom, she allowed me to watch her "doll up" for work. First, she used a curling iron, carefully rolling, then fluffing her curls. Next, she applied powder, rouge, Maybelline eye brow stickum, Tangee lipstick and perfume. Then she swallowed five kinds of pills and rubbed lotion over a new raw spot on her neck before kissing me goodbye and grabbing her purse to leave. But, on that day, she turned back. Reaching into her cosmetic bag, she pulled out a fresh package of Health-Lax. Tearing it open, she broke off two squares, popped them into her mouth and chewed them up.

For readers who might not know, Health-Lax was once marketed as a "mild and gentle-acting" laxative. This non-prescription medicine was intentionally made to look and taste like the old plain, flat Hershey's milk chocolate bars. After watching her eat, I promptly demanded my rightful share.

Patiently, Hazel explained that she had taken medicine and, because I wasn't sick, I couldn't have any. But she was wasting her breath because I didn't believe it. I had never seen Health-Lax before and this "medicine" smelled exactly like chocolate to me. And it had to taste good or she would have made a face when eating it.

My firm conclusion was that this beloved aunt, the one who constantly told me and everyone else how much she loved me, had eaten chocolate candy, right in front of me. Then she had refused to share and lied to me about it. My own school-teacher aunt was doing the very things that grownups had always said were bad.

I had encountered other situations when older kids, and occasional adults, had refused to share goodies with me. I viewed these people as selfish stingy-guts and often told them so. Hazel's treachery shocked me to my toenails and I argued with her. Hard. Then, after I called her what I called the others, I not only received one of her swats on the fanny but was ejected from her room. Because of being too little, I had lost another fight.

Hazel brushed me off with ease but hadn't been with us long enough to be up-dated on my latest activities. Besides, she had no kids of her own to teach her and was an ex-old-maid schoolteacher with many tricks left to learn. What she didn't know was that I had been running away so much lately that Mother had been locking our front door when she worked in the back part of the house.

By locking the front, Mom only had to watch the back. At least, that's what she thought. But I had watched Dad lock and unlock the front door often enough to understood about the key. I knew exactly where it stayed and every time Mom locked it, I took it out, opened the door and took off on a new expedition. I always carefully replaced the key, and for a few trips, had her wondering about her mind. She had only puzzled out my new method two days before Hazel's visit, and I well remember the spanking she gave me that day.

Hazel wasn't cagey enough to conceal her movements so I watched easily through the crack in her door as she tossed the packet of Health-Lax into her suitcase and grabbed her purse again to leave. But, after two steps, she stopped and turned around. Picking up a small key from the dish on top of her dresser, she leaned hard on the lid of the crowded suitcase to make it fasten properly and locked it. Then she dropped the key back in its dish. I slipped away before she reached the door and she never knew I'd been watching.

Mom cooked my breakfast and I forgot about the Health-Lax until getting hungry at mid-morning. I asked for something to eat but her only offer was plain cow milk. I was almost hungry enough to drink it but turned the stuff down as a matter of principle. She knew I didn't like it and was always trying to con me into drinking it. So, I decided to stay hungry, and refused.

Then I remembered the chocolate in Hazel's bag but was smart enough not to head directly for it. Mom would stop the raid if she saw me. I waited until she had turned her attention elsewhere and scampered back to Hazel's room. In two minutes I had her bag open and quickly ate every chocolate morsel in the pack. I tried but wasn't heavy enough to push the top back down and re-lock the bag, but I did replace the key.

I thought I had gotten away clean, and might have done so except for mom's practiced eye. She noticed a smear of chocolate at the corner of my mouth and demanded an explanation. I said I didn't know what it was but she scraped it loose with her fingernail, then smelled and tasted it. Knowing we had no candy in the house, she ordered me to show her where I'd gotten it. Although I hadn't believed the line Hazel used on me, I tried it on my mother because it was the best I could come up with. I said I had taken medicine, then explained, "Because I might get sick."

Mom was no dummy either and, with expert technique, she threw so many questions at me that I quickly confessed. Five minutes later she watched critically as I re-enacted every stage of my crime, even to showing how I had returned the key to its dish. Then, when she saw the Health-Lax wrapper, she lost her cool. It was a "Giant" package.

Pulling me close, she placed a hand on my forehead to check for fever. Then she pushed and poked around on my stomach, asking if it hurt. After the hard pokes, it did hurt and I admitted to pain. This upset her even more, and without waiting, she marched me four long blocks downtown and straight up the bank building stairs to Doc Russell's office.

I didn't dislike Doc, but I didn't like visiting him either. I remembered his shots very well. But I was happier to see him that day because he was in a better mood than my mother. Sitting me down on a corner of his examination table, he listened to her with one ear and employed his stethoscope, listening to my innards with the other. Putting the instrument away, he gently felt my stomach, asking if it hurt. Because he probed gently, it felt OK and I told him so.

Then the tables were turned. Instead of me answering the questions, it was mom's turn. When did I take the medication? She didn't know. How much had I eaten? She didn't know that either. What size package was it? That one she knew but by then he was beginning to grin, because he was looking at what seemed to be a normal, healthy kid sitting on his table.

When he grinned, mother bristled and asked if he was going to pump out my stomach. He said he wasn't, because too much time had passed and the medication had already been absorbed into my body. Still angry, she asked how he thought I should be doctored. He cradled his chin in his hand, pondered a moment and advised her to feed me a lot of crackers when we got home. Mother obviously felt that a modern doctor ought to offer better treatment and, ice edging her voice, asked if he had any other suggestion. He paused a few seconds, and asked, "Well, did you spank him?"

Most doctors in year 2004 are careful not to anger their patients but Doc Russell was a battlefield veteran of World War I who had married his battlefield nurse. She still functioned as his clinic nurse. Both of them had seen trainloads of carnage in the war plus a lot more in the oilfields, and Doc had learned to rely on his instincts. Instinct told him this was a minor situation, and he was hoping to make mom laugh by kidding her. If he had asked me, I would have told him not to bother. She always got madder.

In 1932 America had not coined the term that today's generation calls a doctor's "bedside manner". Even if it had, Doc Russell would have joked with customers any time he wanted. People always said he liked to "pull a person's leg" and he didn't care much if an occasional patient got mad. His practice was so big that he only took fishing trips twice a year. We had one other "real" doctor in Burk, and they swapped out on patients when one of them was ill or had to leave town. Sick people couldn't be sure of avoiding Doc unless they went out of town for treatment, but half of Burk's families, including ours, walked everywhere we went.

Knowing she was bested, mother stopped talking and bustled me out of his office. I knew she wanted to yell at him, maybe even spank him some. Yet, like the rest of our town, I knew she liked him and respected his medical ability. Sooner or later she would stop being mad. She just wasn't ready yet. She was also angry with me and didn't talk to me on the way home. But she did buy a large box of crackers when we passed Parker's Grocery and had me to stuff down so many that it was a year before I ate them again on purpose.

I'd heard Doc tell mother she ought to watch me closely and she took his advice to heart. If I started vomiting or having bad stomach spasms, he had told her to get back in touch. But he smiled as we left and gave me a penny, telling me not to worry, that I would be OK. I believed him, stuck the penny in my pocket, and forgetting all problems, ran out to play when we got home.

But mom wouldn't give it a rest. She stuck to me like honey on pancakes, constantly trailing me about and feeling my forehead and stomach. She refused to believe it when I told her I felt okay and marched me in to sit on the pot every 30 minutes. That night, the second time she woke me to see if I felt all right, I thought she was disappointed when I insisted I was fine. But our communication was always fuzzy when she woke me up and I could have been mistaken.

If I ever experienced a bad gas pain or took an extra trip to the bathroom from eating my Aunt Hazel's laxative, I don't remember it. Mother always talked a lot about the past, but if she ever mentioned this episode later, I don't remember that either. I was glad to quickly forget about it and haven't mentioned it until now. The main lesson here, if one can be applied, is that the Health-Lax Company advertised correctly when they described their product as being "mild and gentle-acting".

CHAPTER 13

PUSHER—1932

READY FOR WORK, Marvin strode purposefully off his front porch toward the muddy and dented Ford coupe with its wooden floored compartment called a "toolpusher" built into the rear. It was a crisp and bright November morning with no breeze. Slow-moving fingers of sunlight probed intently, burning away wide slices of the heavy frost that coated everything. It looked like a warm and clear winter day was developing, but Marvin wore a heavy cowhide halfcoat anyway. Who knew what the wind or weather in North Texas might do?

Marvin had always been good at anything he did, which was why he was "pushin' tools", in charge of three active drilling rigs and driving a company car instead of being a regular oilfield hand. He'd started out on the family farm, using a mule's tail for a compass and by age 10 had told himself he'd never come back if he was ever able to break loose. World War I gave him the chance. At age 15 he ran off from home, lied about his age and joined the army. Two years of driving trucks during the war gave him his "graduation certificate" from plowin', milkin' 'an seedin." By 1928, 10 years and three oil booms later, he was a typical Pioneer Texas Boomer, pushing tools for the Carnation Oil Company in the Burkburnett Oilfield.

As I have tried to show, Marvin was good at most anything he tried, but even he wasn't perfect. Once in a while he got carried away with his program, rushing into it so fast that something broke. Last night, he had planned efficiently, even to parking his company car so he could begin checking it out soon as he walked out his front door. But this morning he was in too big a hurry.

With satisfaction, he noted that none of his tires was flat and there was no puddle under the radiator. Also, the tin can half filled with rocks that he'd set on top of a "tow" sack thrown over a three-coned drill bit and a smaller coring bit had not been moved. The can had been his burglar alarm and, since it was still where he'd left it, this meant that his bits hadn't been stolen. In Burk, that was good news. Theft of oilfield tools was not only possible there, but it happened somewhere in that oilfield every day.

Opening the driver's door, Marvin adjusted the coupe's ignition spark lever and made certain it was out of gear. Then he pulled the crank out of the pusher compartment, inserted it under the radiator, and slowly pulled the engine over twice, drawing fuel into the carburetor. Then, impatiently, he began rolling the crank, determined to keep on until the engine caught. Finally it did, but Instead of acting decently, the little Ford back-fired and the backward-spinning crank handle neatly broke his right arm between the wrist and elbow.

Marvin used the oil-field worker's oldest prerogative and spoke, maybe even yelled, at the coupe, using some words that teamsters employed with uncooperative mules, but that didn't help. His wife and son were away from town, visiting relatives. They wouldn't be back until late that afternoon, and he wasn't speaking with the only neighbor on his block whose car was at home, so he had no choice other than to hike downtown, locate Doc Russell and get his arm fixed.

It took two hours. He walked up to Doc's house and sat in the kitchen with him until Doc finished breakfast. Then Doc drove him downtown to his office and set the arm. After splinting Marvin up, Doc gave him a packet of pills and put Marvin in his car to drive him back home.

Well, being good at most everything had made Marvin develop into a fairly hard-headed person. And after that pain medicine began to take effect, he decided he had plenty to do and decided to go on to work. Making sure that his heavy jacket had a full pint of medicinal whiskey in a side pocket, he slipped it over his shoulders and went out to confront the Ford once more.

More careful this time, he re-set the spark lever and rolled the engine over one time. After that, he intended to roll it over one revolution at a time until it cranked. But the day was hotter now and the spark lever was set exactly right. Soon as the crank moved, the engine fired. This time the crank hung up instead of releasing as it should, and the flailing handle broke Marvin's left arm.

His right arm had been securely splinted by Doc, then suspended from a sling hung round his neck. After experimenting a little, Marvin was able to lean against the side of the house, pick up the newly broken arm with his knee and flip it over into the sling atop his splint, bedding it down safely enough that it wouldn't fall out. He wasn't feeling as much pain as he normally would because of Doc's good pills, and after cradling the newly broken arm securely, he felt good enough to walk over in front of the coupe. Using some more heavy teamster language, he promised to blind the unruly vehicle by kicking both its headlights off their support bar.

He wasn't able to perform as efficient and as clean a job as he wanted to, for fear he'd fall down and couldn't get back up. So, he contented himself with kicking off one light and knocking a few extra dents in the grill, then called the job finished. With lowered head, he walked carefully back toward Doc Russell's office as a new wave of pain and nausea attacked.

Doc didn't fuss. He'd long since passed the point where he figured people might change their ways if he yelled at them. When Marvin told him what happened, he sat him down, felt along the break, and expertly re-set the newly afflicted arm. Thirty minutes later he had worked up a neat double splint harness. Then, bragging a little on his professional job, he helped his patient with a bathroom chore. This, he told Marvin, would end up being his greatest problem.

"And Doc was right," Marvin said later. "Eating, drinking, going to the bathroom, and keepin' myself clean were my biggest problems for the next five weeks."

"When Doc finished treatin' the second break, I told him I would have my wife come in an' pay him next day—the entire bill was just $35.00—because I didn't want him feelin' around in my pocket 'an be tempted into stealin' a crippled patient's money.

"This didn't bother Doc. He just laughed, and asked if I wanted him to take me home again. Well, there was no one there to help me so I told him I'd just as soon go on to work if he would carry me out to the company office."

Artist Gary Tuttle, Humble, Texas

"This impressed Doc a whole lot and by noon he had told all his friends and half his patients in our end of Wichita county about the guy who broke two arms in one day and went on back to work. The newspapers heard about it and sent a reporter out next day to take my picture and talk."

"I enjoyed their attention 'an let 'em print whatever kind of flattering story they wanted, but I didn't tell them everything. I didn't mention trying to kick the lights off of that Ford but one of them had driven by my house and figured out what happened. I wouldn't lie to him about it and that part got printed. The Boss made me pay for puttin' them back on, but at the time, I thought it was worth that small extra expense."

"Another thing I didn't tell the reporters was that my wife wouldn't be back in town until after five that afternoon. At the office I would be able to have someone give me a drink of water or coffee an' feed me a bite of something or other. Also, I knew one or two of my fellow workers well enough to ask them to help me some in the bathroom. They not only admired my work ethic but helped me as well as they knew how."

"When the Boss took me home that afternoon he told me to stay there for five weeks and that he was goin' to pay for all my medical bills and half of my salary. I was tickled to death because Texas had no Worker's Compensation law or hospitalization insurance back then. A lot of bosses wouldn't have given me a nickel."

"After three weeks I took my right arm loose from that harness and found out I could drive pretty good if I took my time. I could look after my drillin' rigs okay if somebody could crank up the car. So, my boss sent a man out every mornin' for two more weeks to crank up both me and the Ford. Then they would point us out to the oilpatch with a map showing any changes in my rig locations. In four or five more weeks, except for a little soreness, those broken arms were history."

NOTE: Marvin lived a half block from our house on Avenue C. His son, was one of the author's regular childhood playmates and graduated from high school in the same class. ES

CHAPTER 14

JIMMY—1933

AFTER THEY GOT to know him, most folks said Jimmy was mean as a snake, but they didn't know him as well as I did. I knew him well enough to be absolutely certain that, if we had been living back in the wild Indian days our old timers talked about, and the Comanches had caught him, they would have thrown him back after putting up with him for 15 minutes.

On the day after Jimmy's family moved in, mother dragged me in to hose me off. While scrubbing, she pointed out that I had a new playmate and ought to treat him nicer than the other kids for a few days so he would feel at home in his new surroundings. Then she dropped eight homemade cookies on a saucer, covered them with a clean tea towel, and trotted us across the street to knock on the new family's front door.

As our mothers talked, my new playmate edged closer. When near enough, he sucked in a deep breath and tried hard but didn't have enough pressure to spit through the screen door into my face. But he came close. One droplet sailed through a rusted spot and lodged on my clean shirt front.

So what happened that day was, my mom simply wasted a good bath and a visit. The new lady kept her good cookies but talked through the screen door and didn't ask us in. And she never returned mom's call. But she did exhibit a tad of judgment by swatting her kid on the rear and fussing at him for messing up the door screen. The year was 1933. The place was Burkburnett, Texas. Jimmy was almost six and so was I.

Unlike his mom, Jimmy visited often. Normally, he was in search of prey. I tried to stay on guard at all times when playing out, because by the time I heard his voice saying "Let's rassle!", it was already too late to prepare an effective defense.

Though he was smaller than me, Jimmy's red hair, freckled skin and tiger-sized heart overcame what was to him a fairly minor problem. He soon became the neighborhood fireball. A great kid to have on your side in a fight, he was a pain in the rear when no fighting was going on. During peacetime he frequently succumbed to boredom and fought with his friends.

Mostly, Jimmy was in a good mood. He smiled a lot, but the smile could be deceptive. He relished combat of any kind and often wore his biggest grin while slinging a hard brown fist at the nearest nose. And you had to give him credit because he wasn't a true bully. He just enjoyed fighting more than anything else and never quite understood why so many kids held grudges after he had picked a fight. To him, combat was the highest form of play.

His dad published the Burkburnett Star and regularly took Jimmy to Saturday night wrestling matches over in Wichita Falls. He was a large man with sandy red hair and Jimmy said he had been captured twice by the Germans during World War I. The first time they caught him, they branded his left shoulder and exchanged him after he promised not to fight against them any more. When they captured him again, they saw their brand and sentenced him to be shot, but the Americans counter-attacked next day and captured him back. Jimmy bragged that his dad was the only U. S. soldier who was captured three times during that war.

I never knew if the story was true but figured it was because Jimmy's mind dealt easier with fact than imagination. Also, we frequently played with a steel World War I helmet, gas mask and haversack that hung from a nail in their garage. Each piece was stenciled with a large blue arrowhead, signifying that they had been used in the Texas 36th Infantry Division. That remarkable combat unit shed tankerloads of American and enemy blood during World War I then repeated those same accomplishments once more during World War II.

When he won at marbles, Jimmy often announced we had been playing for "keeps". When losing, he often insisted we had been playing "funsies". One morning, several weeks after they moved in, he trotted across the street with a brand-new leather sack half full of marbles and challenged me to a contest. He bragged that he couldn't lose because of his big new taw.

That taw impressed me too, and I refused to play unless he agreed on a funsy game. He unhesitatingly agreed and I ran inside to grab up an enameled saucepan my mother had recently discarded. For some reason I had decided it was the best possible vessel for holding my small supply of marbles.

We were both right about that new taw. Ten minutes after we started Jimmy had easily knocked all my marbles out of the cat's eye ring we had drawn on the ground. Then he stuffed all of them into his new bag and stood up. Flatly, he announced we had been playing for keeps and started off in search of more prey.

It shouldn't have, but his action surprised me. Though we often changed our rules between games, we mostly honored our pre-game commitments. But I had underestimated Jimmy's love for winning. We occasionally played for keeps, but most of our parents were dead-set against it, though we never quite understood why. Maybe, we decided, it was because many Texans back then rated gambling to be as sinful as murder, bank robbing or drinking.

Most kids learned the hard way that one price we paid for freedom was keeping grownups in the dark about our games. As much as possible, that is. If they learned much about what we were doing, they wanted to become involved. Once involved, they began to "suggest", which we quickly found out was pure hokum. What they called a suggestion turned out to be interference, plain and simple. Those suggestions were always designed to have us play with their rules instead of ours.

After suggesting, they became very picky, often punishing us for not playing their way. And it was the little things that always set them off, not the big ones. And we never thought their punishment fit our crimes. Penalties could range from enthusiastic spanking to grounding, extra chores and no visiting anybody for a week. Sometimes, they could be all of the above.

I was very angry with Jimmy and desperately wanted to keep my marbles. But I would willingly have lost them before appealing to the grownups. I tried negotiation, reminding him that he was breaking our agreement. He simply increased his speed without bothering to look back. It was either lose my marbles or fight, and since I had just picked up the saucepan, I had an excellent opportunity to enforce my property rights.

Giving Jimmy only a little less warning than he generally gave me, I took several quick steps forward and swung. Fairly hard. Executing a perfect arc, the pan moved to exact point of aim, connecting solidly with the right side of his head, just above the ear. And it dropped him to his knees. For a moment it was so quiet that I could hear the tiny crackling sounds made by slivers of enamel as they flaked off the pan's bottom.

For once, Jimmy didn't offer to fight back. When he turned around, a single tear coursed down each cheek. He wanted to cry but wouldn't. I felt a momentary pang of pity but forced it back. Two tears didn't cover the multitude of sins he had committed. Lips trembling, he lied, almost convincingly. "You didn't have to get mad, I was just funnin'."

"I want my marbles back!"

Wordlessly, he dumped the sack and watched me fish mine out and drop them in my pan. Mine were easy to recognize because they all had pips. Then he gathered his marbles and walked slowly home.

Now that it was too late, I realized how large my crime had been. It was actually so grave that I couldn't guess what might happen. Dad might condone me for recovering what was mine, but past experience had shown me that grownups never swept a crime like this under the rug. It was bad enough when one kid hit another with his closed fist. But one kid knocking another in the head with a saucepan, and from behind no less, was a giant offense, even among kids. Punishment for fist hitting could range from any to all of the stuff our parents might think up, but my violation was so heinous that all of society might get involved. I could even be sent away to reform school. Suddenly I felt way too young to leave home.

For the rest of that day I dreaded what would happen when my parents confronted me. But when dad came home, he said nothing. I decided this was because Jimmy's dad had turned my case over to a judge and they were preparing all the necessary reams of paper to be absolutely certain that I would be sent off to reform school and never return again. When sleep finally came that night, it was pitted with misery. After waking at dawn, I preferred to get up and dress rather than having more bad dreams.

After breakfast, I walked out back, and went through the motions of playing, but could not escape my dread. A time bomb lurked in the near future. It would explode when it chose and there was nothing I could do to stop it. After moping for an hour, I noticed a caterpillar moving slowly across the grass. Temporarily forgetting misery, I picked up a stick and began to lay it across his path, watching to see how he solved the problems I heaped before him. Completely absorbed, I jumped nervously when a heard a familiar voice coming from behind, "Let's rassle!"

Once again I had way too little time for defense. I was barely able to throw up a deflecting arm before seeing Jimmy's broad grin as he wrapped an arm round my neck and picked up both his feet, dragging me to the ground. Giggling with delight, he squeezed with ferocity and spoke.

"Ain't this fun!"

For once, I had to agree because I suddenly realized that the bomb which waited in my future had been defused. It wasn't going to explode and ruin my life. No sheriff or reform school police would come to drag me off to reform school and my parents weren't going to yell at or even punish me. A great life ahead was now possible. All those fears, like many others I experienced in later life, had simply been the result of my over-active imagination. But the battle in progress, like any fight with Jimmy, was very real.

There was no way that Jimmy could ever have been called a normal kid, but in one way, he was like the rest of us. He was as convinced as we were that grownups ought not to be called in to choose our rules of play or to settle our disagreements. But now, my biggest problem wasn't escaping a life in reform school. It was stopping Jimmy before he choked me to death.

It really wasn't that hard. Past necessity had taught me how to break this hold, but I used a different method this time. Reaching up, I slapped that big knot at the side of his head. Not too hard, just hard enough.

Jimmy howled as if a shark had snapped off his leg but promptly relaxed the choke hold. Jumping up, he pointed a finger and eyed me with righteous indignation. Then he shouted with outrage. "I'm going home because you're not playing fair!"

Jimmy was right. I hadn't played fair, but I had suffered at least as much as him during the last 24 hours, and wasn't sorry to see him go. But our argument produced two positive results. First, Jimmy's play manners improved. Never again did I hear him insist we had been playing for keeps when we weren't. Second, though I was tempted, I never struck another kid with anything except my fist.

CHAPTER 15

BOOMTOWN KUKLUX—1933

I ONLY SAW them twice. First, it was downtown on Main Street. Later, it was at the First Baptist Church in Burkburnett, Texas. Because they were different from any people I had ever seen, I watched closely.

It was the fall of 1933 and I was nearing six years old. Excitedly, covered with goose bumps, I stood by my father on Main Street, watching intently as a small circus parade passed by. From eight feet of distance, the heavy stroke on a bass drum's head generates enough noise to shatter a young kid's nervous system, so when the drummer struck, I jumped and grabbed Dad's hand. He smiled then asked if I wanted to be held. But the drummer was moving away and I shook my head "No."

It wasn't a big parade because a dying North Texas oil town, in the grip of America's deepest, most grinding depression, didn't rate a big one. A correct description of that circus would be to say it was a little bigger than a medicine show and smaller than a first-rate carnival.

Very short, the parade featured an arthritic-looking elephant, a pitifully thin caged tiger and a couple of clowns. A man and woman also strutted about the street in trapeze costumes, but I thought they wore bathing suits and capes. Though playing enthusiastically, the five-piece band carried badly dented instruments that needed polishing. And the gold braid on the drum major's uniform was eroded and frayed.

The music was about the same quality as their instruments but we recognized Dixie and the Stars and Stripes Forever, so we applauded. The tastes of most small town Texans back then was mostly centered in their stomachs, and any entertainment, especially free, was appreciated. Our family would only see the parade. There was no money for circus tickets.

In other parades Cowboys rode behind the elephants and other animals. After that, from over across Red River in Oklahoma, came the Indians. Then, behind everything else, the town kids could ride. Most of them looked awkward and clung desperately to ancient, sway-backed plow horses or young, green-broken, pot-bellied colts and ponies. A few boys would follow behind on bicycles, but they had to watch where they went.

Only a few kids had saddles and bridles. They mostly guided their mounts with rope halters that their grownups had hastily twisted from cotton plowline or hackamores then wired the twists tight after they were properly sized. Old quilts, blankets and "tow" sacks were folded up to serve as saddle blankets. Any Indian from across the river sported more stylish parade clothes and rode better mounts than most of the kids.

Sometimes, after sliding off their animals, little kids couldn't get back on and had to finish by walking along the route unless some kind adult boosted them back up. But each of those kids was my hero. My dad had never owned a horse, or even a cow, as long as I knew him. In fact, that year, we didn't even have a car. I figured that I would never have the chance to ride in a parade and I was right.

But this parade was different from the others. There were no Cowboys, or Indians, not even any kids. Instead, behind the last circus wagon, a strange group of men was riding. They numbered about twenty and rode two abreast. Each one wore a white robe made from a bedsheet. It was topped by a pillow-case cap with jagged mask-like eyeholes and a nosehole cut in front. The hoods draped down over the rider's shoulders and each robe was pulled back over the horse's tail to cover the brand on its flank. I had never seen men like these in books, magazines, or at the movies.

Spectators quieted when the horsemen rode by. Some in the crowd waved at riders they recognized but there was no response.

These riders didn't wave or pop each other's horses with their quirts or laugh and joke with each other as the cowboys did. Neither did they yip and yell like the Indians or play pranks, such as kicking the rider's horse next to them or sailing a hat underneath a mount, causing it to emit a moaning bellow and duck its head to buck.

These men rode quietly, double-file, sitting tall, boots square in their stirrups and looking straight ahead. Each man held the reins firmly in his right hand while the left rested on his thigh. A few wore lace-up oilfield footgear instead of western boots and hats. And most of them paid close attention to their head-tossing, snorty range horses, which constantly fiddle-footed while walking on the unfamiliar concrete, as if they were on egg shells. Murmuring softly toward twitching ears, each rider concentrated on keeping his mount's front feet on the pavement instead of high in the air.

Pulling on Dad's hand, I asked who they were. His soft but terse answer, "KuKlux", mystified me. I was a curious kid and had never heard the name before. I yanked again, asking why they wore those funny sheets and masks. He told me to be quiet, he would explain later. Always watchful of his moods, I quieted just as a passing rider spoke softly. "Lo, Ed." My dad's reply was equally soft, "Howdy Abel."

I pulled again, making Dad look down, "How did you know that guy? He had on a mask!" Tolerating my interest, he decided to explain instead of fussing because I had interrupted him, "I recognized his boots." The parade was over and now he tugged my hand. "Let's go over to Burk Cafe for some coffee."

We lived in a dry precinct so coffee or iced tea, rather than whiskey or beer, was the adult beverage of choice. Few families allowed kids to drink coffee because most mothers were certain that coffee would "stunt a child's growth." Some mothers, who wanted their kids to drink milk, told them coffee would turn them black if they drank much of it before they were grown. So when we sat down on our round, swivel-topped cafe stools, Dad ordered coffee. I was allowed to choose between a doughnut, a Coke or a Dr. Pepper, any of which cost a nickel. I loved Coke and picked it because I seldom got to taste it. In fact, I normally got only a swallow or two and had never drunk one without sharing until then.

The cafe was almost filled with friendly, loud talking men and more filed through the front door every minute. Waitresses were the only women present. Dad and I had claimed the last available pair of counter stools which were together and new arrivals quickly filled up the last singles. Men then began dropping into chairs at one of the cafe's many tables. Those who arrived too late for seats walked about, carrying those old-fashioned heavy crock-like cafe cups and saucers filled with steaming coffee. Sipping sparingly, they walked, talked and shook hands, as if attending a formal reception. Both Cowboys and Oilmen wore boots with noisy heels which struck loudly against the worn, linoleum-topped wooden floor. Spur rowels, perhaps seeking attention above the other noise, jingled often.

The men spoke volubly, laughed boisterously and moved frequently to form other groups. Obviously enjoying the meeting, they slapped backs, told jokes, poked stomachs, gouged ribs and passed gossip whenever they found anyone to listen. Then, they moved along, to test their newest stories and best gossip on new victims. Everyone, merchants, farmers, oilfielders and city folks, was obviously enjoying this chance to talk with friends they hadn't seen lately.

Two hard-working waitresses circulated among the tables, constantly fending off barbs of rough humor tossed at them from every direction. They kept their orders without writing and poured hot coffee refills with one hand while protecting their swift-moving and attractively vulnerable flanks with the other.

Then the front door opened and five men wearing jeans, boots and tall western hats, clomped inside. I had seen most of them before. Two had ridden with the cowboys in earlier parades. One of them was our next door neighbor. They all spoke pleasantly and slowed for a moment to talk and shake with people near the door before moving inside to visit with others. Seeing us, our neighbor, walked over and it wasn't until he smiled, saying "Lo again, Ed" and my dad said "Howdy again, Abel," that I recognized him as the rider who had spoken to Dad in the parade.

Abel Horton and his brother, Jimmy, earned $15.00 to $20.00 a month at cowboying for various ranchers who needed wild cattle dragged out of the dense Red River bottom and even rougher pastures in surrounding counties. I liked Abel a lot, and until today I had never guessed that a real cowboy would find some reason to wear a pillowcase mask and drape himself with a bedsheet, then ride his horse through downtown Burkburnett in a parade.

A waitress came up to take his order and Abel couldn't resist having some fun. Yelling like a wild Comanche, he stopped all conversation in the room by grabbing and kissing her hard, right on the mouth. Still kissing, he picked her up by the waist and swung her in circles, telling her how pretty she was and how much he loved her. Finally setting her down, he ordered a cup of "sheep dip."

That waitress was Pauline, Abel's sister, and he was teasing her by making this scene for everyone to see. He also knew it might cause her unpleasant problems with strangers or newcomers who might be encouraged to take liberties. Pauline didn't like it. After taking his order, she darkly advised that he would be wearing coffee on his hat if he didn't keep his hands and mouth to himself. Most of the people knew the family and slapped their knees, laughing loudly, enjoying the prank. But, as I said before, good taste was a rarity and almost anything passed for entertainment in North Texas when I was a kid.

"How come you-all rode today, Abel," Dad asked after Pauline had stomped off, "Anything been happenin' ?"

"Naw," Abel replied, "we haven't even had a meetin' in over a year. I guess this ride could be looked on as pure advertisement."

I next saw the KuKlux three years later on a brilliant Sunday morning. We had just climbed the tall steps at First Baptist Church, and as my eyes adjusted from sunlight to inside lobby lighting, I noticed that the regular deacons and greeters were absent. Instead, there were two lines of KuKlux, wearing white robes. In deference to our church building, each had removed his hood and I recognized the faces of two regular church attenders. Unsmiling, they stood in formation, encouraging no familiarity and staring slightly over our heads. Legs widespread, hands coupled behind them, they stood mute, but we knew they had memorized the face of each worshipper who entered.

Passing in, we took seats in our regular place. After the ushers had passed Sunday offering plates down each row and set them on the altar table to be blessed, every Klansman marched down the center aisle to drop a bill on top. Still unspeaking, each re-traced his steps and marched out. Other than this, the church service was normal. Neither the pastor or any of our deacons mentioned this visit again, and when the service was over, the KuKlux had gone.

While growing up, I only heard of two things the Klan ever did in Burk. One was that church visit, caused by some person who threatened our pastor with physical harm. Because one of his pointed and name-calling sermons had been considered meddling by one or more citizens with extra-tender corns, they had made public threats. But the Klan visit was effective. No harm came to our preacher and no further threats were made after that Sunday.

The other Klan activity occurred when the KuKlux visited a man who lived on our side of town. This man's children walked to school with us each morning, and a rumor had circulated that their father "spent some time" with a dark woman who lived across the tracks. The KuKluxers had heard about it and paid a visit, warning that if he didn't begin to stay at home nights that he would be sorry. Without hesitation the unwilling host denied any wrong-doing and suggested they all visit a very hot place to suck rocks.

After thinking it over, the Klansmen took no action and left. Times were changing, and even if the rumor was true, it was none of their business, and they knew it. As far as I know, the KuKlux never turned out again in Burk, even for a parade.

CHAPTER 16

THE NEAR MISS—1933

PART I, "THE PROBLEM"

OUTSIDE TEMPERATURE HAD climbed past 100 degrees by mid-June of 1933 and our summer quickly turned into a dust-kickin' sizzler. No one was surprised. Few North Texans had ever considered the weather in Burkburnett, up in Wichita County, Texas, to be either friendly or cooperative. It normally fast-forwarded quickly through great, trotted right through nice and moved straight to bad which it liked best of all. So no one thought it was unusual when, on a hot, sticky night toward the end of the month, a fast-moving hyperactive prairie storm blew in with no advance warning.

First, the temperature dropped 25 degrees. This was welcome because it cooled us off. Then came the bad part. A storm cloud burst suddenly, serving up a giant display of vivid chain and forked lightning accompanied by blasts of window-rattling thunder. Ten minutes later a few truckloads of golf-ball-sized hail scattered heavily on our yard. Just behind these gifts of nature, a medium-to-large-sized twister slammed into our end of town and then bounced off after removing a few shingles. No one was unhappy because good news outweighed the bad.

The bad news was, a few houses had lost some shingles and others had a window or two knocked out. Good news was, the storm also dumped a brisk one-inch rain onto our end of the county. Nobody over the age of 10 during that long and drought-ridden

1930's depression, would dare to kick much about a "cyclone" that also brought a one-inch rain unless a person, or a few head of good cattle, got killed.

After breakfast next morning I worked in our yard, picking up windblown shingles for my father. He wanted to nail them back on the roof that evening after getting home from work. Water had stopped dripping into our rain barrel but the ground was muddy and fresh puddles formed by rain and melted hailstones stood in every low spot.

Dad seldom assigned me pleasant jobs, but this one was fun. I felt lucky to be comfortable when working because it was actually pleasant and I knew that wouldn't last for long. Stacking up the loose shingles took only 20 minutes, so still enjoying my work, I decided to drag some windblown limbs out in back for burning. Making a game out of it and stretching out the work, I dragged each limb carefully around mud puddles and was almost finished when I heard a girl's voice calling to me. Looking toward the sound I saw two sisters playing in their front yard, two doors West of our house. When they saw me look, they shouted again and beckoned me over. But I thought about it before going.

We had lived near each other as long any of us could remember, but they didn't like me much and I had long ago classified them as fair weather friends. We got along fairly well if I played with either one alone, but they always ganged up on me when the three of us played together. I looked up and down the street but there were no boys playing outside, so I decided to take a chance and walked on over.

It started out well enough. Their mother, they promptly advised, was in bed, having given birth to a baby boy only the day before. Both of them, Georgia, who was two years older, and Katie, aged 6 like me, were too interested in talking about the new brother to start a fuss, and that was a definite plus. But I wasn't interested in the baby. My mother had already explained to me that he was coming when I mentioned that their mother was getting way too fat around the middle. Yet, even though I had no interest in a new kid on our street, I worked at being friendly and listened politely until they ran out of talk about him.

It was when they mentioned their cat had a new litter of kittens that my interest soared. Unlike small babies, kittens didn't take up all of your parents time. They also didn't cry loudly all night, keeping everyone up and they were normally affectionate if not mistreated. In short, they were everything to a boy my age that babies weren't. They could be fun. We promptly started walking around back to their cowlot, for a viewing, and then, with no warning, Georgia planted her heels, announcing we couldn't go any further.

I figured she was starting up with her usual bossiness, the kind that never failed to cause trouble. I should have gone home right then but I wanted to see the cats, so I argued. Her only reason for stopping was that their father had told them not to play out back. This seemed like an unimaginative excuse to me and I told her so. We had played there often and her parents didn't care. But she seemed nervous and this convinced me even more that she was trying to make trouble. So I hung in hard, arguing for a cat show. Finally, she came out with the truth and said they were afraid.

Georgia had always been boss when we played and, being a normally ambitious male, I sensed opportunity here. If I could edge her out once or twice, then a proper man, like me, could become permanent boss over these fearful females. That development could only improve their company. And, after I pulled out her reason, all they were afraid of was a little old electric "live" wire.

Well, I wasn't afraid of it, and promptly guaranteed both of them complete protection. Following up on my advantage, I demanded to see this new "booger". It pleased me to see that, though she recognized my challenge to her leadership, and was ashamed of her fear, she saw no way to change the situation. After thinking some, she agreed, and we started around back.

Now that her fear was public, I acted bigger than I was and swaggered as we walked. Forgetting the cats, I stepped right out, shoulder to shoulder with Georgia, finally on equal status. Side by side, right through their rain-soaked chicken pen we marched, almost back to the cow lot gate. At this point Georgia stopped, pointed at the wire and dropped back. It draped loosely, a foot off the ground. It was completely motionless and didn't look bad to me.

What happened was that wire had been strung from their house to the cow pen at least 10 years before the three of us were born. It had hung so long in the weather that the insulation was rotted away and hung loosely in ribbons. It had been fastened atop a 10-foot pole on a carpenter's wooden cutoff block that had also rotted through the years. Finally, it had broken away during our storm. Now it draped innocently, directly across our path, swaying slightly whenever nudged by a passing breeze.

I thought for a moment. This was a small thing really, very familiar to each of us and it looked harmless to me. Yet, even though I remembered no exact instruction about electric wires, instinct warned me not to touch it. Greenishly corroded, it seemed to have a concealed power, like a coiled snake or a motionless black widow spider clinging watchfully to its position. I sensed that harm might come to anyone who disturbed it.

But after thinking further, I saw no reason for worry. I was in complete control here and had no intention of touching the thing. So no one was going to be hurt. Then, with the foolishness typical of males at almost any stage of life, I began to demonstrate my bravery and superiority to this pair of intimidated females.

The wire slanted alongside, then gradually crossed the footpath leading out to their barn and those kittens. Years of traffic had worn the two-foot-wide path to a depth of three inches at the point where the wire crossed. Fast-melting hail and rain water had been trapped in the depression, forming a substantial puddle underneath it, and no matter what I had decided, the odds were great that someone could be killed here.

I began to perform by swinging both arms forward and jumping neatly across the puddle. I cleared the wire nicely, but Georgia and Katie still hung back, nervous and unconvinced. They were the smart ones. Impelled to establish leadership, I was the dummy. Swinging my arms mightily again, I jumped back across. More comfortable now, the girls edged closer. Sensing power, I stomped all along one side of the wire, splashing muddy water all over.

Then I jumped back across and tromped down the other side, splashing harder than before, thoroughly enjoying the churned up mess.

Georgia and Katie were kids like me and I knew they also enjoyed splashing water. Smiling encouragement, they edged nervously closer, and I invited them to splash with me. But unlike boys, they looked at their clothes and backed off. Reverting to female thinking, they remembered what their father had told them and announced they had been told to stay away from here.

I had run out of girl-impressing material and, since dummies must always have an audience when being stupid, I raised the game stakes by announcing I would rid our pathway of this fearful wire. Then we could all go to play with the kittens. My audience again beamed encouragement.

Looking around, I saw an old broom leaning against their fence and figured it was the exact tool I needed. With it, I could lift that hateful wire, drape it nicely over their clothesline where it would be suspended two feet away from our path, and we could proceed with our cat project. Holding the broom by its straw end, I balanced that wire on the handle and raised it up above the clothesline.

It didn't require an engineer to know that I was using the wrong end of the broom, but I was only a kid, and like six-year-olds everywhere, had more imagination than judgment. Carefully balancing the wire on the tip end of that broom handle, I was able, several times, to lift it slowly and carefully up to the clothesline. But, at the very last instant, it would always slide away from the clothesline, and drop down the handle toward my hand.

I knew that I was working against a gravity engineering problem but was too young to know its name. Finally, I decided I was just too short to do the job by lifting horizontally with my broom handle. I was never going to get enough wire over the line so it could pull itself on over and out of our path. Every time I tried, the weight of that contrary wire pulled it back toward me again.

What I needed to do, more than anything else, was to leave that wet chicken yard at a dead run. But in my mind, what I needed to do was lift that cranky wire high enough over my head to toss it far enough over the clothesline so it would pull itself out of our way. I understood the problem exactly. I needed to use the tip end of the broom handle and balance the wire on its very nose. Then, when I had it high enough, I could throw it far enough over the clothesline so it would slide on out of the way. But my judgment and the use of the tool were both inadequate for the job.

Three times, just as the wire was high enough, it slid off the handle tip and dropped back over the puddle in front of me. Don't even ask why I didn't use the straw end of that broom and don't ask why Georgia and Katie's father only warned his daughters to stay out of their back yard rather than pulling the switch and shutting current away from the wire. Both are good questions but have bad answers.

Finally, on my fourth effort, I elevated the stubborn wire high enough over my head again and had it exactly balanced on the tip of my broom handle. Then it slipped off and slid once more down my side of the handle, toward my face. My audience, like me, was becoming impatient. I could sense that delay was costing me prestige and my new subjects were questioning my leadership. Possibly they had even seen that I had some fear. Yielding to impatience, I decided to act promptly.

Wanting to end the matter once and for all, I grabbed that downwardly slithering wire in my right hand, intending to throw it over the clothesline and out of our way forever. I knew that it might shock anyone who touched it, but I thought I could flip it mightily over the clothesline and let go before it hurt me. After 70 long years, that decision still ranks among my very worst.

Both my feet were planted in the puddle when my hand closed over that wire. My first indication of horrible trouble was when I received gigantic blows of electric current, blasting straight through my body, into the water below. After the third cycle, I realized this thing was hammering me to death and tried to throw it away, but couldn't.

Electricity had energized every tendon in the fingers of my right hand, pulling them into a tightly closed fist and my hand was frozen round the wire. I remember thinking that electricity was incredibly swift. And if anyone had ever made me understand it would cause my hand to wrap around something and not let go, I would have decided on some other way to impress my audience. But, like many of life's victims, I was the product of bad education and worse judgment.

I could barely hear Georgia and Katie yelling that I was going to die as they sped toward their house. I figured they were correct. I yelled loud as I could, but if any sound came out, my ears couldn't hear it. Since then, I have been told that electric current, running through a well-grounded human body pulls the vocal chords so tight that they can't resonate, but I've never known with certainty whether this is true. Yelling didn't help, so I ran hard against the wire, trying to pull loose. First I ran right, then left, throwing all my weight against it but the wire was too strong. I couldn't break away and rapidly lost strength.

Slowly, I sank into the puddle, where in 50 different spots, electric fire was leaping off my body into the water. My ears were filled with a rapid popping sound, like an everlasting package of fireworks, irregularly exploding. Everything was accompanied by an over-riding buzzing noise sounding like a swarm of gigantic bees. I was also aware of a sweet, scorchy smell, that of burning flesh.

The pain wasn't so bad, nor was my fear, but death was imminent. No one had to tell me I was dying. I knew it. I also knew I had done all I could to break free but was too small for the job. I didn't close my eyes but kept on watching, helpless as multiple points of fire jumped from my clothes and body, onto the wet mud and into the water. Death, running fast, was very near. The meeting would be lonely and nowhere in it was further desire to impress young females.

I don't know how long it was. Time wasn't relevant. I could have been dying for an hour or maybe just a minute when the hammering blows of current stopped as suddenly as they began. Forcing my body, I managed to raise my head up far enough to see my feet. Fire no longer sparked from my body to the puddle and the popping, frying noises had stopped. The world seemed quiet, far too quiet.

I was weak but desperately wanted to be loose from that wire. Working quickly as I could, I leaned to the left and pushing hard with that hand, was able to sit up. I needed both hands to stand and tried to open my right hand, dropping the wire, but my fingers wouldn't release. The tendons had been so badly abused that they couldn't relax when instructed by my brain.

There was no one to help, so I sat in the center of that puddle, working desperately, hoping to displace the deadly wire before it finished me off. With my left hand I pulled the deadened right thumb out of my tightly clenched fist and straightened it out. Happily, it stayed where I released it. Then, working gently because pain was beginning to force its way through the numbness, I unfolded each finger, straightening each one as far out as it would go. As with the thumb, each remained where it was placed.

Pain no longer concerned me. Neither did the 12 or 13 holes on the palm side of my right hand, inside the ragged edges of which I clearly saw and smelled scorched bone. Those weren't big problems. Most important, after getting this chance to live, was getting away from that wire.

Even though I'd been working fast as I could, my mind prodded mercilessly, warning that I moved too slowly. The current could return at any second, sweeping me back into the maw of death. So, even though I'd been taught that open sores should be kept clean, I didn't even try. Rolling over and shoving both palms down into the chicken-littered mud, I scurried away from that merciless wire on all fours, crawling like a baby, fast as my body would move.

The world was still too quiet. So much so that I wondered if the others, like me, had almost been killed. I was shaky, and right then, more than at any time in memory, I wanted to be with my mother. Forcing my body upright, and cradling the filthy injured hand with my good one, I started home. Weary and wobbly, too weak to run, but walking as straight and fast as I could, I began what seemed the longest trip I'd ever started.

Keeping as far as I could away from the wire, I staggered through Georgia and Katie's chicken lot gate and was halfway across the in-between neighbor's back yard when I met most of the neighbors, and Mom was also there. They all shouted questions while trotting toward me but I ignored them, heading straight for Mother. She'd been farthest away when starting, but when Katie told her I was dying, she had moved faster and was passing the rest when we met.

White as me, she grabbed me forcefully, demanding to know how I felt. I was sick and said so. From the look on her face and those of our neighbors, plus a strange "shocky" feeling in my body, I figured that the detestable wire was going to kill me anyway, even though I had peeled my hand away from it. But, whether it killed me or didn't no longer mattered. I was too tired to worry about anything.

While kneeling to support me, mother looked at the muddy hand and when she saw all those holes she set up a yell for someone to carry me to a doctor. When she gave way to fear, I did too. My mouth trembled and I slid to the ground, deciding it didn't matter any more what the neighbors were saying about what Georgia and Katie's mother had done.

That good lady wasn't supposed to be out of bed but had done so anyway after her girls ran in to tell her what happened. Unable to make her hired lady understand what to do, and clad only in a long nightgown, she carried a heavy kitchen chair onto their front porch. Climbing up, she pulled a switch, shutting current away from the cowlot wire and saving my life. But at the moment, I thought she had wasted her time. I felt like I was dying. Closing my eyes, I gave up and laid back. I heard my mother's terrified screams but no longer cared.

PART 2, "TREATMENT"

BURKBURNETT HAD NO hospital back then and, I doubt that it has one now. Neither did it have an ambulance. The nearest available hospital was in Wichita Falls and, back then, 13 miles was often way too far. My family had no car and none of the neighbors had one at home. Georgia and Katie's parents had a telephone, but their dad had driven their car to work. The nearest medical help was at Doctor Russell's office four blocks away, over the Bank on Main street.

I don't think I lost consciousness. I was just too tired to cope any more and tried my best to sleep. Neither am I certain how I got to Doc Russell's office, but I think our in-between neighbor, Mr. Horton, carried me in his arms. It wasn't far and I only weighed 45 pounds. I do remember the Doctor asking how I felt and barely mumbled a reply. I resented his disturbing me.

When Doc began to wash and clean my hand, trying to get a reasonable idea of what was wrong with it, I woke and howled loud enough, I hoped, to make him stop. I thought he would be unhappy with the noise but he wasn't. He was glad to see an energetic reaction and favored me with a genuine smile. Cheerfully, he ordered our neighbor to hold me tighter so he could clean and mop inside all my holes.

After cleaning, and without bothering to use any pain killer, Doc poked into my palm and fingers eight or 10 times with a giant needle, squirting in a gob of saline solution every time. Finally, he drenched the hand with some sort of foul-smelling brownish liquid, wrapped it loosely in gauze and rigged my hand and arm up in a shoulder sling. Then he ran everybody out of his office and sat me down in a chair.

Leaning back against his examination table he watched my face closely and asked how I really felt. I was still shaky but felt better now that he had stopped doctoring and told him so. He chuckled and counted my pulse rate, then listened some more with his stethoscope and rubbed on my stomach to see how tight the muscles were. Finally, he asked if I felt like throwing up. I told him I didn't. Then he asked if I could stand up without wobbling and I did. After a few moments, he asked if I would like an ice cream cone and, if so, what flavor.

In all my life I'd never heard of a kid so sick that he turned down ice cream and I certainly didn't intend to be the first. Suddenly, I was actually hungry and the thought of a strawberry ice cream cone made my mouth water like a bulldog drooling over a T-bone steak. Managing a weak smile, I said "strawberry".

Doc chuckled again and opened his office door. Giving our neighbor a quarter, he ordered him to bring me a double-dip strawberry ice cream cone from Mr. Cannon's drugstore next door to the bank building. There were no patients waiting so he watched closely until I finished eating. Then he left me sitting on his swivel chair, playing with a mechanical, wind-up toy mule that kicked when you pulled its tail, while he went out into the hall and updated my parents on my condition. Dad had been repairing a compressor out in the oilfield, and had just arrived.

Fifteen minutes later they all herded into Doc's office to visit with me. He laughed as loud as the rest when, after he told my parents I wasn't going back into shock, I shook my head "No", and assured everyone I wasn't going to touch that wire again. He told my parents to take me home and recited a long list of instructions for treatment. I could eat lightly he said but should "stay quiet" until noon the next day. As we left he volunteered that Dad could pay my bill at the rate of a dollar every other week and told him to bring me back in five days for a repeat exam.

PART 3, "RECOVERY"

IN THE YEAR 2000, that of our newest millennium, this story would now be over, but I was injured in 1933. Medical science was in a development stage we would now call primitive. Penicillin had not even been invented. The first person I ever heard of being treated with it was able to survive a ruptured appendix. Most people didn't in 1942. Sulfa drugs were developed long after World War II was over and the Myecin drugs long after that.

We lived in a time when, though a few vaccines were available, many people wouldn't accept them because some made patients almost as sick as the disease. Therefore, lock-jaw and diphtheria, as well as measles and mumps, still killed Texans every day. Half the people who "caught" double-pneumonia ended up in a grave. "Blood poison" and gangrene which invaded the bodies of many people were common killers. And, now, we reach the last of my story.

The first two days at home after a near-miss from death were nightmares for the entire family. My nervous system had been so badly damaged that it couldn't shake off what had happened. I suffered from such vicious nightmares that I was more afraid of them than I was of dying, and stubbornly fought sleep away. When it did come, my mind reverted to that death puddle and the feel of electricity coursing through my body returned. I saw, and even smelled, a chillingly lifelike vision of my body, hanging by a stinking, smoking hand, while I yelled soundlessly and that electricity pounded me into nothing. The scene never changed, and each time I saw it, the entire picture was dripping with red, as if everything had been dipped in fresh blood.

The dream always ended with me sitting upright in bed, screaming at the top of my lungs. It was 10 long days before my brain slowly began to mend. And it took months for the hideous dreams to completely go away. They returned at intervals for two long years. No dream in my life has equaled them for content of terror. And because I couldn't sleep, neither could anyone else in the house.

My father, who could be amazingly understanding in many situations, quickly lost patience and it was only my mother's active intervention that kept him from punishing me. He either didn't or couldn't know, just as I didn't know how to tell him, that there was no way I could keep those dreams from happening. Even if I'd known how to say it, I would have been ashamed to admit that I was so afraid of those visions that I feared sleep as much as death. To a little kid, with a ravished nervous system, there was very little difference.

Three days after the second doctor visit, we noticed tell-tale streaks of red blood poison, slowly climbing up my wrist toward the elbow. Mother didn't know what they were, but soon as Dad saw them, he picked me up in his arms and trotted all the way to Doc Russell's office. Doc didn't chuckle that day. He examined the hand, then rubbed and squeezed the swollen area, checking its circulation. He didn't like what he saw.

There wasn't a lot, Doc said, that could be done for me right then. Home care, which he would prescribe, cured many such cases.

And once more he handed me the kicking mule to play with and walked Dad out into the hall where they talked for several minutes, deliberately holding their voices too low for me to hear. Doc told him that, sometimes, nothing except surgery cured cases like mine, and if surgery became necessary, it would be severe.

In the thirties, just as today, adults often concealed things from kids, so I didn't worry a lot, but in looking back, I am certain my parents did. Doc told dad the streaks were already high enough that some doctors would consider amputating my forearm below the elbow. Further, if they climbed three inches above the elbow, my entire arm would have to be taken.

Then he ordered dad to take me home and bathe the hand twice daily, for 30 minutes, in an Epsom salts solution. Afterward it was to be swabbed in alcohol and exposed to sunlight for a half hour or so. When not being treated, it must be wrapped in a clean, light, and airy bandage with no dye in the material. And he wanted me back in two more days for another look. If the marks rose only as much as half an inch, he wanted to see me even if it was at night. Then he marked a circle round my arm with iodine so that any movement of the infectious streaks could be immediately seen.

When Doc next saw me, the streaks weren't quite so red and the swelling was reduced. That, and the fact that they weren't moving upward, was encouraging but they still wouldn't go away. They kept hanging on. Doc applied more of his bad smelling ointment and sent me home for three more days.

On the next visit, the streaks were moving up again. Doc really didn't like that, and back in the hall again he pointedly advised my dad that there was one kind of "minor" surgery that might help but my arm was reaching the point where a real decision had to be made. Options were to try the "minor" surgery, and await development or sacrifice my hand, removing the forearm halfway to my elbow.

By choosing "conservative" surgery the hand might be saved if quick action was taken. If this didn't work, infection would quickly move above the elbow and the lower arm would have to go. Neglecting to amputate at that point would allow poison and gangrene to spread throughout my body, probably killing me.

No parent should be forced to make such a decision, but dad had it to do. He knew that talking with mother would be useless. She was the sort of woman that folks used to call "high strung." A great person, she was a tower of strength in some areas, but was truly helpless with this kind of problem. Doc helped as much as possible by outlining the options. After that, it was up to my dad.

In those days anesthetic meant ether, Doc said, and ether was also dangerous. It could kill any patient, especially a kid, by stopping his heart on the operating table. It could also burn his lungs, precipitating pneumonia. Either occurrence might kill a patient. Also, new infections sometimes followed surgery and they could kill patients as quickly as the illness he already had.

Another problem, Doc continued, was that some patients didn't survive the physical shock of surgical amputation. And there was always the chance that a gangrene infection could return. But, he finished, finally offering some encouragement, there was a good side. He had been a battlefield surgeon in World War I and had amputated scads of arms and legs. Without bragging a bit, he claimed that he knew his job well. And he thought a patient who had lost two-thirds of an arm could function as well in life as one who had lost only a hand. Besides, there was a fair chance that minor surgery would cure me up because I still had a lot of strength and he had decided I was pretty tough.

Dad opted for conservative treatment and Doc's "minor surgery" was scheduled. General anesthesia, the type that used ether to put patients to sleep, had only been around for 50 years. Sometime around 1880, a Nevada surgeon had started using it to put his patients to sleep while practicing a new kind of surgery called an "appendectomy". Other physicians copied his techniques and began using it for other surgical techniques.

Texas back then was filled with old-time frontier people who had heard the screams of patients and had seen the effects of surgery conducted without anesthesia. Most were convinced that half of all patients who submitted to surgery of any kind would die, and they weren't far from being right. Some were so hard-headed that when they "took sick", they refused any kind of surgery, even when a real doctor recommended it. They mostly died, but the ones who didn't and the relatives of those who did, were always happy to furnish their ignorant opinions to anyone, even a sick kid like me. Fortunately, my parents kept me away from this kind of folks before my surgery but, even so, it turned out about to be almost as bad as those pessimists would have predicted.

What he planned to do, Doc explained, was cut seven pairs of vertical slits in my fingers and palm, one on each side of the largest holes in my hand. This was because those holes were my centers of infection. Skin between the slits would then be raised and he would slip drainage tubes under each one. Those tubes would remain in the hand until infection was killed out. The problem was, other than being anesthetized, I might as well have been one of Doc's battlefield casualties. Medical suppliers didn't make kid-sized drainage tubes and his surgery wasn't quite so minor where a little kid's hand was involved.

Problems first developed when they started putting me to sleep. I was very afraid. And those two people, the doctor and his wife, were dressed completely in white. I had never seen them that way. They wore large, scary masks to keep themselves from being gassed by their own ether, and they grabbed me, holding me roughly when I tried to change into a more comfortable position on the table.

I did what most kids would do. I yelled and fought, causing them to summon additional help before I was finally gassed enough so that Doc could begin. For some reason no one could explain, I continued to stir and scream all through the surgery. Dad later told me that he couldn't stand it and ended up walking up and down the street outside Doc's office, listening to me yell.

The first thing I knew, after the fighting and yelling, was feeling Doc's scalpel cutting into my hand. I complained loudly and, just as quickly, he stopped the operation. He was practicing strict patient safety because he didn't think a kid my size ought to have any more ether. But this was a bad development, because he was only half through.

Maybe Doc could have given me another whiff or two, and finished up with no more trouble but he decided I'd been stressed enough and refused to administer any more anesthetic that day. I never blamed him for the decision because he eventually saved my hand and probably my life. Still, it was awfully hard for me to walk back to that operating table two mornings later and lie down again so they could place that white inhalation cone over my face. This time, I asked them not to hold me and they didn't. This time there was no fighting or yelling and Doc finished up in a hurry.

Once again my hand was suspended in a sling because it had now suffered more damage than it started off with. It was also swelled and painful all over, hurting me badly for several more days. The dressing was changed every day and Doc's new treatment ordered us to soak the hand for 15 minutes daily, in a pan of Clorox.

I don't know if Clorox killed the infection or not, but if the smell didn't kill it, I am guessing the infection left by choice. I would have left myself if I could. Besides the constant odor, the chemical ate up my skin. Every time the bandage was changed, rotten layers of skin sloughed off with it. I vomited more than once and the strong smell of Clorox still turns my stomach.

The good news was that I had sunk so low that the only way to go was up. First the swelling, and then the streaks, slowly disappeared. In two or three weeks Doc allowed us to stop the Clorox and we could mop the hand with alcohol again. After three more weeks he pronounced the infection dead and pulled out the drainage tubes. My sling was discarded, and four months after being injured, my hand was actually well except for a permanently bent index finger, "pulled" by heavy scarring, and two nerve bundles which are still numb.

By the end of the year my mind had greatly improved and the bad dream only returned every month or so. Finally, I was as healthy and happy again as other kids my age. For the next five years, every time I passed Doc Russell on the street, he would stop me and demand to see the hand. I would hold it out so he could grab my arm and roll it over, then squeeze, twist and bend everything. Next, he would pull on my fingers and ask me to shake his hand with a hard grip.

Finally, he would ask how my fingers felt and I always said "great." Then he would chuckle and walk jauntily down the sidewalk while peeling a cigar, proud of his work. This continued until a day, I think in 1943, when Doctor Russell collapsed at the family table and died while eating his Sunday lunch.

With Georgia and Katie, I never gained another inch of respect or leadership. Georgia was two years older than me and, at our age, this was a lifetime. Katie, a true sister, never failed to side with Georgia against me.

But it didn't matter any more. My parents and theirs, though they'd been raised in our oilfield boom town together and had sat in classrooms side by side all through school, barely spoke after the incident. But the loss didn't disturb me. New kids moved onto our block. Even though we had disagreements, even fights, we played better together than I had with those sisters.

CHAPTER 17

Storm Cellar—1934

In thinking back, I remember
that my mother wasn't much of a "canner." In fact, she almost
never canned food, complaining that she "just couldn't get it down
right." Neither was she the best cook in the block, which she freely
admitted. But she always followed this admission by observing that
her family wasn't starving. This was true. We might not have
relished every bite we ate but mom's food was seldom thrown away.

My mom was an excellent parent, but complex personalities
ran in our family and she was also many other things. Among the
traits that separated her from many people was a deep-seated fear
of "cyclones." My dad was a man of dependable habits, perhaps the
strongest of which was his healthy appetite. Folks called him a "big
eater." So it was canned corn and beans, potatoes, fruits and preserves,
along with turnips, greens and carrots that my mother dangled
from the end of her stick while persuading him to build us a storm
cellar.

I was an eight-year-old kid in 1935 and tried my best to ignore
the weather because it was almost always bad. North Texas was
always either "too hot" or "too cold," "too still" or "too windy,"
"too wet" or "too dry." And, since the dust bowl was at its very
worst, you could always add "too gritty." Our weather was seldom
"just right."

Mother had moved to Burkburnett, sited on the South bank of
Red River, in 1916. Dad's family came there in 1917 and his dad
worked "here and there" for a living. Both my parents easily
adjusted to the North Texas climate, except for mother and her

"cyclones," but I was never weather-adjusted to North Texas. No one had heard of "El Nino" when I was young, but if they had they would have felt it was dull and uninteresting compared to Texas weather in 1935.

We were always having storms. Big ones. There were the standard ones like snow storms, rainstorms and windstorms. But we also had ice storms, sand storms, twisters, lightning storms, sleet storms, tornadoes and "cyclones." There were also hailstorms and "Northers" plus whirlwinds strong enough to pick up chicken coops or outhouses and strip the leaves off small trees. There were no hurricanes or waterspouts, but we were so busy accommodating to the others that we didn't miss them.

The grownups never told us kids about it, so we didn't realize that this flat and dry country was actually desert until we grew up and left home. And because of its flatness, our tornadoes were dangerous. They mostly came in large rather than medium or small size, and when they met the ground, there were no hills or trees to pitch them back up into the sky. They would settle down, spread out and wander about like giant vacuum cleaner nozzles, grinding and mincing everything in their paths until losing energy and returning to the sky.

Out in the country, most folks had storm cellars and holed up in them during bad storms, even though some neighbors kidded them, calling the cellars "fraid holes." Few town people had cellars, and I don't know why except that Texas was barely two generations removed from the time when families lived in prairie dugouts. Many old-timers had gotten so sick of living underground in cramped quarters that they refused to tolerate a storm cellar. Later, when they moved into towns, they didn't farm any more and had little produce to can so they wouldn't bother to dig one.

As the frontier economy slowly changed into a more permanent society, country families began to build houses. They were mostly frame shacks of one to four rooms but they stood on top of the ground. And as more children were born, they added onto the houses, room at a time, as their owners became prosperous enough to build themselves more living room. The new homes were roomier, prettier and smelled better than dugouts, but country people who moved out of a dugout into a house seldom abandoned the old pit completely. Even though they no longer lived underground, the dugout still had many uses. Some said they were as handy as "socks on a rooster."

Re-named cellars, dugouts were perfect for storing canned vegetables and preserved fruits or jellies. And they were also better, when the weather was bad, than sleeping in wagons when company, temporary workers or harvest help were on the premises for a night or two. But there was also the final reason many kept their cellars. Every Texan knew that if you took to a cellar before a cyclone struck that it would normally pass over without killing you even though it might, out of spite, carry away your house or barn.

So in early fall of 1935, my mother got her way and dad began to dig the hole. He waited until late summer so that any rain which fell would "soften" the clay. I wanted to help but he mostly used me to carry water, coffee, lemonade and tea. I was allowed to fill buckets and carry up all the dirt I wanted, but mostly I was told to "move over" or "stay out of the way."

Dad worked almost every evening after coming home from his job at Wiggins Machine Shop. Digging was slow because of the hard red clay. But, occasionally a heavy rain would leave an inch or two of water in the pit. He waited until water had soaked in and dried out some before digging again. That way the clay would be softened and he wouldn't slide around on the muddy bottom.

Our next door neighbor, Mr. Horton, along with his boys, often visited to chat and watch dad work. They lounged atop the growing pile of dirt at the side of his pit and offered many suggestions, most of which he ignored. They also offered occasional cups of coffee, or glasses of iced tea, most of which he accepted. None of them ever brought a shovel or offered to push a wheelbarrow of earth up to ground level.

Mr. Horton declared several times that he would like to have a cellar like dad's but his bad back kept him from digging one. He performed "day work" around town and we had already noticed that his "bad back" prevented kept him from accepting half the jobs which were offered to him. But any job he liked, no matter how hard, didn't bother it much.

Dad's pit was big, measuring 10 by 12 feet, and went downward for seven. By winter he had finished digging and after hauling in some heavy oilfield timbers for framing, raftering and a ridgepole, he laid them beside his hole to wait for Spring. Tornadoes seldom came in the winter.

In Spring, soon as the pit had dried out, he laid his timbers in place, framed over the top, and nailed corrugated tin across the rafters. Then he threw boards over the tin for reinforcement, piled 10 to 12 inches of red clay on top and tromped it down good. After that he pitched Bermuda grass seed all over it and watered everything down. Leftover dirt was hauled in his wheelbarrow over to an abandoned oilwell pit on the other side of our back yard. There was a deep sink hole where the well's conductor box had originally been located and I heard dad tell Mr. Horton he would have dug the cellar there but he was afraid it would continue to cave in.

The only thing left was to dig the stairs, put on a door and fix the cellar up inside. Since dad liked carpentry better than digging, it finished up quickly. He dug and framed the stairs in short order, then built shelves along the back and sides. Bench seats were built end-to-end along both long walls, and the door was framed up from salvaged derrick timbers which he split to the size and thickness he wanted. Heavy pine siding was nailed on the door frame inside and out while large 10-inch strap hinges attached it to the door frame. Last of all, a ventilator opening was cut alongside the ridgepole, and a stove pipe stuck through it. After a weather cap was tacked on top, dad informed mother, that her cellar was "ready for canned goods."

Her canned corn project worked out okay because my Aunt Pauline knew how to do it. She and mother were partners in this deal, and the canning was done at Holliday, where my aunt lived. Along with three girl cousins, I was drafted to help the women and I didn't even like canned corn.

My job was to lug whatever the women didn't want to carry, which ended up being everything. Then, after shucking those large ears of field corn, my cousins and I were charged with getting "every little bit" of cornsilk from between the kernel rows. After that we washed and stacked the ears so cutters could slice every kernel off into pans for cooking. I wanted to be a cutter but the women vetoed this, assigning me to more hauling. When we finished everyone had dried cornstarch spattered all over them.

Women's tastes baffled me then, and they still do. My cousins, normally neat and prissy, thought canning was great and didn't mind all that cornstarch. I hated both the look and smell of mine and figured the grown folks had, as usual, engineered the best jobs for themselves. But I couldn't change anything because everybody except me loved canned corn and no one listened to my complaints. At home that night, dad proudly carted 18 quart and 12 one pint Mason jars, filled with creamed corn, down into mom's new cellar and lined them up along one of those brand-new shelves.

Okra was next, and mother cranked out a dozen jars of that all by herself. And, because okra naturally tastes bad anyway, no one was ever sure whether she did or didn't get it "exactly right". Peaches, however, were a big problem because, once more, I was the only male around when we canned them. I had to do all the hauling and carrying, even though I was younger and smaller than two of my girl cousins. Once more my Aunt Pauline had the recipe down "pat" and we brought home many jars of pickled and canned sliced peaches.

This time I got to use a knife and help them peel, but only because the grown folks could see they wouldn't finish up three big bushels of peaches unless the kids helped. Using a paring knife wasn't as much fun as I thought it would be, but I didn't mind peach juice as much as cornstarch. And I didn't cut a finger off, as mother had predicted.

That night dad hauled a half dozen quart Mason jars of spiced peaches into the cellar, along with a dozen quart jars and two dozen pint jars of sliced peaches. We now had a respectable supply of canned stuff in the cellar. As with the corn, I hated pickled peaches but could tolerate canned, sliced peaches, so my work wasn't completely wasted.

Green beans and peas came next. Mother and her sister conspired against us kids once again and bought several bushels. We were ordered to shell peas and snap beans until our fingers and thumbs had friction sores and purple colored juice dye all over. Once more I was assigned to haul and dump everything. By then I had also figured out why grown men always managed to disappear when their wives started canning.

Despite growing up in the Great Depression and seldom having exactly what I wanted to eat, I was such a picky eater that my parents often predicted I would end up starving. And I really liked Kentucky Wonder beans when they were cooked up with sliced, creamed new potatoes and canned with a small slice of salt pork in each jar. I detested either green peas or beans prepared in any other way. But it made no difference, I lost out again. My Aunt's Kentucky Wonder green bean recipe didn't allow for potatoes, and those two grownup women didn't cook a single one. Mother pacified me by saying she would add them when she cooked the beans at home but even when she did, she seldom took the time to cream them.

They cooked those beans and peas in large pans and ladled them into empty quart mason jars. The empties were set in dishpans of boiling water to temper. Hot water kept the jars from cracking and ruining when the scalding beans were ladled in. One adult filled jars while another slipped rubber gaskets on their necks, screwed the lids down tight and washed off the juice. Then each jar was set aside to cool. I played pack mule again, all day long. By the time we finished, I decided dad shouldn't have built our cellar at all. I had worked as hard with canning as he had at digging.

Four nights after the bean and pea canning, at 2:00 in the morning, a loud hammering on our back door woke me straight up. The sound was loud enough to carry over the noise of reverberating thunder, which rolled about among the many hail pockets high up in a giant thunderhead poised over our end of Wichita county. Wind gusted first from one side, then another. The gusts grew stronger and lasted longer. Rain fell in sheets for several seconds, then stopped, only to start up again. Here and there, large hailstones began to hammer against our roof and walls.

"Mr. Stevenson," and I recognized Abel Horton's voice above the storm noise, "This cloud's gettin' mean! Can we go down in your cellar?"

"Go ahead," dad shouted back.

Then the light came on in our room and I saw my Mother, fully dressed. She told me to wrap up in a quilt and shouted for dad to hurry. He was grumbling, taking time with his dressing, not convinced he ought to go, but he did pick up speed when our across-the-street neighbor hammered on the back door to ask if his family could use the cellar too.

Artist Gary Tuttle, Humble, Texas

Dad quickly finished dressing then wrapped my sister, Gwynda, in a quilt and, bundling one of us up in one arm and one in the other, he legged it through the heavy forked and chain lightning, fast-falling hail and ripping gusts of wind to our cellar door. Mother ran along beside him, focusing a cranky flashlight on the ground ahead of us.

In oilfield country, people frequently twisted up and lit a sheet of newspaper, then threw it into a cellar before going down. Often there was a loud "whoosh" plus a brief sheet of blue flame caused by burning gas. Our cellar, however, had no gas problems and no one was in danger of being asphyxiated. When we arrived, our neighbors had lit the kerosene lantern and the cellar looked cozy. We felt safe and everybody appreciated being there.

I sat on a tub in a corner where an old mother cat had been allowed to raise a litter of kittens. While stroking the cats, I counted three times and we had eleven people inside. My nose told me we were a "close fit."

Dad had tied a rope to the inside door handle to hold it down but no one was holding it. Suddenly, we heard what sounded like a freight train coming and we all knew that no railroad track lay in that direction. The wind sucked our door wide open, allowing heavy hail and rain to blow in. Dad, assisted by Abel, wrestled the door back down, but the rope was rotten and pulled loose. Dad then pulled a log chain from a corner and they wired it to the door frame, pulling it tight again. Even though they placed their combined weight on the chain, wind pressure occasionally sucked the door up several inches before they wrestled it down again.

After several minutes the freight train noise faded and wind force dropped to a more reasonable level. Hail, which had blanketed the earth to a depth of two inches, began to slow, then stopped. The rain slowed, but continued steadily. This prompted a neighbor to say he hoped it would rain all night. And, since few people in our part of Texas ever fussed about rain, several people nodded their heads in agreement.

Everyone was wide awake and the men were wishing for coffee.

Each family was waiting for the rain to slack off so they could check for damage to their houses. While waiting, they began swapping "cyclone stories" which I loved to hear. The stories mostly involved the worst cyclone experience of the teller's life. Some told tales of wheat straws being driven into the walls of houses and of people being sliced in two by sheets of flying tin. One man remembered a barn being blown completely off its full load of baled hay. After the storm they found an uninjured three-day-old calf on top of the stacked bales.

My mother warned me later that old people sometimes didn't remember things exactly right, and some of those stories were so ridiculous that I realized they were only tales but I loved them anyway. Best of all was one sworn to by a neighbor whose mother's cast iron washpot had been blown away in a bad cyclone. Next morning, while out looking for dead cattle, he had found the kettle in the middle of a pasture, half a mile from their house, almost full of rain water. When he got off his horse to empty it, he found that the wind had been so strong that it turned the washpot inside out. All three of its cast iron feet, which normally stood on the ground, were sticking up from inside.

We went to the cellar a lot during that first year, a little less on the second and much less after that. My recollection is that the storms weren't quite so bad anymore, or maybe we had begun to trust our houses more and had lost some fear. But, in remembering back, I affectionately recall the warm, safe and protected feeling I felt when we were closed in the cellar with our neighbors, each person trying to guess by listening what was happening to his home and property on the outside. When that happened I felt the cellar was worth twice as much work as it took Dad to dig it. And maybe it was even worth all my pack mule work while helping those women to can.

CHAPTER 18

Movin' Out—1935

Until 1935, when President Roosevelt cranked up the WPA, to help needy people, our next door neighbor, Mrs. Horton, was taking in washing and ironing and her oldest daughter, Pauline, waitressed at the Burk Cafe. Those women had to work because their family needed money even more than the rest of us.

The oldest Horton boys, George and Abel, worked as cowboys. Living at home they earned around $40.00 a month between them. Sometimes this large family borrowed food from us, and because of the bad depression with its dearth of jobs, our government had created the WPA as a way to help families whose men could not find work.

I was almost nine, and even though I mistakenly figured I was grown, I was a kid with few illusions when it came to money. We lived in Burkburnett, Texas, once a thriving oilfield boomtown but It wasn't a boomtown any more. The rich and prosperous wildcatters, except for one lone millionaire, J. G. Hardin, had sacked up their winnings and gone. People who stayed behind became unwilling partners in America's longest and cruelest depression.

Neighbors back then had little other entertainment at night than sitting on their front porches to smoke and talk. I always listened closely, keeping quiet and hoping to be left outside with the grownups. One night as we sat outside, Mr. Horton told dad that he and his third son Lon, who was also unemployed, were going to hire out to the WPA which would pay each worker six dollars a day. He strongly advised dad to go with them but dad said he intended to stay where he was.

Next morning I watched as Mr. Horton and Lon walked down Avenue C toward city hall. They came back bragging about their new U. S. Government jobs on which they only had to work three days every week. Each one of them was earning as much as dad. After deciding the work was easy enough, Mr. Horton pulled his 16-year-old son, Roy, out of school and hired him out. Within two weeks, people began to see the Horton men working at shoveling dirt in crews alongside our county roads.

One night dad added up their wages. Guessing at what the women earned, he figured their entire family earned over $70.00 a week, about as much as any family in Burk, except for Mr. Hardin. The Hortons were now what most Burk people would call wealthy and that's why dad ran Mr. Horton off our front porch six weeks later when he knocked after dark and wanted to "borry" a dollar.

Dad earned $18.00 a week as a machinist at Mr. P. A. Wiggins' Machine Shop near the railroad track on West Main. He worked five and a half days weekly and was on 24-hour call. Because Burk's oil business was mostly gone, Mr. Wiggins' shop was the last one in town, and there was no way dad could replace that job if he lost it. Even though Mr. Horton kept telling dad and his two cowboy sons how easy the WPA was, and that they could trim many days off their work weeks and be better off, dad and those cowboys refused to do it.

Two months later, Mr. Wiggins cut his payroll. Since he and dad were the only machinists in the shop, dad was the one who had to go. For the next two months I watched as my father walked down Avenue C each morning with a quarter in one jacket pocket and a peanut butter sandwich in the other, looking for work. Sometimes he was able to work a day or two but it was 10 weeks before he located a real job at the Hinderleiter Tool Company in Seminole, Oklahoma.

After that, every Sunday afternoon, he boarded the noisy, creaky and smoky old Greyhound at 3:15 and rode off to Seminole, where he worked all week. That's why he missed seeing what happened next door at the Hortons. But I knew he would be interested and watched everything closely so I could tell him about it next Saturday.

It happened on a hot Thursday in the middle of July. School was out so I got to see it all. My first indication of change at the Hortons was when the cattle truck didn't circle by at 7:30 that morning. Normally it honked at the corner and slowed down so George and Abel, dragging their ropes and chaps, could hop on board. But on this Thursday, the Horton men all rode downtown and traded off their ancient Model-T Ford sedan for an almost new Model-A flatbed Ford truck with a good set of tires. A brand-new spare had also been mounted on each side of the bed.

Using salvaged lumber they quickly framed a shelter over the truck bed and covered it with heavy waterproof tenting. Curious as a cat, I played nearby and heard Mr. Horton shout to Abel that the womenfolks had finished packing contents from their closets and the kitchen plunder. They were now starting on the bed ticks, quilts and sheets. All this activity had to mean that they were moving out!

Abel had never been a big talker but he had always smiled and tolerated me. Still, because of dad's recent fuss with Mr. Horton, I didn't know if he would put up with me or not, so I tried him out by asking if he could use any help. He looked at me, then paused a moment as if deciding something important. After that he said I could go inside and be a pack mule for the women if I wanted to. Then he smiled real big to show he was only kidding and added that, if he were me, he'd stay outside with him and help boss.

Edging closer, I asked if they were moving. I knew it was a dumb question, but it was more polite than asking where. Abel answered openly, saying they were headed to California, and since he'd always wanted to see the ocean, he was going with the family. They would be out of their house by mid-afternoon.

In those days people didn't require a staggering amount of time to move. The Hortons only had two closets, each made from a piece of bedsheet hung across a length of baling wire strung between nails driven into cornering walls. Much of their furniture was made of wooden boxing material and would be abandoned. People moved often in those days, hoping to starve as little as possible, and the Hortons knew exactly how to move.

More talking and listening revealed that George and Pauline were staying in Burk. She had a boy friend and wanted to get married while George had decided to partner with an old cowman in Oklahoma who needed some help that had a little bit of "cow sense". George had also met a girl from over near Ada and Abel figured she had a lot to do with his staying. Old Mr. Horton, he said, had heard about somebody in California who found a $10.00-a-day job. "Pap, told us that's better than the WPA and he wants a job like that."

Then, grinning again, Abel said that as ugly, beat-up and "puredee" country as he was, he never expected to find a woman dumb enough to marry him. "But," he finished, "it's as easy to be old, ugly and country in California as in Texas, and I really want to see that ocean."

When dad came back next Saturday, I told him about our talk and he laughed out loud, saying he'd always liked that cowboy. But I never told anyone, until now, the thing that happened just before they left.

My mother had been serving them coffee and iced tea all day long, so after packing everything on the truck they pulled into our drive to say their good-byes and to have a drink of ice water to top them off. They had the usual pair of three-gallon, heavily woven, desert-crossing waterbags fastened onto each side of their truck, but it took three hours of steady driving for them to cool off enough for drinking.

Doreen Horton was as pretty as ever. She was thirteen months older than me, and despite the fact that she had always treated me badly, manipulating me shamelessly before her girl friends while building up her self-esteem, I loved her as much that day as I did the day they had moved in. But, like the dumb kid I was, I thought she didn't know. While the adults were visiting, she caught my eye and winked. Then, motioning with her chin, like an Indian, for me to follow, she slipped around the corner of our house toward the back yard.

Puzzled, I trailed behind, finally locating her in back of a tall shrub near our back door. Her cheeks were flushed, her eyes danced and she smiled broadly while impatiently motioning me closer. I was nervous and stopped half a step away. We were still too far apart to suit her so she caught my elbows and pulled me so close that I smelled the gardenia perfume she wore. Leaning into me, she whispered that she loved me also and I could kiss her if I wanted to.

Badly embarrassed, I stood frozen, unable to move. Even though I liked her idea, I was still too young yet for participation in boy-girl love. My mind wasn't ready for real-life romance and the situation was moving way too fast for me. I knew how to kiss because I had seen grownups do it in the movies, but I stood rigid, frozen to the spot, unable to function. Watching her closely, I wondered feverishly if loving women was something a man really ought to do. Right then it seemed awfully hazardous and emotionally dangerous.

Reading my thoughts with ease, Doreen smiled as I visualized Delilah might have done with Samson and told me I needn't be afraid. Then, when I still didn't move quickly enough to suit her, she solved her problem by pulling me tight and kissing me long and hard, right on the mouth.

After this kiss, only my second but definitely the best of the two, Doreen whispered into my ear that she still loved me, as I did her. She also confided she would write, "soon as I can." Then, having finished what she wanted to do, she spun on her heel, and walked rapidly back into the real world.

Still dazed, I realized that I couldn't function in front of all those people, especially my mother. So I stayed where I was. My last glimpse of the Hortons was Doreen's shapely fanny wiggling round the corner of our house toward their California-bound truck.

For too many days afterward I waited for the postman but her letter never came. If I happened to be away when the postman came by, I always casually but carefully, checked with my parents after returning to see if a letter had come, but it was a waste of time.

Six weeks of waiting convinced me that Doreen had, with female practicality, opted for another type of boy-girl relationship.

She wasn't a bad person and had probably believed it when she promised to write but she was still learning about life and about herself. Until it actually happened, she probably didn't know that she was the type of person who could never find happiness with a pen pal. She was the type of person who needed someone she could reach out and touch. I became an expendable item in her developing life.

I had a hard head in my early days, and still can be a stubborn learner, so I didn't profit from this first love experience. Learning nothing about women from Doreen, it wasn't long before I transferred my affection and liberty to a slightly older and shapely black-haired beauty who allowed me to hang around. Two weeks later she threw me over for a twelve-year old with a new red Schwinn bicycle. It was a year later before I located a replacement who was desperate enough to put up with me. Then, I started my schooling again, trying to understand the art of male-female understanding but I haven't graduated yet.

During the next 10 years George Horton frequently re-crossed Red River from his ranch in Oklahoma. Dad occasionally saw him in town, and over cups of steaming Texas coffee, they caught up on family news. Old Mr. Horton, George said, had actually located his $10.00-a-day job and had bought a brand-new Buick. He promptly became a Californian for life and continually advised every Texan he knew to move out West.

In 1943 George reported that Spence, his youngest brother, had been killed while fighting the Germans in North Africa. Roy, 16 months older, had earned a battlefield commission in Italy for bravery, and Abel had not only seen the ocean but was working at the side of it, welding in a West Coast shipyard, and making more money than his father.

The Government had told George he was too valuable as a rancher to be drafted into the Army and had "frozen" him to the cow business. He'd married that girl from Ada but they split the blanket early one Sunday morning after they got home from an all-night dance and she stuck him in the back with a kitchen knife. George's old partner had died and he now lived alone on the ranch. Most Saturdays he drove into Lawton or Burk to see a "show" and to eat some cafe food, preferably fried oysters. Then he bought groceries, picked up the latest issues of "Best Western" and "Ranch Romances", and crossed back over to tend his cows.

If Doreen ever did anything unusual or interesting, George and dad didn't mention it. But I figured she had the looks and gall to sift out half the sailors on California's coast until she found one that suited her exact purpose.

In the year 2005, I picture her as a trim, active and blue-eyed great-grandmother, pretty and shapely for her age. I doubt that she is the rocking chair type. Maybe she lives in Oregon, and I would guess that she drives a convertible in which she hauls loads of grandchildren to places where they all have a good time. I picture them listening closely as she tells stories that make them laugh. And maybe, once or twice, they all have a big laugh when she tells them about the bashful Texas boy who once lived next door.

CHAPTER 19

BOOMER'S KIDS—1937

LIGHTNING BLASTED THAT tank squarely on its top and fire blazed immediately. In Burkburnett, Texas, back in 1937, oil companies generally allowed tank fires to burn themselves out because oil was cheap. Fighting fire was dangerous and expensive so what they did was shut off oil to the tank, pump or drain out what they could and dig a ditch all round to catch any released oil. After that they allowed it to burn to the ground.

Nobody talked about pollution back then and if they had, no one else would have listened to them. Boomtowns exuded pollution in all directions. We lived 24 hours a day with the smell of waste oil burning and the raw, sharp smell of crude oil and petroleum-charged gas. On still winter mornings, gas lay close to the ground and many people were hesitant to build fires for fear that the entire town would explode.

In school we had the additional pollution smells of kerosene and firewood smoke added to the body odor of some students who only bathed occasionally and who wouldn't have used deodorant even if their parents could afford to buy it. Pollution had been a part of Burk for the last 20 years and we seldom heard of anyone getting cancer. There were, however, a lot of folks who died from things like being kicked in the head by a mule, coming down with diphtheria and pneumonia or rupturing their appendix.

Three days after that lightning strike, on our way home from school, Bobby and I stopped once more, along with eight or 10 other kids, to watch the tank die. It looked and sounded the way I figured Hell might and we were entranced. The thing greatly resembled a giant lava lamp of the type that became fashionable 40 years later, but with a burning tank, in addition to the color, you could hear the overwhelming noise of frying, hissing and boiling.

The noise wasn't as loud as Niagara but it could be heard from 200 feet away and a solid core of flaming fingers rose and fell, often reaching 60 feet into the sky. They receded regularly, temporarily replaced by large gouts of heavy black smoke that gradually bloomed and swelled until the fingers of fire rose again, shoving the smoke up to infinity. The boiling and frying sounds never stopped, and that great column of black smoke rose until it flattened out against the bottom atmosphere layer. There, it streamed with the wind, making a long dark plume visible for 20 miles in any direction.

This tank had been burning for three days and the upper side plates, like the outside of a wide flat-topped candle, had burned and rolled eight feet down from the original tank height. But the remaining tank shell was filled with boiling oil. Its top resembled an open flaming mouth, framed by white hot lips. Twisted, curled and horribly chapped by the heat, they continually shrank, like a candle, staying level with the burning oil.

Beneath its mouth, the tank walls were mostly intact but, every three or four minutes, the hissing mess boiled over. Flaming oil then rolled over the tortured lips and streamed down the wall. But the liquid was so hot that it flamed and vaporized again before dropping more than two feet. The rest of the tank's wall, still 10 or 12 feet high, retained its original paint. Much of the paint and most of the company logo, a flying red horse, were intact because most of the heat was released into the atmosphere.

Bobby and I had seen oil tanks burn before, but we stopped every day to watch this one. We liked the noise, the motion and the reflected heat. They tended to "trance" us. Besides, this was the only unusual thing in town right then and interesting happenings in Burk were scarce.

George Thomas, the company's lease pumper, had been sentenced to tank-watching. His company car, a 1935 Chevrolet coupe, was parked closer to the blaze than any other vehicle. His job was to keep citizens, mostly kids like us, from getting too close. He stood watch every day before and after school was out, in addition to his normal lease work. Today he waved us back with a weary motion instead of greeting us with his usual smile. Tank-sitting was grating on his nerves.

"You know, Bobby," I said, deciding to repeat it just one more time, "they say that Mr. Thomas had just been up on top to measure the oil in this tank. He was back in his car, writing down the numbers, when that lightning struck." I looked closely at him while I talked but wasn't certain he was paying attention so, still watching him, I finished loudly, "And there wasn't a cloud in the sky!"

Soon as I finished, but without skipping a beat and never taking his eyes off the flames, Bobby answered: "Yep. I know. Mom told my dad it was his warning from God."

CHAPTER 20

RALPH—1936

RALPH'S FATHER COULD still make
a living at blacksmithing because he was the best tool dresser left in
Burkburnett. Most surrounding cable tool drillers brought their
business in to him. Oil was still king in Wichita County in 1936,
but like everything else, it was awfully cheap. The government,
through radio and newspapers, kept telling us that the Great
American Depression was over, but no one in Burk could tell the
difference. Bankers and lawyers didn't look quite as poor and
threadbare as the rest of us, but they weren't much better off.

Ralph's mother was no longer young. A small woman, she had
followed her husband from a Missouri farm to the Texas oilfields.
When working outside in her garden or hen house, she wore a
"Poke Bonnet" and men's pants and boots. She sold extra eggs at
Boyd's grocery and carefully hid her few pennies of profit as a tithe
to the Baptist church. Her husband spent the money when he found
it and some said he would beat her to find it. She couldn't leave
him because there was no place she could go.

There had been bad signals ever since Ralph, their only child,
had come back home. A large hulk of a man with the mind of a
child, he told people that he received daily "orders" from Tibet. I
learned a lot about his difference when I watched him mow their
lawn for the first time. This was before gas or electric mowers had
been invented, and people who cared how their lawns looked used
long wooden handled reel-type push mowers to clip their grass.
Ralph kept their lawn fairly well mowed but it was never close-
clipped because he always turned the mower upside down and pulled

it around instead of pushing. Every kid I knew had tried this trick. It was easier than pushing, but it only clipped the tops of grass and weeds and our parents always made us do it over. When I pointed out that his mower needed to be righted, he said he knew it. Then, with the only spark of humor I ever saw in him, he smiled. Saying that his way was easier, he kept right on pulling.

When they sent him to town on errands he used his paper note instruction sheets to shoo non-existent flies away from his face. Sometimes he fanned hard with them, mumbling to himself about gnats and mosquitoes which no one else could see but he continued to fight them anyway.

Ralph had been locked away for twelve years in what we called the insane asylum at Wichita Falls. Years later I was told he had contracted a bad disease which the adults did not want to explain to me, and it had affected his mind. His mother, who barely tolerated her home life, was lonely, and had been making regular bus trips over to see him for years. Maybe she reached an emotional limit, or maybe loneliness out weighed her judgment. Anyway, a day came when she decided that Ralph needed better care and she decided to bring him home.

His dad was opposed, even to the point of blacking her eye. Undeterred, she wore the afflicted eye first to talk with her preacher, then to a doctor in Wichita and finally to officials of the asylum. She pressed her case so strongly that they finally gave up and let her have her way.

When mother heard Ralph was coming home, she warned us he would be different from other people, but that we should always be polite. Dad flatly ordered me to stay away from him and told mother to keep our doors locked. Neither of us strictly obeyed his instruction, but it he turned out he was right.

Occasionally, I talked with Ralph across our narrow gravelled road. He was a poor communicator but after he had been there for two weeks I judged him to be mentally younger than me. He couldn't count money, couldn't tell time and couldn't even remember the name of my dog, which was also named Ralph. I figured his mental age to be six and complimented myself by thinking I was an extra sharp nine-year-old.

On the day it happened, I was sitting in our back yard, wearing my good clothes and petting my dog, waiting for our womenfolk to finish prettying up for church. I was being careful because both parents had given fair warning that my day would quickly turn darker if anything they didn't like happened to my Sunday suit. Suddenly, from Ralph's house, I heard a high yell and the noise of heavy, long-running footfalls coming across the street toward me.

Looking up, I saw Ralph's father, wearing his Sunday trousers, a sleeveless undershirt and freshly-shined high-topped shoes. Blood, dripping from a dozen cuts over his head and face was rapidly spreading over his undershirt. Bloody shaving foam had been smeared down his front and his suspenders flapped loosely as he pounded along. No one chased him, but he never slowed while speeding through our back yard toward the nearest telephone, two doors down. Yelling back, he ordered me to go inside and lock our doors.

I had to tell my parents three times before they paid attention. Then, they ran out so quickly that I was barely able to keep up. By then the police had been called and our neighbor had furnished Ralph's father a towel to mop his cuts. Everyone stood in a fast-gathering crowd, which alternated between watching Ralph's house and the road toward town. Our neighbor who owned the telephone had thoughtfully brought his shotgun and no one complained.

Ralph's father explained that his son had been sullen for a week, and was barely speaking. He had wanted to call the asylum to take him back but his wife wouldn't agree. On Sunday morning, Ralph sat down for breakfast but refused to eat or talk. After breakfast, his father began to shave then saw Ralph's image in the mirror behind him. He suggested that his son eat breakfast and Ralph immediately attacked him from behind, scratching him vigorously with long sharp fingernails. Although he was a strong man, the blacksmith swore he was barely able to break away.

By then we could hear Police Chief Bill Starr's wailing siren, and see his 1934 Buick, heading toward us. Church was forgotten by everyone. Moving as one, our group walked out to the road and watched the rooster tail of dust and gravel thrown up by his car as it approached. Deputy Sheriff George Blessing followed closely in his Model-A Ford. The entire law enforcement body of Burkburnett, except for our night watchman, was on its way, and I was having a lot more fun than I would at church.

Both officers wore gray stockmen's felt hats, the kind with a more narrow brim than the cowboy style. Each also wore khaki pants and Western boots, and each listened intently while the blacksmith explained. Bill Starr was the lead officer because we were inside the city limit, and he asked if Ralph had a gun. When told that the family had none, he ordered everyone to stand back and nodded his head, as a signal to Blessing. Shifting his powerful car into gear, Starr drove forcefully across the street into Ralph's back yard. Blessing followed closely, but stopped farther back because Ralph's mother blocked his path. Paying no mind to anyone, she walked aimlessly about, shouting for her son to come outside but received no answer. Everyone crowded up to the cars because nobody wanted to miss anything.

Starr hopped out and shouted at the closed back door. He promised that Ralph would not be harmed if he came out voluntarily. Receiving no answer he removed his coat, laid it on his car hood, and began rolling up his sleeves. Deputy Blessing, observing this, looked thoughtfully at the white paint peeling from Ralph's back door, then announced loudly that he hated to go in because there might be trouble. If there was, he would probably shoot somebody before being killed or injured by a crazy man.

Ralph's mother was wearing her church dress but still had her kitchen apron on. When Blessing spoke she threw up her head and moaned in a low tone, sounding like a fear-driven hound. Then she rolled the apron round her hands and swayed slowly back and forth. Her moans grew louder.

Everyone knew that if these officers decided to kill somebody, they would do it. Nothing we said or did would change it. Finally, Starr turned back and touched her arm to gain attention. Then he allowed her to watch as he drew his pistol from its holster and, laid it atop his coat. Turning, he strode briskly to the door and shouted again to Ralph, but there was still no answer. Nothing could have pulled my eyes off him right then, but I knew Ralph's mother had regained hope because the animal sounds had stopped.

Starr shoved the door open and stepped quickly inside, moving to the right as he did so. Blessing, pistol in hand, jumped through behind him and crouched, protecting Starr's back, as he circled through the house, still calling to Ralph. Everyone moved up close enough to see and hear but not so close that we were in danger of getting powder burns or blood splatters.

First, we heard a yell which was followed by bumpings, grunts and groans mixed with the sound of bodies slamming about. The noise grew louder and there was a crash, as if a big mirror or a window had broken. Then we heard Starr's voice, riding above the noise of combat, yelling at Ralph to give up, and Blessing's blunt warning that he would shoot. The slamming noises continued but we heard no shot.

Suddenly there was a loud yell of angry protest as Starr burst through the door, roughly shoving Ralph ahead, and controlling him by use of a wrestler's hold on his arm and neck. Both were covered with blood and Ralph, though walking on tiptoe because of pressure on his shoulder, was screaming and cursing. He constantly swung his free arm back toward Starr's face. Once, when he connected, blood flew everywhere.

Blessing walked behind with his pistol trained on Ralph. When he saw Starr get hit, he drew his blackjack and took two quick double steps forward. Raising the instrument high, in one smooth, swinging backhand motion, he smashed it solidly just above Ralph's right ear. His collapse was so sudden that the limp weight pulled Starr down with him. Five seconds later, Blessing had pulled Ralph's unresisting arms behind him and snapped his handcuffs on.

Ralph's mother promptly ran to comfort him but Blessing grabbed her shoulder, pushing her back. Without pause she straightened and bore forward again. This time Blessing shoved hard enough to make her fall.

When she began whimpering for her son, Starr intervened, "Let her tend him, Jim, and help me up from here. He's scraped and scratched me so bad I'll have to see Doc Russell to stop my bleedin'."

"You're not scraped and scratched, Bill," Blessing answered, "Look at his hands. You are all cut up!"

"Hell, I cain't see, Jim, and pardon my language, ladies, but I'm feelin' sick." Then to Blessing, "Just tell me about it."

"Bill, this guy has broke up razor blades and taped 'em under his fingernails. He left 'em sticking out about a quarter inch from most of his fingers. You've been cut up all over. And," he added as an afterthought, "you are in need of a doctor."

None of us had heard of this sort of fighting before and we crowded closer to see Ralph's hands, but Blessing had gotten a bellyful and yelled us back. Then he told the shotgun neighbor to unload his gun before he shot himself and to make himself useful by loading Starr up and driving him to the Doc. He also told Ralph's mother to bring them some clean towels.

Ralph suddenly awoke and complained loudly of a headache. He yelled stridently for his mother and when she didn't come he banged the side of his head against the ground until a messy glob of drool and blood spilled from the corner of his mouth but Blessing paid no attention. Pulling out his bone-handled Barlow knife he squatted behind Ralph and grabbed a wrist just above the cuffs. Ralph immediately struggled and kicked out with rage. Wasting no effort at all, Blessing dropped the wrist and grabbed Ralph's nearest ear, twisting it hard.

"You feel this?" he questioned, increasing the pressure. Ralph stopped struggling and began to shout loudly for his mother. Blessing increased the pressure until his shouts turned into yelps of pain. Then he eased pressure on the ear and continued his lesson. "I asked if you feel this?" Twisting again.

Everyone, except Ralph's mother, watched with satisfaction. We knew the guy wasn't normal but were angry at what he had done and figured a dose of discipline couldn't hurt him. In fact, his mother was probably the only one there who cared whether or not Blessing pulled the ear off.

Instruction continued. "Do you feel this?" More twisting. "Yes, and you better quit. My mother will have the law on you."

"I am the law," Blessing stated flatly and twisted until Ralph screamed like a girl. "Now, do you want me to quit or not?"

"Yes. Pulleees!"

Blessing was busy and didn't look up as the shotgun neighbor hauled Starr off in his Buick. Maintaining steady pressure on Ralph's ear, he talked softly and patiently like an experienced school teacher.

"I want you to listen good," he said. "I am going to cut all this tape off your hands and get rid of those razor blades. If you are real quiet and we are both lucky, you may not get cut. But if you raise any more fuss, you will not only get a cut or two but you'll have a headache on both sides because I'll have to put you to sleep again." Then he twisted hard again. "Do you understand?"

Ralph said he did and Blessing turned the ear loose. Following instruction closely, he rolled over when Blessing told him and held his hands motionless while the tape was pared away. Then, at Blessing's order, he stood up and walked over to the Model-A.

Blessing talked softly, but plainly, so there would be no misunderstanding. First he explained that Ralph was going to jail. Then he advised that he didn't want any yelling, kicking, or trying to run away. Ralph nodded that he understood and I decided the Deputy's lesson had proved that, while Ralph might be crazy, he wasn't stupid. He could behave if he wanted to.

At the car door Blessing said he needed all of his car windows and Ralph would not want to hear what would happen if any were kicked out. Ralph nodded, and slipped in the back, with no fuss. We never saw him again.

Seven weeks after Ralph went to jail, his mother walked across the street to visit mine and they sat in our dining room to talk. After the manner of polite Texans back then, Mom served iced tea in heavy stemmed goblets. Intent on their conversation, they forget to send me away and I heard his mother's sobs as she told the last of her son's story.

Ralph contracted pneumonia shortly after returning to the asylum and never recovered. She had ridden the bus over to Wichita for a visit and was told of his sickness when she arrived. They told her he wasn't critical and was getting better but before her next visit the postman delivered a letter saying he was dead and had been buried in a pauper's grave.

Between sobs she told Mom that there was no money for moving him to a proper burial plot and her husband had declared he wouldn't pay for it if even there was. Except for my mother and several ladies of the Baptist Church, she was alone in her grief. Between them, they ministered to her for over a year.

Sympathetic 10-year-old boys are hard to find. My friends and I were very impressed with Bill Starr who, without shooting him, had won his hard-fought battle with a crazy man, even though he was so badly cut up that he almost lost an ear. We were even more impressed to hear that Doc Russell had stopped counting after stitching 70 spots in Starr's face and head.

We weren't as impressed as we should have been by Starr's kindness to a pitiful old mother, which caused him to be sliced up by a lunatic. I was aware that he had done his job properly, even superbly, by not shooting Ralph but my young buddies and I would have been more impressed if he had shot him. It wasn't that we were so cruel, it was that we felt justice should be administered as it was portrayed in our Saturday Western movies.

Only one other thing about Ralph's story impressed me. Several weeks after that first tearful visit, I heard his mother telling mine how smart and intelligent her son had been as a young boy in Missouri. Grown folks liked him, and were constantly telling her how smart and intelligent he was. Her husband had bought Ralph a cart so he could sell ice cream downtown. She had made him some red overalls and a red hat that he wore when selling, and he occasionally earned as much as a dollar a day.

I promptly visualized myself wearing cowboy boots and a Western hat instead of red overalls, with a cart full of ice cream and literally raking up the cash on hot days in downtown Burk. My dad, I imagined, would quickly grasp the wisdom of this profitable idea and put up the money for a fully loaded cart in exchange for half the profits.

Then I realized that dad would see the fatal flaw in this plan quicker than me. He would immediately know that my friends and I would eat up all the profit, if not the entire stock on my first day in business. Nobody in Burk could name a kid my age who could be trusted with an ice cream cart when the thermometer read 110 in the shade and there was little shade to be found.

BOOMER'S KIDS—1937

IT WAS ALMOST 2:30 on a hot
summer afternoon and four of us lay under the shade of small
peach tree in Don's back yard. We had stopped for a brief rest,
enjoying the closeness of our dog-like panting and the stinky sweet
smell of our own sweat, something only 12-year-old boys can do.

Don's mom had not only interrupted but had completely
stopped our touch football game by opening their back screen door
and holding up a large, frosty-cold water pitcher filled with lime
Kool-Ade. Our ages ranged from nine to 12 and we had known each
other forever. We ranged together like a pack of hounds, all year
long and played together as often as our folks allowed.

Each of us quickly drank half of his tall glass, then I slowly sipped
the rest of mine so the sharp lime nectar would last as long as possible.
I didn't know what the others thought but I figured one glass was all
we would get and I was right. When our panting subsided, Don
selected a conversational topic and opened his subject. "My dad was
held up during the oil boom an' the robber took all his money."

"That's nothing," Jim quickly retorted, "My uncle was held up
twice an' one of those guys knocked him in the head. Left him
layin' for dead."

Then everyone looked to me but I had no relatives with interesting
holdup stories and said nothing. Bob leapt quickly into the vacuum I
had allowed. "That aint' nothin' at all! My dad was held up one night
while crossing the alley runnin' behind the bank on Main Street!"

"The holdup guy stuck a gun in his back and had him to walk
way back into the alley where no one could see them. He told dad
to give him all his money, an' dad said he might as well shoot him
because he'd spent every penny he had at the show and was absolutely
broke."

"The holdup guy made him dump all his pockets out and open
up his billfold and even take off his shoes an' shake 'em before he
would believe what he said. Then he got real mad an' cussed dad
out. Said he was of a good mind to shoot him because of his being

broke, but that he didn't really like hurting people and was going to let him go. He told dad to not look back and to walk slowly toward the sidewalk. When he got there, he was to turn straight South on Avenue C, like he had been headed to start with and to just keep on a-going."

"Dad took only took three steps before the high-jacker ordered him to stop, and back up. He figured the guy had changed his mind an' was going to kill him. An' he wanted to run but there was no way the holdup guy could miss hitting him, close as they were, so he slowly backed up to the gunman."

"Once more the robber said he wasn't a mean man, and didn't want to hurt people, but that his big brother was set up on the next corner an' he was a "real mean" man. If he held up someone that didn't even have a dollar, he would shoot them, for sure. Then, telling dad he didn't want his brother to shoot anybody that night, he shoved a dollar over dad's shoulder into his shirt pocket and told him again to walk off slowly, without lookin' back and go on home."

"Well, dad walked slowly back over to the sidewalk, but when he got there, he quickly darted to the right, around the corner of the bank building, rather than to his left, and ran hard as he could across the street, over to the other sidewalk. After he was out of easy pistol-range, he trotted back up to Main Street and circled back home by another road."

NOTE: I have heard three adult boomtowners recite this story with only minor changes in detail. Each insisted it was his own personal experience. Burk's Boomers loved this story. That's why it is being preserved. ES

CHAPTER 21

FISHIN' POLES—1937

IN 1937, WHEN I was 10, we couldn't drive out to a swamp and cut homegrown fishing poles as people in East and South Texas did. North Texas had hard winters which froze grass roots so deep into the ground that bamboo plants couldn't survive them. Even if they could, there were no bogs, marshes or swamps to furnish moisture where they might flourish.

Burkburnett, Texas, where I grew up, was a place where people joked but were halfway serious when they talked about kids who had started first grade without ever seeing rain. Other Burk kids, they said, when visiting in East Texas and Louisiana, had to ask what swamps, bogs and pine trees were. They had never seen such things. We bought our cane fishing poles in stores and filling stations that catered to fishermen and the pole would cost anywhere from a nickel to 35 cents, depending on its size.

Deep East Texas fishermen, in the swampy backwater areas near Louisiana, lived in a more human-friendly climate and had fishing canes free for the cutting. When finished, they stripped their lines off and rolled up the hooks, floats and weights to take home. Poles were left on the banks for anyone who might use them later. In Burkburnett, after you were through fishing you would wind the line, floats and hooks tightly around the pole, stick hooks into the cork and carry everything home to be used again.

One bright and clear Saturday morning in early spring of 1937, my father got up craving a mess of fresh-caught, pan-fried fish. Naturally, he wanted all the fixins' my mother served with them. Fixins' included hot water cornbread, fast-fried in boiling grease, skillet-fried potatoes, sliced blue onions and tomatoes, plus all the iced tea he could drink. If mom wanted to throw in some cole slaw, beans or squash, he liked that too because he was a big eater. Shortly after breakfast, he told me to get ready, we were going fishing.

Dad seldom fished and had no poles. Neither did he have lines, floats or hooks but this didn't bother him. We lived in an age when poverty was the one thing everyone had plenty of, and though the custom often caused trouble between friends, neighbors and relatives, everybody borrowed from everybody else. No family was immune from this custom which old timers called "borryin".

But dad wouldn't borrow from, and seldom loaned to, a man he didn't like and respect. In our new millennium, 60 years later, this still seems a sensible rule to me. But dad liked and respected Sam Garnett and Sam fished a lot. So, within ten minutes, we pulled up in front of Mr. Garnett's house and stopped.

Dad worked as an operator at the Skelly Gas Plant in Burk and Mr. Sam was a pumper, I think for Texaco, but after 60 years, I am no longer certain. Mr. Sam was driving off to his lease when we got there, intending to switch out some oil tanks, but he loved to talk. So, he killed his engine and walked back up to his garage to assist us in selecting poles from his ample supply.

As he pulled them down from above the exposed garage ceiling joists where they were stored, Mr. Sam began telling us about a big batch of fish he'd caught on his last trip. "Why, Ed," he said, speaking to dad, "Charley Wilson and I caught so many catfish last month that I finally got ashamed. Charley didn't want to stop, but I finally told him straight out that we had to quit. Mostly I said this because, even if we gave a big mess to the lake owner, we barely had room in my car to carry the rest home. An' I was right!"

Suddenly, he reached up and pulled down a strong-looking, but medium-length pole and shoved it into my hand. "Here, son. This is just the pole you need. I used thissun' myself on that trip and caught a fish about this big." Then he held out both forefingers, measuring 10 or 12 inches between them.

After all his fish talk, that measurement failed to impress me and my expression must have shown it. He grinned and asked, "You don't believe me?" I'd been taught never to contradict grown people, so I promptly lied, and shook my head up and down. Mr. Sam nodded back in affirmation. "Well, that relieves me," he continued, straight-faced, "because I'm tellin' you the absolute truth."

"That fish I caught was this big," measuring with the forefingers again, "just between his eyes." Then he motioned to my pole. "That there is a real stout pole you have. At first I was afraid the fish would break it, but he didn't. But he would've if I hadn't let him pull me out so far in the lake that I waded in chin-high water for over an hour 'til he wore hisself down some. Even after Charley and me got him up on the bank it took us both to carry him over an' tie him onto the side of my car. He was way too big to haul home in the trunk."

"Well," he continued, "after givin' a big bunch of fish to the lake owner, Charley and me split the rest but I gave him more than I kept. Since I only have two kids at home now, I made him take that big one. Just like me he knew right off that it was more than his family could eat, so he drove over to Electra and gave it to his cousin."

"Just like Charley, soon as he saw it, that cousin knew it was more fish than they could handle too. So, he cleaned and skinned it out, then took it down to the ice house for keepin' 'til the followin' Saturday night so they could have a fish fry at his church. He later told Charley that they fed over a hunnert' people an' still throwed some of that fish away."

"Now, son," he said looking at me, "you are actin' like you don't much believe me again, an' this time you could be right because I know Charlie's cousin. An' I've been in his church over at Electra, an' he was probably stretchin' the blanket. I don't believe more than fifty folks ever showed up at any of their church meetins."

Mrs. Garnett came out then, and when her husband slowed down enough for her to get a word in edgeways, she told dad, "Mr. Ed, don't you pay attention to Sam. He's just runnin' off at the mouth. Blowin'. Truth is, if you could bring us a nice mess of fish, we'd be much-obliged. I've not eaten a good mess of catfish this year."

"Now, Ed," Mr. Garnett defended, "Don't you pay any 'tention to her talk. Fact is, she was hanging' clothes out on the line last week an' my youngest boy had got that pole right there down out of the garage," and he pointed again to the pole I was holding.

"Well," he continued, "my boy was standin' near her an' threw his hook way back behind him, practicing a long cast an' he caught his momma right on top of the head, just like she was a big fish. Well, I heard her a-hollerin' an' run out of the house quick as I could but no matter how hard I tried, I wasn't able to jerk that hook loose. Its barb went plumb through one spot in her scalp and come out another."

Stopping to breathe, he finished, "An' you know what? It was all I could do to hold that woman down long enough to cut the hook out. Now, I hate to say it in front of her this way, but she's been talkin' kinda' funny ever since."

During all this time, Mrs. Garnett was the only person who disputed anything Mr. Sam had said and no one said anything else about his tale as we walked back down to the car with our poles. As we climbed in, Mr. Garnett turned to dad with a serious face and warned, "Ed, don't you go out to Thompson's Tank. Nobody's been catchin' anything there since my last trip."

We drove straight toward Thompson's Tank and started fishing. I was confused. because I had listened to all this grown-up lying and not one of them had laughed or smiled. And they sounded serious to me. Because I knew Mr. Sam's youngest boy, I halfway believed the fish hook story, but it was hard for me to realize my dad was dumb enough to accept Mr. Sam's big fish whopper as the truth. No 10-year-old kid is comfortable with the thought that he might be smarter than his father, but unless my dad was having a really off-day, I couldn't come up with any other good reason why he would believe that yarn.

I made no conversation while he drove. Instead, I continued to re-run all that adult conversation. Still, no matter how many excuses I made up for dad, I finally had to admit he believed that bunch of trash mouth Mr. Sam dished out.

Looking back from 60 years of distance, I can now understand that I was simply hearing three adults having fun by joshing each other and listening to Mr. Sam play games with my mind. I now understand that my dad knew exactly what was going on and that all three of them knew exactly what I was thinking. But I didn't know it then and none of them ever explained. Instead, after a mile or two, dad asked what I thought about Mr. Sam's fish story.

In those days, kids were expected to promptly answer any adult question and it was hard for me to come up with a safe reply. My parents' rules insisted that I shouldn't call Mr. Sam or any other grown person a liar. Besides that, I didn't feel it was safe to even hint that I recognized those lies when my dad couldn't. So it took me some time to frame an adult-safe answer which still said what I wanted to tell him.

Dad kept waiting and the pressure kept building so, after thinking as long as I dared, I sucked in my breath, gambled and pitched out my best shot. "I think Mr. Sam was just a-blowin'. Even Mrs. Garnett said he was runnin' off at the mouth and that's what she called it. Maybe," I finished carefully, "Maybe he needs to go see a doctor."

No one had ever considered me the family comedian. I wasn't prepared for this speech to strike dad's funny-bone, but it did. I jumped when he bellowed out a loud, explosive workingman's laugh. But because of the way people could be back then, he never explained what he thought was funny. I was so relieved that he had not gotten angry that I laughed as loudly as him. But the subject was dangerous to me and I never brought it up again, figuring it ought to be buried forever.

During our three hours at Thompson's tank, dad pulled in seven nice yearling catfish weighing almost a pound each. I caught three sun perch, one large as a man's hand, and stuck them on his home fashioned stringer without any help. This good fishing, I decided, proved my theory that nothing Mr. Garnett had told us that morning held an ounce of truth. But I was premature in judgment. A few days later I heard a pair of his neighbors laughing about the youngest Garnett boy catching his mother's head with a fishing hook. The old fibber had been truthful about the fish hook story, part of it, anyway.

BOOMTOWNER—1937

"YES, WE LIVED there when the
New London school blew up," my Uncle Bill said. "I heard the
noise and knew something really bad had happened. Trotting up to
the highway, I stuck out my thumb and a Texaco gang truck driver
slowed down long enough for me to jump onto his right front
fender. Several cars and two more oilfield trucks and crews were on
the scene when we got there. But only minutes later, a Kilgore
funeral home ambulance and a fire truck drove in.

"People immediately began dragging chunks of concrete and
bricks away by hand, trying to uncover trapped victims to pull them
out. Any help at all was needed and I pitched in with the rest. More
oilfield trucks, some equipped with heavy duty winches and roller
bars, drove up. Their crews quickly hooked onto heavy chunks of
debris, dragging them away to make room for more rescue vehicles
and crews to work closer to the ruined building. Most of the people
we took out were school children, already dead. Some were alive
but badly injured.

Within an hour doctors and nurses reached us. They rendered
whatever aid they could but worked mostly with parents and
relatives of dead or missing people since few of the victims were
pulled out alive. One or two were thought to be dead and were
placed in with the dead folks but were only unconscious. As soon
as a sign of life was found, they were removed from that group.

Ambulances from funeral homes in Kilgore, Tyler, Longview
and Henderson, maybe other cities too, came to help. The few
living victims, lumped together with the dead, were placed into
the ambulances and hauled to the nearest city where medical
treatment could be given. The dead were then taken on to whatever
funeral homes the ambulances had come from. No record was kept
of who went where. This caused additional anxiety and grief for
parents and relatives searching for their loved ones.

No one could tell them where to look unless some worker had
recognized and remembered a victim who was removed. Some of

those unlucky searchers, carrying a tremendous weight of fear and dread, stayed to help volunteers remove more bodies. Others, unable to bear the anxiety, spent much of that first night driving all over East Texas in a frantic search for loved ones. I will never forget the cries of agony when a parent found his or her dead child, or the cries of happiness when a child was found alive, even though barely. It was hard to tell the difference unless you watched the parent's face.

It seemed to last forever but within three days all the bodies were taken out. One group of four or five must have been in or near a chemistry lab because they had yellow spots on their bodies. I heard someone say that those victims had been sprayed with "picric" acid.

Many people came to help. The Salvation Army and Red Cross were on hand plus men and women from local churches. They stayed there day and night, serving food, coffee and cigarettes to the workers. I didn't smoke cigarettes but left with a good feeling toward the Salvation Army because if you asked one of them for a smoke, he or she would give you a pack. The Red Cross doled cigarettes out one at a time. Cots were set up so that, when we were too tired to work, we could sleep for an hour or two. But work never stopped until the last child's body had been removed from that building.

Bill Johnson, Boomer,
Author's Uncle

NOTE: The New London School Explosion may still be America's most terrible domestic oilfield tragedy when measured in terms of lives lost. Occurring at 3:17 PM on March 18, 1937, in Rusk County, Texas, it was a one-of-a-kind happening. Nothing like it had been experienced before and the impact was powerful. Several years later survivors erected a large memorial downtown, with a tablet showing that 289 persons were killed, about a hundred more Texans than were killed in the Alamo. Modern researchers now insist that death certificates for 314 victims have been found. The writer has several friends who were in the explosion and has talked with many others. Most of those people still measure any other bad occurrence against it or World War II. ES

CHAPTER 22

LEAVING CHILDHOOD—1937

(Memoir of Ruth Hudson Long as told by her to the author)

ARISING SHORTLY AFTER dawn, I ran to the closet for a look at my lovely new dance dress. I was nine years old, in the third grade at New London, Texas School and today was the high point of my school year. Standing before the mirror, I slipped the dress on, buttoned it with care and slowly tied the sash, making certain everything lay exactly perfect. After smoothing it down to the last seam, I pirouetted daintily as I could and posed dramatically, one arm upraised, admiring my vision in the mirror. My world seemed perfect, but only because God had been merciful and had not given me the ability to see me far into the future. Before the day was over, I would learn that real people, those who loved me and that I also loved, could die as quickly and permanently as chickens, kittens or puppies.

My dress was created for a special occasion. The end of our school year was approaching and a special program had been prepared for a Parent Teacher's Association meeting that afternoon. It was a traditional elementary school performance and our class was presenting a girl-boy dancing number for the program. We had practiced for weeks and this was the most important school day I'd ever had.

As the bus bounced over rough oilfield lease roads, on its way to the homes of my classmates, I sat as far from the others as possible, guarding the dress from wrinkles or stain. Through my window, I watched as familiar green hills, covered with hundred foot high pine trees and various hardwoods, plus an astounding number of

90-foot-tall steel oilfield derricks slid by. There weren't as many derricks as trees, but in the seven miles between my house and school, you could easily count several thousand. In open spots, native Redbud and fluffy white Dogwood trees, some twenty feet tall, bloomed their hearts out. We were living in the triangle between Tyler, Kilgore and Henderson, right in the center of Texas' giant East Texas Oilfield and the day was March 18, 1937, the day New London's School exploded.

Ours was a large family, living much like our neighbors. Five of us attended the New London School. Two were still too young. Most of my classmate's fathers worked for one of at least 50 different companies who pumped up oil from that 40 mile long, 30 mile wide oilfield. But, despite all the oil coming up, most of our dads earned relatively small wages. But they were glad to have work because most Texans were struggling hard through the middle of America's greatest depression. Most folks felt any job at all beat none. We were eating enough and wore decent clothes and even though we lived in rough-built oilfield shanties, we were like kids everywhere else. Words such as rich and poor didn't impress us. Our happiness came from living in homes where parents gave us love and protection.

Louise, my younger sister, should have gone to school that day but had lost a shoe and couldn't find it before the bus came, so the bus left without her. On the way, my three older brothers skylarked with classmates. This was normal for them, also for me, but I hung back that day, careful of the dress.

When we reached school, I trotted straight to my homeroom, eager to see how nice and pretty the other girl's dresses might be. But my eagerness quickly turned to disappointment when the tardy bell rang because my partner hadn't come to school. For whatever reason, he had missed the bus and lived ten miles away. Like Louise, there was no other way for him to attend, which meant that I had no dance partner and could not perform with the others. I was already holding a soppy handkerchief when my teacher found time to explain and to give me a giant hug.

At two thirty that afternoon, when class was over, I stood at the edge of the school ground and dropped a few more tears while watching the other dancers march proudly out of the Elementary building to the gymnasium. That was where the program would be presented. And during the next several weeks, I would cry often but not because I pitied myself.

Unwilling to play with the others, I sat on a curb at the bus stop, facing toward the gym, propping my chin on my hands. The day was still warm and birds sang merrily. Many students chased each other around the school yard but I decided to be perverse, enjoying my misery. Unsmiling, I sat stiffly, waiting for the bus.

While moping, I thought of how good my classmates would feel during the program. The boys would move gracefully through their dance and the girls' dresses would flounce saucily. It was too far away for me to hear the standard applause always given by loving parents and friends, but I imagined I could hear and sighed mournfully. I was a nine-year-old living in a home with a lot of kids. Approval and special attention were important at that time of my life, but, because I was one of many, they rarely came to me. The thought that my entire class was bowing to thunderous applause, was more than I wanted to think about.

Deciding to forget the gym, I turned toward the main school building which lazily sunned, like a well-fed cat, only fifty yards away. Then, just as my eyes focused directly on it, the building disappeared behind a thick cloud of smoke. The New London school building exploded!

I was less conscious of the noise than what I saw and the first thing I remember was that large cloud of thick white smoke which blocked the building from view. It spread upward and outward above the pines and derricks. Then came the noise, which shook the ground heavily under our feet, but was a muffled rumble rather than a sharp sound such as might be made by a close lightning strike. Bricks, chunks of concrete, pieces of glass and other things nobody should ever see, began falling out of the cloud but most of them struck earth before reaching us.

I later understood that what I had thought was smoke was actually white mortar dust. There was no fire to cause smoke. When the cloud thinned, I saw that our two-story high school building was gone except for its Southeast corner. The rest was strewn crazily about the entire school area or had fallen back into a deep crater. All three of my brothers, Duane, Glenn and Elisha, were in classrooms over there!

My first instinct was to run. So, terrified of the noise, the large piles of brick and stone and of things that might lie underneath, that was what I did. I have no memory of jumping up and running to my playground instructor, but I ended up with her and I didn't walk. I ran blindly. With admirable calm, she gathered us up as a mother hen gathers her chicks and placed us behind a corner of the elementary school wall. It was a place of seeming security and it also blocked many disturbing sights and unsettling sounds from third grade ears.

Students of all ages drifted into our huddle. Nervous and upset, we hovered, seldom speaking and I had no way of knowing how near or far they had been from the blast. Some were injured, though not seriously. A few were only scratched. But all were dazed, in shock, and some were spotted or covered all over with the white mortar dust. All had blank and puzzled expressions on their faces because none of us could fit this horror into our minds. We constantly wondered why it had happened. The new arrivals came to us for comfort, not treatment, and our teacher ministered to each, comforting each as well as she was able.

Sirens and whistles from nearby refineries began shrilling their sharp alarms. In a few more minutes, they were joined by the bells and sirens of the police cars, ambulances and fire trucks. Refineries stopped blowing their alarm whistles late that night, after they were convinced everyone knew about the disaster. But the police and ambulance sirens wailed for two days.

Occasionally, a student would begin to cry but there were no loud, uncontrollable outbursts. Even while crying we knew that there was little to be done. The rest of our world was busy, tending classmates who were in greater need than us. Though visibly shaken, our playground instructor never abandoned us. She continually soothed us, saying that God was "good" and "everything would work out all right," but it didn't. Yet, because we needed to, we believed her and our terror was diminished.

Like some of the others, I begged to leave, wanting to look for my brothers. She refused this, keeping us together, saying that our bus would soon come to take us home. I was actually relieved when she refused. Even though I wanted to see after my brothers, entering the explosion area really terrified me because of what I might see.

When the building exploded, my mother was in our back yard, five miles away, hanging washing on her clothesline. She heard the blast and knew it was a large one but paid little attention. Explosions of all sizes were common in the oilfields. With two small children at home, four in school and one on the way, she had little energy for idle curiosity.

My father and several other men were riding home from the refinery in a company gang truck. As they approached our school, they saw a student walking down the middle of the road toward them, cradling a bloody arm. Stopping, they quickly learned what happened. Since he was almost home and walking well, they sent him on, jumped back in and drove on. Most of them had children there and all had friends or relatives who attended. When the truck skidded to a stop, they jumped out, each desperately searching for his own.

Within minutes dad found Elisha, my brother. He had been killed immediately and his body was blown out into the school yard. Early-arriving rescuers had placed him out of the traffic area with a constantly growing group of young bodies. Dad collapsed when he saw my brother. Later he told me that his anguish was over-powering because Dewayne and Glenn were also in the building, and when he looked at the damage, he felt certain no one else would come out alive. He thought he had lost all three sons.

But he was wrong. Upstairs, inside the Southeast corner of the building, Dewayne was in a separate class that happened to be in the only building corner left standing. When the explosion came, he felt as if the world had come to an end but suffered no injury at all. The choking cloud of smoke and mortar dust cut visibility to almost zero and some of his classmates began shouting about fire. This scared everyone because the stairs had been blown away and the hallway was blocked. Terrified, DeWayne turned toward the nearest window and, taking no time to open it, knocked the pane out with his fist. The one-inch gash he received at that moment was his only injury.

This window was located in a corner near a drainpipe on which he quickly shinnied to the ground. A few boys followed him but most of the girls weren't that active. Everyone was afraid of burning, or that the building might collapse, burying them alive. Many jumped from the upstairs windows to hard earth below. One girl broke her back and several sustained broken arms and legs. Others were knocked unconscious, but none was killed.

Dewayne immediately began looking for our brothers. Within five minutes he found Glenn, completely dazed, wandering around the school yard. He had been struck on the head, receiving a concussion. Up to the time I last talked with him about it, he still had no idea whether he was helped out of the building or if he rescued himself.

Realizing that Glenn needed medical attention, Dewayne began looking for a way to get him to a hospital but couldn't find a ride. A rich oil man, called by many people a "Wildcatter", stopped by. He offered his car and chauffeur to take Glenn to a hospital, but an ambulance driver told him that all the nearby hospitals were full. This news didn't slow that good man a bit. Telling his driver to take Glenn to his own house, which was only a few miles from the school, he advised all the workers and medical people present that he was setting up a medical aid station there. He was going to locate a telephone and call his personal doctor in Henderson, Texas to come to his home with a nurse. Any injured person who came or was brought there would be treated free. Then he had both my brothers put in his vehicle and left.

Good news was carried as quickly as people could bear it because bad news was so plentiful. Therefore, both Glenn and my dad had learned that I was unhurt. Glenn had been told this by another student, and a school instructor had passed the word on to my dad. But no one came to pick me up or bring news to the kids in my group. Few of us had any idea whether our friends or relatives were injured, alive, or dead.

We stayed in that huddle, near the bus stop, waiting for transportation from somewhere, sometime, to take us back to home and safety. Desperately lonely, we badly needed to see our parents but we also dreaded for the bus to come. No one wanted to know who might not be going back.

We stayed there for what seemed like forever. And that loyal teacher stayed with us, reassuring and comforting, but it still seemed to me as if time had stopped, and I wondered if things would ever get better. Later on, I learned that all the roads and highways were choked with traffic. No one was able to do anything quickly. Adults who managed to get to our school had seen that heroic emergency rescue effort was needed and many went straight to work, hoping to save lives by digging out trapped bodies. But we didn't know about those things and were finding it harder and harder to accommodate to a suddenly harsh and unfamiliar world.

Finally, at nearly dark, our teacher called us close and said a bus was ready to take us home. Up to then many busses had either been blocked away from us by heavy traffic or too busy carrying injured people to any hospital within fifty miles to help us. We were happy to leave the school but I worried because I didn't know what to tell my parents about my brothers, and the bus ground slowly along, often stopping to wait for traffic. Finally reaching our neighborhood, it began to drop students off. There was no laughter or conversation. Everyone, including our driver, desperately wanted to be at home with his family but we were also afraid of what we might learn when we got there.

Soon as the bus stopped at our mailbox, I jumped out and ran toward our house. My only thought was to locate my mother, but there were no lights burning inside. I ran on in, shouting for her, but no one was there. Nothing I had felt until then was as bad as my experience at that moment. I badly needed my mother but had come home to an empty house and the walls seemed ready to close around me. Bursting into tears, I stumbled back through the front door, onto our front porch.

Looking up the road, I saw lights at the home of our nearest neighbors, an elderly couple. Running for their house at top speed,

I sobbed all the way. Knocking and shouting, I explained to the lady who opened the door that no one was home at my house. This good woman brought me in and took me into her lap, to rock and comfort me. She didn't know where my parents were but told me I wasn't abandoned and that they would soon return. In the meantime, she and her husband had been needing some company and she hoped I could visit with them until my family arrived.

Shortly after 9:30, the lights came on at our house. I ran all the way home without stopping and burst in through the front door. Everyone was there except for Elisha. Each person's face reflected sorrow and most eyes were brilliant with repressed tears. The thing I remember most was my brother, Glenn. He lay on the couch, his head covered by a large bandage and cried without restraint. I had never seen him cry like that before. Between sobs he repeated over and over again, "He's killed. He's killed. My brother's killed."

Shortly after, relatives and friends came to visit and many bore dishes of food. One of my mother's sisters took charge of me and located something solid for me to nibble plus a glass of milk. Then she sat in a rocking chair and took me into her lap. Slowly rocking, she gave me the affection and comfort I had needed for hours but which my parents had been too distraught to extend. As I listened to her friendly and comfortable conversation, my fears began to fade.

The new gown, twisted and soiled, as well as its reason for being, was long forgotten. Finally relaxing, my brain slowed, allowing my eyelids to droop. Then sleep, the commencement of healing, moved in. I had no way of knowing it that night, but next morning when I got up, I would still be a nine-year-old girl, but was no longer a child. I still had many childlike habits to outgrow, but I had taken a major step toward being adult.

They say that 294 people were killed in this disaster. Twice as many children were injured. Many badly. Several families lost all their children and some kids lost one of their parents. One or two families lost both parents. Our family was considered lucky because only one us was taken.

The explosion was caused by a leaky gas line that allowed a large volume of natural gas to collect underneath the school's basement slab. A dead air space, used for storage, had been constructed under half of that slab. At one end a door opened into the school's shop classroom. For some reason the storage area was not vented. After gas seeped in, filling up the storage, the odorless substance fed slowly under the door into the school's shop classroom. When gas and air were properly mixed, and reached a correct temperature, some person in the shop class closed an electric switch and it happened.

So powerful was the blast that it blew the building's bottom slab up through the roof, allowing tons of debris and numbers of bodies to fall into the crater before settling. Rubble and large slabs of concrete were cleared as fast as possible by workmen using heavy oilfield equipment. This quick action saved many lives. Even so, it was nearly three days before the last body was taken out. In Austin, shortly afterward, the Texas Legislature passed a law requiring natural gas to be odorized so the smell would warn people, hopefully preventing further such tragedies.

Our school re-opened six weeks later and every available space was taken up for classrooms. But when Louise and I approached the building, she began to lag behind and cry. Even though she hadn't been at school that day, she was afraid the building would blow up again. When we reached the steps she refused to go in. I sat out with her all morning and our teacher would periodically come out, trying to get her to come in but she exercised her well-known stubbornness and didn't budge.

At noon the school nurse drove us home. We stayed out of school for the rest of that year. Only DeWayne, who was a high school junior that year, finished school in New London. The rest of us transferred to nearby Gaston school at Joinerville, Texas. In 1945, I graduated from high school there.

CHAPTER 23

Saturday Morning Movies—1937

In Spring of 1937 I was not yet
10 years old. The last third of America's Great Depression was just
beginning and I was working as hard, as a young kid could at trying
to become an adult. Besides the normal problems accompanying a
severe economic depression, our town, Burkburnett, Texas, had
even more. Not only was it a dying oilfield town but it was located
well within the dust bowl and we were experiencing a severe
drought. More than any decade in the history of Texas, that of the
1930's is remembered as the driest.

It was a time when anyone you saw would have loved to be rich.
Visitors could look in any direction they wanted without seeing
any person or place which a few dollars would not improve. And
most of us figured that if it weren't for bad luck we would have had
no luck at all.

In 1917, when my father's family arrived, Burkburnett was a
prosperous Oil Boomtown of at least 20,000 people and thousands
more lived and worked in the sprawling Northwest and Southwest
oilfields there. The city was "bustin out at the seams", much like
the earlier gold and silver mining camps in California and Colorada,
but Burk's miners dug for oil, not gold. By 1936, with oil selling for
under $2.00 a barrel and the wells drying up, most Boomers were
long gone. Now we reeled along, trying to last out the depression,
a small town of about 2,000 people, depending on what day you
took count.

My friends and I spent hours, after school and on weekends,
sitting around and dreaming up schemes to get rich. A lot of grown

folks did the same, but the difference was they had less time to daydream and their plans were less creative than ours.

One Thursday afternoon in late spring, just after school, George and Bobby and I met for our regular "emergency planning session". We had this same emergency session every week, but because we were young and seldom crossed any bridges before we came to them, this one always surprised us. The emergency always involved the same problem which was scraping up enough money to attend the Saturday morning movies. It was a big problem because the admission price was a nickel.

To understand correctly, you must think back to a time when there was no television. Only one of us had a radio in our home and only one other of us had a telephone at home. My family had neither. Even if we had one, we only knew two or three other people with phones that we could talk with. Besides, where good friends were involved, most Texans still felt it was more neighborly to walk over and sit down to chat in person.

Saturday morning movies were the best entertainment offered to kids in Burk and we took them seriously. Each Saturday the Palace Theater offered a bargain bonanza. First, they showed a first-class Western movie featuring stars like William Boyd, Tex Ritter, Gene Autry, Roy Rogers, or, one of my new favorites, Tim Holt. In addition, they showed a chapter from the current serial. This week would be chapter four of an exciting 15-unit mini-series about Flash Gordon starring Larry "Buster" Crabbe, the great Olympic swimmer.

As if those offerings weren't enough, there was always a comedy. It could be Porky Pig or a Daffy Duck, but if we were lucky, it would be the latest production of the Three Stooges, which we loved. We never called our trips "going to the movies", it was always "goin' to the show," and in those pre-television days it was truly the only show in town.

There was another dividend we harvested from going to the show. All that afternoon, and for the rest of the week, we re-enacted our movies in vacant lots, on tops of outbuildings, in garage lofts and while climbing around in trees. Our most rewarding play-times involved creating all over again the Westerns, serials and comedies shown at the Palace. We weren't too bad when aping some of the stars, especially The Three Stooges. And one or two of us did a realistic Donald Duck impression.

Players who had seen the movies always spoke with the most authority as to which boys or girls should re-create the starring roles. They were also absolute authorities on dialogue and story line. In other words, those who had seen the shows would be directors and bosses, while those who hadn't served as peons. Young as we were, we had already learned that being boss, even without pay, was better than being a hired hand.

Few purchases since then have pleased me as much as the nickels I spent in the Palace Theater. Those coins, small as they were, entitled me to take my turn as director. I became a "stander and pointer" who made wide-ranging and rapid decisions involving the actors in our dramas. Lack of talent was a minor problem, we thought, which could be easily overcome by enthusiasm, originality and obedience. Being boss in adult life was never as much fun because the decisions were always harder, and the workers, though quite competent and professional, had serious attitude problems and were never as willing as our childhood stars.

This week we decided to pool our money. George and I quickly voted for this approach because Bobby, in a moment of guileless candor, had told us he had four cents and thought he could get his father to give him another penny. George immediately said he "thought" he had a penny at home and he would contribute it to a pool if we all agreed to share. Then he looked to me for support.

I studied seriously before voting for the pool. In the first place, I had three pennies myself. I had found them the day before when crawling under our back porch to see what the dog was barking at. But I had serious doubts about turning my money over to central management. I knew instinctively that George was lying about having a penny because I'd never seen him with a cent in hand unless he was trotting toward a store to spend it. But in the end, my greed for Bobby's money outweighed caution and I voted for the pool, offering up my three pennies. We now owned seven cents, almost half enough.

George wanted to hold all the money, but even Bobby knew this was a bad idea and we voted it down. George simply wasn't always reliable. I suggested Bobby for treasurer. He was not without sin but his family had a little more money than ours and he was less selfish than George and me. After making Bobby the treasurer, we discussed our fund raising drive.

Several ideas were considered. George proposed that we should separate, walking down different streets until dusk, looking carefully in the ditches and picking up the coins and bills that had been dropped by wealthy and careless citizens. These people were obviously so busy with daily work that they could not properly handle their money and we would meet in an hour to divide our findings. In George's mind, there were enough of these wealthy persons to furnish us with movie fare until next Thanksgiving.

Bobby suggested that if we decided what our parents wanted from us, then contacted them and promised to faithfully perform certain chores for a full month, that they would give us the money. His father had a good job and, since he was its only child, Bobby had a better chance to pick up a nickel or dime from his dad than George or me.

George and I had fathers with regular jobs, but we also had a pot load of brothers and sisters. Neither of our parents cared at all whether we went to the show. In fact, even after rounding up our own money, we always had to ask their permission and arrange chore times around show time. This made Bobby's idea of promising to perform unnamed chores for a whole month sound ridiculous. Our parents knew as well as we did that George I were going to do our work anyway, so Bobby's idea was vetoed. Then, he and I joined forces against George's plan. Young as we were, we still knew that walking around and looking on the ground for lost money was wishful thinking. We did this every single day and found only a penny or two in a year.

Pressure was now directed at me to produce a plan, and I had thought of one, but it had flaws. Still, because no better one emerged, I began to unfold it. And as I talked, it sounded better and my enthusiasm grew. Both of them knew the Rowe family who lived two doors down from me. They were also familiar with Mr. Rowe's uncle, a Confederate veteran aged 90 who lived with a daughter in Bowie, Texas. The old fellow often became angry with his son-in-law and boarded the Greyhound bus, riding 50 miles to Burk and visiting with his nephew.

He came every two or three months, and we knew him by sight, so when he walked down the road from the bus station we always trotted out to escort him to the Rowe house. He had missed the house twice, ending up in the country, so we always ran to help. This wasn't because we were outstanding boys but because he sometimes gave us a penny. I am explaining all this because of a conversation I had just heard between Mr. Rowe and my father after the old fellow recently left Burk headed back home to Bowie.

The Rowes had a two-hole outdoor toilet in a rear corner of their cow lot and I told Bobby and George about it. They knew this already and pointedly advised that I was way off our subject. I admitted that this seemed to be true but made my point anyway.

According to Mr. Rowe, on his last visit, that elderly uncle had dropped his purse down through one of the holes in their outhouse. Many older men, back then, especially farmers, carried their money in long leather purses instead of billfolds. These purses had two or three snap-top compartments and folded double in the middle but were too large to be carried in men's pockets. Most farmers carried them in the bib pockets of their overalls and other men carried them in coat pockets. Coins rode in a small compartment near the top of this purse while bills were folded up and carried deeper down for better safety. Mr. Rowe had salvaged his purse and all of his bills, but the change compartment latch had sprung open when the purse fell in and all the old fellow's silver, nearly three dollars worth, had dropped into the stinking muck below.

George particularly liked my story and rolled on the ground while laughing. Bobby giggled appreciatively, but when the laughter passed away each of them looked questioningly at me because the story, they felt, had nothing to do with our problem. It didn't, that is, until I gave them the real news.

None of that silver had ever been taken out! The old fellow wanted to get it but Mr. Rowe had told him in no uncertain words that he wasn't going to fish for it. He also told his boys to use the outhouse for intended purposes only and not for salvage activities. Since the old fellow couldn't see well enough to dig it out, that entire fortune lay unclaimed in the Rowe's toilet, needlessly going to waste.

Bobby was trusting, but George was skeptical. He just couldn't believe that none of the Rowes had taken that good money out of their outhouse. I told him I wouldn't have believed it either if I hadn't heard Mr. Rowe say so with his own mouth. Then I suggested we should form a salvage operation, to recover the treasure.

Discussion commenced. First, we had to decide if we wanted the money bad enough. Then, there were also the ethics to consider, such as whether it was proper for us to salvage somebody else's money. Finally, there was the problem of arranging the opportunity. No one needed to mention it because we automatically knew this was the kind of project we had to keep hidden from our parents. We didn't know which of their many grown-up reasons they might choose for disapproving the salvage hunt but there was certain to be one at least. Probably several. We knew we had to be cautious, be quiet, and be quick. And we had to do the job after dark.

Unknowingly, we followed the time-tested manner of governments, corporate boards, and prominent citizen groups. First, we talked about our needs, then we discussed feasibility, and finally we considered the ethics involved. Like grownups, we knew instinctively that if the opportunity, and needs were present, ethics and feasibility could always be adjusted.

Continuing to act like grown folks, we decided that we needed the money and the ethics portion received short consideration. We did briefly discuss whether recovering the money would be considered theft because we had all received specific theft training and didn't need the problem of adults calling us thieves. But we decided no theft was possible because Mr. Rowe had made it plain. He and his boys were not going to look for that money. It was abandoned and there was no reason for it to lie in someone's toilet when we could remove it and channel it back into the economy, thus helping ourselves as well as the movie business.

Opportunity was created later that evening by George's father, who allowed him to borrow the family flashlight. George's excuse was that Bobby and I needed to look for night bugs after supper so they could be taken to school next week. That excuse turned out to be a stroke of genius because our parents, just like parents today, would do almost anything to help their kids get better grades in school. After final discussion, we were happy with our plan. Feeling that it would work, we voted to proceed.

It was a simple plan and ought to have worked because we followed our blueprint closely and worked quickly. The flaw was that we took no time for basic mining research. It started well. George and Bobby showed up at dusk with the flashlight, so the first part of our plan, opportunity, was working well. Second, on Friday night we could play later, because there was no school next day. This gave us a short time space when parental supervision would be relaxed.

Soon as it was "deep dark," we took our fruit jars and began checking the bushes with George's flashlight. We located and captured a few hapless bugs, which were promptly thrust into prison and the jar lids screwed on tight. Then we gradually worked farther away from the house. After getting far enough away to be out of sight and mind of the grown folks, we cut into the alley behind my house and turned the light off. Sternly lecturing each other to keep quiet, we made our way up the dark alley to Mr. Rowe's back fence.

That fence was built of two rows of heavy chicken wire four feet tall, planned so it would be hard for kids or cows to climb over. But I had pushed the wire open and slipped through many times before, and along with George, easily climbed in that night. Bobby, who was a year younger and shorter than us, had more trouble but we finally managed to shove the wire down far enough so he could slide over.

The Rowe's cow was gentle but exhibited understandable nervousness when three clumsy boys invaded her pen. But, I had fed her a lot of grass through the wire over several years and, soon as I got in, I pulled a handful of hay from a bale in her small shed and gave it to her. Reassured, she munched along behind us and would have entered the outhouse with us if we hadn't fussed at her.

Only five minutes had lapsed since we first began our search, so things were moving fast enough. Still, we knew from hard experience that parents could snap onto a new pattern very quickly, so we worked as quick and quiet as we could.

We were better at quick than quiet but it only took a moment to turn the old wooden latch button and enter. We pulled the door tight behind us and turned on the light. Even though we no longer lived in houses with outdoor toilets, George and I had friends or relatives who still used them. Our memories were excellent, so we suffered only minor cultural shock as those fresh, heavy waves of strong privy smell pressed against our faces, shoving hard against us and contending for equal air space in the tiny wooden building. With Bobby, it was different. He had no experience with either one or two holers and complained loudly about the odor. We shut him up by saying he wouldn't notice it in a few minutes and reminded him that we were on important business, to which we should pay strict attention. Then we went to work.

Our plan was simple enough. Without mentioning it, I had borrowed my mother's long-handled dipper. We had also brought along a piece of wire mesh borrowed from some brick masons a few streets over. One of us was to operate the dipper which meant reaching it down into the treasure area and pulling up loads of raw mother lode. The lode was then to be screened through our wire mesh to locate coins. My conscience didn't bother me at all as I told my partners that, since this was my idea, I was therefore boss and one of them needed to volunteer as dipper operator.

Without hesitation I extended the dipper to Bobby but he, alertly and sharply for him, pointed out that his arms were too short and that spiders could also be hidden under the seat near those two dark holes. Then I nominated George, but he slowly held up the flashlight. His father, he intoned, had instructed that he alone was to handle it. No one could operate it, hold it, or even touch it, except him.

Since the dipper belonged to me and I was already holding it, I decided that graceful defeat was better than a noisy one and accepted my election to the post of dipper operator. But the honor of this new job did nothing to offset the powerful, almost blinding odor which blasted my face and nose as I bent down to commence operations. Sticking the dipper, my right arm, and half my head into the nearest hole, I almost gagged while instructing George to use the other hole for his flashlight.

Until looking in, I had no real appreciation of the scope of our job. During the planning I visualized that all we needed to do was shine the light inside, locate the bright coins all in a bunch, then dexterously flip them into mom's dipper and promptly leave to clean and divide our loot. But it didn't happen that way. Even though George carefully shined his light everywhere below, the only bright and shining objects we saw were things we didn't want to see, or smell.

And, even though we had told Bobby he would get used to the smell, finally not even noticing it at all, we were wrong. The closer I got to this job, the worse it stank. It was a hot night and I was sweating. My eyes had started to water and it was all I could do to keep from throwing up. Besides, no matter how hard I looked, I saw no treasure. Youthful optimism had met reality and was losing the battle.

Not knowing anything else to do, I filled my dipper and pulled it above the seat for screening. George focused the light, and though we tried hard, screening was impossible. This material was not sized to the mesh and wouldn't pass through. I dumped the first bunch back and sampled another spot. As I carefully raised the second dipperful toward the surface, George suddenly cursed. "Dad-dangitt!" But I knew the problem before he opened his mouth. His father's flashlight was no longer tightly clutched in his hand. Now it rested atop a pile of fresh material in Mr. Rowe's outhouse floor.

George didn't fluster easily when our class bully made the rounds at school recess, but he lost his cool that night in the Rowe's outhouse. His dad's only flashlight was slowly sinking from sight and he couldn't reach it. He ordered me to pull it out and I tried, but my arms were shorter than his. I couldn't reach it even though I was a little nearer. Quickly, I handed him the dipper and he carefully skidded the light over the surface until I could stretch hard, grab hastily, and pull it out. Wordlessly, I handed him the slippery metal object which now emitted a dim, yellow light because its lens needed cleaning as badly as my hands.

There had never been more room for this job than we needed, and our heads were close together. The light was also dim and we could barely see into each other's eyes, but what we saw was enough. No further discussion was needed. Enthusiasm and hope had fled. Our eyes had already voted and the treasure hunt was over.

We turned In unison, and were out of there three seconds later, almost de-horning the astonished cow who snorted and crawfished backward all splay-legged when the Rowe's privy door bounced off the side of her head. Bobby reached and cleared the fence with ease before George and I even got there.

All things considered, we had made quite a lot happen in the short 15 minutes since our hunt started. We got no treasure but we still had plenty to do. Parents were always checking into our activities, and we knew that none of them would be amused if we were caught, not "red" but "dark-handed." Besides, we were sick to death of this project and its smell. Our greatest aim at the moment was to destroy all incriminating evidence, including odor, quick as we could.

In my back yard we coupled up Dad's old red rubber water hose and washed our hands thoroughly. Even Bobby, who hadn't touched anything as far as I knew, was anxious to wash his. I then washed out the dipper until it shone as brightly as ever. But George's flashlight was another matter.

We all knew flashlights should never get wet. At the very best, they were cranky devices, always pooping out and developing shorts or needing new bulbs and batteries at the most critical times. Water was almost the worst thing that could happen to them and, if one ever really got wet, it never seemed to recover. Like a sick sheep, it weakened, gave up and lay down to die, no matter what kind of treatment you gave it.

George's flashlight was really filthy and there was no way he could take it home without a bath. We had no cloths or towels to clean with and had already rubbed it around in the grass. Rubbing only caused it to collect loose grass cuttings which added to the problem. It still smelled awfully bad and a bath was imperative.

George knew nothing about flashlight mechanics. This caused him to be even more anxious because he didn't know what to do. I, on the other hand, had carefully watched an uncle once as he cannibalized two old flashlights, making one good one from the pair. To settle George down I assured him that we could tear down his dad's light and wash it off inside to get rid of the odor. Then we could dry it carefully and put it back together so it would work. He gave me reluctant permission to do it because there was nothing else to be done. But he reminded me again of his instructions to allow no one else to hold it or even turn it on. I reassured him again and started tearing it down.

And we did it! The only bad time was when we were drying and cleaning out the metal shell and its lens, but everyone contributed his shirt tail and we got it perfectly dry. When we had finished, the thing smelled okay, looked good as new and emitted a bright white light. I was as surprised as the others but didn't let them know.

Right in the middle of our work, my mother, who had heard water running outside, asked from the back door if we had found any good bugs. Bobby promptly answered that we had caught "a lot," saving me the necessity of answering. Back then we considered it better form to lie to someone else's mother than to our own. Bobby was being helpful and I appreciated it. My hands were full right then and I didn't need any help from the house. Satisfied, Mom withdrew after telling us to wind up our business because it was nearing bedtime. It was quite a few years before she learned that, all during that unfortunate night, we had been hurrying as fast as we could.

As soon as the light was cleaned, we parted. No ceremony was observed. The only thing we said was what we always said, "See you tomorrow." I eased into the house carrying my jar with four lone bugs in one hand and Mom's dipper in the other. I had learned about germs in school but dismissed all thought of them while replacing that clean and shiny dipper back in the exact place from which I had taken it. When finished, I went to my room, threw my clothes over the bed corner and went to sleep without being told.

After breakfast next morning I was out in my yard, aiming and shooting my BB-gun at various targets and wishing I had saved a few BBs. George trotted up and smiled a greeting then asked if I would like to go to the show. I looked at him with disgust because he knew very well that I was dying to go. He also knew that I had only three pennies which I'd taken back from our defunct partnership. Grumpily, I reminded him of this.

George never stopped grinning. He seemed proud of himself and said he had a surprise. I was dubious, but followed him down the block and to the back side of his father's garage where he showed me three unbroken quart-sized milk bottles that nested, barely visible, in the tall grass. Each bottle could be exchanged for a nickel at C. H. Parker Grocery on Main Street or at any other grocery store in town.

I asked George where the bottles came from, and he looked a little embarrassed. His smile also weakened and I knew we had encountered the theft ethic again. From his attitude, I knew he was riding the line, and had probably crossed over. He had found these bottles on the way home last night, he explained, after returning the brick mason's screen. "In the ditch," he added, but without looking me straight in the eye. He knew that we had both searched many ditches before for valuable items without finding anything worth carrying home.

I chose to believe him, even though I was pretty certain the bottles had been lifted from some neighbor's front porch where they had been waiting for the milkman to come. But I wasn't certain, and my parents had always told me to be certain of the facts before calling anyone guilty, so I accepted George's story. I insisted, however, that Bobby must go with us. He smiled, saying that was why it was so nice that our careless donor had dropped exactly three bottles.

Ethics here weren't really difficult. In the first place, I hadn't stolen any milk bottles. Second, I wasn't certain George had. Third,

I was performing a good deed by insisting that Bobby be allowed to come along, and our parents had hammered at us to perform good deeds, as far back as I could remember. Actually, this was one of my better ethical decisions, and my parents would likely have commended me for it if I had bothered to tell them.

An hour later, George, Bobby, and I could be seen skylarking down the street towards town, each carefully guarding his milk bottle from breakage. We were headed for Parker's grocery to cash them in. After that we would cross Main Street to the Palace Theater and watch a brand-new movie starring an up-and-coming young Western actor named Bob Steele. I had seen him before and thought that he was going to be one of the great ones.

CHAPTER 24

HARVEY—1940

I WAS 12, "goin'-on" 13, when the summer of 1940 arrived in Burkburnett, Texas. Only a few old-timers called Burk a Boomtown any more. The Boomers still hanging around were like my folks, mostly broke. Times were still hard and people lucky enough to have jobs clung to them tightly.

Though our President and many world leaders denied it would ever happen, most North Texans saw World War II coming long before it got there. We were outraged by actions of both the Japanese and German governments. We thought they deserved a good beating, but weren't ready to do it yet. We were more concerned with not sliding back into the Great Depression. The radio, papers and newsreels all assured us that President Roosevelt had cured the abominable thing but prosperity had somehow overlooked North Texas. Few people in Burk saw more than a glimmer of new money between 1930 and 1943.

World War II finally brought us prosperity. Two-thirds of our single men and half our married men were fighting overseas, before wartime payrolls began making it possible for North Texans to live, eat and dress like the rest of America. Finally, 13 years after the 1929 stock market crash, war production and defense plant payrolls made the depression go away.

When Japan bombed Pearl Harbor on December 7, 1941, North Texans were as enraged as when the World Trade Center was destroyed in 2001. Within days, our older brothers, uncles and cousins were enlisting to fight. Within weeks, small blue banners with white stars in them were seen hanging in windows all over

North Texas. Within a year, every family I knew had lost at least one, and some had lost several, friends or relatives in the war and many of those white star banners were replaced by gold ones, signifying that some mother's son had been killed. But it wasn't all bad. Even though gas, meat, shoes, tires, coffee, sugar, cigarettes Coca-Cola and Snicker Bars had been rationed, most folks in Burk were living a lot better than during peace time.

In late 1940, war was imminent and every spare barrel of oil which could be turned into a pipeline was sent to the East and West coasts for loading into tankers. Except for a rapidly declining oilfield, Burk's largest industry was farming. Few people drilled there any more except for a few promoters who couldn't afford good leases and drilled an occasional "pure guess" hole down in the Red River bottom.

Floods carried away their tanks and machinery and washed out their roads almost every year and "river bottom" wells were out of production a third of the time. They had to be big pumpers to pay off. There was still a lot of oil in the ground but the oil business had boiled down to pumping out and selling oil from wells in the aging Northwest and Southwest fields. Most of them delivered a little less oil and a little more salt water every month, and were mere ghosts of their boomtown strength. Thousands, however, still produced from four to 20 barrels of oil every day. They also produced billions of million cubic feet of gas which was refined into high-octane, war-winning, aviation fuel.

My guess is that nearly 4,000 people lived in Burk in 1940. Most of them still earned their livings in the oilfield. The next largest group farmed and the rest were store owners, businessmen, teachers, preachers, plus a couple of lawyers, three doctors and a mortician. Main topics of conversation were when the war would start, weddings, funerals, an occasional new well being drilled and the weather. Monotony was our normal pattern and that was why I perked up quickly when a flatbed truck loaded with household goods stopped across Avenue C from us, right in front of the old Gilchrist house. That truck was moving the Day family into their new home.

Harvey Day was a lease pumper for the Magnolia Oil Company and quickly advised us he was going to retire "pretty soon." Retirement, for most 60-year-olds like him, meant after the war with Germany, Italy and Japan had been fought and won. Harvey told everybody he had moved his family out of a "shotgun" shack in the oilfield to live in a "real" house in town where he could retire in style.

I liked Harvey, but couldn't call him by his first name, as did everyone else. My parents insisted I call him "Mr. Day." He was a small fellow who moved quickly. He also laughed and joked a lot, normally taking time to talk with me. Dad liked him too because Harvey had permission to fish in lakes where most people couldn't and Harvey was a good fisherman who shared with his neighbors. He also told a lot of funny stories but Dad warned that they weren't all strictly true.

After watching Harvey a few days, I decided his pumping job with Magnolia was a snap and began planning to hire out to them when I grew up. Sixty years later, I realize that his job was easy because Burk's oilfield production had become routine. By 1940 pumper's jobs had become so predictable that pumping duties were reduced to tending company machinery, switching out oil tanks and measuring the oil on hand every day. Otherwise, they swept their pump houses out occasionally and quickly reported any breakdown or any leak too big for them to handle alone.

By early 1930, regardless of what people saw in movies and read about in books, the oil companies had stopped hiring fighters, heavy drinkers and men who wouldn't show up for work on time. They were able to do this because jobs were scarce and they could pick whatever kind of employee they needed. So could anyone else who hired help but oil companies went a step further. They were polishing their images and if employees didn't pay their bills, the companies would dock their pay and pay bills for them. If an employee decided to argue about it, there wasn't a lawyer in Wichita County who would take the case because, in 1940, even lawyers figured that decent people ought to pay what they owed.

Harvey was what oil companies called a "steady" hand. Most folks liked him. Women folks, though, valued each other in a different manner. My mother and Mrs. Day approached warily, measuring each other in a subtle, devious feminine way, hard for men to understand. But soon, they were swapping recipes and my parents' vote was unanimous. The Days would make good neighbors.

At 6:00 each morning, good days or bad, you could see Harvey heading out to the Magnolia's lease. He would pull on his ancient and oil-stained gray felt hat before stepping off the back steps. Carefully, he loaded Old Shep, his aged and beloved black and tan "stock dog", into Magnolia's old Chevrolet coupe. Protectively balancing his pint fruit jar filled with steaming black Texas coffee, he methodically cranked the old Chevy until its motor roared.

This coupe was easily recognizable as a pumper's car because the trunk lid had been taken off and a wooden "toolpusher" deck built into the rear trunk. This gave Harvey the ability to haul hand tools, heavy parts, supplies, and other kinds of oilfield "iron", to and from Magnolia's lease. Sipping carefully, so he wouldn't burn his mouth, Harvey eased out on his clutch, backed slowly down the drive and turned toward Magnolia's lease, slowly building speed as he drove.

Unless something bad happened, he would be home by 9:00. His boys had left for school and he was able to sit in complete peace to enjoy a hot breakfast of steak or a pork chop, plus two fried eggs, biscuits with cream gravy, jelly and plenty of hot coffee. His wife's meals, Harvey bragged, were better than anything he could buy at the Burk Cafe.

After breakfast, unless it was too cold or windy, Harvey sat on his front porch, reading the paper. Leaning a wooden kitchen chair back on its rear legs against the porch wall, with his paper folded in one hand and his mug in the other, he read comfortably while Old Shep gently snored at his feet.

Harvey studied his papers carefully. First it was the Wichita Falls Record News, followed every Wednesday by the Burkburnett Star. If you were close, you could see his lips move and hear him softly recite the words as he read to himself. Usually, he mumbled through two, and sometimes three, mugs of coffee before finishing. After that, he pulled his hat brim down, dropped his eyelids and helped Shep with the nap business.

Artist Holly Nowak, Kingwood, Texas

In 1940 God dished out the hottest and most miserable summer Burk people could remember. He also sent us a bumper crop of houseflies, and Harvey claimed he had worn out three fly swatters, 15 cent's worth, during the first week they hatched. But it was wasted effort, he complained. For every fly he killed, 10 came to the funeral and, no matter how much Dad warned me about Mr. Day's stories, I had already learned from killing flies myself, that our neighbor was telling the absolute truth.

He also complained about having to scrub and hose off the paint on his front porch every day to "get shut of all that fly juice". Then he tried using Flit, a pesticide delivered from an old-fashioned push-pull sprayer, but the mist caused his wife's flowers to curl up and he didn't like the smell. When Old Shep began to choke and cough, he discarded the sprayer.

Still, Harvey was sick of flies falling into his coffee, and after noticing that they always congregated heavily on the front screen door, his mind settled into deep thought. During his second cup of coffee he thought a few minutes longer and finally concocted what he thought might be a solution. Turning it over once more in his mind, he double-checked the details, to be certain. Finally, he decided it would work and began to assemble his invention.

In 1940, as in 2005, many people stored junk in their garages instead of throwing it away. People didn't do garage sales and there was no Goodwill back then so the stuff really piled up. Harvey rummaged around in a dusty corner of his garage near the Chevy's front bumper, finally locating a large, old-fashioned, brass-bladed Emerson fan. It was too dangerous to use because the blade shroud had been removed. Without that protective cover, it was vicious and could easily cut the tail off your cat or your finger, whichever came closest the quickest. Still, people in that Deep Depression had learned never to throw anything away that worked and Harvey had pitched it on the flatbed when they moved to town. He also remembered where to find it when it was needed.

Using a heavy jackknife, he cut off the extension cord as close to the fan's base as he could slice, then tossed the fan down. Working quickly, he stripped the first layer of insulation off the severed end of plug wire and split its two legs down the middle. Then he pulled the legs into a tight half-granny knot with each of them sticking out. Then he pared a half inch of insulation off each leg, revealing shiny bright copper wire. Those legs, or posts, were spread into a "V" to keep them from touching each other and blowing out his fuses. When he was finished, if you plugged it in a socket, you had a crude electric "shocker."

Just inside Harvey's front screen door, in the living room, was a wide window with an electric baseplug underneath. All houses had screens back then because home air-conditioning was still a pipedream, occasionally pondered by electrical engineers. A few expensive stores and theaters had air conditioning in 1940 but many of those used large vaults of ice and heavy-duty blower fans to cool the air.

But everybody had fans. One was the cardboard kind, covered with bible verses and pictures of Jesus, which you fanned back and forth to shove the air rapidly around your face. They were generally furnished to churches by the Owens-Brumley funeral home. Lots of religious Baptists and Methodists, correctly assuming the fans would cool sinners at home as well as they did in church, swiped half of them for home use. I didn't figure out for years that this was exactly what the funeral home wanted us to do and a few elderly and otherwise religious grandmothers who kept the fans were still praying for forgiveness when death took them away. The only other fans people had were newer models of Harvey's old Emerson and nothing else would get rid of our sweat in the summertime except hoses, bathtubs, wet towels or water holes large enough to swim in.

Window screens were the only way our houses could have free airflow in hot weather and they needed to be good ones, with few holes. Flies, mosquitoes, toads, snakes, spiders, skunks, mad dogs, grasshoppers and moths were only a few of the reasons we needed them. There were also stinging scorpions and centipedes that scared more folks than all the other pests.

But houseflies were the biggest problem and they were attracted by cooking odors. Because of this, and to find shelter from sun and rain, they gathered heavily on house screens. In the few minutes before a summer storm, they often gathered so heavily on porch and window screens that people inside could barely see out.

But Harvey was on a roll! Deeply involved in the joy of creation, he considered nothing else. Following his vision, he worked quickly. Pushing a corner of the front porch window screen outward, he shoved the bare end of the fan cord outside and plugged the other end into his wall socket. Going outside, he shoved the screen corner shut and, sitting down in his porch chair, reared back to wait for customers.

Propped comfortably against the wall, he held a fresh mug of coffee in his left hand and the shocker in his other. Patiently, he waited three minutes until a suitable crop had assembled. When satisfied, he flicked his right wrist slightly, barely touching the screen door and watched as the shocker emitted some scratchy noises and a few pale, rusty-looking sparks.

But the result was outstanding! Fifty houseflies which had once walked around on his screen dropped to the floor, at the same instant. Some fell onto Old Shep who never stopped snoring. Most importantly, after watching for several minutes, Harvey noted with exultation that not one fly ever moved as much as a wing. Every one of those suckers was dead before he had hit the floor. His invention worked far better than he had hoped.

Harvey never claimed to be an electrician but he had worked long enough in the oilfield to learn a few "do's" and "don'ts" about using electricity. Now that he knew the shocker would work, he walked back to his garage, looking for material to add a safety feature to his design. Locating an old ironing cord with an "Off-On" switch attached, he spliced it into the shocker wire. Now the cord was much longer and it could also be turned off whenever he needed to pour a fresh mug of coffee, go to the bathroom or talk with The Magnolia if it called him.

Harvey quickly developed skill in using his tool and spent eight wildly enthusiastic days busily slaughtering flies by the thousands, though he claimed they numbered into the millions. At first he had been secretive about his shocker, but it worked so well that soon he couldn't resist bragging to any neighbor who would listen.

"At the end of my first day," he puffed, I carried off better than a gallon of dead flies in my wife's dust pan. There was no more swatting and no more washing fly juice off my front porch."

Dead flies were dumped on the ground behind his trash barrel and Harvey swore that several varieties of birds had eaten so many that they had to back up and take running starts before clearing his back fence. I figured, like Dad said, that this was a case of him stretching the blanket pretty hard. But, even though I knew the story wasn't quite true, I enjoyed thinking about those birds revving up their wings, then running and jumping up in the air to clear his fence.

Progress, Harvey later told us, continued without slacking up until the ninth day. On that morning, for no reason he could see, the fly crop thinned down. A bunch! He was waiting longer and longer for an acceptable number of victims, and business was so slow that the job had actually become boring. Either he was killing the flies out, or they were "smartening" up, he didn't know which. But one thing was certain. He was killing less flies now with the shocker than he used to get with the swatters.

A number of flies still circled round but, while they continued lighting all over him and Old Shep, few of them lit on the screens, even if the day was cloudy. Actually, more of them started settling on him and the dog than when he first started swatting. And he knew the situation was getting serious again when they once more began to fall in his coffee.

Shep, Harvey noted, had a greater tolerance for flies than people. He slept soundly, for minutes at a time, with flies walking all over his face. Occasionally, he would raise his head to snap up a particularly persistent offender, but after briskly chewing it to specks and swallowing it down, he dropped his head back down to resume his nap. But, by the tenth day, Harvey and Shep were attracting even more flies and something else had to be done.

As he glumly considered whether to sack up the shocker and buy a half dozen more swatters, Harvey looked down to see a full dozen flies walking around on Shep's peacefully snoring nose. Four or five of them were in the act of landing or taking off at almost any given time and Harvey held the shocker in his hand. He briefly considered shocking his beloved pet but decided against it.

Actually, there were more flies on him than Shep anyway. Fifteen or twenty were lighting and walking about on his bare arms and neck half the time while, at the same time, he only saw three or four on the screen door. He thought about touching his arm with the shocker but decided not to do so. He was certain to receive a solid jolt, but there was no guarantee that enough energy would kill flies after passing through his body.

Glancing down again at Shep, he saw that all the hovering flies had landed and a bumper crop was walking about all over his dog. Before he could even think about it, the tip of his shocker moved swiftly down to flick a white patch of fur on Shep's rear end. And the result was astonishing!

"I didn't think he would feel it much," Harvey always said, "but that dog howled like he'd been stung by a dozen hornets and jumped straight forward. The pain must have hurt worse than hornets because he was facing the house when he leapt up and he jumped right square through the brand-new screen I had put on that door. He also left two trails, one wet and one kind of stringy, all along behind. But that wasn't the worst."

"Shep charged straight across my wife's new living room rug, still leaving those trails. An' at the far corner he turned to dive behind the couch. By then he was movin' out pretty 'peart, full speed in fact, an' hit an electric light cord just before duckin' out of sight. The force of that collision pulled my wife's new French-lookin' lamp off of her end-table. And, Man, when that thing hit the hard oak floor, right at the edge of her new rug, it broke into so many pieces that I could tell right away there was no use tryin' to glue the thing back together."

I heard Harvey tell his tale several times, and by the time he reached this point, his audiences were always whooping and slapping their legs. With the exact timing possessed by all natural comics, he would step politely back, allowing them to quieten so they could understand every word of his finish. "Actually," he would declare, "I wouldn't of shocked Old Shep if I'd thought it would really hurt him, but I definitely for sure wouldn't of done it if I'd noticed he was pointed straight at that new screen door but—you know what?"

"I had no trouble cleanin' up the front porch floor good as new. I also had my screen re-covered within two hours. During all this time, I was offerin' to help my wife clean up her carpet. I even threw in a promise to buy her a new lamp, but she wouldn't listen or say a word to me for the rest of that day. Fact is, I had to eat supper that night at the Burk Cafe. Then I took in a Clark Gable movie 'cause I knew I couldn't get back in the house 'til after she had gone to bed. But, next day, she decided we could drive over to Wichita Falls and I bought her a more expensive lamp. Then she started talkin' to me again."

"Shep was right mad at me too. He wouldn't have a blamed thing to do with me 'til I let him watch while I threw that shocker in the trash barrel. That fixed him and me up okay but he's still in bad shape with my wife. An' I feel sorry for him 'cause he's gettin' old an' likes to lay under the fan after dark but she won't throw him a single inch of slack. She says that, besides smellin' awful strong, he's been bad an' he's not comin' back in her house 'til after the first hard Norther."

BOOMTOWNER—1941

"TOM MICHAELS' CREW had just finished installing a brand-new pump in a little Sinclair pumphouse over at Hull Station near Kamay but somebody, we never knew who, had forgotten one important thing. They forgot to replace a three-inch bull plug after venting the oil tank line when they finished installing the pump. They left the plug laying in a corner of the pump house floor, and thinking everything was okay, they cranked up their new six-horse Fairbanks suction pump and opened the line, starting it to pumping oil. Then they went outside and began to pack up their tools."

"They were climbing into the gang-truck, ready to leave, when the pump began running away, going faster and faster. It wouldn't slow down because it was drawing in too much air, and the faster it went, the more raw oil it threw out onto that pumphouse floor through the bull plug opening.

"Knowing that his pump was tearing itself to pieces, Tom ran back into the pumphouse wanting to pull that spark plug wire loose and shut off the pump but he was too late. He had barely entered the door when that plug wire sparked one time too many, touching off a violent explosion. Raw crude gas vapor had been rising up from all that green oil on the floor and mixing with the hot summer air inside that small building.

The heavy explosion blew him back through the door. It also blew a sheet of raw oil over his clothes and he was on fire all over. The blast force rolled him over and over across the bald prairie like a tumble-bug. But, soon as he stopped rolling, he got up to run because no man can lie quietly while suffering that kind of pain."

"The crew chased him down and rolled him around on the ground, finally putting out the fire. Then they loaded him into the gang truck and carried him to the Bethania Hospital in Wichita Falls because it would have taken an ambulance crew an hour and a half to come out and find them. Those doctors gave him the best medical attention anybody could get, but it didn't work. Tom died next morning about 9:45."

"I had 10 men working for me over in Olney and Tom had about 15 working for him in Holliday, where they had recently built a new warehouse and set up a good-sized pipeyard. Sinclair's district manager told me to move over to Holliday and bring any of the men with me who wanted to keep working for the company. He added Tom's crew to mine and closed the Olney pipeyard. I was to run all the district's work from Holliday. I was glad to get the job. Even though it meant more work, it was a promotion. But the satisfaction of a raise and promotion is not as much fun when it comes about because a good man died."

Cecil Holler Author's Uncle

CHAPTER 25

JOB EDUCATON—1943

I SPOKE TO him but Harlan didn't slow down, or even seem to hear. He gurgled once or twice while passing but kept a bee-line toward his father's office near the back door. His face was splotchy red and he was holding one hand over his eyes. When I saw tears spilling through his fingers onto the rough pine floor I realized he was bawling.

Harlan lived in my end of town and was two years ahead of me in school. At first I thought he might have lost a fight, but his clothes weren't messed up and his nose wasn't bleeding. Then I figured someone in the family might have died, but no one came out of his dad's office to make an announcement. I chased this puzzle around my mind while completing a cleanup of the store's gigantic coffee roaster and grinder. Because I loved the rich and pleasant smell of freshly roasted coffee, I enjoyed this part of my job.

Even though I didn't know what happened, my opinion of Horace had nose-dived. Nothing was bad enough to make me parade down Main Street, crying like a baby, in front of the whole town, as he just had. Still, fifteen minutes later, I felt like crying myself but wasn't about to give anyone the pleasure of watching.

Bill Jones, Harlan's dad, seemed to be a friendly and likable man. He was no longer young, but I didn't think of him as old. He had always spoken and waved whenever he saw me. Like any 15-year-old boy, I needed all the good attention and emotional support the world could offer, so I responded to his kindness, speaking proudly whenever we met. Then, because I hadn't been able to get a raise at my job in another grocery store, I jumped at the chance to go to work for its competition. My reasons were basic. Mr. Jones managed this store, and I really liked him. But most important, he would pay more money.

Before finishing the first day, I had to admit that my new career choice wasn't going to be a picnic. In fact, Mr. Jones was the first person to begin educating me, a 15-year-old grocery store package boy, about several basic and unpleasant boss-worker relationships that lurked ahead in the grownup world.

Before an hour had passed I was missing my old job and all my friends over there. We had worked hard, but performed willingly, even enthusiastically, because we were allowed to have a little fun while working. I missed the honest and cackling laughter of their butcher, Les, as well as the manager's sons, Billy and Bobby. We had played well in school and pulled well together at the store.

Bill and Bob didn't dope off and take it easy like boss's sons often do. They performed their fair share of work, not necessarily because they were outstanding examples of American youth but because their father insisted. He considered all package boys to be equal and expected his sons to work as hard as anybody. He also had strenuous but fair ways to bring any of us back into line if we slacked off too much. We respected him because he was unscrupulously fair and allowed us to enjoy our jobs as long as fun didn't interfere with customers or lose the store any money.

The new store was different. No one smiled there except the manager and he only smiled at the customers, as he had once done toward me before I went to work there. He let me understand in a hurry that he ran a tight ship and never smiled in my direction again. Maybe I was too young and self-centered and maybe I reacted too strongly, but my feelings were injured. After watching him for two days I decided he cared nothing about his workers and was only happy when everything in his store was all work and no play.

Later on, I found officers like him in the Navy and met similar bosses in the business world after that. Most of them were impressive and performed their duties well but their promotions were earned on the sore backs of, and some people said, over the "bleached" bones of their helpers. Few people working for guys like them were happy until finding other jobs.

My immaturity might have affected Mr. Jones' attitude because employers back then expected kids to perform like grownups. I wasn't the best worker in town and wasn't eaten up with maturity, but I wasn't lazy either. Like most youngsters, I tried hard and performed well most of the time. But I was a kid, and kids aren't yet adults and can't always make the best decisions.

Job lesson number one came quickly on my first afternoon. Put simply, this great truth stated that "It's easier to be friends with most people than it is to work for them." I was laboring in the vegetable display area when Mr. Jones taught me that.

He had instructed me to bring a 100-pound sack of red onions from the rear storage area and stock them in the onion bin. This seemed simple to me and I performed the job exactly as I always had in the other store. After locating the proper onions, I carried the sack up front to the bin. Moving swiftly, I clipped the binding strings on top, grabbed the sack's top ears and lifted it halfway up over the edge of the bin. Boosting up with my knee I dumped the top of the sack over into the bin while pulling the sack away. Then I trashed the sack and went back to finish what I had been doing.

Ten minutes later, his voice reeking with displeasure, Mr. Jones summoned me loudly. I trotted over to the vegetable area and stood before him for what seemed a long time but was probably less than a minute, while he complained loudly that I hadn't stocked those onions to suit him. I was, he pointed out, experienced and should have known he wanted me to clean up the floor when I was finished, and to get rid of all loose onion husks in the bin. Also, he had found my discarded sack in the trash pile and we were never supposed to throw those sacks away. His voice wasn't kind and he didn't smile. All the employees and customers on that side of the store heard everything.

Next day the store's butcher told me that Mr. Jones sold all the discarded onion and potato sacks for a penny apiece to an Oklahoma farmer who crossed Red River once a week to get them. He also said that our boss normally found an early excuse to browbeat the latest employee, which right now was me. I thought about this, remembering that at the other store we threw those sacks away, and no one who knew him had ever accused Billy and Bobby's dad of being wasteful.

So, I fished his onion sack out of the trash bin, located his salvage pile and stuffed it in with the rest. Then I picked up the one onion husk which had fallen on the floor and began to carefully rub and peel all those red onions down until they were almost white, stuffing the husks into a paper bag.

Before I had finished, Mr. Jones was back again, complaining that I was taking way too much time to perform such a simple job. He wanted me to remember that time was money and also that I had wasted a new paper sack by stuffing onion husks in it. Instead, he carped, I should have dragged a corrugated box out of the trash bin, saving a new paper sack. So, from the first day, Mr. Jones and I had different ideas about what a "good" employee was.

Harlan came on a Friday afternoon at 4:00, near the end of my second week. During this time his father, instead of mellowing, had gotten worse. I was likely hyper-sensitive, but I thought he complained too often, too loud, with too little reason. In this way, he taught me the second classic lesson about bosses in the American workplace. This lesson pointed out that a new boss can look and act like a dream, but after you go to work for him, he can turn into a nightmare and a horse's fanny to boot.

At the Jones store the last guy hired was always saddled with the sorriest jobs and abuse our boss managed to think up. Some said he enjoyed it, seldom firing the new hands, but occasionally making them so miserable that they walked off the job. I would have left already but I needed the money and new jobs, even jobs like mine, were hard to find in a little town.

Within 10 minutes after Harlan came in I had completed my very best polishing job on the store's big coffee roaster. Then I threw my rags in a box salvaged from the trash bin and walked toward the rear. That was when I saw Mr. Jones walk out of his office and walk briskly toward me soon as he spotted me. Harlan followed but lagged further behind as they came closer. I didn't know it yet but the time had come for my third and last great job lesson from this guy. It only took a moment, and translated simply, it set forth the premise that "blood running through the veins of a boss's son is thicker than that of the store's newest package boy".

"I'm letting you go, Ed," Mr. Jones said. Strangely enough, he was smiling again as he had before I had gone to work for him. "You don't seem to like your work here," he continued, "and we want all our hands to be happy." Then the guy looked straight into my eyes and, still smiling, finished giving me the boot. "Harlan lost his job today and he needs a job, just like you."

"I have figured up your pay," he continued, taking my arm and walking me toward the front door, "it's in this envelope," and he shoved the packet into my hand. "Now I didn't pay you for a full day, but I did add an extra hour, nine cents, because I always want to be fair."

Talking companionably as we walked, he deftly pulled the tie string on my apron and slipped it gently over my head. Then he edged me out onto the front sidewalk and closed the door behind me. I resented this bad treatment but had to admire his skill. And I didn't talk back to him because my parents had always taught me to respect adults, even when they acted like teen-agers. Besides, I suffered so much from stress that I was a half block down the sidewalk before thinking of a sharp or cutting answer I might have used on him.

His final words and sickening smile had been worse than anything else. "You tell your folks I don't want anyone to have hard feelings about this and would like them to keep on trading at our store."

"Fat chance," I responded hotly in my mind but this stinging rejoinder was finally crafted down in front of Heine's drug store. "Nobody in our family will cross your door again as long as you or any of your kin are there." And we never did.

I had never been fired before and was ashamed. I wanted to cry but had made up my mind about crying long before this day. I was ashamed because I didn't know how to explain this to my family and my friends. Few people back then sided with a worker who got laid off unless the company he worked for was having a general layoff, going out of business or changing ownership. Jobs were precious, and people figured that a person who got fired, probably deserved it. My job didn't pay much, but little as the amount was, it subtracted that much money from what my Dad had to earn.

Opening the envelope I counted out $2.08 and decided I could spare a nickel for a short coke at Heine's Drug Store. I was feeling guilty and had the hazy idea that, while drinking, I could sort this situation out well enough to explain it to Dad. If so, maybe between us, we could figure out a remedy.

Halfway through the slowly sipped coke, I re-played again in my mind the final scenes of my disgrace and suddenly remembered something I had overlooked. When I did, I wanted to stand up and shout for joy but kept my cool and my seat. What I had forgotten were the most important words Bill Jones ever said to me and, exultantly, I repeated them again to make certain I remembered correctly. "Besides," he had told me, "Harlan lost his job today."

This was important because it not only explained why Harlan had been crying, but also reminded me he had been working at the Morris five and dime, only a block away from where I was sipping coke and licking my wounds. I had no idea why Harlan was fired and didn't care, but it was clear that someone would be needed to take his place! Quickly, but carefully, so I wouldn't waste a drop, I sucked the last watery stream of Coke through my straw and stood to leave. There was no reason why I shouldn't have Harlan's old job. And, as I quick-stepped toward Mr. Morris' five and dime, I planned my hiring on speech.

Five minutes later I was asking for Harlan's job and 10 minutes after that I'd been hired. I finished the afternoon by sweeping up the five and dime floor instead of the one at the grocery and was making more money than I had before. Besides that, the new job was a snap. I worked there more than a year and never broke a sweat. My pay was fifteen cents an hour, six cents more than I made at the Jones store, and I wondered once if his dad paid Harlan the same wages he did me.

Nothing on the new job weighed over 20 pounds and I never had to wear dirty, bulky aprons as in the old grocery days. Besides that, Mr. Morris' store closed at 9:00 on Saturday nights whereas the grocery never started closing until 11:00. Then, after all our grocery customers had come by to pick up the sacks they had bought earlier and taken time to buy all the items they had forgotten before, we had to mop the floors, re-stock the shelves and scald out the meat grinders, butcher knives and pans in the butcher shop. We seldom left the grocery store before 1:00 Sunday morning, way too late for young package boys to watch the midnight movie that started every Saturday night at 11:30.

I recall my job at the five and dime with pleasure. Two weeks of work under Mr. Jones had taught me to appreciate a boss like Mr. Morris who always treated me like an adult. He never threatened or raised his voice toward me, even if there was no one else around to hear. But mostly, I was grateful because he had made it possible for me to avoid explaining to my family and friends why I had gotten fired.

It was true that I never got a raise while working for Mr. Morris but that was normal for the times. Despite our country's heavy expenses in fighting World War II, there had been little inflation and my money bought just as much when I left Mr. Morris as when I started.

Few Texans in 1943 understood anything about how America's economy worked. They barely understand their own finances. I realize today that I should have appreciated Mr. Morris and his wife more than I did. They exhibited true bravery by keeping that store open at all. Profit from the investment must have been small, but by keeping its doors open, they served our community well and created jobs for two lady clerks, Mr. and Mrs. Morris and me.

My parents had always taught me to accept people and events as being proper until I knew differently. So I thought little about it several days later when I saw a crumpled $5 bill laying on the aisle floor behind one of Mr. Morris' cash registers. Without missing a beat, I picked it up, stuck it in my shirt pocket and finished sweeping.

I had been raised to understand that I wasn't entitled to anything I hadn't earned and it didn't occur to me to keep this money. Without thinking twice, I gave the bill to Mr. Morris after sweeping all the way to the rear. He thanked me and gave a big smile, apparently happy to receive it.

For the remainder of the time I worked there, every three or four weeks, I would find a crumpled bill lying near one of the cash registers. Each bill was faithfully turned over to Mr. Morris, and It was ten years later before it occurred to me that he might have deliberately placed them there to test my honesty. I had concluded that the Morrises owned more money than they needed and had become careless about handling it.

No one at the store ever said why Harlan had lost his job and I didn't ask. I sympathized with him because he ended up having to work for his dad and wondered if he could hang with it. A full decade later, it also occurred to me that Harlan might have, on that long-ago Friday afternoon, forgotten to turn in one of the crumpled up bills he'd found on Mr. Morris' floor. I was tempted, that first time, to keep the bill I found. And, if I hadn't been so heavily programmed against stealing, could have gotten fired on my first few days at work.

So, I learned my last important job lesson that month. Simply put, it states: "There is more than one kind of bad boss." Even though I liked Mr. Morris, and he was considered a good man, he was a bad boss in one detail. No boss should tempt anyone, especially a young kid, to pocket money that doesn't belong to him.

CHAPTER 26

MITCH—1943

IT WAS EARLY in 1943. New Year's was only three weeks behind us and I had just landed the best job I ever had. My family lived in Burkburnett, a Texas town, of about 3,000 folks, but despite its size those people were convinced that their town was as good as any. If you didn't believe it, you could just ask. They would tell you.

Burk was located in a sharp bend on the Texas side of Red River, between Wichita Falls and Lawton, Oklahoma. Since late 1941, most of our young men had been leaving home to fight in World War II. People today might think they were over-patriotic because more than half of them volunteered without waiting to be drafted. But they had two major reasons. First, they wanted badly to whip the Germans and Japanese. Second, by joining up, they were leaving a poor economy that had been offering them low-paying jobs for 10 long years.

North Texas was on the verge of experiencing its first real labor shortage since 1916. That was when it was a boom town that never stopped drilling oil wells despite World War I manpower shortages. In 1943 the same thing began to happen again. More and more young men like Johnny Ozee were joining the Army, Navy and Marines, and that is why Mr. Cannon hired me, a 15-year-old kid, to work in his drug store as a soda jerk. I didn't get the job because I was an above average worker. I was simply his best choice.

Up to then I had been working at the only five and dime store in Burk. It was an easy job with decent people but it had no future. The owner never intended to give me a raise. Besides, I was tired of sorting the trash out of his floor sweep and re-cycling it every evening.

Floor sweep was a mixture of medium-grained sawdust, dyed red, and lightly coated with cedar-scented oil. A three gallon can cost three dollars, and if I picked out most of the cigarette butts, gum wrappers, straight-pins, half-burned matches, dried mud, toothpicks, spit, hair pins, chewing gum and used merchandise tags out of it, he could make a can last for six months. Today, my boss would be commended for recycling waste products, but at the time, I figured he was plain stingy.

Looking back over 60 years of time, I realize that he was fighting hard just to keep his doors open, and I should have been more grateful for my job. But I was a kid and had been talking with guys a little older than me who had medical disabilities keeping them out of the Army but who could work at defense plant jobs. They were making more money than grown men with families who had stayed in Burk and I was a little jealous.

When I learned that Johnny had quit Mr. Cannon to join the Navy and become a fighter pilot, I trotted over when the five and dime closed and hit Mr. Cannon up for Johnny's job. We talked a few minutes about honesty and ethics and he asked if I liked him. When I told him that I did, he said this was good and added that he liked me too. To be certain I hadn't picked up any wrong vibrations, he explained that he always made it a practice never to hire a man or woman who didn't like him or whom he did not like. This habit, he felt, prevented many problems.

Then he said that he would often be away from the store, but expected his employees to conduct themselves when he was away just as they did when he was there. If hired, I was to dress cleanly and appropriately for work. I should unfailingly treat his customers as friends because if they didn't like us they would trade elsewhere. I was always to wash my hands with soap and to prepare his lunch counter food with "no germs." Lastly, I should make honest change and look after the store's interests just as if he and I were the same person. All this seemed reasonable to me, so I agreed and he hired me.

It caused me no concern that I was only making 20 cents an hour, half of what he had paid Johnny Ozee. In fact, it was only five cents an hour more than I'd made at the five and dime but I liked it better in the drug store. Cannon's was the town's main meeting place. Most people stopped there to loaf whenever they had a few minutes free time.

An average Cannon's customer wasn't able to afford many restaurant meals, but he could treat himself to a Coke or a cup of steaming, generally black, Texas coffee once or twice a week. We lived in a dry precinct of Wichita County so Burk had no liquor stores or bars. Burk folks drank Cokes, coffee or iced water and Canton's was their main hangout.

Nobody was expected to tip drugstore help and we didn't expect it. The price of a short Coke or a mug of coffee was only a nickel. So was a doughnut. A guy who was in the chips could order a sundae for 15 cents or a malt or milk shake for a nickel more. If he was a big sport with a spare quarter, he could supervise construction of his own three-dip banana split. The soda jerk would properly drape his ice cream with chocolate, pineapple and strawberry topping, then dust it with nuts and slather real whipped cream all over it and drop a maraschino cherry on top. After finishing, the fountain guy applied the exact amount of pressure to slide that 8-inch glass boat and its delectable contents gently down the marble counter top to where the customer's napkin and spoon waited, ready for use.

Cannon's customers were farmers, ranchers, teachers, housewives, oil-field hands, bankers, Indians and teen-agers. Regardless of who they were, all of them stood a good chance of finding some neighbor or friend with whom to pass the time of day or of walking in and finding a person for whom they were looking. Sometimes, since it was a drug store, the person needed a prescription filled and sometimes he was picking up a message that had been left for him. But, even if he had no business there, he was entitled to sit and participate in a small town bull session.

If a visitor had no money, he or she was still served a large Coke glass full of ice and water. He could also sit on a stool and drink as long as it took him to rest up, to wait for someone else, or just to stay inside a few minutes, sheltering from the frequently harsh North Texas weather. Water refills were given on request, and visitors were politely included in whatever daily gossip was making the rounds. Anyone afflicted with a temporary money shortage bothered no one else because we all knew how it felt to be broke.

Grownup conversation at Cannon's centered on the weather, crops, sports, jobs, and funerals. But it also included weddings, showers and quilting parties, which were termed "puredee gossip" by the men. But almost every conversation, even among the ladies, finished with talk about war in North Africa, the South Pacific or Europe. Everyone had relatives and friends overseas, and never during that war, did I hear a favorable comment about either Germans or Japanese.

For young people, Cannon's was where all the action was. In the summertime they met there to make plans. They came in and out at all hours of the day to visit, and at night to meet before and after dates or going to the movies. In Cannon's, young folks sat in booths, to drink Cokes on the way home from school and after ball games. Half our young folks met in Cannon's every day. Sometimes by accident and sometimes on purpose.

Many of the very pretty and older girls I knew, some of whom strolled up and down Burk's streets on the arms of taller and sometimes awkward young men, then married them later, had spent hours chatting, dreaming, holding hands and sipping Cokes in a Cannon booth. Most of these couples became responsible adults. And despite the youthful brags of many young stags about their super active love lives, I don't remember any girl in my high school class who "had" to get married.

The war was one reason for our good conduct. Every month, many of the young men were leaving home. This left fewer young guys at home to sniff out and find woman trouble. Other young men were only kept home by the pleas of anxious mothers and girlfriends that they graduate from high school before joining the Service. My estimate is that one of those couples in seven married just before the boy left home or was shipped overseas. Despite all this, I was glad to see, when attending my 50th class reunion, that most of my classmates whose opposites were still kicking, still lived with the ones they married back then.

Like most young Burk people, if I wasn't at Cannon's I was wondering who was and what they were talking about. When I had free time, I normally went there first to see who was hanging out. In fact, if my dad would have let me and Mr. Cannon had been that mean, I would have worked there for nothing.

My new job began at 8:00 on the first Monday morning after I left the five and dime. Mr. Cannon started my training by assuming the role of a customer. He had me serve him coffee and one or two other easy things from the fountain. Then he showed me where they kept different items of merchandise like "Kotex." Even at 16 I barely understood what the stuff was for and had absolutely no interest in it. Women were the only ones who used it and none of them ever mentioned the subject to me.

This merchandise, Mr. Cannon explained, pointing and deliberately refusing to say its name aloud, should be sold by one of the ladies on duty unless I was the only employee in the store. If I found it necessary to conduct a sale directly to a lady, I was to ask no questions because she would normally wait until no one was near and then quietly give me all the information I needed. I should keep my voice down and draw no attention to her purchase.

If the lady failed to give me enough information, I was allowed to ask the box size and whether she wanted small, but nothing else. After her purchase was made, I was to stand with my back to the counter and double-bag her package or wrap it in heavy paper so no one could read the label through it. Then I was to quietly hand it over and ring up her money or charge the sale to her account. This program, he stressed, was always to be followed exactly.

In those days, many grown women were too modest to buy Kotex for themselves or a daughter. Some of them embarrassed their sons and younger brothers just as badly by sending them to buy it. Normally the boy took a written description of what was needed and would give the note to me rather than ask a lady clerk for it. Mostly, I helped him out, but if he was a sassy kid, too big for his britches who always gave me or my friends a hard time, I would tell him to buy it from the ladies.

My boss and I continued to like each other because he was good at his business and treated me as if I were grown, not a kid. This made me try hard to do my job properly. Noting this, he took time to brag on my accomplishments, and was patient with me. He didn't yell when I made a mistake and this made me try even harder.

Every morning at 10:00 Mr. Cannon picked up a canvas bag and walked down to the First National Bank at the corner of Main and Avenue C. Then I was left to the mercy of his lady clerks, but they were also good teachers. They taught me to cook burgers and other food items on the grill. After two days of working at the lunch counter, I decided I was not only a capable fry cook, but a person who could easily become a top grade chef.

A week after starting, I wasn't worth as much as I thought, but figured I was grading a strong "B." I'd learned to work at the counter, talk with customers and also take phone orders at the same time. I had also learned to pass the time of day with one customer and keep from trashing whatever I was cooking for another. In addition, I had figured out how to reassure buyers in other parts of the store that I hadn't forgotten them while I finished a malt, a sundae or created one of Cannon's great toasted pimento cheese sandwiches, which was always garnished with an olive and a handful of chips. Best of all, the cash register and I had learned to live with each other, and if asked, I would have said things couldn't get much better.

Within three weeks I had learned to arrange supplies so I didn't run out at critical times. I had also learned exactly when to pop into the back stockroom and re-energize or change out the carbonation bottle before our Cokes and Dr. Peppers lost their fizz. I also knew what the regular customers wanted without them ordering it and had made an entire group of new friends. As a bonus, I was able to spend quality time talking with other friends when business was slack. Even better than that, I had cemented relationships with several cute girls from across the river by putting an extra olive on their pimento cheese sandwich or dropping an extra Maraschino Cherry on their chocolate sundaes.

I proudly learned to communicate in soda skeet language such as calling chocolate milk with a scoop of vanilla ice cream a "baby doll" and occasionally taught this language to chosen friends when they were polite.

One of the "perks" of my new job was free food. Mr. Cannon said I could mix myself a malt or sundae during each shift, along with a free burger or sandwich. To me, this was as good as good could get. After a month, I finally decided that even selling Kotex was better than picking trash out of floor sweep at the five and dime and wouldn't have swapped my job for any other.

Later, when hot summer arrived, there were days when the outside world was too busy to stop working and visit in Cannon's. On those days I had little or nothing to do and was happy to talk with a new friend, Mitch, who had started dropping in almost every day.

Mitch was a Kiowa Indian, aged 21, who worked most of the time in the oil fields as a pipeliner, roughneck or roustabout. Whenever he needed money, he would hire out for any oil company which was hiring roustabouts, pipeliners or roughnecks at the time. He didn't care who the company was or what kind of work they had, he was good at any of it. When he had plenty of money he would quit and stay with his parents across the river in Oklahoma.

Mitch was "between jobs", he said, the first time I saw him. Then he sat down and ordered a lemon Coke. He wore khakis and a "hard hat" half the time, and a Western hat, jeans and boots the rest of the time. Unlike most Indians, he wore his hair cut short, with no braids.

I liked him because he treated me as an equal. He said his father was a real Indian chief who no longer lived on the reservation. His grandfather had been a "wild" Indian but was not a chief. Mitch's dad had been made chief by tribal ceremony and still performed those duties, even after moving his family off the reservation. Mitch had been small when they left. The only explanation his father gave for leaving was he saw no future in being a "blanket" Indian.

Mitch was several years older than my group but there were no Indians of his age in town to hang out with. So he visited with us in Burk and we enjoyed his company. If any kind of discrimination had ever bothered him, he never mentioned it. He was of medium height and well-muscled but not heavy. He could move quick as a cat when he wanted and it always impressed me when he reached out to grab a passing fly from the air with his fingers. Mitch always smiled and was easygoing, but no one treated him lightly. Something about him warned them it wouldn't be safe.

He was the only Indian I ever knew who whistled songs. Other Indians could whistle anything they wanted to and imitated bird calls better than we did. They also whistled at running rabbits to make them stop and stand up to look behind them, but they never whistled real music.

Mitch was different. He whistled all the latest tunes when walking Burk's sidewalks and didn't care if it was in daytime or night. He liked modern songs but also lustily whistled classical pieces he had heard on the radio or memorized from movies. I thought he performed "Flight of the Bumble Bee" as well as a 10-piece orchestra.

I never met Mitch's father but knew he was an unusual Indian. For instance, he told Mitch that their family would be cheated out of their fair share of America if they stayed on the reservation and kept attending "Government Schools." He felt an Indian should work hard, just like other Americans, so he could be proud of himself and "hold up his head." He had tried to enlist in the army the day after Pearl Harbor but was turned down because he was too old. This irritated him a lot because they had said he was too young to fight in World War I.

Mitch respected his father and agreed with him on most things. He figured his dad was earning a better living than their reservation relatives enjoyed, but he thought reservation Indians had more fun. He had learned enough in white schools to know that his relatives believed a large amount of superstition, but agreed with his father that this didn't make them bad people. They were simply people with wrong opinions. His father insisted that a correct opinion was more important than anything else. We talked a while about this and decided that maybe girls were more important, but we had to agree with his father that a right opinion beat a wrong one any way you wanted to look at it.

Mitch didn't agree with his dad about the war. He thought this was a white man's war instead of an Indian fight, and he had the Indian's pure love of running free. He was back home at the time because he had plenty of money "right now". He had quit his job to visit with cousins on the reservation. They planned to travel up into the Arkansas mountains to visit some relatives, also to explore some places they hadn't seen lately.

This sounded like a fun trip to me and, boylike, I told him I'd like to go. He said to round up twenty bucks and come on. Then I remembered that I needed to hang around and take care of my job. Mitch looked straight into my eyes and smiled as he watched me realize something he had known most of his life. It was that white people were never comfortable when they tried to live or act like Indians.

Oklahoma reservations were only a few miles across the Red River from us and many Indians shopped in Burkburnett. The average Indian man spoke English well enough if he wanted to, but often ignored white people who tried to talk with him. Indians cherished their dignity and talked only with people they trusted and liked. They came across the river to buy groceries or hardware, and I never knew of one to cause an ounce of trouble in Burk. They seldom went to movies or ate in cafes, but they loved rodeos and parades as much as we did. Their sharp eyes missed nothing as they walked along the sidewalks. Mostly they looked straight ahead, focusing on objects a block down the street.

Indian men always entered a store first, seldom speaking, but sometimes nodding at the store manager. They wore tall black hats with straight, unrolled brims. Their hat bands were mostly beaded, but occasionally they were made from braided horse hair. All the men wore long braids, one on each side, with an occasional white-tipped black hat feather. Western shirts, blue jeans, and boots or moccasins finished out their dress. Vests and coats were optional, depending on the weather.

Women followed behind their men, and in hot summer, wrapped up in white sheets instead of blankets. They always wore

braids and a headband. Normally the band was beaded, but,
sometimes it was made of braided fabric or animal fur. Behind them,
in descending order, came the children, normally fairly clean and
properly dressed. They were always quiet and well-behaved.

Once inside a store the man, often called "Chief" by store
clerks, would silently make a right turn and walk to the farthest
wall. Then he would turn left, and walk down the aisle to the rear
of the store. The entire family followed behind him like cars hooked
to a train engine. First the mother, then the oldest child, and on
down to the smallest.

At the rear of the store, the man made a U-turn into the next
aisle and slowly walked back up front. Then he went to the next
aisle, turned toward the rear again, and continued this pattern until
he had covered the entire store, one aisle at a time. The children,
walked behind, looking at and smelling different items but touched
nothing. Occasionally a young one would forget his instruction
and reach for a colorful item but the next older child would slap his
hand away. Those babies never sobbed or cried.

Mitch said the reason those Indians covered every aisle first
was, like us, they seldom had enough money. The man wanted to
see if the store had stocked any new items before spending
anything. He also told me that Indians, when with their own people,
laughed, sang songs and played tricks on each other. They also got
drunk, fought with and sometimes hurt or killed each other just as
whites did. But, when with white people they were too proud to
relax or talk much. He also said young Indian children never sobbed
or cried out when at home, on the reservation, or anywhere else.
He would not talk about the ways that parents trained their children
not to cry.

I saw a lot of Mitch during the next few weeks because his
Arkansas trip didn't work out. But he wasn't upset, they would
take it later. I liked him better all the time because he was one
Indian who would tell me almost anything I wanted to know about
Indian life, including his knife fights, gunshot injuries and his love
life. He had physical scars to back up those fight stories and the love
stories sounded real enough that I figured they were true.

Mostly though, I liked him because he was an Indian who acted more like a white person than an Indian. My friends liked him too and some of the girls tried getting better acquainted with him but he paid them no attention. When I asked why, he said that Indian men and white women, mixed together, were "bad medicine". He wouldn't talk further about that either.

We talked about the war and Mitch told me the main reason he didn't enlist was he had a tremendous fear that he would die or be killed in this "white man's war." He didn't call it a premonition. He said it was "an Indian feeling" that he would never see home again if he joined up. His father had agreed that the feeling could be true.

He wanted to know if I thought he was wrong for moving his draft registration from Texas to Oklahoma and back to Texas again whenever the draft boards called him in to take a physical. I finally decided it was right for him because ours was not an Indian war.

Most whites, I told him, would not think poorly of him for dodging the draft because he was an Indian. But, if he were white, they would call him a coward and a "draft dodger." Everyone I knew had strong patriotic feelings and so did Mitch. He told me if he heard anyone speaking badly against America's war effort, he would make them either fight or run, whichever suited them best. Months later, when silence was no longer necessary, I told Mitch's story to several US veterans, including one who had been a German prisoner of war. None of them blamed him.

Between the summer heat, working hard and trying to solve my love problems, I didn't miss Mitch a lot when he stopped coming by. My problems were big because they involved two rhyming words, "romance" and "finance". Both were becoming scarce at the time. The dime an hour raise Mr. Cannon had recently given me wasn't doing the job. Though I could only afford one, I had foolishly accumulated an extra "hot" date. Trouble immediately arose because, even though my finances were limited, I couldn't decide which girl to keep.

Summer moved toward fall with no change. School was beginning, and instead of saving money during the fat months, I went back to school flat broke. But one of the problems was solved. I didn't have to cut off either cutie. Each one resolved this problem with her own shears. While I was throwing money to the winds, each had managed to ignore the other. But, when the well ran dry and I was no longer broke but deeply in debt, neither of those sweet cuties gave me a nickel's worth of credit for past performance. Each griped constantly about the other and a "Blue Texas Norther" swept into Camelot.

One afternoon between customers, I took advantage of some slack time to clean up our back bar mirror. This had to be done once a week. In getting ready, I heated a pot of water, bringing it to a slow simmer, and was swabbing off the heavy plate glass mirror, as well as the glass shelves which held our Coke glasses. Also included in the cleanup were our three electric malt mixers with their tall metal cups. To do this job properly I needed 20 minutes of uninterrupted time and was hurrying so I could finish before more customers came in.

While working, I pleasured myself by wallowing in self-pity over my ridiculous love life and was drying off the last mixer when I looked into the mirror and saw that Mitch had slipped noiselessly inside. He sat alone at the counter, glumly staring at, but not seeing me. His fists propped his chin and he was the most pitiful looking Indian I ever saw. I decided some of his relatives had died.

You could normally hear this guy whistling for 50 feet before he hit the front door, but he hadn't made a cheep that day. I asked if he was okay but he ignored my question. He also waved off my offer of his customary lemon Coke, and said he didn't want to talk. Even though I was young and immature, I wasn't stupid. If he sat there long enough he was going to have to tell somebody what was wrong and sooner would be better. So I fixed him a tall lemon Coke anyway. Sliding it over in front of his stool, I went back to work. He waited until I was almost through before speaking. "Well, it's all over," he announced, "I just came in to say goodbye."

I moved closer to listen. After several sips and some more dark reflection, Mitch began telling me that the thing he'd always dreaded had finally happened. The Texas and Oklahoma draft boards had pooled their information and caught him red-handed.

Each board had labeled him a draft dodger and both had sent him registered letters saying that criminal action would be taken unless he reported next Wednesday for an army physical in whichever state he wished. It could be either Wichita Falls or Lawton, they didn't care but each letter advised that he should bring a packed bag because they were certain he would pass his physical and would be in the United States Army in less than a week. Mitch's physical was scheduled for the next day in Lawton.

I mixed a vanilla Coke for myself, and we sipped together, finally deciding that the draft boards had a right to be mad. After all, their dignities had been flaunted and they could have jailed him if they wished. We'd seen it happen before. Still, to a freedom loving Indian, the army was only a little better than prison.

I suggested he try to get sent to the Navy rather than the Army, but he ruled that out. He told me he could run or walk a long way if he had to but he had no idea at all how far he could swim. He felt a lot more comfortable at handling troubles that happened on dirt.

We visited a few minutes longer before he rose to leave. He needed to be home early, he said, because his best girl was coming over for dinner. We shook hands, and I told him the lemon Coke was on me. He thanked me and promised to send a letter, but I felt that this would be a little too much like a white man, even for Mitch. When I said I would see him later, he didn't answer. He looked into my eyes and nodded.

Neither of us mentioned his "Indian feeling" but both of us thought about it as he moved toward the door. He didn't swagger or whistle while walking and he never sent a letter. I didn't blame Mitch for being scared. We both had relatives and friends who had been killed in this war and we knew it was no game. It was deadly serious and its real name was death.

A few weeks later, at 11:00 on a bright November morning, I drove my father's 1937 Nash 4-door over the Red River bridge into Oklahoma. It was three days before Thanksgiving and no Texas farmers near Burk were selling turkeys that year. Most of America's turkeys had already been bought by the government and sent overseas for our servicemen's Thanksgiving dinners. Dad had heard about one Oklahoma farmer selling turkeys and sent me to buy one.

After passing Randlett, I turned onto an old-style Oklahoma red-gravel road. Those roads made scads of 90 degree turns because farmers and ranchers objected when roads cut across their land. County Commissioners back then built as much road going around property lines as through them because farmers often gave them free right-of-way if they went around. If they cut through a ranch or farm that didn't want the road, the landowners would go to court and the government always lost. Many of those 90-degree turns were straightened out by strangers driving through after sundown. A sizable number of late-driving, hard-drinking locals also ripped up their share of barbed wire fencing after late Saturday night parties.

I had just rounded a hard 90 degree turn where the road followed a property-dividing gully for about a mile. Just as I straightened out, I saw something moving near the gully, on my left, half a mile ahead. At first I thought it was a cow, but it was taller, and after watching I could see it was a person wearing a brown jacket. Finally, a man climbed out of that gully. He walked to the fence, laid a gun over the top wire and straddled over. Laying the weapon down, he turned and began pulling something through the fence. It hung up often and he frequently bent over to free it up.

Interested, I slowed down to see what he was pulling, and just as I was even with the guy, he finished pulling it through and turned toward me. Even though he had on a cap, I recognized the flash of Mitch's smile when he saw me. Without thinking further, I shut off the motor, and as country folks often did back then, left dad's car in the middle of the road while stepping out to talk.

Most guys either lost or gained weight when they went in the Army, and they always came back home for the first time with shaved heads, but Mitch's weight looked the same. He had never worn long Indian hair, so, because of the cap, I saw little change in his looks. Each of us grinned big and we were happy as a pair of puppies to see each other again, but we formally shook hands. In those days girls and women could hug and squeeze each other but not men. After saying our howdies we hunkered down on our heels, unconsciously adopting the habit of Plainsmen and Indians for centuries past and began catching up on each other's news.

As Mitch talked about his stint in the Army, I looked at the rifle which lay on the ground by the fence. It was a pitifully used up single-shot .22 caliber. Its stock had been repaired with rawhide, and there was no rear sight. It was rusted all over and you had to look closely to see it had once been a Winchester. Then I saw a big pile of rabbits lying where he had pulled them through the fence and guessed he had killed about 40.

Mitch stopped talking about his experiences and wanted to know what was happening on the home front. It took me less than five minutes to bring him up to date on my new job at Riley's machine shop. I also told him that, despite having money once again, my luck with girls was still pretty sad.

He nodded sympathetically, wished me luck and stood up, saying he needed to head for the house so the women could start preparing his rabbits. I asked why he had killed so many, and he said they were having a "stomp dance" at the reservation that night and he was furnishing some meat. A local rancher, he added, was furnishing a cow but he grinned when he said it. I knew that rancher's reputation and both of us knew he would die before giving a cow to the Indians, but the tribe was eating barbecue that night anyway.

Mitch was staying with a cousin three miles up the road and my offer of a ride sat well with him. By the time I arranged a pair of tow sacks on the trunk floor to soak up any loose blood, he had dragged his rabbits near enough that I only had to stoop over and help him boost them in. He had taken several rusty hanks of baling wire, and after shooting each animal, had wrapped a wire loop round its hind legs, then added each new rabbit to the string, and pulled them along behind as he crossed the fields. This was what I had seen him pulling through the fence and he admitted they were heavy. I figured he had shot at least 60 pounds of rabbits, dead weight, and most had been struck in the head.

After we turned onto the road and headed toward his cousin's house, I complimented Mitch on his marksmanship, saying I figured he had shot at least 40. He told me there were 46 and he would have killed more but he had run out of ammunition. He'd taken only one box of shells with him. Each small box held 50 cartridges and I figured that shooting 46 rabbits with fifty shells was great shooting. But Mitch said he should have shot 48. He had missed two. One of his small cousins had shot twice at a chicken hawk, and only 48 shells were in the box when he started his rabbit hunt.

Mitch figured any good shot could have done as well, but I glanced at his pitiful rifle and shook my head. I wasn't a bad shot myself, but If anyone had told me this story, I wouldn't have believed them. I couldn't have shot that well, even with my own gun.

As we neared his cousin's house I asked Mitch how long he would be on leave and he said he wasn't going back. This alarmed me. I thought he might have run away from the Army, but he insisted that they had given him a medical discharge. I asked what was wrong and he said the Army doctors had told him his eyes were too bad.

He didn't know why they figured that and added that he didn't care. He knew he was color-blind, and that might have had something to do with it, but he also knew he couldn't hit anything with the weird M-1 rifle they had given him to shoot. The way they made him hold it, wrapping up his arm in that silly sling, he couldn't even hit a barn at 20 feet and didn't try very hard.

All he knew for certain was, a day or two after he had shot that big rifle, they called him to the administration tent and gave him a medical discharge, a hundred dollars in cash and a bus ticket home. Then he flashed his big smile and said his father had advised him to always obey orders in the Army, so he left in less than 30 minutes, before they had a chance to change their minds.

As I backed out onto the road, I heard him whistling "Flight of the Bumble Bee" and, in the rear view mirror I saw him dragging his rabbits toward the house and motion to an older woman to take over his kill. Several weeks later I heard that he had married his fiancee and that they had moved over near Anadarko.

If I had known then what I know today I would have driven over to visit, but I didn't. Like many young people, I put off way too many things which I should have done, always telling myself I would do them later. Because of this poor habit, I never visited and haven't seen Mitch since the day he shot those 46 rabbits.

CHAPTER 27

NOLY—1943

SWEATING A LITTLE because it was hard work, I was pushing a wheelbarrow load of metal shavings out back and passing just behind Boss's perch along the front of his long-bedded heavy-framed metal lathe. Boss was about my height but he weighed a solid two hundred and thirty pounds and there wasn't an ounce of fat on him. He was just strong. Very strong. Boss was bent over, carefully chucking-up a steel cylinder casting which weighed ninety pounds and which, when finished, would power a 40-horse power Marion oilfield compressor. I would have bet anybody that he had no idea I was near but would have lost.

"Wait up, Kid," he said, when I was exactly one step from his back. Boss was always serious and seldom joked with me. I stopped, watching closely as he turned to face me and made a mental note to remember that this guy had eyes in back of his head.

Looking carefully to see whether he had my attention, he said, "Noly's down in his back and needs somebody to drive him and his truck to East Texas this Friday so he can deliver a rebuilt pump to his customer." Keeping his eyes on mine to insure communication, he went on, "Ask your folks tonight if they mind you usin' your brand-new Texas Commercial Drivin' License to help Noly out." I said I would, and picked up the wheelbarrow handles again, but he wasn't finished.

"This okay with you?", he questioned, eyes holding fast to mine, wanting to read my thoughts.

"Yes, Sir," I answered, looking back and grinning, "In fact, I'd enjoy a trip."

"All right," he said, watching me seriously. Then his mouth
widened into a half-hearted smile. "Cain't say I blame you."
Glancing at his lathe, he became a real person to me when he
explained further, "I'd like to get out of here early Friday myself,
but I've got to deliver this cylinder, rings and all, along with four
others just like it, next Monday morning at 8:00. To make that
happen, I have to work most of Sunday before finishing up."

Then Boss turned back to his lathe to pass a large tong-like pair
of machinist's calipers from one end of his cylinder casting to the
other, and making small adjustments at the lathe's tool holder,
preparing for his first cut. The first cut, I had learned, was always
fast and always rough. "Chatter marks" didn't matter because the
main purpose of a first cut was to even out most of the casting
irregularities and trim off the rust so that the piston could be
properly rounded off on the lathe.

"Go on," Boss instructed, without looking back, "Enjoy the
trip if you can." And it surprised me that he would consider whether
I might or might not enjoy any part of my job.

Everybody in town called him "Noly", and with his wife and
two children, he lived two blocks from my house. Like most of the
adults I knew, Noly had followed the 1916 oil boom into Burk,
arriving there 10 or 12 years before I was born. He was no taller
than me and didn't weigh as much but he could move quick as a cat
when he had to and folks said he would "fight a circle-saw" and
probably win. But during the time I knew him, I never heard of him
fighting any circle saws, or people either.

Because of a meager education and a bad back, Noly lived by his
wits and fed his family pretty well by using his quick mind, an ever-
acid tongue and a stout Dodge one-ton pickup truck. He called
himself a "trader" but trading didn't set very well with many people
as a proper vocation back then and some folks, behind his back, also
called him an "iron rustler" along with other less complimentary
names.

About half the time, I was in love with Noly's daughter and
hung around their house a lot whenever she was in a good humor
with me. Noly and I understood each other to the extent that I

listened to most of his stories and laughed at his jokes, even though
the stories weren't always believable or the jokes funny. His part of
our deal was that he didn't run me off unless I really got to be a pain
in the neck. Occasionally he listened to my troubles when other
grownups wouldn't and I was grateful for that. Most adults back
then spent more time yelling and quieting boys down than worrying
about their problems.

In 1943, Noly was earning a better than average living for his
family by scouting around the country and buying up or trading for
worn out, broken and junked out oilfield machinery. Whenever
he bought something good enough to repair, he brought it to my
boss. The shop would completely rebuild whatever it was, then
polish and paint it until it looked brand-new. Boss and Noly had
also stored a large quantity of junk iron, too badly broken to repair,
in the shop's open yard right next to one of Boley Pilkerton's oil
wells. Anyone who needed spare parts would cull through the junk
and, if they found something they needed, would pay Boss and
Noly sky-high prices to own it.

In December of 1941, right after Pearl Harbor, all newly milled
iron and steel was quickly channeled into war production. For the
past 10 years Japan had been buying most of America's scrap iron
and steel. But when they began to shoot it back at us, the
government suddenly wanted everyone to donate all the scrap iron
they could for re-smelting. Boss didn't donate. He stored all he
could on his lot because he was no longer able to buy iron and steel
for shop use. Even when he found some, he had to wait weeks,
even months for the War Production Board to approve a purchase.

Because that junkyard was ugly, Boss and Noly would be called
environmental contaminators today. But in those days, people who
lived in dying mining towns, whether of gold, silver or oil, were
more interested in making a living and winning the worst war in
America's history than in making the town look pretty. Besides,
anybody with one eye and a lick of sense already knew that North
Texas had been overlooked when God and his helpers ladled out
countryside beauty. There wasn't much about scrap iron, or any
other junk, which would seriously damage our town's appearance.

Gossipers hinted that maybe Noly didn't always pay for the stuff he picked up and hauled off to be sold. I didn't know, but I figured they were wrong. I felt he had to be honest because the town only had about 4,000 people and everyone would have known it if he was arrested, but he never was. So, for a period of several years Boss's shop had been rebuilding Noly's machines, getting them ready to sell. Noly had located many customers and hauled those rebuilt machines up into Oklahoma, down near Houston and back to Kilgore, in the very heart of the giant East Texas field. "Over in East Texas," he told anyone who would listen, "people pay off in cash, not promises."

I worked for Boss after school and on Saturdays as a "cleanup kid". His shop was located near the railroad track on West Main Street and was the same one in which Dad had worked for Mr. P. A. Wiggins when I was small. When Noly came down with that mean, twisting backache he didn't come to me and ask for help. Instead, because I worked for Boss, he asked Boss to talk with me about making the trip with him.

I was a junior in high school, having just turned sixteen. My social life was undeveloped at the time, so I didn't feel deprived when Boss asked me to drive Noly. In fact, I was proud. I liked the idea that they would trust me to drive and was also happy to see East Texas. I'd only been there once before and barely remembered it. But I recalled 80-foot pine trees and wide, heavily-watered rivers plus many lakes and streams and more green color than a North Texas kid ever knew existed. Most of the wild greenery I had seen in North Texas consisted of tumble weeds, mesquites and salt cedars growing in mostly dry streambeds that we called rivers or around our small stock tanks.

Noly was paying me full wages, 15 cents an hour, which added up to $1.50 for each 10-hour day we were out of town. I liked the wages, remembering that only a short time before, when the war started, grown men wore out their shoes walking around and looking for any kind of work at all. When they found one it was generally hard labor which seldom paid more than $1.25 a day. Sometimes, it paid less than a dollar. And all I had to do this weekend was drive Noly's truck wherever he told me and listen politely when he talked. For that, I would earn $1.50 a day, plus meals. To a kid my age, this was a great deal.

My folks said the trip was OK and Noly picked me up at school on Friday but he never moved out of the driver's seat. I was disappointed because a few of my buddies, had waited around to watch me drive off. They snickered when I had to walk around and get in on the passenger's side. I watched Noly closely and could see that his back was stiff and hurting. In fact, he swallowed a large-sized metal box of Bayer aspirins every day I was with him, but seldom turned loose of his steering wheel. I finally decided he had only hired me as a last resort driver, in case he dropped in his tracks and couldn't get up. But he insisted that I stay awake all the time and talk with him. And I pumped gas whenever we needed fuel.

Noly had an opinion on everything. All you had to do was ask and you would get it. He also talked compulsively. Looking back, I can remember three of his opinions and four or five of his stories which turned out to be true but, at the time, I had no idea which was which and I'm not certain if he did either. Grown folks in Burk said he was pretty windy.

I already knew he didn't like cowboy boots because his son never stopped complaining that his dad wouldn't let him have a pair. Most Texas boys I knew lived for the time when they could pull a pair on. But, on this trip, Noly talked to me about "reform school" and I learned why he didn't like Western boots.

"Don't ever get sent there," he advised, talking about reform school. "I went there when I was about your age. Healthy or sick, you have to work hard, an' all the guards wear cowboy boots. When I went in I had a smart mouth but they taught me to control it before I left. An' they ruined my back in there, stompin' it with them damn boot heels. I've always admitted to usin' a sometimes spiteful mouth, but I didn't deserve what they gave me."

He stopped talking, and for a moment, I thought he might tell me why he was sent, but he didn't and I knew better than to ask. Instead, he said wonderingly, "You know, I figure a year of miserable time, like I spent in there, can be as long as 15 regular years." Then, thinking longer, he finished softly, speaking only to himself, "I didn't know it then, but do now, if they ruin your back, it's the same as ruinin' your life." Then he gripped the steering wheel hard and looked far out through the windshield, into the night. I didn't answer because I understood that, for once, he wasn't asking for one in order to start an argument.

We arrived in Gladewater just after 11:00 that night and drove straight across town to what Texans used to call a "rooming house". The owner, a widow lady, was about 45 years old, with an attractive, dark-haired daughter. They welcomed us cordially, glad to see us. They also seemed to respect Noly more than Burk folks did, but this didn't concern me one way or the other. I liked him, and decided their attitude simply reflected a difference between the way East Texas and North Texas people valued folks.

These two women sat us down in their dining room, giving me a Coke and him a cup of black coffee. They offered to make us roast beef sandwiches and were even going to carry Noly's bag and my grocery store sack of clothes upstairs to our room but he turned them down, saying we would go out to a cafe for a late supper and would haul our stuff up later.

They told us to use the second upstairs room on the right, then gave us a key to the front door and went off to bed. There were lots of Texans then who thought nine o'clock was way too late for decent working people to be up and about. A lot of them distrusted someone who didn't "go to bed with the chickens", but I wasn't that kind. I figured it was an old-folks attitude and had decided by the age of 10 that most things happening during the day were dull and boring when compared to night-time activity. I was seldom ready to go to bed until absolutely worn out.

Noly must have felt like me about the night. He was happy to sit and eat slowly, talking about anything at all, with me or with local residents who walked by. After we had finished eating he lingered, sipping through several cups of black coffee and didn't stand to leave until they began stacking chairs on the tables to sweep up. We went back to our room at one thirty and I was nominated to carry all the stuff, quietly as possible, up to a neat and clean room furnished with a rocking chair, a dresser and one double bed. I took the half of bed Noly didn't want and we slept comfortably until 6.00. The charge for our room was $3.00. Next morning, after a restaurant breakfast of bacon and eggs, pancakes slathered with real cow butter and lots of ribbon-cane syrup with cups of black coffee, we drove the 15 miles over to Kilgore. Just before we reached his customer's oilfield supply house, Noly pulled off the road and got out. Walking around to the passenger's side, he swapped seats with me. Then he instructed me closely about where to drive and how to back up under a chain hoist so his pump could be easily unloaded. With me pulling the hoist chain and the others supervising, it took only 15 minutes to unload. When we had finished, the buyer asked if we wanted a check or cash. Noly firmly told him, "Cash" and I watched closely as the customer pulled out his billfold and counted $475.00 into Noly's hand.

I had never seen anybody outside a bank hold this much money before. And it fascinated me. The customer asked Noly to count the money back, to be sure it was correct but was assured expansively, "If I can't trust you, I can't trust anybody." Then Noly gave him a healthy slap on the shoulder, folded the bills carelessly, and stuffing them into his shirt pocket, offered to buy coffee for everyone.

Impressed, the customer grinned, then shook his head sideways. "Later", he answered, "I've got a delivery to make." Then, looking at me, he asked why I was driving and listened carefully as Noly described his bad back. While talking, Noly looked over at me once or twice, in warning. Then his customer wanted to know how long it would take us to bring him two more pumps.

"Well," Noly responded, "These things are gettin' harder to find." Then he took a long draw from his cigarette. He held the smoke for a long enough time that it could be called a period of "thoughtful consideration" and exhaled through his nostrils. Flipping the shortened butt carelessly aside, he answered, "I figger six weeks. And, they'll have to cost more, because my expenses are up," he finished, jerking his chin at me. "They'll be at least $50.00 more, anyway."

"Bring me two more. Okay?"

In the year 2003, after making hundreds of sales and trades myself, I am convinced that Noly played that customer better than a Grand Prize winner plays his fish in a modern Bass Tournament. But, even then I suspected him because those junked out pumps were lying around for the taking on half the oil leases up in Burkburnett. Our oil was dwindling and a lot of wells were being shut in. Those old used pumps had little market value above scrap iron price unless Noly and Boss rebuilt them.

"You got 'em," Noly forcefully answered. Then he lifted his hand, flashed an attractive trader's smile, and began reciting his standard departure lines. Catching my eye, he jerked his chin toward the truck, instructing me to jump in and "crank her up."

When I had it running, he shook hands with his buyer, limped slowly around the truck's headlamps and eased carefully into the passenger's seat. After we had pulled 30 feet away, he told me to stop and back up. Then he deftly sunk his salesman's hook deeper into that customer's jaw, absolutely insuring that the order just given us would be readily received.

Soon as we got back to the customer, Noly stuck his head out the window and asked if the man needed those pumps "really bad." The guy nodded his head "yes" and Noly promised to have the first one back within 3 weeks. "I know," he assured him soothingly, "where I can, for sure, buy one pump right now." Then he flashed the guy a high sign and elbowed me hard in the ribs, to drive away.

Three blocks down the street, he pointed to a wide spot and motioned me to pull over and stop. Slowly, but with only a slight limp, he walked around the truck and slid easily under the wheel. Then he pulled that money out of his shirt pocket and counted it carefully before storing it safely in his billfold. With a bright smile he looked in my direction. "My back feels a lot better now." Then he pulled his Dodge onto the road and I never sat in the driver's seat again.

I have learned since then that few people are in a better mood than a trader who has just "cut a hog". Noly was no exception. His face had brightened considerably and he announced that he was ready to give me a brief tour of the biggest oil field in the world. "Out here," he declared forcefully, "Money grows on trees."

From what I could see, East Texas was truly having a big boom. Drilling rigs were running all around Kilgore, Greggton, New London and Overton, also over toward Longview. Thousands of pumping oil wells were scattered everywhere and there were hundreds of rigs boring for oil. And there were no groups of men sitting around talking about finding jobs as we had seen up in North Texas. When we passed through Kilgore, I saw wells pumping on many city lots. I also saw two in a school yard and one at a church. This sort of thing had also happened in our Burkburnett boom, thirty years before.

Noly's tour carried us back the long way to Gladewater across a large river which was not anywhere as wide as Red River but it had 50 times as much clear green water flowing through its beautiful deep bore. Noly said it was called the Sabine and pointed a half mile further South to a spot where the water widened and cypress knees stuck up along the shore. That spot, he testified, was Sabine Pass where Dick Dowling, an Irish bartender, had collected a group of countrymen from the neighborhood around his bar and defeated the entire Yankee Navy during America's Civil War.

I loved history and was impressed. But it was ten more years before I learned that Sabine pass lay a few miles below Port Arthur, Texas nearly 125 miles downstream from Gladewater. But Noly could have known the truth all along and just moved the battle site up toward Gladewater for my benefit.

I was almost 60 before learning that Captain Dowling was, in fact, an Irish bar owner from Houston, who did not defeat the entire US Navy, but did repel every ship they dared to sail against him. His makeshift group of confederate irregulars were mostly Irish laborers from Houston, most of whom were customers at his bar. Captain Dowling's bones are interred under a handsome life-size statue of him in a cemetery on the Southeast side of Houston.

For the remainder of that day Noly drove us throughout the East Texas Oilfield. He made sales pitches at every supply house or machine shop we passed, and he picked up one order for a re-built cross-head slide steam pump plus another for the kind of pump we had just delivered. Business was improving. To celebrate, Noly carried the landladies and me to a movie that night. He also treated us to popcorn and Cokes.

Up to now, I have neglected to mention that, by the time I was sixteen, I was as large as many grown men and people said I looked old for my age. Anyway, when we came out of the movie, four lonesome young soldiers were standing out on the street, under the Marquee. One of them, appreciating real beauty when he saw it, directed a long wolf whistle at our landlady's daughter.

This girl was two years older than me, and probably because her mother was present, tossed her head saucily, stuck her nose in the air and ignored him. Grabbing my arm, she leaned heavily against me, talking with animation, as we continued on down the sidewalk toward Noly's pickup. Everyone hates rejection, and this GI was no exception. Electing to protest, he committed a drastic error.

"Go on ahead, lady," he shouted at the girl. "Ignore a good man who fights for his country and is broke, then make love to a "Four-F" draft dodger!"

Noly, sore back and all, moved so fast that the action was blurred. He'd been 10 feet away when the soldier spoke but covered the entire distance in two steps. Because of height furnished by the curb, he was nose to nose with the guy by the time he had finished his complaint.

"Who do you think you are, loud mouth?", Noly yelled directly into his face.

"You may be a fighter but I'm not convinced. I don't see any ribbons or purple hearts on your shirt. What I do see is a bully who picks on women and young boys. This is a nice young girl here, no streetwalker, and that is her mother right there. And this boy is only sixteen, a junior in high school, and, frankly, I think he can stomp your butt. But, If you want to fight somebody, just pick on me because I'm right here." Then, eyes boring hard and breathing hard, he stuck his nose right against the soldier's face, causing him to pull backward.

Stupefied, the youngster mumbled an apology and trotted off, trying to catch his buddies who had started off before Noly was half finished with his yelling. From then on I respected Noly, even more than those Gladewater ladies did. And I never failed to assure people that I liked him anytime they passed a bad remark about him.

By 8:00 on Sunday morning Noly and I were headed North, out of East Texas, back toward Fort Worth. We stopped in "Cowtown" for dinner and he called the owner of a big machine shop trying, he said, to drum up some more business. We reached Burk at five that evening and, as I pulled my sack out of the truck, Noly asked how much I made at the shop when working three eight hour days. I told him and he paid me. Then he thanked me for coming and drove on home.

Next afternoon, when I came to work after school, Boss was waiting. Shutting down his lathe when he saw me, he told me to follow him up to his office for a talk. After closing the door he asked, "How was your trip, Kid?" I said it was good.

He moved straight to his subject. "How much did Noly pay you?" I told him and Boss snorted. "I hoped he wouldn't be that tight, but suspected it. You were gone over 50 hours and are entitled to more money."

Reaching into his billfold, Boss handed me a 10 dollar bill. "I charged him this when we split out the money. Go ahead and take it. You gave up a full week end and you earned it."

"Actually," he continued, saying something that told me more than he knew, "Noly and I got paid $425.00 for that last pump and we cleared over $150.00 apiece." Then he thought a minute and said somewhat wistfully, "I can't exactly check Noly out on this deal because that guy in Kilgore insists on paying in cash rather than by check, but anyway, I made Noly treat you right." Then he opened the door and sent me back to work.

A week later Boss waited for me again. This time he was angry. "Come on up to the office, Kid, we need to talk some more." I followed along behind, wondering at every step what sort of sin I had committed.

"Now, Kid," Boss said, "You can see I'm mad, but I'm not mad at you. What we're going to talk about is just between you and me an' nobody else is to know about it. And, one more thing. You work for me. If you don't tell me the truth, I'll have to fire you. Understand?" Wordlessly, I nodded my head up and down. "All right", he finished, never breaking eye contact with me. Finally satisfied, he nodded his head in satisfaction.

Then Boss began to ask about the prices Noly had paid for things on our trip. These questions were hard for me to answer because I knew that when Noly told boss he received $425.00 instead $475.00 for the pump, that he was holding back on his split-out with Boss. I sympathized with Noly, but not with his stealing. My parents had always told me not to lie and to always tell the truth. Now, just a kid, I had been caught up in an argument between grownups and wasn't sure just what I should do. I decided that telling the truth, as I'd been taught, was the way to go, but I hated getting Noly in trouble.

Whatever Boss asked, I answered. I told him our room rent was $3.00 a night and that gas was 19 cents a gallon almost every place we bought it. I also said I'd never ordered an expensive steak, but had eaten a chicken-fried special at one meal and it had cost seventy cents. Boss said Noly had turned in higher figures for some of these things and when he had finished he looked seriously at me again. "You sure you're telling me the truth, Kid?" Miserably, I nodded my head "yes" and looked away.

Boss never cursed, but he suddenly growled, "Dang that Noly, I'd ought to kick his butt, but I'm not—I'm just goin to run him off. I won't tolerate a man who won't 'divvy-up' square."

Then he said he had caught onto Noly because the Oil Well supply man from Gladewater had called him that morning. That buyer said he needed one more pump, but thought, if he ordered three that he ought to get the old price of $475.00. By saying this he spilled the beans on Noly's scam.

Boss said he wouldn't mention anything to Noly about talking with me and admonished me again not to tell anyone else. I promised and he sent me back to work. Keeping my promise, I kept my secret from then until now when it can no longer matter. Both men have been dead for years.

At 4:30 that afternoon Noly slid his Dodge pickup up in front of Boss's office and hopped out. I worked from a spot where I could watch, and five minutes later, I saw him walk rapidly out and jump back in. Zipping away, his Dodge only hit the high spots as he drove East on Main. He was mad.

On my way home that afternoon, I hoped Noly would be gone because I had to walk right by his house, but it wasn't my day. Half a block before getting there I saw him standing out on his driveway, washing down his pickup with a garden hose. I felt guilty because of telling Boss correct answers to the questions he had asked, even though I had no choice. Now, since Noly had no job, his family, taking my girl with them, would probably have to move out of town.

Kidlike, I had convinced myself that all this trouble was my fault. Noly, I figured, would know that I had told on him, even though I was certain Boss wouldn't tell him. If he did guess I figured he now regretted that he had taken up for me against that soldier and wouldn't allow me to visit his daughter any more even if they stayed in Burk. I slowed down some but kept my path toward his house because there was no choice. I could walk around the block and avoid meeting him today, but we lived in a small town and would meet sometime. Besides, I had already learned that running seldom helped.

When Noly doubled up the end of his hose and walked over to shut off the water faucet, I knew he'd seen me coming. Apprehension grew as I watched him drop the hose and walk out to the sidewalk where he waited, arms across chest, looking straight at me. He didn't look happy.

"Well, Kid," he greeted, lips stretched into a tight, dry grin, "You won't be seeing me around the shop anymore. Boss and I have split our blanket." Then he moved straight into the subject that I didn't want to talk about. "Did he ask you about our expenses?" Miserable, I stared at my shoes, not wanting to answer, but finally raised my face, looked him in the eye and nodded my head "yes." Then I quickly looked back toward the sidewalk.

Apparently not caring how I felt, he bored deeper. "Did you tell Boss the truth?" Without looking up, I nodded my head up and down again. Noly threw his head back and laughed, which surprised me. "I figured you would."

"Look up here," he commanded. "You did exactly right. Boys should always tell the truth." Then, when he thought about what he had said, knowing that I knew he had lied to Boss, he finished up: "Well, Traders should always be truthful too, but sometimes they aren't. I lied to Boss because he was holdin' me too close to the edge on our deal."

I was relieved that Noly wasn't mad at me, but still felt guilty. And I had always been ashamed of keeping the $10.00 Boss gave me. To make myself feel better I pulled out my billfold, and jerked the ten out, offering it to him. "Take this", I said, "Boss gave it to me, but it's really yours. You paid me for our deal soon as we got home. Maybe this will help with your move."

Noly took the bill in his hand and studied it carefully. Turning it over, he looked at the other side a moment and handed it back. "No, Kid, you keep this. Boss was right. I should've paid you more."

Then he laughed and said. "Hey! Give me a smile, it won't break your jaw. Nobody is looking at the end of the world here and my family's not movin' anywhere. For over a year I could've had a better deal than Boss gave me with Wilson Supply Company over at Wichita Falls, but they didn't offer me enough difference to change over."

"I've already lined up a new deal with that shop owner over in Fort Worth," he continued, "the one I called on the way back from Gladewater. Remember?" Once more I nodded a reply.

"Well, that feller is takin' only a third, not half of the profits, and he's splittin' expenses right down the middle. Since most everything I sell is in East Texas, or right here in this county, the distance to and from his shop doesn't matter. I make that drive once a week anyway."

I was too relieved to do more than grin and nod, glad not to be feeling guilty any more. I thanked Noly and started on home, but he called me back.

"Now, Kid, if you still have a mind to do something with your $10.00 bill, I'll tell you something."

Seeing that I was giving him full attention, he finished, "Only a few minutes ago I heard my pretty daughter mention that she'd like to see the new movie playing up at the Palace theater next Friday night. I also remember her saying it had been too long since you had taken her anywhere.

"Now don't you be dumb enough to go an' tell her what I've just said. No single girl, or married woman either, likes a man to know what she thinks about him unless she tells him in person." Then he flashed his brilliant trader's smile, "But, I don't see any reason why, if she is going out on Friday night anyway that you shouldn't take her. Leastways, it might as well be you if you think that's a good enough reason to break your $10.00 bill."

BOOMER'S KID—1944

"BACK IN 1922 my dad was walking to work at 11:30 on a dark, dark night. He was working graveyard tour at a gas plant half a mile past downtown Burk. He was two blocks past the street lights and stepping along, fast as he could without falling down, when he heard a moan coming from the ditch over near the fence on his right."

"He stopped to listen but heard nothing else and the situation made him nervous. He would rather have gone on but knew he hadn't imagined that moan so he asked, 'Who's there?' No answer came."

"Edging toward the ditch, he questioned again, 'What's the matter?' A voice answered weakly, 'Help me, I'm hurt'."

"I need to explain here that my dad wasn't walking in the dark because he enjoyed stumbling around. He was doing so because his flashlight batteries had played out three blocks before he reached that voice. He really didn't want to go over to that person on the ground because he could imagine all sorts of things, mostly bad. And it was so black he couldn't see his hand when holding it up against his face. But his conscience was stronger than his fear and he wouldn't leave another human alone in that ditch, maybe to die."

"Mustering his courage, he told the ditch-person to lie quiet, that he was coming over. And when he judged he was close enough, he bent over the spot where he thought the man's head should be and asked what was wrong. But he had held his arms a little behind him as he bent over because he wasn't very sure where the man's head was located."

"How are you hurt?", he asked.

"There was a rustle of movement and a hard, deep voice flatly challenged, 'Give me your money or I'll blow your head off!'"

"Well, dad didn't know for sure if that man had a gun but he sure didn't want anybody to shoot him or knock him in the head, then rob him and leave him alone in that ditch to die and he just happened to be carrying that lunch bucket in his right hand, the strongest.

Soon as the man spoke, dad knew exactly where his head was, and before either of them had time to think about it, he swung, not with the flashlight, because it was on his weaker side, but with that lunch bucket, since it was positioned exactly right. It connected solidly, hitting that robber in the head so hard that lunch flew everywhere. At the same time, dad dropped the bucket, and struck out at a dead run."

"It was a quarter mile on out to the plant but dad never slowed 'til reaching there. There was no shot behind him, so he figured the robber either didn't have a gun, or that he had hit him so hard with the bucket that he couldn't shoot until he was out of range."

"They called for the law to meet them where it had happened and three of them drove over from the plant to meet with the officer, but that high-jacker was long gone. By turning the car a little they focused the head lights around and located his lunch bucket but it was too badly bent to fix. He looked for his food but the only thing left was a small yellow onion.

Dad figured it was good that some hungry guy had robbed him because maybe, after filling up his stomach and doctoring his head, he would re-think the future and pick out an honest business. Maybe one where he was a little luckier. Everybody soon forgot the whole thing, because robberies happened every day in Burk that year. Everyone, that is, except dad. He re-tells the story whenever he thinks about it and it gets longer every time."

A. C. Todd

CHAPTER 28

LINEMAN—1944

FINALLY, THE LAST day arrived. School was out and it was the beginning of my last summer vacation. Next year I would be a senior. I was taller than half the boys in my class, also heavier than some grown men in Burkburnett, Texas. Occasionally day dreams led me to believe I was seven feet tall with a seven-footer's strength and ability, but reality always bounced back within seconds. In fact today, when I should have been feeling great, my ego was as low as it could get.

The problem was, even though I was almost a senior in high school, and liked to think of myself as grown, the truth was, I was only a kid. Maybe I was a little taller than average, but nothing more, nothing less. Not only that, I was a broke kid in whose left front pants pocket rode a single quarter, the only asset standing between me and bankruptcy. I'd been earning my own spending money since I was 11 and ordinarily kept a small amount of money but on the last day of my junior high school year, my total wealth was 25 cents.

Today kids solve this problem by wheedling money out of their doting parents. I would have wheedled too if I could, but it did no good. My parents had little more money than me. Dad had placed me on solid notice that year. Whatever spending money I needed must come from my own labor. "I'm not made of money," he intoned solemnly and added, "Whenever you believe you need to buy something, go find a job and earn what you need."

Dad's action laid down a pattern for my life and helped me to become a self-sufficient adult, but at age 16 my earning patterns were awfully streaky. I'd been looking hard for a summer job but hadn't found one and few things are more pitiful than a lanky teenager with only a quarter to his name.

Still, there was some reason to smile. School was really out. Most of us boys had decided summer would never come. Spring had dragged in late, only two weeks behind an unusually hard, near-Arctic, Texas winter which had cramped our souls so badly that our hearts and bodies begged for outdoor activity long before winter turned loose.

We were sick of books and gymnasium sports because we'd been way too quiet and way too good for way too long. Now we could party—if we had any money to party with. But school was out. We were sure of it because even the teachers and our principal were packing up their stuff.

On the way home I noticed that even the girls were smiling, stepping out as smartly as a group of circus ponies. Patiently, they had followed the rules of confinement all winter long, seeming happy with their shackles, but now I could tell that they had been craving the outdoors almost as much as we boys. Their heads tossed in happy cadence with tripping feet and their eyes flashed excitedly as they talked intently, comparing plans for the summer. Forming into loosely knit groups as we traveled homeward, we realized we were finally free. Intentionally, we slowed our pace, which allowed us more time to enjoy the walk together. Even though almost bankrupt, I could still be happy because summer had finally arrived!

A few boys already had summer jobs but most, like me, were still looking. Half the boys and most of the girls, didn't bother to look. And some of those boys whose parents gave them money whenever they wanted it were still sponging off their folks at age fifty.

In 1944, if boys really wanted jobs, they generally found them. With girls, it was different. Few young ladies found jobs even when really trying. America was still convinced that young girls needed to spend their maidenhood learning to be housewives and mothers. The only jobs which paid them enough to be independent were in defense plants, near large cities. And those jobs were mostly filled by daring girls who had left home before graduating from high school or by young women whose husbands were fighting in the war. The average girl in my class wasn't ready for that kind of life.

Small town girls were limited to clerking jobs in local stores, secretarying or waitressing. Waitress jobs were considered a little worldly for proper girls and weren't highly regarded by strict parents. So because of the way people were back then, most girls stayed home in the summer and tried hard to learn the duties their mothers felt future housewives needed to know. Outstanding girls hoped for college and careers, but most only dreamed of the day when a man would come along. They would know him because he was handsome, very considerate, rode a white steed and would talk seriously to them of love, marriage, children and a home of their own.

America had been fighting World War II for more than three years and people sensed that the spines of Germany and Japan were cracking. We were on the edge of conquering the enemies that pessimists had said were virtually unbeatable when the war started. "It," people would say, meaning the war and nodding meaningfully to one another, "is almost over." And families who had postponed normal vacation activity for years while waiting for the depression to subside and for "our boys" to come home, began planning for a happier future. In the meantime, because most young men were fighting, boys who wanted to work could locate jobs. Some of them were interesting, but the girls were mostly out of luck.

There was the usual amount of skylarking as we moved homeward. Most of the student pranks were harmless, but there was always the usual bonehead who opened his notebook, scattering pages along the road. Juniors and seniors felt themselves a bit advanced for this sort of thing but didn't openly condemn their younger brethren. Sometimes just one kid scattered pages and sometimes a dozen but I can't recall a year when there wasn't at least one.

We were mostly a moral people then, many of us amazingly innocent. Some of the worst sins in my crowd involved smoking and splitting an occasional beer on Friday or Saturday night. We also used "bad" language and often fought each other when we thought we had a good chance to win. But no boy in my class seriously considered maiming a classmate when fighting or committing robbery, burglary or rape.

Sex problems sometimes arose from late night daters hanging out in parked cars, but gasoline was hard to get and, because of war shortages, most boys had trouble finding cars for dates. All boys thought constantly about and some talked a lot about girls. They often lied to each other about what they did or intended to do on dates, but most were actually dreaming. Few of us actually had sex. I would guess that girls were somewhat like boys but none has ever told me whether they lied to one another, amplifying date activity.

Even though young, we were very aware of life's tragedies. America's Great Depression had ushered us into serious times earlier than usual. Then we had war that killed and maimed our loved ones and neighbors in alarming numbers. Yet, we were innocent of drugs and AIDS hadn't even been invented yet. Those unplanned horrors loomed in America's future, 30 years ahead.

World War II still presides as America's most horrible disaster and its death rate was approximated only by that of America's revolt from the British. Those of us who lived through it were molded and stressed by its hideousness. Even now, in a new millennium, we measure all disasters against it.

Many of my classmates stopped at Cannon's drug store to visit a few minutes longer, and to formally toast the arrival of summer over a Coke, malt or a sundae. I decided to save my quarter and turned away, headed North on Avenue C toward home.

I was angry with myself because I'd had a good job in a local dry goods store until three weeks before school was out. It was paying me twenty cents an hour. But I had received the promise of a better-paying job in the summer and had quit the one I had, allowing my future to be decided by a stranger, as my grandfather used to say.

I had saved up 10 dollars and figured it would last long enough to treat me to a short vacation until summer arrived, but that was a mistake. Not only did I run out of money but the summer job fell through. Once again, I was enduring the hateful disgust of poverty that never seemed better. It was always worse, every time it happened.

My friends, intent on celebrating, failed to notice when I left. Once again, I realized how quickly the world ignores people who allow themselves to become financially naked and I felt sorry for myself. With slumped shoulders, I walked toward the future, and if anyone had told me that my financial problems would be solved in two more blocks, right in front of Mr. Brooks' house, I wouldn't have believed them. But it happened.

Mr. Brooks had been my friend and hero ever since a day in fourth grade when I watched him barely elude death from a falling utility pole. He worked for the light company and his house was halfway between our house and town. He always spoke seriously with me, as if I were adult. I admired him greatly and never saw him without remembering the day I stood on the edge of our school ground and watched intently as he and a helper chopped down a rotted-out utility pole.

When the pole fell it leaned unexpectedly toward Mr. Brooks, who tried to move but his feet suddenly tangled in a bundle of loose wire lying on the ground. He fell hard onto the dried clay earth directly underneath that pole and would have been crushed to death except that, at the last possible instant, he twisted his body out of its path. The pole struck ground so heavily, exactly where he had lain, that it made a big noise, bouncing three feet into the air, raising a thick cloud of dust. But he never got a scratch.

Although barely escaping the maw of death, Mr. Brooks was cool as a cucumber and thus became my instant hero. Working with care and saying nothing, he untangled the heavy copper wire from his feet. Then he stood and began slapping the dirt off his clothes with his hat. When he saw me gaping, he grinned and spoke: "Always remember, Kid, a miss is as good as a mile." Then, he flipped a twig off his hat brim, pulled it down tight on his head and nodded to his white-faced helper. Wasting no more time, they returned to their job as if nothing unusual had happened.

Mr. Brooks was standing in his front yard when I got to his house. Today I realize he was waiting for me, but it didn't occur to me then. Without ceremony he asked what kind of job I had for the summer. I said I'd hired out for one that had fallen through and was down to my last quarter. He asked if I would like to be a lineman and when he told me the job paid $1.25 an hour, plus occasional overtime, I fell in love with the idea. Fifty dollars a week was 30 dollars more than anybody had ever estimated I was worth until then. I wasted no time in letting him know I would appreciate having that kind of job.

Mr. Brooks said a friend of his was contracting some pole and line work for a rural electric association, near Jolly, a farm community 10 miles South and a little East of Wichita Falls. His friend, Jim Porch, needed a lineman trainee. I asked Mr. Brooks if he thought I could do that kind of work and he said I could if I didn't mind hard work. The job started on Monday morning at 7:00 but I needed some equipment. He could loan me a pair of climbing hooks, but I also needed a lineman's safety floater belt, and did I have one?

Well, I had no idea what a safety floater belt might be, so he knew I didn't have one. He described it as a wide leather belt that fitted closely about a lineman's waist. It had pouches and loops to hold necessary hand tools but also had a heavy leather safety band which snapped on and off the belt at either end. Both ends of the safety band could be passed around a pole and snapped into a wide ring on the other side, thus anchoring a lineman, even a trainee like me, firmly to the pole on which he worked.

I didn't know if the belt problem could be solved but promised to look for one and get back to him quickly. At home Dad remembered seeing an old lineman's belt hanging on the tool room wall at the Skelly Oil Company gasoline plant where he worked. We drove over and, sure enough, it was still there. Dad asked his boss, Andy Frizzell, about borrowing it and Mr. Frizzell said it would be okay for a while because it was an extra piece of equipment.

Dad's boss was happy to help because everyone back then knew how hard any family's life could be when a wage earner was out of work. America had few welfare programs in 1944 and, even if it had, my family would not have applied. To us, and many old-time

Texans, accepting charity was a disgrace. Most of our neighbors and friends back then would help a person they didn't much like, to locate and keep a job. Our Great Depression was supposed to be over and we had a labor shortage because of the war, but money was still tight and decent people would help each other to find work whenever they could. Mr. Frizzell complimented me for wanting to be a lineman and told me that this type of job, performed properly, would help America finish the war almost as quickly as if I joined the Army.

At 7:00 next Monday morning I stood at the corner of Main and Avenue C in Burk, waiting for a gang truck to pick me up. One hand clutched my borrowed belt and hooks and the other held a brown paper sack lunch. At 7:05 the gang truck arrived and hauled us from Burkburnett, through Wichita Falls, then to Jolly and seven miles off the main highway down a county road. At 10 minutes to eight it dumped us alongside the road. When I looked South I saw a line of shining, freshly creosoted, utility poles, thirty feet tall and it was a long line, stretching off into what seemed like the middle of next week.

Our contractor, boss and foreman was Jim Porch, a short but powerfully built old-style lineman who tolerated no nonsense and wasted little time with teaching. Chewing many tobacco cuds had permanently puffed his right cheek outward, making it look like an abscessed tooth, and he always carried tobacco in his mouth except when on a pole. He later told me he'd quit "chewin' on poles" because he was tired of hiring "grunts" and truck drivers who walked off the job because he accidentally spat down on them once or twice.

Porch asked my name and wrote it down on a pocket pad. Then he told me to help his grunt and the truck driver. I was also instructed to put on my hooks and start climbing poles. He wanted me to learn how to use my hooks and belt so I could start climbing poles after lunch. Then he scampered up a 40-foot anchor pole, and working alone, using only a rig-ax, wire cutters, pliers and a brace and bit, he installed a double cross-arm on its top. He also "braced" it out and attached a set of "standoff" insulators. These, he shouted down, after seeing that I watched, were the kind of things he had hired me to do.

The line of poles ran downroad at this point, headed South. Since it was a new REA (Rural Electrification Agency) line, no power had been turned into it. I'd been worrying about electricity and was glad to hear that the lines were dead.

My morning was spent in fetching, helping and trying to analyze this new business. The truck driver showed me a lot of unusual tools, carefully explaining their names and uses. Between work periods and these lectures, I climbed up on several poles but never more than halfway to the top. I learned a little about using those hooks, which were treacherous. If you were a beginner like me and leaned either knee close to the pole, the hook on that side would kick out and you would "skin" toward the ground. When beginners skinned, they normally fell all the way.

Our poles had been "set in" a day before by the pole crew. Because the sun was hot, fresh Creosote continually wept from the wood, and forming tiny rivulets, oozed groundward. I had worn a light, short-sleeved shirt and my arms had no protection when I skinned a pole so that by noon the insides of both my arms were covered with friction burns. A number of the scratches were deep and overlaid with globs of raw creosote. When I had time, I pulled out the biggest splinters but there were a hundred smaller ones which had to wait until I got home. The front of my shirt was black and had several long rips as did my belly. By lunch time, I was a sorry-looking trainee.

While we ate the truck driver told me that he earned 95 cents an hour, which was 30 cents more than the grunt but also 30 cents less than I was getting. This man had a wife and two children at home and Jim Porch had offered him my job but the guy was afraid to climb poles and turned it down. He was never jealous of me. Instead, he was respectful and did his best to teach me all he could about my job. I have always remembered this kindness.

This was my first introduction to the real grownup world and I was shocked to learn that adults, like kids, could be treated unfairly. There was no question that any sensible person would automatically know that the truck driver was a better employee than me and ought to be worth more money to our boss. But that didn't matter. The company paid me more than him or the grunt because I would climb poles and they wouldn't. They paid more because I risked more. Today, companies call this "accepting responsibility" but it means the same thing.

That truck driver needed every dollar he could take home, but because he couldn't climb, he took home less money than a wet-behind-the-ears school kid. I've never mentioned the man before but I've never stopped being grateful for his help. He deserved more than life was giving him.

After lunch Jim Porch picked up a burlap sack half full of porcelain insulators and looked at my belt to see if I had all the tools I needed. Dropping the sack in his truck bed, he motioned for me to get in. As we drove out toward "end of line", where the poles stopped, he handed me a sack filled with metal cotter keys an inch and a half long.

I needed, he said, to attach a metal bracket to the top of every pole. Then I would screw one of those porcelain insulators onto the bracket. Finally, I was to line up the holes which passed through both the bracket and the insulator base. Then I should insert one of the cotter keys through all those holes, and spread its two legs apart. That locked the insulator onto the bracket. Then I was to climb down, go to the next pole and repeat this operation, working back up the line, until every pole had been "capped".

At end of the line Jim Porch dropped the sack of insulators on the ground and also set out a metal two-gallon "Gott" water can loaded with ice and water. He told me I would find a bracket and bolt at the base of each pole and an extra insulator in my sack "in case one breaks."

"I'm leaving you out here by yourself," he announced, "because you don't need anybody to laugh or snicker if you happen to skin a pole while learning to climb and use the hooks. You also don't need help because this is a one-man job. I'll pick you up at five."

Very nervous, I clutched an insulator and bracket in my left hand, and heard his truck crank up as I started up the first pole. His truck paused and I turned back to see him stick his head out the window. Forcefully, he spat out a big gob of tobacco juice and delivered the longest speech I had heard him make so far.

"You may skin several poles. Ever'body does. When it happens, don't get scared. Just climb right up again. Rest up when you are really tired, but I don't advise much rest at first. It just gives you more time to build up fear."

Spitting again for emphasis, he finished, "Don't leave any pole unless it's finished. I will check all your work for a while which means that I have to climb every pole you do. Climbing poles is hard work at any age an' if I have to climb up and clean up any of your messes after two more days, you'll not be workin' here on day three."

Then, for the first time, he grinned at me and I was surprised that his jaw didn't break. He had noticed how scratched and dirty I was and offered some advice, "You'll find tie strings and short lengths of wire in that insulator bag. If you'll tie the insulators and brackets to your belt and put the bolt in a belt pouch, you can use both hands to climb. Also, you ought to wear a hat and long-sleeved shirt tomorrow. Then he gunned the pickup away, raising a sizable rooster-tail of red Texas road dust floating high behind.

Those tall, black and diabolic poles, besides being covered with splinters and raw creosote tar, had only been dropped into their holes the day before. A little dirt had been shoved in but it wasn't tamped down so, from the time I started up, each pole would roll in its hole and rock from one side to the other, depending on the direction I shifted my body weight. The higher I climbed, the harder they pitched and rolled. And the sad, honest truth was that I felt exactly like that truck driver. I'd never climbed a tree as tall as these poles before because I was afraid of heights myself. Each time one of those cranky things heeled over in its socket, it scared the wadding out of me.

I skinned the first pole three times before reaching its top. Then I climbed it three more times to pick up tools and parts I had dropped. And there was another problem. I hadn't learned yet to lean back into the safety belt and lock my knees while working to give my thigh muscles a rest so, by the time I had finished the first pole, my legs were wobbly. Still, I remembered what Jim Porch told me, and figuring he knew what he was talking about, I jumped right on the next pole. This time, I had better luck. I only skinned it twice before topping it and only climbed down twice for stuff that I dropped.

After resting for ten minutes and swigging from the water can, I started up number three, but had already begun to work smarter. This time I tied three insulators onto my belt so that, if I dropped a couple I wouldn't have to climb down for them. And this pole was only skinned once. I dropped two insulators, but held onto the bracket and didn't have to go down for anything. By then I was griping to myself at whoever had strung those brackets along the bases of the poles. If they had left two on the first pole I could have carried one on to the next and wouldn't have had to climb down again unless I dropped them both.

It took an hour to finish the first three poles but I had learned not to be terrified each time my weight shifted and the pole rolled over with me. By then I had learned to hang loose and roll with the pole instead of grabbing with my knees. This kept me from kicking one or both of the malicious hooks loose, and suddenly I understood. If both hooks stayed in place, beginning linemen didn't skin down that tar-oozing monstrosity.

Two hours later I had finished seven more poles but fatigue had set in. Sun had burned my neck, my face and the outsides of my forearms to a deep beet red. Also, fresh black creosote had absorbed and magnified both sun and heat, allowing it to scorch the blackened inner surfaces of both forearms. It also stabbed through the ripped spots on my shirt each time they gapped open.

I had so many sore spots that I could touch one almost anywhere, and was so tired I could barely walk. I squatted to drink and leaned back against a pole for a few minutes rest then climbed for another hour, finishing six more poles. But, by then, I was moving slowly and jerkily. Carefully descending the last pole of that hour, I had finally finished number 16. I had no watch and was only guessing it was close to 5:00 when I saw the dust trail of Jim Porch's pickup, a mile away, coming toward me. This raised my spirits because I had never been certain whether he might decide I wasn't worth coming back for. Right then, I was awfully sick of that sun-drenched, dried-up rural road in Clay County Texas.

Porch stopped the truck and asked how many poles I had done. I told him sixteen and was proud of myself now that the day was finished. His face didn't change expression but he told me to throw my insulator sack and water cooler in the bed and climb aboard. The gang truck had already left for Wichita Falls and he drove me back to my house in Burk. All during this drive he complained about the power company we worked for. They weren't delivering his materials on time and were trying to niggle him down on his contract fee.

When we arrived at my house, he stopped to let me climb out and told me to get a good night's rest so I would be fresh for next day. I was to meet him downtown again on the same corner. I said I would but was barely able to climb out of the truck and was already considering other jobs because this one seemed a lot tougher than me.

He must have read my mind because after I hit the ground he let off on the foot-feed and stuck his head out the window. Spitting out a tablespoon of juice, he spoke. "Kid, I don't make a habit of bragging on people. Mainly, I guess, because no matter how good I did it, nobody ever bragged much on anything I've ever done. But you did good out there today. I didn't think you would get half as many poles finished as you did. You've learned a lot an', if you hang in a few days, the job gets easier."

"If you keep on like you've started out, you'll make a good hand, and I sure do need one." Looking me straight in the eye, he finished: "I'd appreciate it if you could see your way clear to come back an' work for me in the morning."

Then he was all business again. Pulling back his head, he eased out on the clutch and advised me once more to wear a hat and a heavy shirt with long sleeves. "Sun and splinters," he admonished, "will kill you in this business before electricity or falling."

Waking at 5:15 next morning, I tried three times before finally standing up. It was worse than the second morning of spring football training. Five whole minutes were spent before I could stand up straight. Every one of my muscles, joints and my two or three hundred scrapes, scratches and splinter holes was hurting. A lot. Then, there was my sun and creosote-burned skin. I was running a fever and it was hard to force my stiff and sore fingers to pull on clothes over such an unhappy body. Dragging in to breakfast, I suggested to dad that maybe this job was too tough for a kid my size and I should find something else."

Dad seldom interfered with my business and I bless him for it today but I hated him on that day because he promptly made it plain that he didn't favor me quitting. He also pointed out that I was learning a trade in which a man could earn a good living for his family.

Then he threatened me. I could use my own free judgment, he said, and quit. But if I did, he figured I would have less fun at home than I would working for Jim Porch. And his last words before leaving for work were that a man should always give a new job two weeks. If he couldn't tolerate it after that, he could quit, but only after he had located a replacement.

I had learned at an early age to pay close attention to what dad said. He wasn't always right, but he was always boss in our house and those of us who crossed his path lived with the consequence. After thinking things over, I decided to go to work.

At five minutes to seven I was at the pickup point, carrying my hooks, belt and lunch. Jim Porch was waiting, and I was slightly encouraged because, even though I hadn't thought I could when I left the house, I walked all the way to our meeting place. I also noticed that, the farther I went, the better my body worked. This gave me hope that I might finish the day. At least, I felt more like trying. Opening the pickup door, I climbed in and one happy thought surfaced as we rattled off toward Jolly. If I made it through this day, I would only have to slave eight more before my dad would let me quit.

This thought sustained me until, right in the middle of day six, the second Monday, I realized that I was having fun. Not a lot, but a tad. From that point on my job became a "piece of cake" which made me happy, but the happiness only lasted until Friday. That evening, when Jim Porch handed me my check, I was fired from a job for the second time in my life. And I didn't like it that time any better than I did the first. Jim had never been tactful and he didn't seem a bit disturbed when he gave me the gate.

"Kid, your job here is finished," was what he said.

I opened my mouth to ask what I'd done wrong but he raised a hand to stop me: "It's not you, Kid. You weren't perfect but you did good enough. It's those sidewinders in the REA office. I finally got me a gut full of their crap and have "spotted" my contract. I'm startin' a new job, with a good company. It's with Texaco, In the East Texas Oilfield near Kilgore. I'll be makin' more there than these people will let me make and the oil company will give me a retirement program to boot. If you were older I would carry you with me, because they said I could bring a trainee but I don't figure you are ready to leave home yet, so I'm layin' you off."

Then he told me to help the crew pick up all the loose hand tools and clean up our trash. Those were the last orders I received from him. He said he was stopping at a beer joint on the way home to drink a couple of cold Lone Stars and to celebrate his freedom from our light company and he would buy the truck driver a beer if he wanted one. The grunt and I, since we were under 18, could only drink "pop."

That was my last day as a lineman and I haven't climbed a pole since. Years later, I learned that modern utility companies take a year, sometimes longer, before allowing new employees to climb 30 and 40-foot poles. But Jim Porch was a war-time contractor. He needed a lineman, not a trainee. Neither the Germans or the REA would allow him a year to nurse one.

Because he needed a person who would climb poles, Jim Porch took me and had me fairly well pointed until he blew up and told the electric company to "stuff it." At first I hated his job, not only because it was harder than anything I'd ever done but because I was afraid of it. That evening, because of my Dad's interference in my business and Jim Porch making something out of me that I hadn't been before, I was actually sorry I wouldn't be riding back to Jolly at 7:00 next morning to help him string wire.

CHAPTER 29

THE SWEETHEART—1945

IT WAS A hot Texas night in mid-May, 1945. Early hatched June bugs roved in tireless circles, bumping randomly into the glass safety cowls covering the floor lights on Bell Oil Company's drilling rig. We were driving down well No. 3 and had just finished the first half of a trip by pulling all our drillpipe out of the well.

It took less than five minutes for us to break off, or unscrew, the old worn down Hughes bit and connect a new one tightly on the bottom of the pipestring. Then we started tripping again, running pipe back in the hole. Our driller was mad at the daylight digger and, as always when his bit wasn't cutting downward, was in a foul mood. I called it a "foot-stompin' rush" but H. B. described it better when he said Digger was in a "butt-kickin'" mood. We minded our manners, listening closely and jumping quickly when he shouted our instructions.

I was throwing the sweetheart chain and had just flipped its four loose coils upward, above the pipe connection on top of the string, and jerked them tight. As I flipped them up, Digger goosed the draw works motor. It roared loudly and began winding the other end of the sweetheart chain onto a winch drum. I watched carefully, feeding the muddy chain loosely through my left hand as the four coils spun our new pipe joint down into a tight connection on top of the drillstring.

Digger liked for his pipe joints to "snug up" so tight that the entire string spun round in the iron-jawed slips when the pipe threads locked together. After dusk, sparks flew everywhere when that happened. He liked that too because it assured him that a tight connection had been made. Every oilfield driller knew he would never find work again if he allowed a drillpipe joint to loosen up and back off, dumping half his drillpipe down his well.

The sweetheart chain was connected to a winch on the rig's drawworks engine and we always used it on trips to tighten the drillpipe joints because it did the job very quickly. Using a set of tongs to tighten the joints was much safer but speed was worth more than worker safety to most drillers. Drilling crews called the chain a "sweetheart" for the same reason they sometimes called a tall man "Shorty". It wasn't sweet at all. Roughnecks like H. B. and me hated the thing because it had the nasty habit of nipping off finger joints after spitefully catching and squeezing a chainman's luckless hand against the drillpipe. And that night, we learned it had at least one other bad habit.

Our entire rig was covered with mud and we were dirtier than it was. We could barely stand up on the muddy derrick floor which was made of steel. This was because eight or 10 "wet" joints had been uncoupled when the daylight crew started pulling pipe out of the hole shortly before our crew came out to work. The wet joints sprayed from 50 to 100 gallons of drilling mud in a 40-foot circle and our digger, mad because his crew was having to finish up another crew's trip, wouldn't stop to cleanup until he had a new bit rolling at the bottom of our well.

Besides the trip we shouldn't have been making, the daylight crew had left us with another problem. Somehow or other, they had managed to jerk the sweetheart chain in two, and whoever spliced it back together had left the tail six feet too long. Too late, we found that this made the chain almost impossible to control, and as I started running down the third joint, I felt it running much too fast through my muddy glove.

Increasing its speed, the chain began to snatch and grab at my fingers. When it tried to loop round my thumb, I released it, to keep my hand from being jerked off around the drillpipe. Soon as I did, the chain's long tail whistled rapidly around the pipe string, gathering speed as it went. Our digger hadn't seen what happened and was still sucking it up and this added even more to its speed. It literally whistled as it spun around the drillpipe.

H. B., opposite me, was working 'breakout' tongs and was lucky. He dropped flat and the long tail swished over him. It missed his head but forcefully slapped the brim of his hard hat, sailing the headgear up and off the derrick floor. It landed out in the cow pasture, 30 feet from our rig.

I had no choice. Normally a helpful tool, our sweetheart had become a monster, and though shortening as it neared me, was still gathering speed when it got there. If I moved toward the drill column it could wrap round my body and pull me into the drillpipe, so I backed up, but wasn't as lucky as H. B. The wadded up tail end struck me full in the stomach, hard as a mule's kick and drove me a step backward, knocking out my wind. I didn't lose consciousness, but sank slowly to the derrick floor and barely recall the Digger rolling me over and asking in a worried voice, "Can you breathe, Kid?" I couldn't answer because I had no wind left.

It seemed forever before my paralyzed stomach muscles relaxed enough to let me breathe. When they did, I pulled in so much air and held it so long that I shuddered when exhaling. After a gulp or two, the shimmering waves of darkness and nausea receded but I still had to focus closely to see solid objects through the dozens of dark spots floating around in my field of vision.

Digger told me to lie still and ordered H. B. to "watch me" while he trotted back up to lock the brake and shift the rotary table into motion so our drilling mud wouldn't tighten up and stick his drillpipe in the well. Drillers could get fired for letting that happen, too. Returning, he picked me up, easily as a baby, and carried me down the metal stairs to ground level. Walking out as far as the floor lights reached, he laid me down and began his examination.

Working quickly but gently as a trained nurse, he loosened my belt, freeing my waist. Breathing immediately improved. Then he unbuttoned my shirt, probed around my middle and told me to say when it hurt. After he had probed deeply in my gut and I assured him nothing deep inside was hurting, he rolled me onto my right side and jabbed a work-hardened forefinger up and down my back until I yelled that it only hurt where he was prodding. Then he nodded his head, stuck out both hands and helped ease me up to a sitting position. Watching my eyes carefully to see if I was verging into shock, he began to ask questions and watched my face closely as I answered. Finally, he stopped.

"You scared hell out of me for a minute, Kid. I was afraid that chain had cut you in two but you are lucky. All it did was brand you. Look at your belly," he commanded, his eyes never leaving mine.

Unhappily, I looked down, and through the floating spots, I saw a nine-inch string of blood blisters, each clearly showing on my stomach where a sweetheart link had struck hard enough to print through my heavy khaki shirt. There was also a dollar-sized bruise on the skin over my right hip but my luck still held. The hip bone, which had taken a good lick, was sore as a boil and was swelling rapidly but wasn't broken. The blisters and my hip continued to blacken as I watched, but there was no cut or even a drop of blood to be seen.

Ten minutes later I was standing to sip scalding hot coffee. Ten minutes after that I was back on the floor, flipping the sweetheart and we were running pipe back into the hole. But we worked slower this time so I could control the chain better. We also tied a pair of worn out work gloves on its tail to slow it down in case I had to turn loose again.

After he had reached the bottom and his bit was rolling again, Digger put H. B. and me to swabbing mud while he trimmed the sweetheart's tail to its proper length. He took this opportunity to give the daylight driller a good "long-distance" cussin'. He had decided his competitor was guilty of riding a "wore-out" bit and losing drilling footage because he hadn't wanted to use the poorly repaired chain.

He also figured the daylighter decided to offset his loss of footage by running on a dull bit until almost time for us to show up, so we would lose footage by finishing their trip. By refusing to take out time for repair or cleanup, Digger ended up logging more footage on our shift than the daylighters did on theirs. The chain part hadn't upset him as much as having to finish up the daylighter's trip but it also angered him because it had pushed him into making a bad decision, causing my injury.

When he was through trimming and griping, Digger cautioned us not to mention what he had said to the other crews or anyone else. Drillers, he advised, had their own ways of evening things up with each other, and they were the only ones to decide when and if any getting even was necessary. The job, he admonished, belonged absolutely to him, not to beginning floor hands like us. Then he finished his lecture by warning that loose talk could place him into a position where he might have to hurt the daylighter.

An hour later, H. B. and I had finished using the rig's water pump jet to slice all the mud from our machinery and off the derrick floor. Drillpipe weight was standing smoothly on the bit again and Digger was making a lot of hole, which was his absolute greatest aim. To do this, he had trimmed down so much on the amount of drilling mud he used that we were digging mostly with water and I later found out this was really dangerous.

If the drillbit had struck a pressure pocket, we could have had a blowout. A big blowout normally shoved the drillpipe up and out of a well high enough in the air that it would fold up and separate like wet joints of spaghetti while falling back to the ground. But, by using gouts of water, Digger could drill twice as fast. The guy wasn't Bell's number one No. 1 by accident, and he was protecting his reputation that night. Speed was more important to him than safety.

Happier now than at anytime since we had started our tour, pronounced "tower" in the oilfield, Digger allowed H. B. to ride the brake for a while. He was teaching him how to read the gauge that showed how much weight needed to be placed on the bit to drill the most hole possible and still keep it straight. I stood behind, watching and listening.

Artist Gary Tuttle, Humble, Texas

The three of us slowly sipped from fragrant thermos cups of steaming, black Texas coffee, that almost all oilfield hands used to love with a passion. All, that is, except for Charley, our Indian derrick hand. He never touched it.

The "Chief", had made a good derrickman, Digger said, but he obviously liked his own company better than ours and we seldom knew what he was thinking. When I looked over at him, Chief was squatted on the floor across from us, expressionless, leant back against the mud pump and deep into his own thoughts. He stared at, but probably didn't see, hear or feel the monotonous grind and derrick-rattling motion of the rig's heavy steel rotary table.

Recovered from his storm, Digger tapped H. B.'s arm when he wanted him to increase or decrease weight on the bit. Shouting over the heavy machinery noise, he was telling us another lousy joke, at which we had learned to laugh heartily when he finished. Suddenly, he interrupted himself in mid-sentence. Reaching over, he snatched off H. B.'s hard hat and examined it closely. The rolled edge on its aluminum brim had been flattened and shoved inward a full inch where the chain had smacked it. Digger turned the headgear over in his hand and traced one or two other dents with his thick blunt forefinger. Then he grinned broadly and handed it back.

"Well, Shooter" he told H. B., "you and the Kid ain't there yet, your hats are still too new. But both of you are gainin' a little on being roughnecks."

CHAPTER 30

Signin' Up—1945

H. B. and I had started working in the oilfield two weeks before the night I had my scuffle with the sweetheart, and we had gotten our jobs purely by accident. We'd been hunting for three days with no luck at all, and had dropped in at the Burk Cafe for a late lunch. Temporarily forgetting the job hunt, we were finishing our burgers and fries and had started a good natured competition for attention from their cute, young waitress when I overheard a pair of Continental Supply House salesmen talking about Bell Oil Company. I punched H. B. in the ribs just in time for him to hear them say that Fred Rogers, Bell's local farm boss, was hiring a roughneck crew.

We looked into each other's face and two pairs of eyes assured each another that we were on the same wave length. Waiting no longer, we swallowed our coffee, stood up and laid down two quarters apiece for our meal. Then we said goodbye to that sweet young waitress and walked out. The fact that we didn't leave a tip worried neither her or us. We were nearer her age than most of her customers and she liked us. That made it okay. Besides that, she was making more money than us and the three of us knew it.

H. B. and I had worked around Burkburnett, Texas ever since we had learned that, not many, but a few people had money, and would sometimes pay us to do jobs they didn't like or were unable to perform. Those jobs seldom lasted long, and because we were kids, we were always last to be hired and first to be fired. So, we had developed the habit of keeping our ears open, always listening for news of any job.

For 10 years before World War II began, only half the grownups in Burk had jobs that could be called "permanent." And even after the War began to loosen up our job market, the best a kid in Burk could hope for was to land some sort of job that people called "regular". Most regular jobs were in stores where we worked after school and on Saturdays. Most people didn't work on Sundays back then. They rested and went to church. Sunday workers could normally be boiled down to doctors, preachers druggists and oilfield people.

Regular jobs were certainly the best, but we quickly learned that no job was perfect. Long before we could be called adult, management taught us that we would seldom receive a warning when it planned to lay us off. What it did was wait until the very last minute of the very last day to "let us go" for fear we would loaf until quitting time. At 5:00, or 6:00, whenever the day was finished, management paid us the buck or two we had coming and told us not to come back. H. B. and I considered this to be normal treatment and were seldom upset. But this had taught us never to stop looking for a job, even if we already had a regular job. We worked because we needed money, seldom asking the amount of pay or the kind of work we would do. We took jobs when we could and worried about the details later.

H. B. and I struck out for Bell's office on foot because we had no cars. At the ripe age of "17 goin' on 18," we figured we were way too old to ride bikes. It was early May, 1945, and already hot. World War II would soon be over and to rush the end along, America had placed six million men in uniforms. That month, America was pointing more guns, planes and ships at the Japanese and Germans than the rulers of those countries, even in their worst nightmares, had ever dreamed could be built. That was the kind of world we lived in when H. B. and I graduated from High School. Two weeks later, we were "grabbin' iron" on the floor of an oilfield drilling rig.

We liked riding more than walking but had learned by the age of 10 that walking four or five miles was no real hardship. And because we were young and healthy, it was much easier than many of the problems we learned to tolerate. So we put this hoofing time to good use that afternoon by slinging rocks at fence posts after leaving the city limit. Sometimes cars stopped to pick up walkers but we didn't hang a ride that day. We kept on, "pickin' 'em up and layin' 'em down" until reaching Bell's office 30 minutes later.

Deep down, we knew we were just kids, but we were also full of vinegar and had convinced ourselves that we were as good and as tough as most full-grown men. After all, we were 17, old enough to join the Army if our parents signed the papers. Both of us would register with the draft board soon as we turned 18. Barely out of high school, we were young and sassy, convinced we were Supermen, and the entire world, ready for us to conquer, stretched ahead.

H. B. had been a star basketball player and received more attention than me but most of the adults we dealt with still treated us as they always had, like kids. We were convinced that most people over 30 were fuddy-duddies who had slipped into early senility and were losing their firm grip on life. Grown folks' patronizing attitudes rubbed against our grain and reinforced our opinion that most of them were already over the hill.

As we walked along, each trying to sling rocks farther and straighter than the other, we wondered what oilfield roughnecks really did. Men earned livings for families by working on drilling rigs, and we figured that this kind of job might earn us some respect from the adult world. We had no idea what Bell might pay, but it would certainly be more than anything we earned before.

Most families in Wichita County had relatives working in the oilfield and many still do. H. B. and I figured we'd learned a lot by listening to and watching those seasoned oilfield hands, but like everyone else who only watched the oilfield, we were looking in from the outside and were ignorant. Adopting the supreme confidence God gives to the very young, we visualized that roughnecking was no big deal. Certainly, we guessed, it ought to be just as easy as football practice or Mr. Douglas' physics class. But we guessed wrong.

Arriving at Bell's office, we sat on a bench in the outer lobby until Fred had time to talk with us. When he asked us in, we were surprised to find him as polite as if we were grown men with families. This made a big hit with us because, as I've said, we had only received small doses of adult treatment from the grownups with whom we'd been dealing.

After a tad of re-acquaintance conversation, Fred, who knew us by sight and whose son was two years behind us in school, studied us for a few seconds, then decided he would "try" to use us. This was the oilfield way of saying we had a chance to be hired. But there were conditions. We must promise to stay with the company until it had finished drilling the string of wells it was starting. We also had to promise to "put-out", which, in oilfield language meant "work like the devil."

Finally, Fred warned, we must show up for work not only every day, even on weekends, but a few minutes ahead of "on time." We had no problem in accepting everything he stipulated except that early-arrival business. Getting somewhere before time was a brand-new way of thinking for us.

Then Fred said Bell had decided to start us out at $1.67 an hour, and from that moment on, we promised to do anything he asked. Nobody, nobody ever, either us, our parents or our doting grandparents, had ever dreamed we were worth that kind of serious money until then!

Fred had us fill out an application for the company file. He also told us we must be wearing metal hard hats and a pair of steel-toed safety boots before we could even set one of our feet on their drilling rig floor. But, and he shook a wagging forefinger at us, we weren't hired yet. Our application and talking to him and the hats and shoes were the easy part. The hardest part would be pleasing the "Digger." We had to talk with him, and if he didn't want us, Fred wouldn't hire us.

He finished by saying we should be at Bell's pipeyard next Monday morning at 6:45. We were to be wearing work clothes, hard hats, those safety-toed shoes and carrying a shirt and street pants plus a sack lunch. Then we could talk to the Digger about roughnecking.

Oilfields back then were full of drillers that people called "Digger." It was a term that aptly described their profession, but Bell's driller had adopted "Digger" as his real name and let everybody know it immediately, without waiting for a place to throw it into the conversation. I didn't ask how H. B. felt about him, but he impressed me. A bunch!

Digger was a year or two over 45 and weighed about 195 pounds, but was only 5 feet, 8 inches tall. He was bell-shaped when you looked at him from the front or back and rolled forward when he walked, like a grizzly on its hind legs. But he carried no fat and was very, very strong.

Despite his shape and size, Digger's movement was graceful and he surprised us later by climbing about in the derrick as handily as a monkey. We also learned that he could move with blinding speed when speed was needed. He always wore clean, neatly pressed khakis, occasionally mended, along with a clean, but heavily dented, aluminum, hard hat. And his leather-laced, safety-toed, 8-inch-top Redwing boots were exactly like our new ones.

We arrived at 6:45, as Fred instructed. Nobody was smoking, talking or sitting down. These guys didn't go on the payroll until 7:00 but they were already working busily as a bed of red ants. Digger was actively directing the loading of Bell's new homemade drilling rig onto a large Dart truck so it could be hauled out to the well location and could be "strung up."

When we told him who we were, he motioned us back out of his way. We waited respectfully until he had the truck drivers and their swampers pointed. Then he pulled out and read the time on a big railroad-looking pocket watch with a short leather fob attached to its swivel. Buckled to the fob's outer end was a silver-looking drillbit ornament with the name of Hughes Oil Tool Company stamped on its face. Hughes Tool gave these watch fobs only to seasoned oilfield drillers.

Noting the time, Digger ordered all the truck drivers and crews to follow Bell's No. 2 driller out to the well site and back the rig up to its drilling pad. He would arrive fifteen minutes afterward to supervise its exact placement and start rigging up. Stuffing the watch back into a protected pocket under his wide leather belt, he turned to us, eyed us closely, and spoke without pleasure: "Now I've got my schoolboys, as Fred told me I would, and it's my job to dig oil wells with them."

Then he regarded us soberly for 15 more seconds. At the time, I had no idea what he was thinking. Sixty years later, I am certain he was forcing himself down to the "lick log." Probably, he was reminding himself there was no one else to work for him so he couldn't run us off even if he wanted to. He had to make the best of this bad deal that Fred and World War II had given him.

Then his face cleared. He flashed a big smile and spoke loudly: "Well, I've done okay before with worse-lookin' guys than you. Up to now I've always used experienced men but we don't have any of those right now. Just you. So you won't be boys any longer. Bell is paying you men's wages and I am going to treat you like men."

"And I expect you to act like men while working for me," he continued. "If you do, I'll make you into good roughnecks. But, if you are counterfeit, I'll run you off."

Making his first point, Digger began to work on point number two. "Sometimes you will find your jobs to be fun, and sometimes they will be very hard and unpleasant. No one knows in advance. A lot of depends on you, an' a lot on how good or bad the drillin' goes. But mostly, it all depends on how I feel at any given time. The most important job you have with Bell Oil and Gas is keeping me happy. If you don't intend to do that, I'm advisin' you to go back to the dry goods store an' try to get your money back on those new boots."

Standing back, he looked us over again, allowing us time to digest what he had said. Then he stepped forward and stuck out his huge right paw for me to shake. "My name's Digger Daniels." He was no longer smiling but he carefully listened to my name and his bright blue eyes bored straight into mine. "If you work for me you can't quit until this job's finished unless you whip me. Unless, that is, you run off. I'm a-goin' to call you "Kid."

Then he shook seriously with H. B. while listening to his name and nodding his head. "Same goes for you," he told him. "I think

I'm goin' to like workin' you, just like I enjoyed watchin' you play basketball. Your name is fine, but I'll call you "The Shooter."

Lastly, he turned to our third crew member, one of the whitest Indians I'd ever seen. "What's your name, Chief?" The Indian told him "Charley." In answer to more questions, Charley said that he was a Comanche from the reservation over near Lawton, Oklahoma.

Digger also noted Charley's pale skin and asked if he was used to working outside. Charley said he had been "up North", but we all knew he could also have been in a white man's prison or jail. Digger nodded, watching him closely and finally made up his mind. Sticking out his paw, he squeezed Charley's hand firmly and told him to work hard and not ever drink a drop of liquor while he worked for Bell. If he followed those orders, they would get along fine. While turning toward the office, he talked back to Charley over his shoulder, "You prob'ly already know that I'm goin' to call you "Chief"." Then, motioning us to follow, he lumbered gracefully into Bell's office where we would sign the payroll sheet.

We got no medical exam because most oil companies back then refused to waste time and money on them. If a hand was needed and someone showed up who walked without a cane and promised to work, they would give him a chance. Most bosses had learned over the years that men can be like mules. You can't always tell for sure whether they really are, or really aren't, worn out until you harness them up. Most of the men who applied for jobs had families needing food and shelter, so bosses often gave doubtful men a chance to perform. It was only a tad of trouble to fire a man later if he didn't fit the job.

H. B. and I became Bell employees, Driller's Helpers, by charging $29.50 worth of boots, hard hats and khakis at the Manhattan clothing store, by listening to Digger's speech and by writing our names down at the spot he pointed to in the payroll book. Becoming roughnecks was harder.

CHAPTER 31

WEEVIL SCHOOL—1945

BY EARLY 1945, people had focused long and hard on winning the war and many of them were worn out. Those on the home front had exceeded every goal set by our nation to win, but in doing so some had worked harder than their bodies and minds could stand. Few home front Americans showed more bravery than their sons, brothers, spouses and friends who did the actual fighting, but most of them worked longer hours and sometimes harder than many veterans who whipped Germany and Japan.

For way too long, way too few Americans had labored way too hard, in way too many industries, with way too few patched and worn out tools, to perform way too many difficult jobs. And in Burkburnett, people took this war as seriously as Texans ever take anything. Finally, with the end in sight, the mainsprings of many people had been wound so tight that they could no longer relax. For years, they had accommodated to war-induced schedules by working until nearly dropping. In that way they found sleep easily when finally going to bed. But for some, the strategy backfired.

They had gone so far, so fast and for so long that they couldn't wind down. Stress had warped their systems and some of those unfortunates never recovered. Unable to slow down after the emergency was over, they kept running at high speed until they sickened and died, thus becoming casualties of war as certainly as if a sniper's bullet had searched them out.

Most North Texans were lucky, and quickly swapped their thinking away from war. They were the ones who promptly charted a clear path toward happier times. A surprising number of them, along with a dwindling but active number of war heroes, are still enjoying life. Interested as teenagers, they have lined up with the rest of Texas to peer over the rim of history into a new millennium.

Our nation would have found World War II much harder to win if it had not been for Texas oil. The nation still needs Texas oil and natural gas in 2004 as much as it did back then. But the oil industry suffered during that war because most young men were in uniform. Bell Oil, which owned Fred and the Digger and the rest of us, had been lucky until H. B. and I came along because, although Burk's oilfield had been losing steam for ten full years before the war began, a bunch of older but highly experienced "Boomers" lived there permanently.

"Losing production", a phrase generally meaning "more and more salt water", is an oil man's face-saving phrase for admitting that his wells are drying up. All of Burk's wells were dying but thousands of wells were still producing small amounts. A few are still pumping today. If it hadn't been for old retirement age boomers, Burk's production would have stayed in the ground. The old guys had stopped following booms because they wanted to stay at home with their families and friends while younger men were off fighting. Now that the end was in sight, they began to quit and that was why a pair of kids like H. B. and I were taken on.

While hauling us out to Bell's lease in his Buick for our first day in the oilfield, our Digger chewed on a large unlit cigar. Between sentences, while delivering a long induction speech to us, he spat chunks of tobacco, along with an occasional tablespoon or so of juice, out his window. Because it was hot, the Buick's windows were rolled down so we could benefit from wind motion while riding. But the wind was strong and the ride was also dusty and noisy. This was normal for the times because it had only been 10 years since cars were given heaters. Air-conditioning for America's cars was still a dream, and wouldn't be normal for 15 more years.

Rolling along at 35 miles an hour with all windows down, H. B. and I sucked in big bunches of hot road dust. There was also an occasional grasshopper or wasp, plus a lot of spit and tobacco flakes.

This material blew in through the rear windows, propelled by wind motion. Often, it struck us in the face. It got in our eyes too, if we weren't careful, but we remembered that staggering new hourly wage and didn't even consider fussing. During the entire trip, Digger never stopped lecturing.

By hiring us, he plainly stated, he and Fred and The Bell had embarked upon an uncertain experiment. "No one knows," he announced mournfully, "whether a man can drill an oil well with only a pair of boll-weevils like you an' a cigar store Indian, instead of a real crew of driller's helpers." We had heard the "cigar store Indian" term before today, so we knew he was talking about Charley. We had also seen "drillers helpers" printed on the papers we signed earlier, and knew that was what we were, but we didn't learn until later that a "boll-weevil" was any fresh, inexperienced hand who hired out in the oilfield.

We were, he assured us, awfully poor help, who didn't even know our "backups" from our "breakouts". And like small children, we would need watching every minute for fear we would kill ourselves or some innocent bystander. Even worse, through sheer ignorance, we might do something to damage the Bell's brand-new drilling rig. And If that happened, he gloomily predicted, we would all be fired.

After constructing this framework for his lecture, he raised his voice louder, gathered emphasis, and explained the reasons for his dissertation. First, he wanted us to understand that he was accustomed to being Bell's number one driller. He had earned this position by always making "more hole" than any of the others. Now, he feared, unless he could make somethings out of three nothings awfully quick, he would fall "plumb to the bottom of the sack".

If that happened, Digger assured us, his pride would be offended, making him very unhappy. Pride, he said, along with his God-given guts and strength, had taken him off a poor Oklahoma farm into a passing circus when he was only 16. The move had also prevented an abusive step-father from killing him.

After 20 months of working as a circus roustabout, raising tents, driving stakes and feeding ungrateful animals, Digger had "waved goodbye to all those clowns" and hired out in the oilfields of Illinois. After six weeks of pipelining at $2.00 a day and digging miles of ditch with an idiot spoon he became sick and tired of throwin' dirt. Swapping jobs again he moved onto a derrick floor. "And, from here," he announced proudly, "I never intend to leave." Within two years he had "made" driller and five years after that he became "lead-off" driller wherever he hired out. Still remembering our fat future paychecks, as well as our physical well-being, H. B. and I minded our manners and offered no back-talk.

The monologue continued. Digger had good reasons for saying the things he did. He wanted to make certain we understood that his job, and ours, depended upon us hitting oil once in a while. The more strikes we made, the longer our jobs would last and the better our chances would be to receive a bonus.

We had been hired, he explained, by a small independent oil company with tiny pockets when compared to the big corporations. Small fish living in shark-filled waters, had to work harder and smarter to survive. Bell's Chiefs, planning for a more prosperous world after the war, had dreamed up a new kind of drilling rig. It had been constructed slowly from discarded, rebuilt and rusty but still solid machinery plus loads of second-hand oilfield pipe. Over a two-year period, using their own welders on days when there was little work for them to do, Bell had assembled this new vision in their company pipe yard at Burkburnett. Now, with the rig completed and the war nearly over, Bell had begun a hopeful thrust toward a prosperous future.

This new experiment, after being lovingly assembled, was painted Navy blue, with attractive orange Bell-shaped logos added here and there. And their invention had drawn a large number of oilfield lookers. Some were complimentary, but just as many wagged their heads pessimistically and predicted that it wouldn't work.

Even though starting off as a pile of rusty junk and trusting its entire future to a rebuilt drawworks engine and a mud pump with a two foot long housing crack brazed shut by Bell's company welders, the new rig looked good. It had sleek lines and was narrow

enough to truck easily down the highway. Best of all, It was one of
the very first rigs designed with a ready-built "lay-down" derrick,
which, with minor concept changes, later became known far and
wide as a "Portable Jackknife Drilling Rig."

No one was certain if Bell's new machine would function
properly or how deep it could drill, so Bell leased a small "dry hole
tract" in the old Southwest Burkburnett field that offered a small
chance for a hit or two. Management wanted to drill a few shallow
wells as a shake-down procedure, and to get a feel for how the rig
would perform. Digger made it crystal clear that he wouldn't allow
our laziness or inexperience to ruin his position as top driller. If the
rig was a good one, he wanted to be its lead-off driller in bigger and
better oilfields, maybe out near Midland or Odessa or the newly
discovered fields in New Mexico.

Getting this subject off his chest, Digger took a short recess to
peel a new cigar. Then he opened class again, contributing further
to our oilfield education. We learned that he didn't like the evening
tour, at all. Top drillers were given their choice and normally picked
"daylights". The number two driller picked between the evening
tour and graveyard and the number three guy's crew got whatever
shift was left. Digger was offered his choice of tours but had picked
evenings, from four to midnight, because he'd been told that his
new crew probably would be schoolboys. Past experience had
shown him that young guys were more dependable on evening
tour than on any other shift.

Younguns' he declared, were poor help on daylights because
they "tom-catted" all night long and never got enough sleep. They
were even worse on graveyard because they got home before 9:00
in the morning, wide-eyed and bushy-tailed and seldom bedded
down at all. They had lots of money to spend and plenty of daylight
time to get into mischief while other men were working.

Seldom sleeping in their own beds, he accused, they "nose
around all over, smellin' for women." He knew this, he admitted,
because he had done those same things when he was young. With
lots of money and all day to look for ways of drinking too much
and crawling into the wrong beds, Digger continued, these

younguns' managed to "plow up plenty of snakes along with their partyin'."

H. B. and I had been raised by strict parents and had little or no experience with women, but we'd heard racy stories from older guys about some of the active and popular young women in Wichita County plus a few over across the Red River in Oklahoma. Some of those ladies' husbands were off fighting the war, a long way from home. But there was another sizable group of popular ladies who were married, but had no children. Their husbands worked long hours and some of them were out of town for weeks at a time.

Most of them were still girls, barely women, and were often lonely. In addition, they were pretty and healthy. Some had jobs but, with no children to hamper them, could often take off from work. Because of loneliness, a few were persuaded to accept company during long, cold Texas nights. An impressive number of them learned to enjoy male company during the war, developing what Digger called high-rollin' habits. This caused multiple problems in war time marriages as well as for young stags swarming around.

"Most of those husbands," Digger intoned, "are smarter than their wives think." Then he told us about several bad cases when absentee husbands and overseas GI's had come back home to find young roughnecks busily performing acts of charitable homework.

H. B. and I already knew about some of these cases, but Digger brought us up to date anyway. He explained how these love-ins often ended up in fights. If it wasn't with a husband, it was with another young Romeo who slunk around. Young males who participated in these affairs often collected bullet and knife scars. Sometimes they got hauled off to jail and occasionally a killing developed. In the worst cases all these things happened at once and everyone read about it in the Burkburnett Star or the Wichita Falls Record News.

None of this activity, Digger pointed out, bothered him one iota unless it affected his drilling footage. When that occurred, the matter became personal, and if any of his young guys "dug up so much fun" that they neglected coming back to the derrick for a day

or two, then it was his job, as a self-respecting oilfield driller, to fire
them. Mostly he only "scolded" these returning sinners before
sending them down the road. But he would deal out a black eye or
two if any of them was foolish enough to offer any back-sass.

The point of all this talking, he finished, was to explain that
our rig was never to stop running. When any person was fired, got
sick, suffered an injury or was off the job for any reason at all, the
rest of us must cover his job until he returned or another hand was
hired or made. And, if we couldn't keep the rig running, Fred would
fire all of us and hire a driller who would. We depended on each
other by reason of necessity and good sense. There were no
acceptable excuses for anything, anything at all, that kept his rotary
bit from cutting hole. Just then, with perfect timing, Digger's
sermon finished as we turned off the road out into a pasture where
our rig was being sited.

"I have just told you how drilling a well works with me", he
concluded, while braking his vehicle to a stop. "You have started
out to be roughnecks and, if you will do what I tell you, you can be
real hands pretty quick. But regardless of that", he concluded, "while
you are on my rig, you can give your souls to God, cause your butts
belong to me." He watched closely as we stepped out, searching
faces for any sign of disagreement. H. B. and I looked carefully at
each other and thought of nothing we should add to our driller's
one-way conversation. Charley, our Indian derrickman, acted as if
he'd never heard a word, but was the first man to grab a sledge
hammer when Digger pointed out a guy wire stake he wanted
driven down.

CHAPTER 32

STARTIN' OUT—1945

WE HIT THE ground running, soon as the Digger's car stopped rolling, working hard as we knew how. He had told us to help out, so we immediately started to run and fetch, reaching and grabbing for any experienced hand who shouted for help. Within minutes we had learned a new batch of oilfield words. They weren't curse words. We already knew those. They were names, words and phrases heard only in the "oil patch". We also started learning ways to perform tasks that we never knew existed until then.

By 5:00 that evening Bell Oil's fancy new rig had been strung up and we were dog-tired. H. B. and I together had dug four "deadman holes", each five and a half feet long and five feet deep. Deadman holes had to be long enough to hold five foot sections of eight-inch sized oilwell casing pipe. The pipe sections, called "dead men," were laid out in the bottom and served as anchors for our derrick cables.

Each anchor had metal eyes welded onto one side and the rig's balancing cables, called "guywires", were threaded through the eyes then wrapped round the pipe. After two wraps the cable was fed back through the eyes, then married tight to the cable and fastened with metal clamps. Then we shoveled the dirt back in and tromped it down tight as a few old-time settlers did on fresh graves in country Texas cemeteries.

Forty or 50 people had showed up to witness Bell's rig-raising. Even the welders who built it were watching intently. Digger took his time, enjoying every moment. When everything suited him down to the last "bristle", as H. B. said, he cranked up the big rebuilt Waukesha drawworks engine. Listening to its motor idle for a minute or so, he slowly revved it up to maximum, testing its sound and power. Satisfied, he throttled it back to a muted roar which, even at medium speed, was loud as a half dozen Hell's Angels goosing their Harleys.

At the proper moment, Digger shifted gears without an audible grind or scraping noise. Braking lightly so that the heavy pipe-lifting cable would wind properly on its drum until it started pulling real weight, he gradually increased engine speed. At first nothing happened, then the derrick bent slowly in its middle, and a second later its crown began to rise. Digger eased out on the brake, allowing real weight to lay cable on the drum. Carefully, he watched everywhere for the slightest sign of trouble as Bell's new Jackknife derrick lifted off its cradle, the crown block reaching slowly toward the sun.

When the derrick was vertical, Digger held it steady with power from the drawworks engine while the two free-riding derrick legs were pinned into their brand new boots, which were welded into opposite corners of the derrick floor. The locking pin for each leg was made from solid steel shafting, two inches thick and eighteen inches long.

While the derrick feet were sliding the pins into those boots, a roughneck with a heavy slam hammer stood near. When the pin holes moved into exact alignment, each pin was tapped through the boot, thus locking the leg tightly to the derrick floor. Pins were then locked in place by a cotter key through a hole drilled in their outer ends. This made it impossible for them to drift out and destabilize the derrick. Spectators applauded noisily after Digger throttled down his engine and pulled off his hard hat to mop his bald head with a blue bandana handkerchief. Bell's new rig had been trucked out to the oilfield and raised. Nothing bad had happened yet and the new creation was already more successful than bad mouthers had predicted only an hour before.

After the derrick was raised, Digger showed H. B. and me how to twist the heavy cable turnbuckles with long spud wrench handles to reduce cable length and balance loose "swag" out of the guylines. Then we placed a metal clamp on each cable, marrying its tail back against its body above ground. Rigging up was now completed except for breaking in the Digger's heavy new catline, made of hemp. It would be used to drop our steel pipe racks into position. After that, if all the fresh welds, bolts and scrap metal parts on the new rig held together, oil drilling could begin. Digger and the other drillers would use this new-fangled portable derrick to raise and lower millions of pounds of the five-inch steel drillpipe that had been trucked out and dropped off to drill this well.

H. B. and I had done a lot more than dig deadman holes. We also leveled the rig's "doghouse" which was a portable metal building measuring 10 by 12 feet. It held the driller's well logs, his cutting samples, extra drillbits, hand tools and all kinds of spare parts. It also protected our travel clothes, wallets, lunches and other valuables from varmints and weather.

Besides the doghouse, we had helped lay the two-inch water line running from the well to a stock tank located half a mile across Bell's cow pasture lease. The day before we got there, three truck loads of water pipe had been strung across the prairie between our rig and the tank. Bell figured that drilling crews could lay water line as easily as pipeliners, so coupling up that water line was part of our job. It was hard, sweaty work and lasted four long hours.

Two men, each using a set of iron-handled pipe tongs five feet long, that actually looked like giant pliers, worked on opposite sides of the pipe. One shoved his tong handles up to grab the pipe for a downstroke while the other pulled his set down. Then the first man would reach up to grab a new hold while the second one pulled down. Each operator worked as fast and hard as he was able. When one pipe joint was connected, both men trotted up to the front and latched onto the newest joint, threading it down quickly as they could. Other workers lined up the pipe joints, doped threads, held stabbing boards and fitted pipe ends into collars, so the tong operators wouldn't have to slow down between joints.

All the drillers, company officials, and any other hand who could drop what he was doing hurried over to enjoy watching this work. Tong work was as hard as any in the oilfield and many drillers used it as a test to judge how stout and tough their new roughnecks might be. In fact, we learned afterward that some drillers would replace a hand who didn't last for ten minutes of continuous, heavy tong work. My test and H. B.'s began when the Digger motioned toward a pair of stout and experienced hands, to run down a few joints of water pipe. This was a demonstration to show the weevils, us, how the job needed to be done.

After five minutes he relieved one of them and placed H. B. in his place. Five minutes later, he told me to work the tongs opposite H. B. but, guess what, unlike the old timers, weevils were not relieved. Instead, Digger watched closely until each new hand worked himself into the ground, and gave up. By then, even a pair of oilfield supply salesmen had stopped off to watch as Charley, H. B. and me, plus two roughnecks hired by the daylight and graveyard drillers, worked hard to earn places on Bell Oil Company's derrick floor.

H. B. had started several minutes before me but I had to give up first. He was bigger, also stouter, and everyone knew it. I lasted for 15 minutes and wanted to keep going but finally asked for rest. H. B. quit right after me and Digger put Charley in his place opposite another new hand. Charley only lasted for 12 minutes but he looked to be hungry, not in top condition. Still he out-did a new guy from another crew. After that, Digger assigned us to other jobs but, every 30 minutes, he placed us back on the tongs for a 10 minute shot until that water line was tonged down.

At 1:15 Digger gave us a 30-minute lunch break. Ten minutes later, mine and H. B.'s lunch sacks were empty. At 2:00 Digger sent the graveyard crew home because they had to relieve us at 11:45 that night. The daylight crew was sent in at 5:30 because they had to relieve the graveyarders next morning at 7:45. Besides rigging up the drilling rig, all the smaller engines, including our water pump and power plant had to be watered, gassed, and adjusted. Everything had now been done and we were ready to start drilling. By then it was a half hour past sundown and both mine and H. B.'s stomachs felt like our throats had been corked for a week. We only brought one lunch apiece and had been kept hopping.

Digger yelled loud as he could when he needed our bodies, and we jumped to do his bidding. We were clumsy and awkward but tried hard to master new tasks on heavy, unfamiliar machines with tools we had never used until that day. Digger never slowed and acted as if one meal a day was plenty for any roughneck. We never even thought of complaining because we'd already learned that the only way we would get to be roughnecks was by "yelling and doing." He yelled and we did it. We were raw and our performance was poor. Looking back over 60 years, I figure Digger was as frustrated as a racehorse pulling a plow.

By 7:30 I could hear H. B.'s stomach growling above the drawworks motor as we followed Digger's shouted orders for starting his new well down toward a bottom that was as yet unknown. Using water and pump pressure only, not even attaching a drilling bit, he first drilled or "flushed" down the "rathole." That hole was drilled through a hole Bell's rig builders had cut through the derrick floor, barely inside the left rear derrick leg. The rathole slanted down 25 feet into the earth, and was drilled with pipe weight and water pressure only. The pipe weight flushed it down so fast that it seemed to be in free-fall. After that, he drilled the "mousehole" through a square hole right next to the "rotary table" which was located in the exact center of our steel derrick floor.

H. B. and I learned quickly on some things, slower on others, that our rig's heavy steel rotary table turned the drillpipe. The rotary in turn, was driven by a powerful Waukesha "drawworks" engine fired by butane instead of boiler steam as was done on old-fashioned steam rotary rigs. Our drilling rig's rotary table turned round and round, driving our "kelly" which was screwed onto the top joint of drillpipe. Fastened right on the bottom of this drillpipe was a Hughes Tool Company "rock bit" which slowly cut through ancient rock and shale formations, deepening the well.

That kelly was a wonderful invention. It was an extra strong steel pipe, 24 feet long, which screwed onto the top of our drill pipe. Its walls were made of triple-thick steel, but instead of being round like other pipe, they were square, from top to bottom. This was so a two-pieced set of steel "slips" which were square in the middle, to fit around the Kelly, but were round on their backs, to fit the round place in the Rotary Table, could turn the kelly. When H. B. and I fitted and dropped them into place, Digger shifted his drawworks into gear, turning the rotary, which turned the kelly, which turned the drillpipe, which turned the bit at the bottom of our hole.

The rest was easy. As the well deepened, the kelly drew nearer and nearer to the derrick floor and it was time to add another joint of drill pipe. That was called "making a connection". Drilling stopped while the Digger switched his drawworks engine from drilling to the cable drum and lifted the Kelly high enough up in the derrick so that its bottom joint was three feet above the derrick floor. Then we pulled the Kelly's slips out of the Rotary table, replacing them with drillpipe slips which held the drillpipe up, keeping it from falling into the hole, while we unscrewed the Kelly and dropped it safely into the Rathole.

Unhooking from the Kelly, we latched onto the pipe "elevator" handles, or "bails" and pulled a joint of drillpipe from the Mousehole, connecting it tightly on top of the drillpipe. Then we pulled out the drillpipe slips and lowered the new joint down to floor level and set the slips again, to hold up the drillpipe while we unhooked the pipe elevators and picked up the kelly again and screwed it tightly onto the top of the drillpipe. Then Digger picked up his pipe weight, H. B. and I pulled out the pipe slips, freeing the string and it was lowered gently down until the kelly was back inside the rotary. H. B. and I replaced the rotary slips and the rotary began to turn, deepening our well. All this activity was performed at top speed and, when we had learned how to do it right, H. B. and I could make it all happen in four or five minutes even though it took me more than an hour to write about it.

The point of all this explanation is to allow modern people to understand how Pioneer Texas drillers dug oil wells. It also points out that way down at the bottom of every oil well, at the end of the very last joint of drillpipe was a tri-coned rotary drillbit, weighing over 80 pounds. It had been patented by the Hughes Tool Company out of Houston, and was designed to roll and cut hard rock formations. While it was turning, our bit drove the well deeper and deeper. When it stopped, Bell Oil Company was losing money fast and Digger turned as cranky as a cat on a stove lid.

Everything else about drilling an oilwell was simple. A heavy pump sucked mud out of the slush pit, forcing it down through a swivel joint on top of the Kelly. That mud traveled through the Kelly, into the drillpipe, on to the bottom of our well. Then it passed through the center of that Hughes bit, rising back to the surface outside our drillpipe and back into the well's slushpit. The heavy mud flushed up bit cuttings, dropping them through a screen into the pit. All this mud, gallons and gallons of it, was driven by, you guessed it, a high pressure, steel chambered mud pump! But that part of drilling wasn't yet clear to H. B. and me, or Charlie either, until after we had been making it happen for six or seven weeks.

Dusk was settling in and Digger had us fire up the electric generator, turning on the rig lights. I didn't know or much care how H. B. felt right then, but I felt as if it was a week past my regular meal time. My stomach had wadded up tight and I had decided there was no chance to eat again until after midnight, when we "broke" our tour. Because of our inexperience, everything had taken twice as long as it should have but Digger had finally reached the point of picking up his heavy steel drill collar. This massive chunk of iron helped to stabilize the well's direction, and when turning at normal speed, helped to keep our drillpipe from twisting off. It was inserted into the pipestring one or two joints above the bit. After that we screwed or "made up" a brand new Hughes bit on the bottom joint of pipe. We were getting ready to run all this heavy steel into our well when lights of an approaching pickup flashed over a rise two hundred yards West of us and slanted downhill toward the derrick.

When Digger saw them, he shoved down on the brake lever controlling the cable drum and locked it down tightly. This left the drill collar and bit hanging right in the middle of our derrick floor. Then he popped the drawworks engine into neutral, idling it down near stalling speed and smiled broadly. "Shut 'er down men" he shouted, "here comes Fred with our fried chicken suppers."

H. B. and I looked at each other and smiled widely. It wasn't only because we were about to enjoy a badly needed meal. And it wasn't only because we'd been working hard, all day long, like real grown men, and were proud of what we had accomplished. It was because our boss had just called us "men". We had been trying to make that point with grownups most of our lives.

We wolfed down our large workingman's dinner. Fred, having put in many years on drilling rigs, had personally supervised a waitress at the Burk Cafe as she sacked it up. He'd made certain that each of us had four big pieces of chicken and a large dish of peach cobbler. He'd also made certain each man had a double-handful of brown French fries thrown into the sack along with an extra buttered roll.

H. B. and I, and maybe even Charley, though we were never certain how he felt because he seldom spoke to anyone on purpose, were convinced that Fred had saved our lives. Our eyes were as round and honest as a hound dog's when we thanked him for our dinner. We really meant it!

Later on, when our jobs often became pure slavery, we remembered that chicken dinner and kept on doing what we were supposed to, even though we hated it. And, 15 minutes after we ate, when the Digger told us to "hit the floor", we were in better condition to grow into real roughnecks than we would have been without that good meal, the taste of which I still recall with pleasure.

CHAPTER 33

FISHIN'—1945

AFTER WE HAD drilled four wells and shifted Bell's rig over to location No. 5, H. B. and I decided we were already decent roughnecks. We figured our Digger knew enough about drilling to make great ones out of us, but after working for him a week we also decided that he was going to call us worthless weevils as long as we lived. looking back, I can see he was smarter than we thought. He knew better than us that at age 17 our minds could accommodate a large amount of knowledge. And we might even put some of it to good use if we were properly motivated. To him, proper motivation meant we needed to keep on striving for the goal of being recognized as roughnecks.

Digger motivated with the best. He started out by yelling and intimidating, then he drove us as hard and as long as we could go. Later, after he had us really working, and after we'd learned enough to be of real help instead of driving him nuts, he lightened up and motivated more by example. Yelling less, he began to smile more and frequently told us jokes, but he wasn't good at it. Listening to them was almost as bad as his yelling. Still, we were quick studies. Remembering which side our bread was buttered on, we laughed like hyenas whenever he finished one. We laughed even louder at the worst ones. Indian Charley occasionally tried a smile and it made H. B. and me laugh. We knew it really griped him.

At the time, we didn't know how lucky we were because Digger was a practical driller. After watching the other crews, it became obvious to us that most drillers insisted on as much spit and polish as sea captains. They never intended for a floor hand to sit down and rest for even a tiny second. Their crews moved constantly during each eight-hour shift, obeying orders to mop, hose, wipe, paint, oil, tighten, and double-check gauges. Like the tyrants they were, they kept their roughnecks moving by assigning them any activity at all, even to digging unnecessary trash holes. Those drillers always bragged that no man ever sat down on their tour, pronounced "tower".

Digger thought those guys were silly and told us so. He liked a clean rig, and wanted his paint to shine enough to keep Fred happy, but he didn't believe in make-work. His interest was in "makin' hole". "All the rest," he averred, "is pure winder' dressin'." Then he would spit out a wad of cigar gook and announce that he couldn't see where a good hand ever got any better just because a driller had "wore him plumb out" for no reason at all.

If we had drilled more footage than our schedule called for, and a hard rain shower blew in, Digger would lift the weight off his bit, throttle down the drawworks and slow the rotary table down to double-slow. Then he would call us into the doghouse out of the weather where we would sit on those heavy corrugated board Hughes tool bit boxes and sip coffee while he told us jokes and tales about difficult oilfield fishing jobs he had solved.

On a drilling rig, fishing happened when some foreign object, especially a piece of metal, such as a hand tool, a loose bolt, or the cone of a bit, fell into the well. This object quickly worked its way down to the bottom and lodged underneath the bit, jamming it up. Hughes Tool Company bits were the best ones made and were the only ones our driller used. They drilled through dirt and most rock formations very well but even Hughes had never made, or claimed to make, a bit that would cut through metal.

Once in the bottom of a well, a foreign object, stops all drilling. The well is shut down because the bit can't do its job, and the object has to be "fished" out by the crew. When fishing, the crew pulls the bit, stacks all the drillpipe and takes off the bit. Then they attach a basket-like tool to the bottom of their drillpipe. Running the basket and pipe back into the hole, they try to capture the offending object and bring it up. Each crew continues to fish or "trip", day and night, pulling pipe up and running it back into the well until the foreign material is removed. If it isn't cleaned out, the well is abandoned.

To roughnecks and drillers, every fishing trip seems longer than the last and there is no rest in between. When a new tour reports for work it walks onto the derrick floor and starts fishing wherever the other crew lays down their tools. Even the least reverent departing crewmember always prays fervently that the fish has been hauled to the top and the bit is on the bottom again, cutting rock, when they return.

Drilling oil wells costs disgraceful amounts of money and fishing dramatically increases this cost. Owners whose crews are fishing have no idea at all whether they will finish drilling the well, let alone whether or not there might be oil at the bottom. This tightens their jaws and makes it almost impossible for them to smile. Because of this, the careless roughneck who drops a tool or foreign object into the well, causing a fishing job, is normally fired. Most drillers waited until the fishing job was over, but only to give the offender a good taste of the hard work and trouble he'd caused. After that, he was "put out on the grass". And no experienced roughneck ever took up for a floor hand who was fired because he dropped something down a well.

After drilling four wells, H. B. and I figured we had "made" roughneck but were only kidding ourselves because on Well No. 5, we "bought our Fishin' Licenses". Everything had been good up to then. We were in the hole that night, cutting an easy structure allowing us to add a new stalk of pipe each hour. Adding a stalk was called "making a connection" and we'd just finished one when Digger told H. B. to "ride" the brake while he climbed down to the slushpit to catch some drilling samples.

We were never certain exactly why Digger might lean toward one or the other of us, but we knew he had decided that H. B. had a feel for drilling. So when leaving the floor, he normally put H. B. on the drawworks, to ride the brake, which was how pipe weight was fed onto the bit. This arrangement suited me down to the ground because I didn't like riding the brake. My neck always ached from constant craning to watch the weight gauge that Bell's rig designers had set in a bad location. Digger could face the gauge while reaching behind him and instinctively feed weight properly, but weevils had to watch the gauge and the brake handle both. He was always poking fun at H. B. and me when he saw us stretching our sore backs and necks.

Keeping correct pressure on the gauge was important because if you "crowded" a bit, weighting it too heavily, even a good bit would spitefully drive sideways, and drill a crooked hole. Crooked hole drillers learned early that oil companies hated wells whose walls weren't plumb. And in the oilfield, exactly as in the Army and Navy when an employee goofed up, costing the company money, he learned that rocks and all kinds of trash, some of it big globs of horse plop, always roll downhill. Fast. By the time this fast-moving material traveled from the home office all the way down to a well site, it had gathered a big load of energy, and the bad-will that came with it was very distracting.

Often, a badly bent hole or a fishing job created so much fuss and damaged so many feelings that a whole crew was fired. Sometimes, a driller would simply walk away in disgust. But, whatever the result, none of those things helped his reputation. Everyone in the oilfield knew that a driller's word and his ability formed his reputation in the oilfield. Most drillers would fight over them.

As H. B. watched the gauge, Charley and I took oily "waste cloths" and rubbed dust off all the paint surfaces we could reach without climbing above the first derrick girt. This was easy work, and needed no concentration. I amused myself by watching H. B. crane and rub his neck. Tiring of that, I watched Digger, a big-waisted man, as he squatted at the edge of the slushpit, leaning over his stomach and reaching out with a small wire tea strainer, to collect bit cuttings from the swirling pool of fast-rising mud.

Digger smelled the samples and tasted them a lot, looking much like what I learned years afterward a gourmet cook would look, only he wore an aluminum hard hat instead of a tall white one with a big cottonball on top. After testing, he frequently dropped scoops of cuttings from his strainer into small sampling bags and wrote down the time and depth and other pertinent information. The bags looked like, but were twice as large as the old-fashioned Bull Durham five cent sized tobacco sacks.

Tiring of watching him, I shifted my vision to the rotary exactly in time to see the kelly rise up five or six inches in its drive bushings then drop back down. At the same time, I heard the drawworks engine suck fuel through its carburetor and roar, trying to compensate with extra fuel for the need to deliver more power. As I watched, the kelly rose and dropped again, but Digger had moved onto the floor before it finished its third hop. In those few brief seconds, he had traveled from the back side of the slushpit, around the rear of the doghouse and up ten metal steps to the derrick floor, a solid one hundred and fifty feet.

Pushing H. B. away, he shoved the brake down tight, revved his drawworks up and slowly released the brake, easing the entire drill string up about four feet. Then he watched carefully, as the pipestring rotated, slowly but smoothly, looking quite normal. He squinted upward into the derrick to see if anything was twisted or in a strain but everything looked okay. The massive traveling blocks moved smoothly and were hanging straight, just as they ought.

Nothing above-ground seemed haywire, so whatever was wrong had to be downhole. Carefully, Digger lowered his string downward and, soon as the bit bottomed out, his kelly began to hop and walk, just as before. The drawworks engine continued stuttering in time with the kelly's movement, racing and slowing, trying its best to adjust to those drastic power needs.

Digger picked up the pipe again and slowed his kelly down to nothing, barely letting it rotate. Holding it several feet off bottom, he locked the brake and increased his mud pressure, hoping it could circulate fast enough to carry up whatever foreign material was in the bottom of his well. While the well circulated, he walked back down to the slushpit and dipped with his strainer to see what might be washing up, but nothing showed.

Bluntly, he yelled out, asking if anyone had dropped a hand tool or even a stick of chewing gum into his well. We all shook our heads "no." Then he speculated loudly enough for us to hear that our bit had probably dropped a cone off and we would likely have a fishing job. Welcoming no conversation, he sipped coffee from his thermos and waited fully ten minutes while the drilling mud circulated.

When his cup was empty, he eased the bit back down to bottom and the kelly immediately began to rise and drop, walking hard, so he gave up. Slowly pulling the string up until the top drillpipe joint was several feet above the rotary table, he told us to set the pipe slips. "Pull on your gloves, men," he yelled, as he shut the pump down, "We're agoin' fishin'."

We had our pipe on top and racked back in an hour. It was a hot night and we were sweating. Digger hung the bit and drill collar over the hole and locked his brake. H. B. and I hit the water can while he came down onto the floor with us to examine the bit. All three cones were still attached. A few teeth were scarred and dented but the cones were still tight and the bit showed little damage. Digger thought it ought to cut without any problem but something hard, he didn't know what, was "Ridin' off my bit."

Then he ordered Charlie to drag another bit out of the doghouse, and we placed a pair of 2 X 12 inch boards over the rotary to keep anything else from dropping into the well when the old bit came off. As soon as we backed it off the pipe string, three pieces of macerated white steel fell onto the boards. Then, when Digger rolled the bit over, we could hear the noise of loose metal clinking inside. Something was obviously wrong.

Digger fiddled with the bit cones but they were jammed and wouldn't turn. Then he saw a piece of white metal sticking out from the bottom. Standing the bit on its cones, he whapped the frame with a slam hammer, then he turned it upside down and emptied out three more pieces of the same metal. Close examination revealed that they were solid steel chunks, originally about 5/8 of an inch square, and each was three to five inches long.

Every piece had been chewed, stretched and distorted, but had originally come from the same steel object. We had no idea what it had been but we also knew it hadn't hatched itself out 1,200 feet underground, then waited around for us to come along to dig this well. Modern men had crafted that steel. We could tell by looking at the twisted pieces.

Examining further, we found marks on the end of one piece showing where it had been perfectly squared off with a metal bench saw. Cutting torch marks along the sides of other pieces showed that a fabricator had cut the steel lengthwise then ground excess slag from the edges. Our Hughes bit had chewed lengths off that piece of underground metal and stuffed it inside the bit through the fluid hole at the bit's bottom then shoved it up into the drillpipe. It had pulled and stretched each piece, gnawing them until the surface was mostly white metal. Only small amounts of rust or original mill markings remained.

Digger had a weird fish and was puzzled. None of his hands had dropped tools into the well because this metal had obviously been fabricated. It was part of some metal structure but he couldn't figure out what and ordered us to carefully search over the rig for any missing parts or holes where a piece of metal could have dropped off. We looked but found nothing wrong. Chief, who loved climbing, had been given a flashlight and sent up in the derrick to look around but he found nothing amiss.

Digger matched up the metal pieces lengthwise as best he could and ended up with about eighteen inches of stretched and twisted malleable steel, but more was still down in the well. The bad part was we didn't have a fishing basket and couldn't get one from Bradford Supply at Burkburnett until next morning. Glumly, he considered whether, for the first time in years, he would have to shut down his well, and detested the idea. That was another of the many things that could happen, and help to shove No. 1 drillers off the top.

As Digger squatted on the floor, muttering over his jigsaw puzzle, I felt a call from nature. Figuring this was the best chance I would ever have to answer, I walked across the floor past our rotary table and toward the stairs. A fresh gust of wind twisted the suspended drill collar on its cable and a large glob of mud dropped onto my left boot toe. Irritated, I glared up at the slowly turning collar but forgot the boot when I saw something else!

Light glinted off fresh metal where that mud had sloughed away and I could see that a vertical slot had been cut into the sidewall of the drill collar. This slot was still mostly full of mud but I wiped more away and could see that it measured about five-eighths inch in width and was almost that deep. I didn't know exactly how long it was but knew it had once held metal instead of mud. Probably it once held our fish. When I called out, the Digger grabbed his flashlight and trotted over for a look.

Within seconds, he had figured out the puzzle. Cleaned up, the slot measured thirty inches and was the same width and depth as the metal pieces we had dug up. Drill collars were expensive and hard to locate after the war. So Bell, saving time and money, had designed and built its own. Company welders had fashioned the heavy tool from old junked-out equipment and the pieces of metal we had pulled out of that bit had been chewed loose from what had once been a vertical stabilizer that had broken loose from Bell's homemade collar. A welder's seam had separated, allowing the stabilizer to loosen. Slowly it worked out of its slot and dropped downhole, lodging under the bit.

Measuring our metal pieces against the length of the slot, Digger calculated that two-thirds of the stabilizer had already been pulled up. Fortunately, the steel wasn't tempered or it might have torn the bit apart. But the cones were still tight and Digger figured they should cut. We weren't, he decided, going to shut down our rig to wait for fishing tools. Instead, we would use that stout Hughes bit to see if we could drill up the rest of that stabilizer.

And we did it! Within minutes we had the old bit back on the drillpipe. Fifty minutes later, it was on bottom again and rolling. After an hour, Digger, by working carefully and slowly adding and picking up weight when necessary then letting his Kelly bounce and walk when it insisted, finally watched his bit settle down. Carefully, he added weight and began to drill. Thirty minutes later, the bit was still cutting, though slowly, and we pulled up our pipe again to see what we had caught. All the remaining metal had been chewed up and pushed up above the bit into the drillpipe and the pieces dropped easily onto the derrick floor when we broke our bit off. Our stout Hughes bit had "drilled up" that fish!

Once we were back in the hole, Digger relaxed big time. Calling us over, he thanked us, then put H. B. on the brake and reached for his thermos. When the Chief saw that, he eased over to the farthest derrick corner and squatted in his regular spot to watch, probably without seeing, the rumbling action of our rotary. I watched H. B. craning his neck and once more felt lucky that Digger wasn't trying to turn me onto a driller.

After two good sips of hot coffee Digger sighed with pleasure and relief. Laughing aloud he turned toward me and shouted above the rig noise. "Well, Kid, "you saved Bell a bunch of money tonight and you saved me a lot of footage. The both of us thank you. You an' H. B. aren't roughnecks yet, but you are both gettin' closer."

Then, feeling extra generous, he looked back at me and said seriously, "I'm gonna' start callin' you 'Hawkeye', instead of 'Kid'."

CHAPTER 34

Runnin' Casin'—1945

By the time we struck bottom on Well No. 7, H. B. and I realized why the Burkburnett oil boom was over. It was simple. Ninety nine percent of all the oil had already been found. Our first six wells were dusters. Digger had solemnly pronounced each to be "dry as a popcorn fart," but this one showed a little promise.

No one was certain whether it would amount to anything, but the Gods from our home office in Tulsa and the regional office in Burk visited the site, huddled to share their wisdom and reviewed the evidence. Finally, they decided to set casing. This meant that we would run eight-inch pipe down the well two hundred feet or so, then fill it with concrete, creating a plug. This would stop leakage near the surface and protect the shallow water sands. After concrete had set, Bell would drill the casing core with a "spudding" machine and begin doctoring this new treasure to see if any oil could be milked out. If enough was found, tanks would be set and a pumping unit and other hardware would be installed. But, even after all the expense and trouble, this new well, if it produced anything at all, could turn cranky and fizzle out in a week.

We arrived at 3:45 next afternoon, ready for work, just as all the details had been decided. Fred Rogers, the man who first hired us and Harry Martin, our home office superintendent, walked slowly out to meet us, accompanied by the daylight driller. H. B. and I had no idea that it was oilfield custom for the No. 1 crew to run casing, but our bosses had decided that the daylight guys, Bell's No. 2. crew, would run this casing because they were more experienced than us.

H. B. and I didn't know enough about oilpatch custom to be insulted at being shoved aside and were as surprised as Fred and Mr. Martin probably were when our Digger found out what they had done and raised his voice. Well, he didn't actually speak. What he did was yell loud enough that everybody could hear and they automatically stopped to listen. Even though Digger was mostly defending his overtime pay, he was also protecting his territorial rights and delivered a classic "stand up on your hind legs and growl Texas speech." When he was through, H. B. and I figured he had given a good and loud performance enough for anybody's driller.

"Now looka here Fred," Digger shouted. "An' you too, Mr. Martin. I am your No. 1 driller and you haven't talked to me about any of this. My crew may be new but it has put down more hole than either of the other two who drilled this string of wells. We can do anything out here that they can."

Looking straight into their eyes, he continued: "Now, either I am your No. 1 driller, or I'm not. That's up to you to decide, but one thing I know is that I can put my quick-handed Chief up on the "stabbin' board" and use Shooter an' Hawkeye here to twist casin' for him an' they won't cost you an extra penny 'cause I won't let 'em. They'll run that pipe of yours down-hole as fast as anybody else, maybe even faster. So why won't you let us do it?"

Fred and the home office boss offered no argument. Saying nothing, they looked at each other for a moment, and communicated in a way I couldn't see. Maybe—Just maybe, Mr. Martin nodded his head a quarter-inch. I was never certain. Anyway, Fred turned to the daylight driller and sent him and his crew back to town. By then, H. B. and I had figured out that something unusual was happening and began to be proud of Digger, but our pride only lasted an hour. Before finishing, we wished that he had let us go home and thrown that casing job to the daylighters. It was bad stuff for roughnecks.

Bell's old casing was "pure-dee" junk. It wasn't their fault, because, even if they could have afforded new casing right at the end of the war, there wasn't any to buy. Steel companies hadn't swapped over from war to peacetime oilfield pipe production. Bell's management knew

this and had tried to overcome the problem. They had been buying up
used casing for two years before hiring H. B. and me.

Pulled out of abandoned wells 30 years older than this one and
bought from salvage yards all over North Texas, that pipe was as
sorry as old experienced hands had ever seen. They wagged their
heads and muttered when the casing trucks dropped off their loads.
That old casing "belched" rust, inside and out. It was dented, bent
and double-straightened in some places. Large holes in some joints
had been patched with welder's "half-soles" in hope that they
wouldn't leak too badly. And we had to clean, brush, dope and
chase the bottom threads on every joint before gently "easing" it
into a tight connection at the top of the string.

Oilfield people didn't wear sunshades back then. As with
hardhats and steel-toed boots, the first sunshade and goggle wearers
were derided by fellow workmen who called them "sissies" and
"candy butts". Ten years later, after a few years of drilling in the
deserts of Iran, Iraq and Kuwait, roughnecks threw away their
prejudice. Happily they embraced dark sunshades, and even goggles
for eye protection, but that didn't help H. B. and me. We needed
them in 1945.

Working on the derrick floor, we had to look straight up at the
Chief on his stabbing board, 20 feet above us, while he moved the top
end of each casing joint around until he thought it was positioned
well enough to connect without cross-threading. Thousands of rust
flakes, some big as half dollars and in all shapes and thicknesses, rattled
endlessly down onto our hardhats. They also fell in our faces, down
our necks and into our eyes as we looked up.

When the proper moment came, Chief would nod at us and
we could look down for a few seconds while slowly turning the
joint of casing with our chain tongs, hoping it would thread properly
and make a tight enough connection to hold fluid pressure. We
almost never connected on the first attempt and many joints were
so wormy and rotten that we gave up, threw them over the side and
picked up another stalk.

When a connection attempt failed, we backed the casing joint
out, chased its threads again and started over. This meant taking an

extra dose of rust in our faces. I still have a small blind spot in my left eye which I know has outlasted the casing we ran on No. 7 that day. Filing a claim for insurance never crossed my mind. We were all beaten down and happy for our job to be over when we headed home that night. After midnight, I bathed, washed out my eyes as well as I could and piled into bed.

Next morning things were different. Even though H. B. and I had only slept a few hours, we were proud of ourselves and stepped out jauntily when we arrived at the well location. Our rig was being moved three tenths of a mile North to the next location where it would be rigged up to drill Well No. 8. Rigging up would be finished by 5:00 that afternoon, and both the other crews would go in. Digger and us would start the new well off. We had already logged five hours overtime before running the casing so all our rigging time, plus every hour we worked until the end of that week would be counted as overtime.

Digger had explained all the overtime to us when taking us home the night before and we felt rich. Until then H. B. and I hadn't figured we would ever have that much extra money in our hands. Digger had also instructed us to bring double lunches today so we would have enough energy to carry us through until 11:45 when the graveyard crew showed up. I prepared "sensibly" by fixing a triple lunch, "just in case." When I left home, at 7:00 that morning, I carried a peck sack almost full.

The older hands didn't gripe openly because Fred had come out to the location early. He'd been checking out the swabbing operation on Well No. 7 and came over to No. 8 as soon as the teardown crews arrived. He also promptly bragged to all hands about how quickly the weevil crew had run casing down on Well No. 7, and this pulled the ground out from under the older hands. But we knew by their sour looks and pouty faces that they were ticked off. I didn't blame them. They had a good case.

Two weevils and an Indian, none of whom fed families, had pulled down a hatful of overtime. Any man who worked for Bell could use it. H. B. and I walked around on eggshells, risking no arguments. But the Digger was different. Maybe he had decided to do some "evenin-up" against his fellow drillers. Anyway, he razzed them all day long whenever he thought about it. His targets suffered in silence, working hard, faces averted and heads down, saying nothing.

CHAPTER 35

MAKIN' ROUGHNECK—1945

MOST FOLKS DON'T know it but drilling oil wells takes barrels and barrels and barrels of water. Deep wells in desert-type country have large water tanks that are filled every day or so by water hauling tank trucks. But our bosses had no spare money and were drilling wells the cheapest way it could be done. They had leased 1,000 acres of cow pasture from property owners nine miles Southwest of Burkburnett and intended to drill twelve shallow wells "El Cheapo", as oilpatch folks used to say.

Bell's leasing agent felt that the smartest part of his lease trade was arranging to pump free water from a five-acre stock tank located in the middle of their lease and so did Bell. H. B. and I, and most of the other roughnecks, disagreed. We figured that was the worst part of the deal because we had to use those long handled pipe tongs and spend half a long hot day changing the water line over to a new well every time we switched locations. The line was never buried, because after finishing each well, we dragged it around, dismantling part of it and re-connecting it until it would match the new well's location. To roughnecks, laying pipeline, even on top of the ground, is a hateful job. Most had put in some pipeline time before moving onto derrick floors. Most had also sworn they'd never pipeline again. They reinforced this attitude by telling anyone who would listen that pipeliners were just roughnecks with their brains beat out.

H. B. and I normally did most of the tong work because the older hands had laid down their share of water line when they were weevils and weevils were always given hard jobs until they graduated into roughnecks. We had just finished drilling a circle of seven wells around our stock tank and were moving Bell's rig about a half mile farther out to begin a wider circle.

Well No. 7 had produced enough oil sand that some of the samples smelled and tasted like oil so Bell decided to set casing and spud it in soon as we had torn down and skidded the rig out to location No. 8. Our bosses had decided that No. 8, was in a "best guess" direction for their underground oil sand to drift, if it found any oil at all, so in a fit of optimism worthy of Burk's old-time boomtown atmosphere they began calling No. 8 an "offset". But they grinned a little when saying this because an offset is normally drilled close to a heavy producer.

Digger was still evenin' up with the other two drillers so, on this move, he took H. B. and me off the tong crew. He knew very well that this would tickle us pink and it would also aggravate the other two crews. Nobody liked that hard and heavy tong work. But these guys hated it even more because they felt they were past a point in life where they ought to do pipelining work at all.

At least half of them, after leaving farms or ranches where they seldom saw a dollar, had started oilfield careers by roustabouting. Roustabouts mostly used shovels to perform lease work, like cleaning out oil tanks, digging ditches and holes every day and loading up and hauling off truckloads of thick and filthy waste oil material. They also built lease roads and patched lease fences and installed new gates.

After roustabouting, pipelining was the next most logical step up the oilpatch ladder because it paid a little more. It was back breaking labor but was steadier than roustabouting. After pipelining, the oilfield workers who thought they were the best and luckiest, if they could hack it, graduated to derrick floors. The work was dangerous, and a floor hand had to be sharp and active, but he was seldom bored and he made more money than most oilfield hands. Most roughnecks never intended to leave the derrick floor and hated to pick up a shovel.

Digger hadn't pulled us off the tongs for our benefit. He did it because he was Bell's No. 1 driller and wanted to emphasize that point to the other drillers and their crews. He was still top dog and could do what he wanted. So, he made the Chief, into a truck driver, gave him Bell's flatbed truck, and told us we were the Chief's swampers for this move. We enjoyed these cushy new jobs, that mainly involved loading the truck with small items, such as supplies, derrick timbers, hand tools, and small machinery.

We really got a kick out of waving and shouting "Howdy" every time we drove past a gang of older hands who, on every other move, had watched with pleasure, criticizing our techniques, as we sweated on those pipe tongs. Just as we threw the last load of gear onto the truck, Digger slowed his Buick down long enough on his way over to the new site to yell out, reminding me to pick up his suction pipe board. I promised I would, but like the kid I was, promptly forgot.

People won't understand, so I will explain that while this board had no importance anywhere else in the world, it was important on our well and anything important to the well was important to our Digger. All it was, was, a battered two by eight-inch timber, 10 feet long. We always laid it across the nearest slushpit corner to our mud pump and tied a rope around it to raise and lower the mud pump's suction line.

Though seemingly trivial, the board was a necessity. The slushpit had to deliver the exact amount and thickness of drilling mud that Digger needed whenever he wanted it. And he was so picky about mud that most of the time he had the Chief mix it two hours before he intended to use it.

Just past five that afternoon, after we had finished stringing up and were ready to start our hole, Digger missed his slushpit board. The other two crews, the evening tour guys and the graveyarders, had been sent in. Because Digger was pushing us hard to start making hole, we were as busy as overworked roughnecks ever got. And our well was located on a flat prairie. No loose boards lay around and there were no trees from which we could chop a limb.

Digger plunged into one of his storms and announced that there was no time for anybody to drive or walk over to the old location and bring his board home. For an hour he complained loudly enough to be heard over the drawworks engine about kids and weevils but he didn't use my name so I guessed he wasn't going to fire me. Not yet anyway. Still I wasn't absolutely certain, so I jumped awfully quick whenever he shouted orders.

What Digger did do was encourage me, working alone, to drag a 20-foot joint of water pipe over to a spot where one end stretched across the proper corner of our mud pit. After I had pulled and shoved it exactly where he wanted it, he further encouraged me, still working alone so I could be "proud of my work", to attach the heavy rope and adjust the intake line to a level he wanted.

This was a mean job and Digger knew it. He had me to re-adjust the suction five times before it finally suited him. H. B., enjoyed my predicament, laughing and calling me "Mudpuppy" for the rest of the night. We had no way of knowing it then, but before many more hours had passed, any of us could have called him the same name, but none of us would have been that cruel.

That joint of water line was three times as long as our board had been and was constantly in everyone's path. It lifted off the ground, following the rise of fresh earth, at the edge of our derrick pad, and half the people rounding that corner would trip over it. Some loads were so heavy that it was easier to carry them around the long way.

Making his point well, Digger left the pipe where it was when we broke tour so everybody on the graveyard and daylight tours would be as mad at me as he was. When we came back next day no one had gotten worked up enough about the situation to move it. Digger first looked at it, then at me and wagged his head, announcing that the oilfield was going to the dogs. Then he stepped over it himself and climbed up the derrick stairs.

By 8:00, four hours after starting, we had drilled deep enough that the strata was tightening up. By then, we were adding a joint of drillstem every hour and Digger decided to mix a heavier batch of mud to hold his string tight in the hole in case we drilled into an air or gas pocket. If we had hit one of those, with thin mud, our pipe could be shoved out of the hole by heavy gas pressure. This was called a "blowout", and if falling joints of drillpipe didn't kill somebody, the ensuing gas explosion and fire probably would. Anyway, when digger opened the water line to start mixing his mud, the pump sped up for a few seconds, then stalled out. He had me to crank it up two or three times, hoping it would clean its line out but it wouldn't. It only delivered a trickle then died again.

This happened about once a week and was normally caused when the water intake line dropped too deep into mud at the bottom of our pond. Sometimes too many crawfish or minnows slipped through the pump's intake screen and traveled through the line, plugging the fast-moving pump impeller. Digger had me to pull off the water intake line and clean it out but it was clean as a pin. Nothing was wrong there.

The problem had to be at the water tank where our pump sucked in its water. There was no way to cure that except to walk nearly three fourths of a mile, all the way past Well No. 7 and on down to the lake to clean out the intake because Digger wasn't about to let anyone drive his Buick. Once at the lake, the water line had to be lifted out, and whatever sludge or crawfish or frog eggs or swamp grass that plugged the intake up had to be removed. Then the screen was clamped back on and it was raised high enough to keep it well out of the mud for a while. Then the person who did all this had to walk back to our well.

This was a one-man job but Digger normally sent two men to fix it. Tonight, though, still making his point with me, he changed his method. He had me busy at brushing and doping drillpipe threads, a tedious and messy job, and told H. B. to walk down alone to fix the pump. He also ordered him to bring back our suction board so "Hawkeye", me, could "get rid of that damned pipe."

H. B. grabbed up the flashlight but it didn't work. Someone had set it face down in the doghouse without turning it off and the batteries were dead as doornails. Even though he rummaged around hard in the doghouse shelves and bins, Digger found no replacements. So H. B. had to hike almost 3/4 mile each way across open prairie on that dark and moonless night. We used to say a night like this one was as dark as the inside of a black cat. Digger told H. B. to follow the water line, so he could kick it with his foot and not get lost.

I watched H. B. start off across the prairie, kicking at the water line every three or four steps. Forty minutes later, Digger pulled out his watch, looked at it and began working up a case of nerves. He had ordered Chief to haul mud sacks and he was finished but there was still no water for mud. Ten minutes later, he had Chief help me and we made a new connection, adding another drillstring joint. But, when we went back in the hole, it was really time to mix up our mud. Digger told me to crank the pump again but there was still no water and he didn't like it. H. B. had been gone for an hour, so Digger walked over to me. "Kid", he said, lapsing back from my current nick name of "Hawkeye", "you think Shooter's in trouble?"

I stood up and looked into the blackness, down the water line where H. B. had walked. After thinking about it, I replied that H. B. was as able to take care of himself as me and ought to be all right. Clearly worried, he looked into my face for a second, then turned and walked back to his post near the drawworks engine on the derrick floor.

Five minutes later, he was back. Punching me in the ribs, he said, "Kid, I want you to go find the Shooter. Chief can finish doping up this pipe. And, hurry up, I'll be waiting on both of you to make the next connection."

I knew that any time Digger delayed making a connection, that he was interfering with his "drilling footage" and he figured there was a good reason or he wouldn't do it. I nodded my head sharply, dropped the dope brush into its pot and trotted out as far out as the rig lights could shine. After that I slowed down in a hurry.

I had good night vision and didn't have to kick the line to know where I was going, but it was so dark that even I could only see four or five feet in any direction. I followed the line anyway, just in case H. B. might have fallen near it, and hurt himself. Or, he might have stepped on a rattlesnake big enough to make him too sick to walk and could be down on the ground. But I wasn't really worried until I suddenly remembered something he'd told me lately about being "blind as a bat" when he was out at night. This had been a problem ever since he started wearing extra-thick glasses a year earlier. This caused me to worry and I picked up my walking speed whenever I could. I was about a hundred yards away from our last well when I heard him.

What I heard was the sound he made when tripping and falling to the ground, 50 feet over to my right. I thought a cow was threshing around in the brush until I heard him fussing at himself: "Dumb Ass," he mumbled.

"H. B. Is that you?"

"Yeah, Ed," relief rising in his voice, "I'm glad to hear from you. Hoof yourself over here and help me."

I thought the suction board might have tripped him because I knew he had passed Well No. 7 and was on his way back from the lake. Kidding him, I said, "Can't you carry that board by yourself?"

Forgetting his anger and fear now that he had some company, H. B. chuckled, "Yeah, I can, but I cain't see where to carry it."

By then I had reached him, barely in time to stop him before he walked into a tall prickly pear plant. His sleeve was slimy and covered all over with what my nose told me was a mix of drilling mud and raw crude oil. "How come you've got crude all over your arm?"

"Ed, it's all over me. I walked off into the old slushpit."

"Are you hurt?"

"No, but I'm beat out and can't see. I lost my glasses and have been wandering around all over, trying to get to a place where I could see the rig lights or find the water line. Seems like I've been workin' at it half the night. And now I know that I can't see our derrick from anywhere without my cheaters. An' this dang board," he finished, "feels heavier than a crosstie."

I reached out and took his board then turned him toward the rig. "Reach forward with your right hand and grab my belt," I told him. "We'll be back at the rig in 20 minutes." And we were.

I was amazed when we walked under the rig lights to see how bad he actually looked. His face was pale as a ghost while all the rest of him was colored a greenish black mixed in with mud. Because he had impatiently been waiting to make a new connection, Digger saw us from the derrick floor. Realizing that something serious had happened, he locked his brake tight, throttled back the drawworks and trotted down the metal catwalk stairs to meet us. Chief, curious as a cat but saying nothing, followed him down.

H. B. had mud and oil everywhere a roughneck could except in two places. When he knew he was falling, he had rolled over and dropped in backwards, so his face and the front half of his hard-hat were clean as could be. All the rest of him was covered with muddy oil and slime.

"Damn, Shooter," Digger broke in after H. B. had explained what happened, "how did you get out?"

He knew, as we all did, that the slushpit was six feet deep and brimful of heavy mud with an inch of crude oil across the surface. Swimming in that kind of mix was impossible. Any person or animal, after falling in, normally had only three or four minutes to live. H. B. was resting on the rig steps where we set him down and gratefully raised a steaming cup of coffee to his lips. Slowly sipping, he told us his story.

"I thought I was a goner", he began "and jumped far as I could when I knew I was going in, because I thought I was only a short distance from the corner. I knew if I got my glasses dirty that I wouldn't be able to see, so I turned over and went in on my back, but it didn't help a bit. It's so dark that I couldn't see any better with clean glasses than dirty ones. This night is just too black. I couldn't tell if I was lookin' up or down."

"But I could feel where down was by the direction I was sinking, so I turned onto my stomach in that mud and, still holding my head up, I reached up with my right hand, far as I could, like in swimming. And—you know what? My fingers came down right on top of that suction board!"

After managing to hold on, the rest was simple. H. B. pulled himself out by clutching the board with both hands and climbing the pit wall with his feet. Freeing himself from the clinging mud, he rolled like a coon over on top of the board and "ooched" carefully to solid ground. "I sure was glad to lay flat on solid dirt," he finished.

He had lost his glasses, but that didn't worry him much. He was happy to be alive. Working carefully, he pulled the board back away from the pit. Then, carrying the infernal thing, he began to walk as straight a line as he could, a full hundred steps away from the pit before trying to walk in ever-widening circles, hoping to locate our water line.

We all knew H. B. could have sat down and waited for someone to come get him, but he wasn't put together that way. He'd been sent to clean out the pump intake and to hurry back with that sorry board. And tired as he had been, he never stopped. He kept holding onto that thing because Digger had told him to bring it and there was no quit in him. By the time I heard him fall, he had been stumbling around in a quarter-mile sized thicket of mesquite brush and prickly pears on a pitch-black night with no glasses for over thirty minutes, but he was still trying his best to do what he'd been told. I was proud of him and Digger didn't say it, but I could tell he was too.

Chief, as usual, listened closely. Watching everything intently, he memorized what was happening, but as always, said nothing. When H. B. was finished, Digger filled his coffee cup once more and handed it back. Then he looked at his watch and told H. B. to keep his place and sip coffee until Chief and I finished making the new connection.

After the connection we would reduce the water jet pressure and H. B. could take off his filthy clothes and soap down. Then we would hose him off so he could put on his travel clothes and rest until we broke tour. And that was exactly what we did, except that later Digger had the Chief to help me drag the pipe joint out of our way and install the suction board where he wanted it.

After the graveyarders relieved us, and we were walking out to Digger's car, he told H. B. he was very happy that slush pit hadn't swallowed him up. Then he turned to me, and spoke roughly, which I knew by then was the only way he knew how to tease.

"Hawkeye, I was ready to run you off over that suction board, and I don't ever want you to leave it out on one of my locations again. But," he concluded, "I'm sure glad you left it over on No. 7 this time."

We walked on for several more steps while I tried to decide whether he expected an answer. I was still deciding when H. B. crossed in front of the Digger and stopped me. Back then, men in Texas society didn't enjoy hugging each other, and most of us from that generation still aren't comfortable when doing so. Instead of hugging me, H. B. stuck out his right hand and we shook hands hard while he looked deep into my eyes. Speaking as seriously as any man could, he said, "Me, too. Thanks, Ed!"

Embarrassment shaped my response, causing it to sound artificial and a little foolish. "That's okay, man," I blurted, "Any time."

CHAPTER 36

Movin' On—1945

Eleven days after H. B. crawled out of the pit, everything about our job began to change. Digger was driving us home after we broke tour, and at sometime between Midnight and 8:00, the Graveyarders were supposed to bottom out on Well No. 10. He figured it would be a duster and Fred did too. They hadn't ordered out any casing. But little things were different also. The rig was to stay on location for an extra day or two before being torn down and our crew, would take two days off. It was possible Bell was abandoning their lease. Naturally, they didn't intend paying us for time off because drilling crews from the first day of oilfield history were only paid when working. But I didn't care. I needed rest. We had worked for 13 straight days, including one double tour. I didn't know about the others but I wanted some extra sleep.

In addition to being overworked, I had another problem. For the last two days I'd been trying to build up the courage to tell the Digger I was quitting. I had decided to enroll at Hardin Junior College in Wichita Falls. So after he dropped H. B. off and was turning into my dad's drive, I gathered up my nerve and decided to tell him. To be on the safe side, I waited until his car stopped and opened my door, so I could run if he decided to hit me. Then I began.

"Digger, I don't want you to get mad, but I've got to quit. Are you goin' to whip me?" Nervous as a cat on a stove lid, my right foot on the ground, I had my weight nicely balanced. Ready to jump, I waited for his answer.

He chuckled deeply and I relaxed. Then, I tightened up again but was way behind him. His large right paw snatched out, quick as a striking rattler, and fastened onto the nearest part of me he could reach, my left wrist. To him it wasn't squeezing hard, but the grip was so tight that all the blood flow was stopped. There was no way I could have broken loose without using an axe.

"Why do you ask, Kid?", he questioned softly. "Do I need to give you a whippin'?" I wasn't trying to be funny when I answered that I didn't think so, but I didn't know what he might think. That was why I'd asked.

Digger turned me loose and chuckled again. "Kid," he said, "I don't never whip nobody unless they make me. You and the Shooter and the Chief just got my regular hirin' on speech for boll weevils. I've used it for years 'cause it keeps me from having a big batch of the roughneck problems that I see other drillers tryin' to work around."

"Really, soon as they catch on, most new hands with good attitudes, like you an' the Shooter, work harder an' better than the more experienced and crankier roughnecks. Now, tell me," he said, pulling back his hand and using his softest, most gentle voice, "why are you quittin' out on me?"

Rubbing the numbness from my wrist, I told him about wanting to go to college. I also mentioned my one cousin who had absorbed three years of college and might even graduate. Two of my aunts also had a few semesters of college time. He knew one of them, my Aunt Hazel, who had taught a nephew of his in our school. Hazel had been attending summer college, one semester at a time for as long as I could remember. She was a good teacher, about 40, and had taught in Burkburnett's schools for years but hadn't yet gotten her degree in 1945. My dad had attended a Baptist College in Decatur, Texas on a football scholarship for one year but no one in my family had ever finished.

I explained to Digger that I was curious about college and wanted to see for myself what it was like. I also admitted that I couldn't blame him for being mad because I had promised to help drill all of Bell's wells, but the way I saw it, I ought to try college out and would like for him to release me from my promise. Then I stopped to wait for his answer and it took so long that I wondered if he was ever going to speak to me again. Looking back over nearly 60 years of time, I realize that he was deciding exactly what he wanted to say and was trying to frame it properly so I would not misunderstand.

"Kid," he finally said, "you are doin' exactly what I think you ought to do. You need to work somewheres else besides in the oil patch. To do well in the oilfield, a man has to be a good driller, and you are too smart to make a good one. Guys like you generally end up bein' bored when they have learned mostly all the things a man has to know to be a good driller. An' that's dangerous. Bored men often daydream and lose track of what they are doin', or worse, get impatient and make mistakes, like trying too pull too much weight on a string of pipe that is stuck and pulling the derrick in on top of a drilling crew."

"I wish," he continued, "that I had got better educated. But all the schoolin' I had a chance for was the sixth grade. My second driller taught me the arithmetic parts to drillin' an' how to tag samples and write readable logs. Because of that one generous man, I've been able to make a good livin' in this business, and it's a better livin' than most men can earn for their families. But there are lots of better ways than the oil patch where educated people earn livings. Educated men, like Fred and Mr. Martin, always end up being bosses."

"Now, the Shooter is a good, hard-workin' hand. And he's smart too. Like you, he has made me a good roughneck. You guys had really made it after three weeks, but I did you a favor by not tellin' you that you were already good hands. When you are my age, you will be able to understand that I was right to do it this way. It kept you from getting big heads and sorry attitudes. It also kept your minds open to more learning."

"The Shooter," he went on, "is a person who was born to work outside. He is plenty smart enough to do college work but it would just bore him to death, like drillin' would you. He has a good feel for drillin' and I can teach him all he needs to know on the derrick floor. Fred likes him too an' can teach him enough more to make a good tool pusher out of him if he stays on with Bell."

"But you, Kid, can have the best deal of all. You can go to college an' do lots bigger an' better things than the rest us will ever have a chance for. That's why," he finished earnestly, "I think you ought to go on off to college. Not just because you want to do it, but because it's the right thing for you to do. Don't take this the wrong way, but I think you ought to quit an' I'm officially lettin' you go."

Thirty months later, after a short semester in college and a two year stint in the US Navy, I returned to Burk for a family visit. During my three brief weeks at home before re-entering college, there came a morning when I had an hour to kill so I drove out into the old Southwest field. I had no trouble in finding Bell's old dry-hole lease.

Driving completely around that giant pasture, I recalled my roughneck days and took pleasure in remembering the nicknames Digger had given us. There were no pumps or storage tanks on the ranch, so I guessed that Bell really did spot its lease shortly after I drew down my pay. Thinking deeply into the past, I steered the car by reflex, while remembering the Digger's loud yells at us but also thinking how carefully he had taught us everything we would try to learn about roughnecking, and the care he took in keeping us from being hurt. That was when I realized he had been a much better driller than I knew at the time.

To complete a loop back to Burk, I turned East toward the Wichita Falls and Lawton highway and soon noticed a tall deep-test drilling rig, slowly grinding atop a hill, half a mile inside a cow pasture on my right. As I neared the brand-new cattle guard which protected the well's freshly built gate opening, I read the company's name printed over a large red star on the white metal sign fixed onto the barbed wire fence. It said "Texaco" and, before I knew it, the car's front wheels turned through the gate with virtually no help from me.

Traveling slowly over deep fresh ruts in the bumpy new rig road, I pulled up to where the crew cars had parked and got out. Walking closer, I listened to the harsh noise of the drawworks engine that drove their rotary and the sound resonated up to a strangely satisfying ear-blasting level. By listening to the drawworks and looking at the kelly, I could see that this driller was in the hole.

He was also drilling into a hard formation because after five minutes, his kelly had not dropped perceptibly.

Walking closer to the rig, I stopped to enjoy the raucous blast of sound and vibration as the ground shook in time with their slowly grinding rotary table. I would have liked to climb onto the derrick floor but knew I wouldn't be welcome, even if I had proper safety gear, because I had no business there. After listening five more minutes, I had soaked up enough noise to develop a small ear ache and was about to turn away when I saw a tall hard-hatted worker looking down at me from the derrick floor. Suddenly, he waved vigorously and trotted down the derrick stairs.

By the time he had jumped three steps down, I could tell by his body movement that this guy was H. B. But it sure didn't look like him. I was watching a man at least four inches taller than the one I used to know. And he wore no glasses. Yet, when he had gotten within 40 feet, all my doubt vanished. I recognized his familiar happy smile and the round shape of his face. This was H. B., and no doubt about it!

We shook hands, both talking at once, because we hadn't seen each other since I quit Bell Oil. Within minutes we were as comfortable together as we had been in high school, and it took only a short time for me to tell him about dropping out of college and joining the Navy. Then it only took him a few minutes to tell me about fitting contacts into his eyes to replace those thick glasses he had worn earlier and the many hours he had saved by no longer having to look for them. He also told about marrying one of the prettiest girls in our class and said they had hatched a baby boy who was now over a year old.

After I left, H. B. had moved out to Odessa with Digger and Bell's new rig. He had worked for Digger over a year, until Bell sold out everything, guts, feathers and all, to a bigger Independent company. Digger hired out as tool pusher for some other company. But while H. B. had worked for him, he had moved him off the floor and into the derrick. He had also given him a full round of experience with mixing mud and taught him how to spot a rig on its pad and string it up as good as any veteran oilpatch hand. H. B.

had worked a full year for that new company until he and his wife got homesick. He drug up then and they returned to Burk.

The day after they came back he learned that Fred had hired out to a Wichita Falls company and they had made him their drilling superintendent. Ten minutes after H. B. had called on him at his office and they had talked halfway through a cup of steaming black coffee, Fred had hired him to work on the rig where H. B. and I now stood and talked. Their company was contracted out to the Texas Company to dig a string of 10 deep exploratory wells in that corner of Texas and he would be able to sleep at home nights for the next three years.

"This is a lot bigger rig than the one we started out on," he said, "Come on up and I'll show you."

I pointed out that I wore no safety gear and the rig was busy. "Your driller," I protested, "will run us both off."

H. B. grinned happily then reached for his watch pocket and pulled out a new and expensive looking gold watch. As he started to answer, I could see that his watch, just like Digger's, was fitted with a braided leather fob. And, just at the outer end of that fob I saw a silver replica of one of Hughes Tool Company's rock bits.

"Well, Ed," he answered, "we've got an hour and a half to go before making a new connection, and there's no way that driller's going to get mad at us because I'm him. In fact, Fred says, the way this new company is growing, after Wilson Power Rig Company delivers us the next brand-new rig, he will have to make a tool pusher out of me whether he wants to or not."

H. B. looked straight into my face, grinning his infectious best, and kept on talking. He knew I had always enjoyed hearing him talk and, for my benefit, he was now saying the kinds of things I used to enjoy so much hearing him talk about. "Fred gripes all the time, Ed. He says none of the good young oilfield prospects want to work in the oil patch any more. Nowadays, he says, rather than signing up for the army, or taking a healthy working man's kind of job in the out-of-doors, the good ones get fat and lazy after graduating from high school. He says the hardest work most of them will ever do is go off to college, and maybe try to play some football."

CHAPTER 37

CASIN' PULLIN'—1947

TWENTY MINUTES BEFORE sunrise glinted off the blanket of ice which covered North Texas, I shifted into neutral and pointed the headlights at an old oil drum that we had been using for a water barrel. Stepping out just as George's ancient pickup rolled to a stop, I left the motor running so its heater would warm the others. Also, I was afraid it might not re-start and didn't want to ride all the way to Olney, Texas in George's old Dodge truck with a broken right door glass.

Slamming the dented and rattley door behind me, I moved carefully across the icy ground, stopping only to grab up an old mesquite fence post I'd seen laying there two days before. Reaching the barrel I whammed it several times against a two-inch-thick mantle of ice. And after breaking it into chunks, I was able to bucket out enough slush to make room for filling up two five gallon water buckets.

It was late November, 1947 and daylight had barely arrived. We were moving George's casing pulling rig and it was my week to fill the truck radiators. Anti-freeze was high-priced and still hard to find this soon after World War II. And even if George would have bought any, his rotten old radiators and hoses would have leaked it off before daylight anyway.

George figured it was easier and cheaper for his help to avoid frozen engine blocks by draining the radiators on cold winter nights. Next morning we filled them up again. Both of his old trucks leaked and boiled over so badly that they had to be filled up in the summer anyway, so he judged there was no reason to change his program during winter time just because his help might get wet feet or suffer a little from cold weather. If asked, he would say the workers stayed outside anyway. They would get cold in the winter and hot in the summer anyway, so why should he worry about anti-freeze?

And me? My main problem wasn't that I was cold and about to be wet all over. It was worse. I'd signed up to work for what my granddad used to call a "one-horse outfit". And I didn't know it yet, but I'd made a mistake.

It never occurred to my co-workers that they should get out to help. They intended to stay inside, keeping the heater warm while they criticized my radiator technique. Long before I hired out to George, they had applied oilfield illogic to this part of their work. Deciding there was no reason for three people to get cold and wet on winter mornings while performing a one-man job, they had gambled on the task. On the first and 15th day of every month they drew straws to see who would fill truck radiators for the next two weeks. And it was me, a devout winter-hating Texan who had drawn the short straw and lost.

Three weeks earlier when I was discharged from the Navy in Corpus Christi, thermometers were registering a warm 78 degrees. This morning, in Burkburnett, 400 miles North of Corpus, my dad's front porch thermometer showed 19 degrees when I snapped my Zippo lighter at it to see how much cold I was having to tolerate.

Moving fast, to finish soon as possible, I hauled two five gallon bucketfuls over to the old Dodge truck which carried a set of gin poles laid over its cab. After sticking a flashlight under the hood, I could see well enough to reach in with pliers to close the petcocks located on the bottom ends of the engine block. The old hood wouldn't prop up high enough for a person to stand on the front bumper and pour, so I had to stand in front of the grill and raise each heavy bucket up to chin height. Keeping the bucket lip as near the radiator opening as possible, I gradually lifted the bottom and poured, hoping to get all of that icy water into the radiator but my hope was ridiculous.

The wind blew in constant gusts and I wasn't the best bucket hand in that end of the county, so a persistent cascade of water ended up blowing or splashing off the grill onto my clothes. That straw I pulled had won me the coldest day of 1947 up to then, and before I was through, my entire front was soaked.

Inside the pickup, I could hear snatches of jokes and comments as the others watched with interest. I didn't like it, but knew I would lower myself in their estimation and brighten their day if I complained or showed anger. The best course was to move precisely and keep my cool. Actually, the keeping cool part was no problem.

Few oilfield workers back then expected to extend to or receive sensitivity from fellow employees. Each of those work hardened men had problems of his own and they seldom cared whether newcomers had an ego or not. All boll weevils were treated alike— bad. New guys had to earn any respect they got, and if a boss noticed a new hand's ego bumping into his idea of how the job ought to go, he wasted no time in tromping it out of his way.

A good case could be made that no oilfield hands in those days, me included, exhibited job sensitivity more than once, maybe twice, in a year. We were the way we were because Texans in those days expected each person to "stomp his own wasp nests", "hoe his own row" and "clean up his own cow patties." No real man asked for help if he was able to perform his job alone.

I was an ex-roughneck and wasn't very proud of this casing pulling job anyway. The business rated close to bottoms in oilfield measurement because we were really in the junk iron business. The wells we pulled had been abandoned for years. Some hadn't been pumped since before I was born and our job was to jerk out their scrap iron guts then haul them off for sale.

"Casin' pullin'" was dirty, dangerous, unromantic, unimaginative and low-paying. Also, in the winter of 1947, neither our government nor any boss had ever considered furnishing a crew with psychiatric counselors in order that our "grief and anger" could be properly channeled whenever, not if ever, one of us was hospitalized, maimed or killed.

Our bosses, and even the federal government, would have laughed loudly at such an idea and so would we. Given a choice, we'd much rather they bought us a beer. Because of those reasons, plus personal pride, I expected no sympathy and didn't even consider the possibility of re-drawing straws. We had made a deal, then I gambled and lost. "Next time," I reasoned, as icy water splashed over my clothes and seeped down to my belly, "Maybe I'll win."

Despite a poor oilfield economy, George's one-horse pulling rig had stayed busy all during the war. Wildcatters had paid him big prices for salvaged casing. Now that the war was over, there were more drillers and less casing. Steel companies, when switching back to civilian production, had misjudged oilfield needs and waited way too long to start manufacturing oilfield pipe.

Instead of falling off after the war, the demand for oil blossomed. Drillers were stomping the ground impatiently and cursing while they called everywhere, trying to locate pipe, tubing, casing, motors, pumps and a hundred other war-scarce products. Meanwhile, they catered to George's ego, giving him all the cigars he would smoke, and stood in line to buy every joint of rusty, bent-up second-hand pipe we stripped out of the ground.

As I began pouring the second bucket, I once more asked myself the question that I continued asking throughout my working life. "Ed, why did you hire out to these people?" And, when everything had been considered, my answer was always the same. "I've never not needed money and this is the best job I can find."

Thirty gallons of water afterward, both radiators were filled and I walked, rather than ran, back to the pickup so I wouldn't seem to be giving in to the weather, and crawled under its wheel. Now it was my turn to judge while the others hopped out to start the old Dodge and George's equally ancient Ford truck. The Ford's heater wasn't working when George bought it and only the most naive optimist would believe that he ever intended to spend the money to have it fixed. Today, its driver was going to freeze. My boyhood chum, Freddy, drove the dodge and a guy whose first name was "Shirley" would herd the Ford.

Shirley was orphaned at an early age but was stout and quick and was George's "lead-off hand." Having flat feet and little education had disqualified him from military service and he had worked for George all during the war. Freddy and I had grown up seeing Shirley around town. He had hitch-hiked into Burk at age 12 and had earned his living in the oilfield ever since. He was normally quiet and never picked fights. But, even if we hadn't been knowing him all our lives, Freddy and I knew instinctively that no person in his right mind would josh Shirley about his girlish name.

I yelled over to Freddy that I was wet and cold, and, since my pickup traveled faster than the trucks, I was going to stop off at the Pioneer Cafe in Wichita Falls to drink some hot coffee and dry out some. The trucks could only drive at 40 miles per hour and I promised to catch up with them before they got to Olney. I could get away with this because Freddy was the boss's son. Also, it came to me, that his being my main high school running buddy was another reason I'd hired out to George. Shirley was our foreman but wasn't technically in charge until we got out to the rig, so he made no complaint. I waited to see that their trucks cranked up OK then gunned the old pickup into Wichita.

Kid-like, I hung out in the restaurant long as I dared, soaking up the warmth and smell of good food. I also enjoyed big-dogging in front of a cute young waitress who listened closely to my highly intelligent opinions, covering economics, foreign affairs and fun dating. But her interest really blossomed when I told her how pretty I thought a certain blonde waitress looked on that cold and windy morning. Luxuriating in that toasty atmosphere and enjoying her attentive company, I swallowed four cups of steaming, black Texas coffee and ate a generous bowl of fresh-baked cherry cobbler followed by a large slice of mincemeat pie. By then my clothes were dry and I'd lost my chill.

The atmosphere was so good that I stretched my time a little close. When I finally stood up to leave, that waitress watched closely as I "weighed out" but I wasn't sure whether her opinion of me was truly good or bad because she didn't give me her phone number. Giving up on the phone number, I carelessly flipped a quarter onto the counter, telling her it was for a "top-flight" waitress then squared my shoulders as I thought John Wayne might have done and shouldered bravely through the door into a frigid world.

It was 10:00 when I caught up with the others. I was 15 minutes overdue but my luck held. George's Dodge had blown a tire two miles before reaching Olney and I caught them just as they had finished replacing it. Honking and waving, I slowed down enough to shout that I would drive ahead to the Sinclair Station in town where George had arranged for discounts on his gasoline bills and was waiting impatiently.

George was parked near the road on the station's service apron and I quickly spotted him pacing nervously back and forth beside his brand new 1947 Ford pickup. When we left Burk he had sent us ahead to start up the larger trucks and drive on to Olney. Those trucks traveled more slowly than his pickup. George stopped at the Continental Supply Company in Wichita Falls to buy a new set of "dogs", regular people call them "jaws", for the breakout head on his pulling machine, and he figured this plan would save time and also keep him from driving at the slow speed of his trucks in that new pickup. He had bought his last one back in 1939 and it galled him to creep along in the new one at 40 miles per hour.

George said nothing to me but complained to Freddy as soon as the trucks pulled in. We were 30 thirty minutes late. I was glad I hadn't spent any more time in the Pioneer and arrived in Olney behind them. George would likely have fired me when we got back home. It was now a few minutes past 10:00 in the morning but a stranger who listened to George would have thought the sun was setting.

Freddy wasn't disturbed. He was used to his father's moods. Besides, he knew he wouldn't be fired. His mother protected him fully, even out on that rig. He constantly argued with George, often contradicting him in front of anyone who happened to be around, almost daring his Dad to fire him. Freddy hated his job because he really didn't like any kind of work, especially if it was hard. Shirley and I weren't relatives and we needed our jobs, so we minded our manners and walked carefully when George was in a pet.

Freddy had always been wild as a jackrabbit and was immune from being fired because no one was sure whether he could or would hold a job with anyone else. Besides, George knew he needed watching, both day and night. By hiring Freddy, George could eyeball him during most daylight hours. And, even though it was difficult, he occasionally got some work out of him. Any labor Freddie performed would help to offset the money his mother constantly doled out behind George's back.

After George had complained enough to salvage some ego, he opened the door of his new truck, ducked his head and started to climb in. But Freddy shouted loudly, asking more as a challenge rather than a question, when we would eat lunch. "Dinner's in the pickup," George replied after turning back. "You can eat when the rig has been set up." Then he ducked his head again but Freddy's second question pulled him back. "What did you get us?"

"Baked chicken dinners. Four of 'em, an' some fried pies. An' there's Cokes in the water cooler." Then he leaned toward the truck once more but Freddy still wasn't finished.

"I'm tired of chicken all the time," he complained. "Why don't you ever buy us some steak?"

"I will next time. Now, come on. We need to work." With that George jumped in, slammed the door and burned out, the pickup's shiny rear wheels throwing up enough gravel to rattle off the nearest gas pumps.

Freddy looked at me and grinned in triumph then climbed under the Dodge's steering wheel. He and I had been friends all through high school, and I liked him, but I never stopped being thankful that I didn't have to live with him.

Our well site was 15 miles West of Olney, but, within two hours we had blocked up the rig, raised its gin poles and strung up the draw works. Then we dropped the rig floor in place, leveled it, and drove down the guy-wire stakes with sledge hammers. Finally, we had the cables tied off, the turnbuckles tightened and were able to knock off for lunch. George helped when extra hands were needed, but Freddy was mostly useless except for running errands and fetching tools. Before lunch he pilfered a fried pie and walked around munching on it but George ignored him.

I was hungry and glad when our 30 minute lunch time finally arrived. For a short period we could shelter from the cold wind while eating our almost frozen chicken, potatoes and green bean lunch. George ate before we did and used lunch time to replace the new breakout dogs and rig up his heavy rope "catline".

After lunch, Shirley carefully placed three sticks of nitro jelly into a metal carrier, shoved a couple of percussion caps into their tops, and using a tiny wire line, lowered this package to the bottom of our well. When it was in exact position, he dropped a small pipe collar down the wire to hammer the caps. This exploded the dynamite and blew the casing end loose just above the foot valve at the well's bottom. After that George began to pull up on the casing string, trying to loosen it in the well. If it didn't loosen quickly, we would move a joint further up the string and blow it off again but he didn't like doing that because it wasted a good joint of salvage, plus the expense of a dynamite charge.

Most of the time It only took a couple of hours to complete a well after we started jerking casing out. These were shallow wells, occasionally having as few as 40 recoverable joints. By taking only thirty minutes off for lunch, we should have finished before dusk, but our job started off bad. Those new jaws George bought didn't work well in his old break-out head. Stiff and unmanageable, they hung up after unscrewing each joint even after it was unscrewed from the string.

George wasn't saying much but he had swelled up like a horned toad and was mad enough to spit blood because this trouble started with the very first joint. And he couldn't get the dogs to release, even after shutting down long enough to remove and re-set them. They were just too new and needed a few hours heavy break-in time to loosen them up.

So, after each joint was screwed off the string, work had to stop until we could hammer the breakout machine's head with sledges or wham it against anything handy to make those jaws release. When they finally opened up, it was my job to "tail" the freed joint over the side and lay it to rest with the others. But if this trouble continued, we weren't going to finish by dark. And George, like every other employer I have known, had a great distaste for losing money, unless he was playing poker—that is. Losing at poker was normal for him.

We finally learned that the best way to loosen our breakout head was for George to use the catline and pick up both the machine and the tightly held joint of casing three or four feet. Then he dropped them hard on top of the pipe string and, after four or five good hits the dogs would release and the casing joint would pop loose. If it didn't, we hammered the breakout head with sledges until the dogs released the pipe. When the joint sprang free, I grabbed its bottom end, tailing it across the floor and putting it to bed.

After laying back each joint, we pulled the breakout head back down over the casing string again. Then George would pull the string up through it high enough to clear another joint and we would use the cranky breakout head to screw off another joint. Unscrewing a joint was called "backing it out." After each joint was backed out, George banged the breakout head against the string again until the dogs turned it loose. Then we laid that joint back with the others and kept on pulling.

After 20 or so joints, the jaws occasionally broke loose without banging and we worked a little faster. It began to look as if we might finish before dark, but George still crowded hard, making sure. I could almost hear him thinking: "You never know when something else will happen." And, with his junky equipment, nursed and patched through four years of war, he had a good point.

After 30 joints we began to establish a rhythm. The pipe would spin loose, the breakout jaws would release and the head would drop down under the top collar. George then raised the loose joint a foot or so with his catline so I could catch its tail end and guide it over the edge of the floor to lay it back. It was only taking several minutes to dispose each joint and I could measure by sound and by guess when to reach for each one. And that was exactly when everything came unglued.

The breakout dogs hung tight once more. Working quickly, George repeatedly picked up on the catline and dropped the casing joint and breakout head down on top of the string. After the fourth bang the dogs released and the casing joint sprang loose, rising about a foot. I stuck my left hand into its bottom end and started pulling the joint across my body to tail it over the floor. The problem was, it was getting dark. George hadn't seen the joint spring free and he banged it one more time.

I was in trouble because I was off balance, pulling across my body. I also knew that the end of that joint, where I had carelessly stuffed all my fingers, was going to strike the heavy metal top of the breakout head before I could pull it across. I could lose all four fingers here. Acting on instinct, I rolled my hand over, palm up, and twisted my wrist away from the joint, allowing the casing joint to free fall. Then it banged heavily against the metal breakout head but I got all my fingers free. All, that is, except one.

I thought I was lucky. Nothing much was hurting except the end of my left little finger. It felt the same as it had when I had grazed it hard once with a hammer head, bruising but not cutting the skin. Shirley, who stood beside me, looked straight into my face and said, "Boy, that was close." Then he grabbed the swinging joint of casing, pulled it past me and tailed it across the floor for me.

I grinned, agreeing with him that it "sure was" close. Then I held up my hand to look at the heavy leather glove. My hands were small and the glove's smallest finger was a full inch longer than my own. But, even in the late evening light, I could see that the glove's finger was split straight through the center, from its end, halfway down the middle.

Looking closer, I saw several bright drops of blood rolling on the oily leather surface, so I pulled it off to take a look and what I saw wasn't appetizing. The top joint of that small finger was spread apart, forming a perfect "V". The 1/4-inch-thick pipe wall had split it as precisely, as if it had been sawn, straight down the middle, from the tip halfway into the second joint.

George was busy with something else and hadn't noticed anything wrong. But Freddy, quick-eyed, jumped across the floor when I pulled off my glove. He began to yell, then jumped up and down in the middle of the floor until George saw him. Deliberately, George shoved down on the cable drum's brake arm and throttled back his draw works engine low enough to hear. Then he looked questioningly at his son, waiting for information.

"Ed cut his finger off!"

George looked over to me and comprehension dawned when he saw my glove lying on the floor and me cradling a slowly dripping hand. He considered for several seconds then directed his son. "Put him in the pickup, the old one, not my new one, and carry him to the doctor in Olney." Turning back, he revved up his drawworks and began to raise the string of casing.

I've never been certain whether George didn't want me bloodying up his new pickup or didn't want Freddy to drive it. Probably, it was a little of both. As we bumped out of that cow pasture, I looked back at his small, rusty pulling rig in the right door mirror. George had climbed off the driller's seat onto the well floor and was helping Shirley to set the slips. Neither of them was interested in a psychiatric session to minimize any injury their psyches might have received because of witnessing my accident. And they wouldn't have consented to one if the casing had cut my head off. All they wanted was to finish up before dark.

There is no point in reviewing hospital details, other than to mention that Freddy turned green around the gills and had to leave before the surgeon finished my amputation and stitching job. Also, I made a date with the surgical nurse to go to the movies that night but wouldn't have made it even if George hadn't instructed Freddy to carry me back home.

Most important was, besides paying my medical bills, the Insurance Company gave me $125 for partial loss of a finger. Some folks suggested that I could hire a lawyer and get more money but, for half a finger joint, I didn't want to listen to any lawyers. No one I knew would hire a person with my kind of injury to work for them, so I drew down my wages and quit George. Buying a train ticket, I rode through a hard winter snow storm to Denton where I enrolled as a student at North Texas State Teacher's College.

Shortly afterward my parents moved to Pampa, Texas and I never lived in Burkburnett again. It wasn't easy, but I followed college rules long enough to earn a degree. And the day I hurt my hand turned out to be the last day I drew pay in the "oil patch." That's probably why I still own the rest of my fingers and toes.

CHAPTER 38

Doc—1952

HE WAS ALREADY a legend in the East Texas Oilfield when I met him, but he would probably have selected different reasons for fame than the ones chosen by his friends and neighbors. I first shook hands with Doc in 1952 at Les Foshee's garage, at the side of Highway 64 in Turnertown, located between Henderson and Tyler, in Rusk County, Texas. We got acquainted while standing almost in the middle of the giant East Texas Oilfield, which many people insist is the most productive oilfield ever to be drilled in America. And during its best years, from 1934 to 1945, they are certainly correct.

Only a few years before we met, Doc had bought an empty house and moved it onto a vacant lot four hundred feet East of Les's garage. After having it leveled up and painted, he hooked up the utilities. On the night that he moved in, he started sleeping regularly in a bed for the first time since coming to East Texas seven years earlier.

Everybody called him "Doc" and most folks liked him. They also needed him. He was the only real physician in that end of the piney woods who could treat the hundreds of oilfield families living in tents and "shotgun" oilfield shacks scattered over that end of the field. There were a few herb doctors and preacher-physicians who treated customers by digging up roots to feed them and "laying on their hands" plus several chiropractors who had hung up signs near the road in front of their tents. But if a worker or his family needed more dependable medicine than faith healing or joint jerking, he went to find Doc, the only licensed and college-trained physician around.

The next nearest medical doctors were located from 15 to 30 miles away, depending on where you were when you "took sick" or got hurt. To reach one, the patient had to travel over muddy, one-lane, partially surfaced roads to Kilgore, Longview, Henderson or Tyler. During the early part of that boom roads were always badly congested and virtually impassable, even in good weather. After a heavy rain, which happens often in that country, wagons and trucks stuck tight in the mud, blocking traffic. Drivers and teamsters who couldn't get help often unhooked their teams and rode them off, postponing delivery until the weather was better.

Most people who lived or worked in that part of the field, including me, were treated by Doc at one time or another. I came there in late 1952, way too late to be considered a Pioneer East Texas oil person. In fact, I had quit the oilfields by then, and having worked hard for a college degree, fervently hoped I would never go back to "jerking iron" again.

In 1931, when Doc came, he was a bachelor and had already stopped telling people his age. He had also started using hair polish and constantly told people that a man's birthdate wasn't the main thing. Good eating habits, he insisted, and top physical condition were much more important.

My wife's father, Raymond Crawford, was a druggist who had moved to Selman City only a few weeks after the discovery well was drilled. That was in September of 1930 when a little known and rheumatic Wildcatter and con artist, named Columbus Marion "Dad" Joiner convinced himself that oil could be found in Rusk County. Drastically short on funds, he leased his acreage more than once, some of it even several times, before he was finally able to complete the first producing well in the East Texas Oilfield. It was named the "Daisy Bradford No. 3". Because of equipment and labor failure he had been forced to abandon his first two attempts. No person alive could even guess that his third attempt was to be the first of thousands of producing oilwells and that the field would grow to be the largest oilfield ever found until then.

My wife's grandfather, Ad Crawford, was a sawmiller who recognized commercial possibilities in this new field. He promptly

bought land near Turnertown and opened a lumber yard. He intended
to sell lumber and materials as well as become a building contractor.
He and Raymond also erected a building in which Raymond, a
registered druggist, would operate a drugstore of his own.

Local people were mostly land-poor farmers who had seen
almost none of the world's great wonders. They were highly
impressed by Mr. Joiner's well, even though it wasn't a big gusher.
America's 1930 decade was one in which many East Texas farm
families would not see as much as $400.00 in a full year. Even those
with little imagination understood that an oil strike, even one as
unimpressive as this, would cause money to circulate and that a
measure of prosperity might follow.

"Major" oil companies, evaluating Dad's discovery well, only
yawned at first. None of their geologists could see the likelihood
of a big oil discovery there. This lack of interest allowed the vast
East Texas Oilfield to become an "Independent Oilman's Paradise"
and it cost the big players millions of dollars before they finally
entered the field, hoping to catch up.

Doc, along with thousands of hopeful Boomers who outran
the Major oil companies to East Texas, came six months after Dad's
discovery well and started scouting around, trying to judge how
real the boom was. Deciding it would last, he elected to stay.
Twenty years later, he told me that he'd been trying to decide
whether to set up a practice in the oilfields or head on North to
Alaska. His advice in 1952 was that I ought to go North. Alaska, he
felt, was still loaded with opportunity for young men but the East
Texas Oilfield was playing out. In 2004, a new millennium, we
know that Doc was right about Alaska, but he was wrong about the
East Texas Oilfield. It is still pumping up millions of barrels of oil.

The boom's new doctor immediately bargained with my wife's
father to supply him with "fresh" drugs. He had no problem in
convincing himself and tried to convince my father-on-law that he
should be allowed to buy them at cost. Raymond laughed about
this later, saying, "We didn't do any business that day." So, besides
the hair coloring thing, Doc's reputation for being "tight as bark on
a tree" was established early.

After looking hard and not finding a suitable, or maybe a cheap enough office location, Doc talked with Raymond again. He needed, he pointed out, an office near the main roadway and Raymond's store was located at the edge of what would later be Highway No, 64, near the busy Turnertown intersection. That was where the best roads crossed as they branched toward Henderson, Tyler, Kilgore and Longview. Those same roads also led North to Dallas and East to Louisiana.

Doc's new proposition was that Raymond could make room for a small treatment office near the back of his store. This allowed patients to walk through for treatment. The extra traffic, he reasoned, should enable Raymond to give him free rent. Raymond decided that Doc had studied as much finance as medicine in college and they didn't trade that day either. Several days and a lot of talking later they shook on a deal. The field's new resident MD was allowed a 10 by 12 foot office building beside the store with an outside entrance.

Raymond never mentioned what Doc paid for rent but it was likely very little. He was a generous person if he liked you, and Raymond liked Doc. Also, he had bought a few lots behind his store and was selling them to people who wanted to put houses on them. He figured that having Doc around was good for the community, like the water well Raymond had drilled and was allowing folks to lay pipelines to, charging them only enough to pay his operating expense. Their final agreement was that Doc could buy emergency drugs from Raymond at a 25 percent discount. Doc would prescribe all the drugs he didn't want to inventory and tell patients that Raymond would "treat them good" as he wrote out the prescriptions.

To Raymond, their deal was primarily a community service. Every person you saw in that end of Rusk County was living, working and going to school in the very center of a crowded and dangerous oil field where derricks far outnumbered the single-walled shanties nestling throughout those piney woods. Teams and trucks passed by all night and all day, hauling loads of pipe, oil rigs, pumps, tanks, compressors, boilers and derrick materials over roads that people also used for driving their kids to school and reaching their jobs. Many oilfield people had no cars and either walked or thumbed rides wherever they went. Traffic was always a mess and people had few real choices. Most had to look for Raymond or Doc when they got sick or were hurt.

Gushers blew in at all hours of the day and night and many oilfield people worked so hard that they wouldn't take time to visit Doc or Raymond even when they were extremely sick. People took fewer days off from work in those days and used whatever family remedy was available, along with plenty of whiskey and paregoric. Occasionally a hard-working oilfield hand would delay treatment for so long that he simply worked himself to death.

Raymond, like most merchants in that depression, quickly attracted a large number of customers he didn't need. He described them as "slow-pay" to "no-pay-at-all". Despite the increasing number of wells being drilled, the millions of dollars being spent, and the sudden creation of many oil-rich millionaires, the average oilfield worker was almost as poor as an East Texas farmer. Those were the "Deep Depression" days and no family had too much money.

Oilfield hands were mostly ex-farmers who had fled a life of near-starvation on farms to search for jobs that paid any kind of cash money. What they found were jobs that were hard, dangerous and unpredictable. They often put in 12 hour days or longer, while some country merchants and restaurant owners worked even longer hours than that. Oilfield hands who didn't learn their jobs quickly, or were too small and weak, were quickly weeded out. Raymond and Doc extended gobs of credit to workers who never earned enough to come back and pay their bills, even if they later had the money.

Money got even tighter when some of the new get-rich-quick oil companies began to file for bankruptcy because oil prices had dropped so low. The oil business had suddenly gotten to be like farming. Every producer in the business had developed a bumper crop but there was a problem. There was so much produce, in this case oil, that the crop didn't bring in enough money to pay expenses. At one time during the East Texas boom oil dropped to a dime a barrel and the Texas Governor called out the National Guard to enforce smaller production quotas assigned to oil producers by the Texas Railroad Commission. This set off a deluge of illegal night time oil bootlegging. They called it "hot oil" and it often sold for as little as a quarter a barrel even then, while a barrel of good clean drinking water would always bring $2.00 out in the field and was much harder to find.

Until 1941, when World War II erupted, there were always more oilfield workers than jobs. Men stood everywhere, each one ready to grab a shovel when a worker threw it down, got killed or was "run off" by his boss. Despite these conditions, Raymond always gave credit to sick people, even when knowing they might never pay. Doc complained about it, but did the same. Both of them felt they were practicing vocations rather than businesses.

Raymond didn't know until after they finished their trade that Doc was sleeping in his car. But he learned about it after Doc's new office was ready. Instead of renting a room or setting up a tent as many Boomtowners did, Doc moved out of his car and onto the top of his homemade examination table. He slept there for several years.

Most people were surprised that the arrangement lasted as long as it did. But they had misjudged Raymond's patience and Doc's ability to sleep soundly for the sake of a good deal. But Raymond liked Doc. Besides, Doc was the only real physician around.

Doc and J. C. Penney might have made good tent mates because each of them fell in love with every penny that came to his hand. After reading about Mr. Penney, I would judge Doc was the thriftiest. Doc's fees weren't steep, but, since he seldom spent money, those small payments quickly mounded up. Yet, to his credit and despite his love affair with each and every dollar, no patient ever complained about him or about Raymond refusing to treat or give medication to any sick person, black or white, because they had no money. If Doc had done that, Raymond would likely have made him move.

Within a few weeks, Raymond slowly became the closest thing to a nurse that Doc had. Many times during those boom days, emergencies consisting of knife, gunshot, car wreck, heart attack and job-injured persons were hauled to the drug store or to Doc's new office under the pines.

Any time a case became unwieldy and Doc needed help, regardless of whether it might be day or night, he sent one of the walking wounded over to hammer on Raymond's bedroom or store window. At night Raymond quickly rose and dressed, hurrying on down. During the day he stopped whatever he was doing and trotted over to assist Doc, laboring as hard as he was able, until the job was finished. Many patients were carried off or limped away while listening to Doc's ringing advice that they should eat a banana every day in order to live long healthy lives. Then he recorded their fee and stuck it in his pocket. Neither he or Raymond ever considered that Doc ought to offer payment for this emergency room help.

After World War II began, Raymond opened a post office in his drugstore and Doc quickly bought the maximum amount of US Saving and Postal Notes that any one person was allowed to buy. Periodically, he asked Raymond to issue him more than regulations allowed but Raymond never would.

Sometime later, Doc married and added a room onto his house. Soon the newlyweds had a baby girl and added another room. Doc always came to Raymond and bought the maximum amount of postal notes that each of his new family additions could legally own. When a second baby girl arrived a year later, he methodically performed this chore again.

Doc issued scads of free medical advice and some was ahead of its time. A few people thought it was strange, but a large part of today's medical community agrees with some of Doc's advice. He readily accepted as fact that vitamins were "helpful", but he always recommended that his patients eat a banana every day. He also favored ingestion of raisins, apples, oranges, nuts and any other fruits. Consumption of cabbage and "lots of green vegetables" and bran were also approved, and finally, "lots of exercise."

When patients complained that they could seldom afford these things, he snorted and said they could substitute good grass for green vegetables. It, he pointed out, was free and so was exercise. But fruit, he insisted, ought to be eaten as often as they could find and afford it.

Doc ignored remarks from men patients who pointed out that the oilfield exercised them "plenty." To every smoker he pointed out that they had a bad habit, hard on their lungs and blood circulation systems. Mostly, those patients ignored him because even when their families were hungry, nine out of 10 oilfield workers either smoked or "chewed." A small number of real old timers "dipped."

Early one morning in 1942 a pipeline contractor learned that Doc practiced what he preached. This man was laying a new gas line past Doc's office and had a lot of other jobs to perform, so he arrived as soon as the sun rose, hoping to finish and be gone by 10:00.

The thermometer stood at 25 degrees and digging would be unpleasant. But, even though he was anxious to begin, the contractor delayed his work long enough to step quietly onto Doc's porch and tap on the front door. He'd been raised in Texas and knew that old-time property owners could exert stringent methods to enforce their property rights. Most people were of the opinion that old-fashioned southern politeness, as well as common sense safety-first logic demanded that visitors advise any landholder before setting foot on his property. And doctors were no exception.

Steam radiators, central heating and air conditioning had been invented back then and could be found in some American homes, but not in the piney woods where people still lived very near to pioneer conditions. Many of these families had only recently moved out of bedrolls, tents and log cabins into single-walled oilfield dwellings. Their small houses were heated with homemade oil furnaces, wood stoves or open gas space heaters fed by raw and smoky gas tapped directly from some nearby oil company pipeline.

Only a few people allowed fires to burn all night because most of those heating systems were dangerous if left untended. Besides, these people had been trained all their lives to waste nothing at all. Waste was a sin. Few Texas men of that generation would spend money on house shoes or pajamas, though a few had bathrobes. Every one of them felt bitter cold each winter morning when he hopped barefooted across to a window and blew warm breath on it, trying to warm it enough to clear the glass and peer out to read his thermometer.

They felt the cold even worse after sitting up in bed and pulling on a pair of frozen shoes, then with laces dragging, clomping across a half frozen, brittle linoleum floor which crackled underfoot to light a life-nurturing fire in whatever type of stove the house owned. Sometimes they simply toughed it, figuring that shoes were as cold as the floor, and built their fires bare footed. Whichever way they did it, by the time a fire was roaring, further sleep was out of the question.

Before knocking on Doc's door, the contractor glanced through the front door glass, which was not frosted that morning, and saw his customer, seated on a straight-backed chair, in the exact middle of the living room floor. Each bare foot was planted flatly on frigid linoleum, Doc wore only a pair of men's legless underwear trunks, in contrast to most East Texans who wore long-handled underwear during winter. An empty banana peel lay near his chair and his face was beet red as both arms flailed wildly round and round.

"At first I thought he was dying," the contractor said, "but he stood up, grabbed a wool bathrobe from a hook and walked barefooted over to answer the door when I knocked."

In no rush after putting on his robe, Doc patiently opened the front door. After listening quietly to what his visitor had to say, he gave permission for work to begin. Then he noticed his visitor's puzzled expression and understood that he must have seen through the glass.

Showing no hint of embarrassment, Doc offered a crisp and unsmiling explanation: "I perform deep-breathing and motion exercises each morning. Cold temperatures cause contraction of the body's blood circulation system. Rapid arm motions exercise it. Bare feet on a cold floor will mildly shock and further stimulate the nervous system, exercising it in similar manner. Bananas are among our better foods and I try to eat one every day. Eating good foods, many fruits and exercising properly can help people to live long lives."

Most people in the Turnertown area had favorite stories about Doc's tightness with a buck, like the one about how he and his wife frequently took their daughters to eat lunch at a local boarding house. Most adults bought their children a plate and loaded it up, then purchased an adult plate for themselves. The parent then sat beside his child, conversing and monitoring his table manners. Doc didn't do it that way. He bought one adult plate, loaded it up to the brim and held a daughter in his lap, feeding her out of his plate. Both father and daughter enjoyed those meals, laughing frequently and "visiting" companionably with other diners,

This boarding house was one of the old-fashioned types where you ate until you were no longer hungry. Oilfield hands called it "pitchin' 'til you win". When a dish was emptied, a diner held it up and a waitress promptly filled it. When your plate was empty, you could load it again from the nearest handy dish. Folks always said Doc ate "like a pipeliner" but he always took time to offer medical education during any meal when the opportunity arose.

I graduated from college in 1952 and jobs were scarce. Any American who made $6,000.00 that year was among the top 10 percent of American wage earners. I took a job selling insurance in Henderson, Texas and was making a lot less than the ten percenters. But even though I had a job, I couldn't locate a decent rent house so, Marge and I decided to build a brand new home, which ultimately cost us $4,200. We jumped at the offer her parents made, allowing us to stay with them in Selman City during the two months it took to build our home.

On the day I first met Doc, I couldn't go to work because my clean and snappy 1948 Chevrolet 2-door deluxe sedan had a worn out pressure plate caused by a bad "throwout" bearing in the clutch. Finally, it laid down and had to be fixed so I took it to Les Foshee, the most reputable and hardest-working mechanic in those parts. He agreed to fix it up and guaranteed his work for $42.50. This was a fair price, but I was only earning $30.00 a week.

Having nothing else to do, I visited with Les while he worked, and we were giving each other an old-fashioned pair of ear aches, when Doc drove up in his wife's late-model Chrysler sedan. I noticed that Les didn't seem extra happy to see him but after frowning, he cleared his face, laid down his wrenches and wiped off his hands. Walking outside, he used hand motions to direct as Doc drove up onto the steel metal tracks over Les's outside grease pit. Doc quickly shut off his engine and later, when I knew him better, I understood that he did this to save every possible drop of gas. Stepping to the ground, he questioned Les, "Did you save it?"

Les nodded wordlessly then crawled into the grease pit to shove a drain pan underneath the big car's motor. Doc bent down to stick his head under the fender and look into Les' face. "Is your price still 'four bits'?" Les nodded again, never speaking, he loosened the oil plug, allowing hot motor oil to drain into a catch pan.

Having gotten Les started off, Doc noticed me, and sensing opportunity for a new patient, came over to shake hands and introduce himself. We talked for a few minutes and he pointed out the location of his office. I enjoyed talking to him and decided he was a pleasant-enough East Texan, although somewhat formal. But I was a newcomer and was puzzled when Les smothered a chuckle after Doc asked me how often I ate bananas and if I exercised regularly so I could live to be "a hundred." I was new to the community and decided to wait and see rather than to ask what Les had thought was funny.

After oil stopped dripping from the Chrysler, Les opened the hood and pulled out the filter. Then he selected a re-cleaned filter from his worktable, and stuck it into the engine. Replacing the oil plug, he walked across his shop, picked up a second drain pan, already full of motor oil and carefully poured every drop into the Chrysler's empty engine. Then he cranked the motor, and raced it a few seconds to check for oil leaks but Doc peered underneath and told him there were none so Les idled down. Doc paid Les fifty cents, backed off the rack and drove quietly away.

I looked quizzically at Les to see if he intended to explain but he didn't, so I finally asked. "Did I just see you put a used filter in that doctor's car and fill up his crankcase with used oil while he stood there watching you, and then he paid you real money to do those things to his car?"

"You sure did," Les answered, grinning uncertainly because he didn't know me very well yet, "and I'm agoin' to keep on charging him."

Then he explained. "Doc changes out the oil in his work car every 2,000 miles and I put new oil in his car yesterday. Today I took the oil and filter from his work car and put them in his wife's car. He figures that, since she drives very little, his used oil will keep her car going and not hurt its engine. So I always save his old oil and filter from every change and put them in her car. That way," Les finished, "he only pays about $10.00 a year to service the oil and filters in her car motor." I didn't answer because nothing else needed to be said.

Three years later, Marge and I moved from Henderson to Tyler where I began a new career in the insurance claims business. We weren't among the top ten percent of America's wage earners that year either. We kept track of many friends from Henderson and in the oilfields, but I had heard nothing at all from Doc until a day in 1959 when he called me "long-distance and person-to-person." This kind of call cost more than a normal long distance call so, I knew he was anxious to talk with me.

More than once, when I lived in Henderson and was selling insurance, I had tried to sell Doc some fire insurance on one or more of his rental properties but he wouldn't buy from me. He favored Government Employees Insurance Company, saying that they were cheaper than my companies. But his attitude was different now, because his money was involved and he talked fast, anxious for my help.

It turned out that Doc owned the Sinclair filling station directly across Beckham Street from where I worked. It was also where my office purchased gas and oil for our company cars every day. This building had, Doc told me excitedly, suffered an explosion earlier that morning. Government Employees Insurance had instructed him to call our office for an adjustment of his loss, and he had called me direct because we were old acquaintances. He wanted to be certain I would give his claim the prompt attention and fair payment he knew it deserved.

As Doc talked, I took down his policy information and started building his file. Writing while listening, I finished up at about the time he finally ran out of things to say. That was when I told him that I'd seen his building several times that day and hadn't noticed any trouble. But he insisted an explosion had occurred. He had "damage and trouble" at his property and "needed" my help. I ended our conference by saying that I would personally investigate, and quickly call him back after I knew enough to know what his policy would let me do.

It was February, clear and windy about 20 degrees outside. But the sun was shining so I decided to effect a change of pace for a few minutes and work on Doc's loss. Pulling on a heavy jacket, I grabbed my camera and walked across Beckham Street to see what sort of damage might be there. I was almost up to the gas pumps before noticing anything unusual at all.

The first thing I noticed was that both large doors to the service bays were open and Leroy, the station's operator, was mopping the inside floor near their grease pit. Next I noticed some light smoke residue on the wall near that pit and Leroy's brother, James, was sponging the paint with soapy water and a mop. Last, I saw that large chunks of thick plate glass were laying all around the gas pumps in front of the station entrance. They had come from a heavy plate glass window near the front door.

Walking over to Leroy, I stopped and waited. He was a hard worker and, if I hadn't been a good customer and we hadn't liked each other, he would have made me follow him around to get any information at all. But, because it was me, he threw the mop down and led me into the sales office where they had turned up their fire, trying to keep the room as warm as possible. He poured each of us a cup of steaming black Texas coffee and we sat down to warm near his stove while we talked.

"What's goin' on?"

"Well, we had a small flash fire near the grease pit at about 10:00 this morning."

Then he explained that James had been working on a customer's pickup and that their brand-new clean-up employee, on his first day at work, had set a pan of parts-cleaning-fluid onto the floor directly in front of the open-flame gas heater near the edge of their grease pit. By this time in the story James had finished cleaning the wall and came in from the cold to help us play the coffee pot.

James finished the story, explaining that he had closed both the bay doors because it was cold, and he hadn't noticed what their employee had done. After a few minutes, the cleaning fluid got hot, cooked out a fog of flammable vapor, and there was a sudden bright flash accompanied by a loud "whoosh" and a heavy fog of smoke. The heater had ignited that warm vapor.

The new helper, terrified, broke and ran. Unable to open either bay door quickly enough to suit him, he charged through the connecting door leading into the sales office, where we sat, and turned toward the front door. But it was firmly closed. Not taking time to open it, the guy vaulted to the top of Leroy's desk and jumped straight through that heavy front plate glass window. Shards of glass were still spinning on the concrete apron when he faded from view after sprinting up the hill toward Front Street.

Only an adjuster would have asked the obvious question I put to them. "Was he hurt?" They looked at each other and laughed, then James said they hadn't heard from him, so they didn't know for certain, but no doctors or hospitals had called and he certainly looked pretty active when charging up that hill. They easily put out the fire by dropping a flat sheet of metal across the top of the fluid bucket. Then they called Doc who instructed them to contact a "reasonable" plate glass repairman and have him replace the window. Leroy had wanted to clean up the broken glass but Doc insisted that they wait until an adjuster could see the damage. I finished my coffee, took a few pictures and left, telling Leroy to finish cleaning up whenever he wanted.

Before leaving I asked if they thought an explosion had happened. Both of them looked hard at me, then at each other and laughed some more. All that had happened, Leroy giggled, was that their ex-employee had gotten so badly scared that he left before even taking time to quit.

Back in the office I called Doc and told him the bad news. His policy, I pointed out, covered fire damage, but his deductible was $250.00. Knowing very well that his main interest was in replacing a $200.00 plate glass window, I reviewed for him that this glass was definitely covered for explosion under his policy but that no explosion had occurred. Leroy and James had cleaned up his smoke damage, and charged him nothing, so there was no payment due under his policy.

Doc was miffed and asked if I was mad at him for never buying any insurance from me. I explained that life was way too short for me to be mad at, or try to get even with the people who hadn't wanted to be my customers. But he wouldn't laugh with me and finally stopped talking. After thirty seconds of dead air space, I wished him well and quietly hung up the phone.

Completing a combination opening and closing report to Doc's insurance company, I told them what had happened and advised that Doc's claim had been denied. I included my boss's bill for my work and closed the file. Our bill was paid within several weeks and I heard nothing further from the company, but Leroy did.

Not satisfied with the way I had adjusted his claim, Doc had contacted his company, asking them to send another adjuster who would handle his claim better than me. They sent another adjuster who visited the scene, asked the same questions I had and left. Leroy had been receiving regular calls from the glass man who was still unpaid, but about three weeks after the second adjuster visited, Doc gave up. Complaining loudly about his insurance company not paying off, he finally sent a check to the glass man but only after demanding, but not receiving a 20 percent wholesale glass discount.

Sometime In 1958 or 1959 I heard that Doc had been diagnosed with cancer of the stomach. After experiencing severe pain and indigestion which he had been ignoring and which didn't go away, his deep-probing fingers finally located a big lump low in his left abdomen. Taking his own X-rays, he found a cancerous tumor, the size of an orange, in his lower stomach. Bearing his X-ray plates with him, he drove to Tyler where a fellow physician confirmed the melancholy diagnosis. Additional exploration convinced them that surgery was not a viable option and they were twenty years ahead of a time when other methods might have affected the situation.

Four months later, that good doctor who had spent most of his adult years treating a vast number of East Texas' poorest and least-advantaged oilfield people, the same person who wouldn't tell anyone how old he was, and who had scrimped and saved so he could live comfortably to be a hundred, was borne to his grave. I figured Doc was born around 1895, and that he was 63 or 64 on the day they preached his funeral.

CHAPTER 39

THE ODD COUPLE—1954

As I TURNED onto the Courthouse square that day in Henderson, Texas, I was so hungry that, as Texans sometimes say, "my stomach thought my throat was corked". And I knew exactly where I would eat. People from everywhere crowded into Floyd's Diner on Wednesdays because of the special country fried steak lunch that he cooked up better than anyone ever did except our mothers.

It was 2:00 when I arrived and the lunch crowd was long gone. Eric was the only customer there and he sat alone at the counter, sipping coffee and swapping friendly barbs with Floyd. To make certain everyone had plenty of room, I left a seat between us, nodded to Eric then to Floyd as I sat down on the hard, flat circular diner seat.

Eric operated a paint and wallpaper store half a block South of Floyd's place and had been raised in Rusk County. We were not only members of the First Baptist Church and Kiwanis Club together, but he was also my wife's boss. I noticed that Eric wore a white shirt and Sunday suit, which indicated that it wasn't a routine day for him. But I was interested in a very unusual story and didn't bother to ask why. The story was strange enough that I wanted ask someone who could tell me more about it, and since Eric was raised in Henderson, I figured he would know. Soon as I ordered my steak, I broke into their conversation, and told them what I had heard.

It was a strange tale involving an elderly and prosperous Henderson farmer who, 10 years earlier, had separated from his wife. For years, the story went, that couple had labored hard, carefully walking the narrow edge of poverty on a marginally producing 200 acre farm, fifteen miles Northeast of Henderson. But in 1930, their world changed completely in a very short time.

That was the year when an old hunch-backed arthritic oilfield wildcatter, Columbus "Dad" Joiner, drilled persistently, and on his third attempt completed the Daisy Bradford Oil Well No. 3 in Northern Rusk county. In doing so, he ushered the Giant East Texas Oilfield into existence, creating hundreds of millionaires. That field, 74 years later, still produces large quantities of high quality crude and nothing since then has been the same in either Gregg or Rusk Counties.

Six weeks after the discovery was announced, that farmer and his wife were visited by a wildcatting promoter who offered them a dollar an acre to lease their minerals and a 1/8 interest in any oil brought up from their property. But there was a hitch. They would have to wait "a few weeks" before receiving the lease money because it had to be paid for out of any oil that came up. If there was no oil, he paid nothing but they got their minerals back.

This wasn't a strange proposal for the times. Wildcatters lived in a condition of being broke because their plans and schemes always outran their money. This was so, even though a few of them were paid cash money by cities or other groups to drill test wells near their community. Successful wildcatters normally stayed broke because, even when the oil business paid them some money back, the cash always arrived way behind the promise. Even the richest of Boomers seldom had enough money at any given time to rent drilling rigs, pay out lease money and meet their drilling crew's payroll all at once. And the wildcatter who visited our farming couple had talked the drilling rig owner, the crew and even the rig builder into accepting half of their pay in oil, if there was any. They also agreed to let him "slow-walk" them an extra month before starting payment.

After thinking about it, the farmer decided there was probably no oil under his farm at all. But, if there was some, he would never get a nickel as long as it stayed underground. It had to be drilled for and pumped up before being worth anything. Wildcatting, he decided, was a gamble just like farming. Each business had to be carefully planned out and the plan executed properly. With wildcatters, buying a lease was the same as a farmer buying seed. Drilling was like plowing and planting, and pumping the oil up, if there was any, was like harvesting. After all those three things had been done, both a farmer and a wildcatter would be forced to sell their crops for whatever the market would pay.

When a wildcatter dug a dry hole, or a farmer lost a crop to hail or drought, each of them had to borrow money to buy more seed and gamble again. This farmer had little faith in having oil because the Daisy Bradford well was over a mile from his farm. The farmer and his wife signed the wildcatter's lease, then watched curiously as rigbuilders erected a wooden derrick and a rig was hauled in. Next day the wildcatter's crews strung cable onto a massive set of pulleys they called a traveling block. Then, using heavy five inch drilling pipe, they began to punch a well through the topsoil of his farm.

Seven weeks later, at 2:00 in the afternoon, the drilling crews shut down their rig, drove off and he never saw them again. Next morning trucks came out to load the heavy drilling machinery and hauled it away. The only sign left of any drilling action was the 80-foot-high derrick standing forlornly on its pad.

Hearing nothing further, our farmer assumed the worst. It was a dry hole, the kind he had heard oil people call a "duster". There had been no announcement by the wildcatter and no gusher, so no crowd of onlookers crowded onto his place to gawk at a fountain of oil being wasted. What happened, was exactly what he expected, a dry hole. His wildcatter had shot a blank and left without even saying goodbye. He consoled himself by thinking that he still owned his minerals, but it now appeared that they weren't worth having anyway. Forgetting it all, he turned his attention back to farming.

Three months later, several trucks hauled three lease storage tanks out near his derrick and workers installed what they called a tank battery. Then they tied it into the well. They didn't even bother to install a pump. Next day oil tanker trucks began driving up every four hours. The drivers were in a constant hurry and ran fast, wanting to fill up quickly with oil and haul it off. Two weeks after that, a pipeline was laid out to his well and the wildcatter returned. Rigbuilders, he told the farmer, were coming out next day to build another derrick on the other side of his farm. The farmer asked for his lease money but was told to be patient. Oil was now being sold to pay all the bills that were due and a bank account would be set up for him "in a little while".

That wildcatter had finally hit a home run. He was now a rich man but had less pocket money than when the farmer first met him. His well was not only a good one, but a "Jim-dandy" he said and he hadn't been able to tell anyone until now because they had kept it a "tight hole". This meant they were not telling anyone about their strike. Soon as he saw the well was a good one, he went back to his banker, got more money and hired lease agents to grab all the nearby land they could sign up before word got out. The word got out anyway, as it always did. Within two weeks other wildcatters and oil company lease men swarmed in to sign up leases. But the wildcatter no longer cared because he had spent up all his leasing money. The farmer would soon receive his lease payment, the wildcatter assured him. Then he climbed into his battered old car and drove away.

Not certain whether he was being flim-flammed, the farmer elected to wait a few more days before hiring a lawyer. But to be safe, he started recording license numbers of the tank trucks that loaded up and wrote down all the names he read on the truck doors. Four weeks later, on a Friday morning, the First State Bank president in Henderson, Texas sent him a message by a feed store truck driver. The banker wanted to know what to do with a $19,300 royalty check that some oil company the bank had never heard of before had sent to him. The farmer had no idea what to tell that banker because he'd never owned a bank account before.

For years, this man and his wife had lived during a time when a man with decent credit could buy almost any East Texas farm, including a good livable house, a dependable well, and a solid four-wire fence, all nicely cleared of brush and timber, for 20 dollars an acre. In fact, cash money would buy that same farm for less. Hundreds of such farmers in the thirties were called "dirt poor" because they barely raised enough money each year to pay property taxes.

With a sack full of leases and an excellent line of credit, the wildcatter came back two weeks later to say he intended to drill a third well on the farmer's property. A week later, the bank sent our farmer word that it had gotten another check, larger than the first. This couple now had more cash money on deposit in that bank than many small town Texas banks owned in assets. A month later, they were told that a fourth derrick would be built on their farm. It was now 1931 and that was the year our farmer decided to quit farming.

Sending word, to a local "used horse dealer", the farmer sold everything on his farm that walked, "for one money". That is a trading term which means that one price bought everything, even the chickens. The only animal held back was a loyal family stock dog. He would go to town with them. They owned two sows, a boar and four piglets plus a two mule team and three milk cows plus several geese and the chickens. The trade provided for payment, half in cash and the rest when they moved away and no longer needed a milk cow. It also included the family wagon and a free ride into Henderson with the stock buyer when they left.

In town, they arranged with their new and highly accommodating banker to buy a brand new Buick. They waited in his office for 30 minutes for the dealer to have it washed, filled with gas and driven over. After solving their transportation problem they asked their banker about locating a home in Henderson. Happy to serve these excellent new customers, he described a bargain-priced home owned by an elderly recently widowed lady who owed the bank some money. She wanted to sell her home and move to Dallas to live closer to her children.

It was a nice home for a city the size of Henderson. Much larger than the farm houses they were accustomed to, and it was only 15 years old. It was set on brick piers with four solid brick columns out front to support an attractively long southern styled front porch. It also had a two-car garage, a new roof, and was freshly painted and papered throughout. Besides that, it had a good well with a 40-barrel water tank set on a stout 10 foot tower. If they wanted to keep a cow, they could also buy up to 40 acres of road frontage right next to their house, for $30.00 an acre.

Anxious to please his rich new customers, the banker drove them out to view the home and visit with its owner. On the way, he advised that the electric company was laying a new line down this road because many people were wanting to build in the area. If they bought now, within just 90 days, they could have it wired for electricity and would be able to use one of those new-fangled vacuum cleaners and own a refrigerator which would make all the ice they would ever use.

Less than an hour after visiting, the couple had bought this house and twenty acres of adjoining property for $2,600.00. It was easy to do because their oil wells were now pumping up more money each week than they had been seeing after farming hard for an entire year.

And so they lived, attending church regularly and rearing the last of their children. All the young ones who would attend were sent off to college. The rest were loaned, but not given, enough money to start businesses for which they had reasonable talent. Both the farmer and his wife felt strongly that their oil windfall could dry up any week and their children needed a trade with which to make their own way so they would not have to depend on a "chancy" industry.

But the money kept on keeping on, piling up daily. World War II had arrived and there was very little which they could buy with it. America was geared for wartime weapons and machinery production. No cars and few refrigerators were being built for the civilian market. And about a year after the war began, that farmer and his wife began to experience severe marital problems. Some thought it might be another woman or man but it wasn't. The problems finally grew so bad that they could no longer share the same home.

Because they were religious people, there was no divorce. Instead, the man built a smaller home across the road, a hundred yards South of the house where they had lived since leaving their farm. After obtaining a legal separation and filing it in the courthouse, he moved into that new house to live alone. His wife stayed in the other, also alone and my informant confided that no one ever learned why they split up. The only thing he knew for sure was that neither of them had spoken to the other for two years before he moved across the road.

Like many country wives of her time, that lady had learned to drive a team but not to drive a car. But she had many friends and a large family of children. Seldom did a day pass without one of them paying her company. Friends and relatives took her on shopping trips, to church, to the movies or any other place she wanted to go. Whatever money she needed was provided by terms of their separation agreement and she lacked for nothing.

Because they were simple people with frugal tastes, each one continued to live modestly and spent much less money than their wells pumped up. Until 1954, they continued to live across the road from each other and seldom missed a day in meeting. But they never spoke.

Each morning that lady rose at daybreak. First, she scattered a panful of feed to the chickens penned behind her back yard. Then she prepared and ate her own breakfast. After that, she walked down to her husband's home and prepared whatever breakfast he had written down on his list. While he ate she tidied up, made his bed and commenced preparation for his noon meal. Walking back to her house, she tended her own chores until time to return and set his noon table. His evening meal, which they called "supper" was prepared and served like his lunch, which most Texans of the time called "dinner".

When he needed groceries, she ordered them delivered to his home and was on hand to store them away. Each week she carried her vacuum cleaner down to dust and sweep his house. Using a laundry basket, she hauled his dirty clothes up to her home for washing then walked back down with them, cleaned, folded and ironed. This pattern continued, with never a conversation between them, until two days before the day I sat down in Floyd's Diner to talk with Eric. On that morning, the millionaire ex-farmer, now 89, suffered a massive stroke. All alone, he died and she had found his body in bed.

Finishing the story, I looked into Eric's face and said: "Where I came from, up in Burkburnett, Texas, those folks would be considered real strange. Did you know them? And, if you did, do you know what caused all that trouble?"

Eric looked into my eyes for several seconds then stood up before answering. "Yep, I knew 'em. The lady you are talking about is my mother's sister and I'm headed over to Crawford's Funeral Home right now. Neither one of them ever said what caused their troubles and none of us would ask." Then he pulled on his hat, pushed the diner's door open and paused for a final word.

"In East Texas", he said, "talking about family affairs in public can cause as much trouble as talking politics, but I have one thing to say about that man and will always stand behind it. If he is lucky enough to go to heaven, he probably won't like it there because they aren't going to treat him as well as she did down here."

From the time I started telling my story until Eric walked out, headed for the funeral home, I had forgotten all about my dinner. In fact, I was so interested in the couple's story that I continued staring blindly at the door, watching as Eric ambled down the sidewalk. Floyd's voice brought me back into the real world.

"Ed, you have let your steak get so cold and soggy that it's ruined. Here's you some fresh coffee. I'm fixing you up a new plate and will give your steak to that skinny black and white cat that drug in yesterday."

CHAPTER 40

Trigger—1954

THEY CALLED HIM "Trigger" and I never knew why. I only talked with him once, and having once lived poor, easily recognized some of the scars a man develops who has lived cheek to jowl with poverty and barely won the battle. But I would have thought he was a knife man because he'd probably never saved enough money to own a pistol. They said he had worked for 10 or 12 years in the East Texas oilfield as a roustabout for British American Oil Company until suffering a severe heart attack and having to retire. But, whatever his past, it hadn't broken his spirit. He had an up-beat personality and could tell a great story.

The year was 1954. Marge and I, along with Marlinda, our baby daughter, were living in Henderson, Texas. Without having a lot of luck, I was trying to feed us by selling life insurance. Rusk County back then was full of folks who didn't care if they ever bought a life insurance policy or not. And they especially disliked it when I cranked up on them before 10:00 on any day, especially Monday. It was barely 9:00 that morning so, with an hour of free time to kill, I dropped into Reed's Jewelry Store to talk with the owners.

It wasn't a Mr. Reed, but three brothers named Green who owned and operated that store. They sold more jewelry than any store in town and also stocked a large amount of china, table silver, crystal and other expensive gift items greatly prized by southern ladies. Except for graduation, the June bride rush and Christmas, the Greens normally had a lot of talking time, and after they had turned down my life insurance offers, we still liked each other and got along well. The four of us were "passing the time of day", halfway through a cup of coffee and had already worn out the weather, crops and health talk when Trigger walked through their front door.

That perked the Greens up. They all liked him, and within five minutes I did too. Without meaning to be, the guy was really funny and the fact that he wasn't trying to make us laugh enriched his conversation even more. He was of medium height and weight, looking to be just under 40, fifteen years or so older than me. Best of all, his idea of good conversation completely by-passed the standard weather crop topics. The jewelers all grinned real big at him and Raymond, the oldest, opened up conversation by asking him to "bring us up to date."

"I'm just trying' to keep my ole' heart workin', that's all," Trigger answered. He was dead serious but grinned like a possum while talking. "The Doc says I got a leaky one an' told me not to bother it with too much drinkin'. An', man, I'm really dry. I've not had a drop now in three months."

They wanted to know what his heart was doing and he said it was what it didn't do that bothered him. "Bothers the doctor too", he added. "I got too much blood pressure he says, but that ain't what scares me. What gets my attention is when I'm walking down the sidewalk, like just a few minutes ago, an' the dern thing just quits out on me. I keep on walkin', sometimes six or eight steps before it cranks up again, jus' like nothin' ever happened. But, you know, it makes me study a bit 'cause I don't think I can do over 20 or 30 steps if it doesn't hit a lick or two."

We knew this was serious because people's hearts aren't supposed to act that way, but he laughed and joked so we laughed with him. Raymond asked if his heart had acted up when he was young. Trigger said it had never tried to give out on him except one time when a guy "whapped" him on the head with a trace chain. "That time," he announced, "It completely quit." Of course we all wanted to hear about it and his story went way back to the heart of the big depression, almost 20 years before.

"Back in the mid 1930's I was 16 years old an' would take out of school whenever I found a day of work here or there," Trigger began. "An' my chances of findin' a regular job were slim to none. We had so little money that if I'd of been a smoker I'd of had to quit. Drinkin' was no bother to me because I was young an' hadn't yet learned to like it. But if I had of been, I couldn't have bought enough to get drunk. Just had no money a-tall."

"Corn likker, we called it 'White Lightnin', averaged over three dollars a gallon, an' just about ever'body except bootleggers was too broke to drink. A dollar was a standard day's wages then—if you had a job, that is. Our family tried to have meat one day a week, generally at Sunday dinner, but nobody could afford meat an' bootleg whiskey at the same time. One of them had to go."

"Well, things started changing' in 1935 when President Roosevelt's WPA cranked up. All you had to do was go down to City Hall or the County Barn and sign up. An' that work program started just in time for us. My family didn't just want that money I was goin' to bring home, we had to have it. I left school an' signed up on the very first day. An' we wondered if the family could starve for just a few more days until I brought some money home."

"The WPA, Works Progress Administration, put gangs to work building bridges, heavy rock fences, highways, state parks, roadside parks, highway curve barriers and things like that. There were also CCC, Civilian Construction corps, guys who were sent out of state to live in camps like soldiers, workin' way off from home, but I didn't do that. I stayed in East Texas, sleepin' in my own bed at night. I liked working in Rusk county better because I could personally take my money home every week."

"WPA'ers carried their lunch to work, mostly in rolled up paper sacks. Some only had a biscuit or two with hog lard smeared on 'em in place of butter. A few tried to work with no lunch at all, but couldn't hold out long. You see, that was a time when no school kids would have had food fights, all their ammunition would be eaten up. Our dogs lived on just a few bones, a dried up piece of cornbread once in a while an' whatever they were able to run down an' swaller. Any man who tried to take a rabbit away from his dog and eat it himself, knew that his animal would do its very best to put him in the hospital."

"Well, on my second day of work, we knocked off for dinner and this big guy, about 40, who had just hired on that day, walked up to me before I got sat down and asked what I'd brought to eat. Well, I had a tomato, a raw potato an' a lard biscuit, an' told him that. He snatched the sack out of my hand, stuck my potato in his pocket to take home, ate my tomato and gave me the biscuit back. Everybody saw this but nobody interfered or took up for me. East Texas folks back then were expected to stomp their own snakes and knock down their own hornet nests."

"While I was eatin' my biscuit real slow, so it would last long as possible, this guy yelled out to me, loud enough for ever'body to hear, that I was to bring him a potato tomorrow and another tomato, too. If I didn't, he promised to stomp a big hole in my fanny."

"Well, this was a real problem. First, I'd always been a lot better at talkin' than fightin' an' anybody could see, by using basic common sense, that I wasn't goin' to be able to whip this guy. He outweighed me by a hundred pounds and would chew me slap-up in an even fight. Besides, I didn't even know whether we had any vegetables left at home. We'd been livin' from hand to mouth for three years, and even if we had that extra food, I needed it to keep up my workin' strength. We hadn't yet got any WPA money an' couldn't buy even a one-day supply of food. Next morning I learned we still had a few vegetables left and Mom packed me another tomato and potato. I gambled an' left them in the sack, hoping the big guy might steal somebody else's lunch an' I'd get to eat mine, but it was a bad gamble."

"I also added another bad gamble to the first by not offerin' my sack up to him when he came over after it. I held it behind me, tryin' to reason with him but he never said a word. He just wound up 'an hit me right on the nose, knockin' me flat. That was when It came home to me that my mother had either lied or was badly mistaken when she continually told us boys that 'it took two people to make a fight'. This guy had just proved her wrong. All that's needed for a fight is one bully an' one victim."

"While I was tryin' to stop my first-class nosebleed, this high-jacker sat down an' watched me eat my biscuit while he polished off my tomato. When we were finished, he said he liked me an' was goin' to do me a favor by teachin' me how to fight. I pointed out that I didn't feel much like fighting' because of my nose, but he said I wasn't hurt, that a broke or swelled up nose was no worse than a bad cold. Then, while we was still sittin' down, he hit me again. Right in the mouth."

"He came onto me fast an' wasn't kiddin'. We were rollin' on the ground an' I had to fight to survive so I hit him as hard and as much as I could, but I was too excited and wasn't usin' any coordination. My licks were doin' no more good than jelly beans hitting' an army tank. I quit trying to hit and bit him hard on his nearest ear. He yelled out loud, an' pulled loose. Then he butted me square on the chin with the top of his head 'an the fight was over, 'cause I was out cold. When I woke up he was pouring' a half bucket of spring water in my face and holdin' his bloody ear with one hand but he was laughin' down at me."

"He said I had done pretty good but that he didn't want me to bite him anymore an', if I didn't, he would let me keep my potato from now on. But I still had to bring him a tomato tomorrow. An' after dinner tomorrow we would do some more fighting."

"Well, I wasn't that scared of him by then. At least—not exactly. But like my pa used to say, I was fastidious. I really hated rollin' on the ground, gettin' my clothes all dirty an' tearin' 'em up. Today, if something like that was to happen to me, I would just quit my job an' go somewheres else to work. But, like I said, we had to have the money I was makin'."

"Next day I came back with a full lunch 'an started eatin' when they yelled "dinnertime". The big guy didn't hurry over an' I swallered ever' bite, tomato an' all before he got to me. Now, I knew he was plannin' to eat 'my tomato for dessert. An' I also knew we were goin' to fight, because he was gonna hit me soon as he learned what I had done. So I stood up, watchin' closely as he neared. But I'd been doin' some thinkin', an' the guy didn't know yet but he had already done me part of that favor he promised. I had already learned a little about fightin'."

"Actually, I was lots smaller than him but I had found out I could move faster. So, when he swung on me, I moved sideways real quick 'an he fanned the air. Like lots of big guys, he hadn't found many people willin' to fight with him after he got half grown. He'd been whippin' up on smaller people for a long time and was spoiled rotten. Missin' that first lick made him mad an' he swung at me so hard with the other arm that, when I dodged again, he almost fell down. That made him drop his guard and I swung, hard as I could, measuring' out the distance carefully, an' connected solidly, low in his right side."

"That lick knocked his wind out an' he went down to his knees, so I ran behind real quick an' hit him in the side of the neck with both fists, hard as I could. That really rocked him an' his head dropped over toward his shoulder. When he reached up with both hands to hold his head up straight, I hit him full on the nose. An' that worked good too. Blood flew all over. Some of it got onto me, an' right then, I enjoyed the feel of it."

"I figured I'd best make hay while the sun was shinin', cause there wasn't any tellin' what he would do, or try to do to me, when he got up again. I hit him in that same side, twice more, an' he rolled over onto the ground, but was still trying to hold his head straight with both hands so it wouldn't roll around. I hit him full in the belly again an' was about to give him some more in the face, but one of the older men came over and stopped me. He said I might kill the guy an' could already have broke his neck. Well, I didn't want to maim or kill anyone, so I asked the big guy if he was through."

"He grunted back that he was. I asked if he still wanted to teach me to fight. Still holding his head up straight, he looked right into my face an' said I did okay, an' that he was finished with teachin' me. After that everyone went back to work except him. He sat on a stump for an hour, without moving', still holding' his head with both hands to keep it from laying' over. Later, the gang boss helped him in the truck, drivin' over here to Henderson, lookin' for a doctor."

"Next morning' I carried a sharp maize-headin' knife to work with me 'cause I didn't know what he might try to do. But he never came back to that job. I guess my boss thought I was in the right because he never fussed at me."

Then Trigger stopped talking and announced he had to leave. The Greens pointed out he hadn't told us about the trace chain stopping his heart, but he said he had run out of time and would tell us that one next time he saw us. A week or so later, while reading the Henderson Daily News, I read about the funeral of a man whose nickname was "Trigger." I called Raymond Green at home to ask if he was the same guy.

"That's him," Raymond answered, "Died in his sleep, they said. And I'm sure going to miss him."

"Did he ever finish the story about his heart completely stopping?"

"No, he never came back after that morning."

"You figure he was telling the truth about that fight?"

Raymond chuckled and paused a few seconds before answering. "I don't know, Ed, but it sure sounded good." And after 10 seconds of silence he added, "If his story wasn't true, it certainly should have been."

CHAPTER 41

LOTTA BULL—1964

IT WAS 8:00 on a Monday morning and almost dark outside. I was the only person at work except for our newest secretary, a girl so young that she hadn't yet developed respect for a real Texas storm. Outside, the sky steadily darkened and heavy thunder rumbled ever closer.

I had come in early, planning to work out of town, but might as well have slept in. Every time I tried to make an appointment, my subject was too busy watching the sky to do any business. Rather than lose a battle with the weather, I gave up, electing to fight my Dictaphone and work inside until the weather broke.

Ten minutes after starting my first Dictaphone report to one of our company customers, my intercom buzzed and the new secretary asked me to pick up the phone to accept a new assignment. This was normally her job but the caller had asked for Mr. Newsom, one of the owners. When told he wasn't in, the caller wanted to talk with our "Livestock Specialist." And that was how I began to work on one of the strangest Insurance claims I ever witnessed or heard about.

Marge and I had been married for seven years when we moved to Tyler in January of 1956. We had been living in Tyler for six years, and I had been working as an insurance adjuster from then until April of 1964. Most people back then said Tyler was a good place to raise children and we had learned this was so. We liked Tyler, not only because of its good people, but because we had finally tapped into a measure of prosperity and were beginning to share in the American dream. We had built a new home, then furnished it and still had enough left over to open an honest-to-goodness savings account.

I answered the phone pleasantly but could have saved my trouble. A starchy and distinctly Upper East Coast male voice inquired if I were the office's livestock adjusting specialist. Actually, we adjusted almost no livestock claims back then. In fact, no one in our office fit the description this caller had in mind. Most Texas livestock in the 1960's was for riding, milking, plowing or eating and the average horse or cow only sold for around $75.00 a head. No farmer or rancher in his right mind would buy life insurance on his animals at those prices. In fact, during some of the dry years, a few livestock owners would have felt lucky if several of their animals simply rolled over and died.

I was the best adjuster in town to fit this caller's purpose because I had recently adjusted the death claim of a $3,000 race horse brood mare and everything worked out all right. So rather than cause this stiff and unfriendly voice to give its assignment to a competitor, I told it what it wanted to hear. Technically, I wasn't lying when saying I was the person with whom it needed to speak. Actually, I was one of only a few adjusters in Tyler that morning who was sitting at his desk, ready to do business.

In tones reeking of authority, the voice droned off its name, its street address on Maiden Lane in New York City, plus its telephone number and a claim number for the file. I didn't know then, but afterward learned that most US insurors representing this large European insurance company rented office space on Maiden Lane. The voice demanded to know whether I could devote immediate attention to its file, and since my out-of-town trip was impossible, I said I could. Then it asked if I knew where the Billy Byers Ranch, near Tyler, was located. I said I did, and the voice spewed more information into my earpiece.

The BB ranch was their policyholder, the voice intoned, and was a very substantial account. The ranch owned a highly prized and registered Black Angus Bull which had died during the night and its company had "five thousand" of exposure on the animal. I was to take my camera and a vet out to the ranch to supervise a postmortem examination and report back as soon as a cause of death had been determined. In fact, it expected my call before noon, Texas time, which was one o'clock in New York.

Looking out the window, I could see that our part of Texas might be blown over into Louisiana or washed down into the Sabine River at almost any minute. I mentioned this fact to the voice and added that most vets had built-in dislikes for working outdoors in bad weather. His company, I continued, could easily spend its entire $5,000 in paying a vet enough to muddy up his nice cowboy boots on a day like this. The post mortem, I thought, would best be postponed until the storm blew over.

The voice then raised its sound level, and made imperative noises, almost as if it had been waiting for a chance to assert the authority needed to work with any adjuster who lived South of New Jersey. It crisply advised that their company didn't have $5,000 in coverage on this bull. It had insured him for $50,000. In addition, they had 12 more registered Black Angus cows on their policy, each of which was insured for $10,000. Then, either for heightened effect or to draw breath, I wasn't certain which it paused, but I didn't wait. Raising my voice and speaking positively, I promised that a vet would be secured and the desired postmortem conducted.

Somewhat mollified, but only slightly, the voice gave me a phone number for the Byers Ranch and the name of its manager, Tommy West. It mentioned that he was a graduate of Texas A&M University, as was the vet hired by Byers ranch, then inquired as to whether that college had an "adequate" veterinary school. It expressed relief when I answered in the affirmative.

Sweeping on, the voice instructed me to obtain a "capable" vet who would act as a person of the "carrier's choice", which meant they wanted to buy him. Then we would meet with the ranch vet who was waiting, as we spoke, to begin a post mortem examination. After the vets were finished, I was to instruct the ranch to preserve the carcass until Maiden Lane decided what else might be needed. Proper tattoo numbers for the bull were given me, and I was to positively identify him as the "insured animal" by reading those exact numbers inside each of his ears. I was also furnished additional identifying data and warned once more that a prompt call-back was required. Then I heard a click in my earpiece, followed by a dial tone, and understood that our conversation was over.

Dialing quickly, I called Jeff Holder, the vet who treated my dachshund and horses. I told him that I needed to hire him quickly for a post mortem exam. Jeff then began to reel off a bunch of unnecessary weather information and suggested we ought to wait. It was only after I mentioned that he could name his own fee that he decided he might be able to find his hat and slicker. Then he asked where this high powered All-American bull was located, and when I told him he became genuinely enthusiastic.

Jeff was well acquainted with the deceased animal as well as with its owner. He also explained that Billy Byers, the bull's owner, had awfully deep oil money pockets. Those pockets had made it possible for him to bring such a famous bull to our city. Talking on, he filled me in on the bull's past, as if a prominent citizen had died. He was especially impressed about how, when the bull was brought to Tyler, Mr. Byers had reserved a suite for it at the Blackstone Hotel downtown. The animal, whose registered name was Prince TT-105, had been bedded down for a full weekend in the hotel's master suite so that everybody who wanted to get to know him better could drive downtown and satisfy this desire.

Jeff then described how the bull's attendants had been dressed in tuxedos and used gilded shovels to flip Prince TT's many indiscretions into gilded barrels half filled with perfumes and deodorant. During that decade, this kind of activity was considered effective advertising by Black Angus cattle breeders, most of whom had big gobs of money like Mr. Byers. But the bull had arrived a year before I moved to Tyler and Jeff's report didn't interest me. Breaking in, I reminded him about the weather, observing that we ought to drive on out to perform the surgery before Old TT floated down river.

Because I was in a bigger hurry, I arrived at the ranch before Jeff and was quickly ushered into the manager's office by his very attractive young wife. Manager Sands was red of face and yelling into his telephone when I walked in. His final message advised the other party that if it would drive down to Tyler and repeat what it had just said, he would happily stomp its donkey right through the ranch parking strip out in front. With that, he slammed down his phone. Mr. Paul Turman, the ranch vet, kept both his smile and his seat, so I judged it was all right to hang around. Still, I watched carefully as Tommy Sands swung his chair in my direction.

Shaking my hand, he introduced himself, and apologized for his display of temper. I was glad to see a smile and answered with one my own. Then I said I wanted to know what the other guy had told him so I wouldn't make the same mistake and end up flattened out on the ranch driveway. He shook his head, saying that would never happen, and began to talk. And the more I heard, the more unusual this claim became. First, Billy Byers did not own all of the dead animal. He had originally bought half, then sold half of his half to a wealthy attorney friend who owned a ranch up near Terrill, Texas. But, and this was the strangest part, Tommy Sands had just finished yelling over his telephone with owner number three, who owned half of the dead bull.

That owner ranched up in Oklahoma near Tulsa, and had allowed his insurance on the bull to expire, which was a severe error in judgment. Then he had compounded his error with another by accusing Tommy West of mishandling the animal, possibly contributing to its death. That was when he stepped on the wrong set of corns, and it was the tail end of that phone conversation I had heard when walking in.

I was fairly certain that Maiden Lane knew nothing at all about the other bull partners, or any other insurance policies on this bull or they would have mentioned it. Most large insurance policies, whether on animals, men or even buildings, have a schedule showing the total amount of coverage on the insured object. This excellent rule was designed to keep men, buildings and animals from being over-insured. By cutting down on over-insurance, the company was short-circuiting a policyholder's temptation, in case he encountered a sudden need for quick cash, to arrange premature death or destruction of such insured objects.

I asked Tommy how much insurance the Byers ranch had on their bull. He said they had one policy, for $50,000. This agreed with my information and everything in Tyler seemed normal. Then I asked if the Terrell rancher had any insurance and was told he might have insured his one fourth interest for $150,000. When I asked about the rancher in Oklahoma, Tommy hadn't seen their policy either but had heard it was written for $400,000, and he had just been told it was expired.

Then Tommy explained that the Oklahoma owner was claiming the Byers Ranch was, for some obscure reason, responsible because their $400,000 policy premium had not been paid on time, so it looked as if one lawsuit was already developing here. He also said that when he brought Prince TT back from Oklahoma several months earlier, that the Oklahoma owner had been allowing the bull to pasture in with herd cows, which is a careless thing to allow with such a fabulously expensive animal. Bull fights often result in killings and severe injuries. And Prince TT had been in poor range condition when they brought him back to Tyler. In fact, it took 60 days before Tommy was able to perk him up and begin extracting and freezing semen once more.

Thunder suddenly boomed, rattling the walls and windows. My vet had arrived, and I suggested the vets begin their postmortem. Tommy told us TT had died in the middle of a pasture a half mile off the highway and about the same distance behind his office. The animal was above the water line and ought not to float away. To preserve everything properly, he had spread a large tarp over the bull and left a ranch hand on guard to keep buzzards, crows and dogs away.

Tommy asked if the vets wanted the bull moved under shelter, but they decided it was better to work out in the open. If the weather interfered badly they could cover him with the tarp and finish after the storm was over.

I rode out with Tommy and each vet followed in his own vehicle. That was because each wanted to have his personal equipment handy. Tommy shoved the Jeep hard, searching out the shortest road around trees, rocks and ridges. The Jeep's spinning wheels threw up a constant rooster tail of crimson clover buds, soupy mud, and occasional tufts of cow plop behind us. My seat belt was fastened, but I still had to hang on tightly to keep from being thrown sideways in my seat. The vets lagged far enough behind so their vehicles would receive as few splatters as possible.

Tommy had just pointed out TT's tarpaulin 20 yards ahead when a drove of Chester White hogs ran in front of the Jeep. Tommy slowed precipitately and began to curse while sliding to a stop near the tarp. At first I didn't understand why he was angry, but I then saw that every hog's nose was bloody way up to his eyes and that Old TT's tarp had been partially rooted aside. When they began to circle back for another try, Tommy began to kick any hog within reach and it finally dawned on me that those plump white pigs had been dining on our post mortem subject.

Tommy was still angry when the vets drove up at the same time as one of Tommy's foremen who was riding a handsome chestnut-colored gelding. The foreman was carefully balancing an axe across his saddle bow and rode directly to the ranch veterinarian, handing it to him blade first. Despite all the equipment they had brought, neither of those vets had thought to bring one. Suddenly a bright flash of lightning flared and a prodigious clap of thunder exploded. The rider waved at the storm, starting to complain about the weather but Tommy stopped him short. "Why did Jimenez leave this bull?"

The foreman apologized for his hand, saying he had gone up to his cottage for a late breakfast. Tommy cut him off again. "Have you seen those hogs?", he yelled. The rider admitted he had, "just now" when delivering the axe, but continued to defend his employee, as a good foreman should.

Tommy over-rode him again, warning that he was taking his own job in both hands by protecting Jimenez but to proceed if he wanted. The foreman thought briefly and said he had to admit there was no good excuse for the man to leave his post and maybe he ought to be fired but that he would like to keep him if possible. Tommy dropped his head for several moments, considering, then nodded in assent. "But," he stated flatly, "I want Jimenez to work two long 10 hour days in a row. Afterward he is to come up to the office and show me all the things he has done.

The foreman nodded, and lifted his reins, anxious to be gone. Reading its rider's mood, the Sorrel whirled quickly and smoothly, raising up into a canter, but Tommy stopped them with a short yell. "Buck!"

The chestnut slid on its hind feet toward a stop and, while still moving, reared up and spun round on its rear hooves. After each white-stockinged forefoot dropped lightly onto the turf, both horse and rider were facing us again. Buck's answer was serious: "Yes, Boss?"

"Pen up those damned hogs. I don't want any more problems from them while this is going on."

"Yes sir," Buck shouted, but not loud enough to be impertinent. Then he effortlessly picked up the chestnut's front feet, turning it away from us again, and as daintily as before, the horse lifted into the same lazy canter that moved them rapidly over the ridge. Tommy and I looked at each other and he shook his head, grinning, but said nothing. Both of us recognized and admired expert horsemanship when we saw it.

Barely glancing at the lowering cloud, our vets quickly went to work. Tommy had other business and left, saying he would return later. The tarp was removed, and the vets decided that, while the hogs had torn out 10 or 12 sizable hunks of beef, Old TT hadn't been damaged so much that it would compromise the postmortem.

Each vet donned a butcher's apron, and seizing TT's top legs, rolled him over onto his back and propped him where they wanted him to stay with some nearby rocks. As they worked, I shot still pictures, snapping the camera whenever there was something to shoot. Next, they propped his front legs apart and split his wish bone open with the foreman's axe. With one vet on his right and other on his left front leg, they pulled his chest cavity open and began to slice and peel with their butcher knives. Fascinated by their skill, I continued to shoot pictures as a pile of used parts rapidly arose on Old TT's right hand side.

They were working at a good clip and I judged from the parts pile that they were halfway through when we heard a horn blowing imperatively. Looking uphill I saw Tommy's Jeep speeding rapidly toward us at what might have been a new speed record for that pasture. Sliding to a stop, he told the vets to stop their butchery until he and I came back. Motioning for me to hang on, he powered into a wheel-spinning 180-degree turn back uphill toward headquarters. On the way he yelled that I had a long-distance call waiting, which explained his rush. This was years before cellular or portable phones were developed or he would have had the call transferred down to me.

I held on again as the Jeep churned and bounced up the hill, but finding a safe moment, I peered into my side mirror to see a strange view of our vets. Side by side, they sat on TT's rib cage, the pile of bull parts between them. Each had fired up a cigarette, and their heads wagged earnestly as they pointed up at the sky.

This just wasn't my day. The newest voice, when I said "Hello", wasn't as foreign sounding as the New York speech had been, but it was just as ridiculously overbearing. Its owner was a Dallas insurance adjuster whose firm specialized in livestock claims. He represented the company that insured Old TT for the rancher up near Terrill. He flatly ordered me to stop all activity, especially the postmortem examination, until he could fly to Tyler.

I advised him we were facing horrible weather and had already started the post-mortem, so it was way too late to stop. I also told him that no responsible charter pilot would fly to Tyler on a day like this, and driving would take too long. Time, in a case of this sort, was of the essence. Our vets needed to proceed before deterioration set in, possibly hiding clues to the animal's death.

The voice complained again. Loudly. It mentioned lawsuits and conflicts of interest but I didn't back down so it finally granted reluctant permission for us to continue working. Still, it insisted, it would arrive at the ranch later in the day and demanded a conference with each vet plus an opportunity to take its own pictures. It would also need to confer with all witnesses and wanted me to arrange this. Finally, it required a copy of all my pictures and copies of reports from both vets.

I didn't enjoy being treated like a flunky, and took advantage of a lull in the long list of demands to point out that no one in Dallas was signing my paychecks. But, like the East Coast voice, this one paid no attention to anything I said. It simply re-stated its demands. I knew my boss would give this competitor almost anything it requested because of what he would term "professional courtesy," so I agreed to the demands just to get back to work.

Tommy hauled me back down to the pasture and everyone agreed it was a minor miracle that the ranch hadn't yet been flooded or blown away. I told the vets to crank up again, and they'd been at it less than five minutes when a fast-moving twin-engined C-47 cargo-type airplane topped the nearest pine ridge at low altitude and waggled its wings while roaring over our heads. Then it circled swiftly into a landing pattern over the ranch airstrip. One of the vets had flown in it before and identified it as belonging to Billy Byers, the ranch owner. But I had already figured that out because of the huge red "BB", shaped like the ranch's brand, which the plane bore on its tail.

Tommy had told me earlier that his boss was in Phoenix for a week but, obviously, when he was notified about his prize bull, he disregarded the sorry weather and ordered his pilot to hurry home. I saw Tommy's Jeep swerve from its path up to the office and turn toward the air strip. Fifteen minutes later he barreled back down with Billy Byers and his pilot holding on as well as they were able.

Each vet knew Mr. Byers personally and each enjoyed shaking his hand and calling him by his first name. Tommy then introduced me to him, and I was surprised to find that this wealthy ex-wildcatter was a genuinely polite person who showed no addiction to his obvious personal power. Kind and considerate, Mr. Byers also asked quiet questions of Tommy, who answered promptly. Both of them spoke in low, relaxed tones and it was obvious that each respected the other. They worked well together.

After 20 more minutes of carving, the vets murmured excitedly and bent to peer closely at a small bull part. Then they nodded and smiled, congratulating each other on locating the exact cause of TT's death. I took two or three shots of part of an artery which they had spread open over TT's open carcass. There was no sign of poisoning, gunshot, or foul play, which was good for the ranch's position. Old TT had apparently ruptured his aorta and died from slow internal bleeding. Veterinary opinion was unanimous. Even if the problem had been diagnosed early, considering the level of veterinary science back then, nothing could have saved Prince TT.

As the vets spoke, tablespoon-sized drops of rain began to fall and the number suddenly mushroomed. By common consent, everyone ran toward their vehicles. My camera and film were stuffed into a water repellent bag, and I snapped my plastic raincoat tightly against the water, then began climbing into the rear of the Jeep. But Mr. Byers wouldn't have it. He insisted that he and the pilot should ride in back, which had much less protection from the weather.

Two ranch hands arrived as we drove away. Buck had sent them over to build a fence around the carcass. They began to work soon as we were out of the way. With apparent unconcern, they started digging postholes as if it were a bright and sunshiny day instead of one filled with blustery fifty-mile-an-hour wind gusts, giant flares of lightning and torrents of rain. Tommy's Jeep skidded to and fro as he goosed it hard while forging toward the top of the hill. As we reached the summit, I asked if he intended checking to see whether the hogs had been penned, but I already knew what he would say. He looked at me obliquely, judging whether or not I was serious. After seeing my grin, he shook his head "No".

It was 1:30 when we pulled up to the long breezeway running alongside the ranch parking strip to the office door. And because Tommy had raised the Jeep top before it started raining, we weren't completely soaked. But the storm was worsening. Rain now fell in solid sheets and lightning flared into our eyes. Repetitive thunder blasts sounded like a heavy artillery barrage. Violent wind gusts bent large tree tops toward the ground and walls of rain alternated between falling straight down and blowing parallel to the earth. This was exactly the kind of weather that caused many old-time Texans to hunt their 'fraid-holes'. Comparing this storm to normal rain showers was like comparing a common herd bull with TT-105. They weren't the same thing at all.

I had barely sloshed inside the office when Tommy's wife reported that I had a phone call waiting. It was the guy from Dallas again. Still cranky, he demanded that we cease and desist with the autopsy until he and his vet could arrive to witness all the proceedings, which would be in two more hours. I didn't help his feelings any when I said the autopsy was over and there was no evidence of foul play. First he accused me of lacking professional courtesy, then warned me not to tell anyone else what I had just "confided" to him until I was holding written reports in hand from each vet.

Tired of his badgering, I pointed out that I had not requested any job training from Dallas and that he should conduct his own investigation and allow me to care for mine. I also confided to him that I was ignoring any more Dallas instruction. Obviously miffed, the voice demanded to speak with the ranch manager, a demand which I welcomed. With a genuine smile on my face, I watched Tommy's puzzled expression as I turned and shoved the telephone into his hand.

While Tommy was trying to make sense out of Dallas, I called my office on another line, to talk with my own boss. I brought him up to date on the file and told him about both voices. Then I suggested it might be better for him to report to the New York voice, bringing it up to date, because the more I talked with it, the more likely it would be to discover I wasn't the five star top-rated livestock specialist it had requested. Jimmy agreed, saying he would handle it.

Tommy and I finished talking at the same time. Then speaking loudly enough to attract all attention, he announced that everyone who cared to stay had been invited by Mr. Byers to lunch on a big Black Angus T-bone steak, complete with baked potato, tossed salad and all the trimmings. Peach cobbler and homemade ice cream was for desert. Mr. Byers then spoke up, adding his endorsement to Tommy's invitation and saying that his cook had prepared that peach cobbler especially for him, but we were welcome to eat all we wanted if we could finish our steaks first and beat him to it.

The storm was still going full blast and it was obvious that nothing could be accomplished outside. We all looked at each other, and reading each other's expressions, unanimously voted for steak. I hadn't been hungry until my stomach heard the steaks mentioned, and it suddenly seemed that breakfast had happened somewhere near the middle of last week.

Since this was his home, Tommy sat at the table's head with his attractive wife on his right. Mr. Byers sat at the foot and I sat on one side with Jeff. The ranch vet and pilot sat opposite us. We were served by a black woman in a white dress who first brought red wine and decanted it for anyone who wanted. As it turned out, the pilot was her only customer. The rest of us opted for hot mugs of steaming black Texas coffee or goblets of iced tea.

Because those steaks were excellent, lunch moved swiftly and conversation was light. Only one serious matter arose, and it came about because of a vet congratulating Tommy for having recently extracted and frozen a large quantity of Prince TT's life-giving fluid. Mr. Byers' voice hardened for the first time since I had met him. Raising his head, he asked Tommy how many vials of semen were in the freezer. After learning, he ordered Tommy to personally destroy each one "right after lunch".

The Angus Breeders Association, he explained for our benefit, had a strict rule against practicing artificial insemination techniques with biological fluids from deceased animals, whether registered or not. Furthermore, he wanted no talk to circulate that might discredit the ranch and either his or Tommy's personal reputations. Tommy promised to "attend to it", and I knew that this would be handled exactly the same as the hog penning. Mr. Byers would not feel it necessary to ask whether his order had been observed. He already knew.

After at least three inches of rain fell in an amazingly short period of time, it suddenly slacked off, and within 15 minutes, storm clouds had blown away. The sky was bright again. As we finished dessert, our host summoned his chef before us. When the tall black man appeared, Mr. Byers sincerely congratulated him for preparing an excellent meal. The cook, well-entitled to be called 'Chef', removed his hat, and just as sincerely, thanked his employer for the honor.

Both vets left when lunch was finished and mine, it developed, was angry with me. He had privately come to me, asking how much he should charge for preparing the written report my company wanted from him. And I was truthful when saying that I had absolutely no idea. I knew nothing about pricing his work and only a little more about adjusting livestock claims. But he assumed that I had failed to help him when I could, and lined up with all the other people who were mad at me that day.

I did not leave with the vets because I had more work to do. Specifically, I must identify the dead bull, which meant I must read the tattoo marks in his ears. One life insurance contract insured him for $50,000 and another for $150,000 but neither would pay a nickel until I proved that the real Prince TT-105 was dead. This meant I had to personally examine those marks.

Water and mud were everywhere, so Tommy found me a pair of over boots which surprised me by fitting my shoes. Then he drove Mr. Byers and me back to the carcass. I was surprised to see that the bull was not only covered tightly with a tarp, but that the crew had built a tight five-strand barbed wire fence all around him. Buck was present and explained to Tommy that cattle had been smelling the blood and "fooling" with the tarp from the time it had stopped raining. Every ranch dog and two curious horses had acted as if they also might grab a bite of rare beefsteak, but they had all been driven away.

Because of this, Buck had stationed Jemeniz at the pen with a shotgun and sleeping bag. He was to stay there at all times except when relieved for meals. Buck also said he had located enough chicken wire to lay over the barbed wire and felt this ought to keep dogs, wolves and hogs from slipping past his guard. He finished by looking straight at me and stating that if a bear showed up, scared off the guard and climbed over their fence, we might as well have a funeral because there wouldn't be enough of TT left for the Insurance company to worry about.

I happened to be wearing a new suit that day. I wasn't wearing it because I considered it proper clothing for ranch work. It was because our company insisted that all its adjusters wear shirts, ties and coats when working in the field. The theory was that we should look presentable enough to walk into any man's office or place of business. To avoid ripping either leg off my new suit pants, I exercised great caution when climbing that tight new fence. After I had cleared it, Tommy shoved me a clipboard, my pen and flashlight. Then, lightly and easily, because he wore heavy Levis and rough pasture boots, he stepped over behind me. Together, we pulled out the pegs and rolled the tarp away from TT's head.

He had been folded back together and rolled over onto his right side. As I knelt behind his head at the top of his neck, his left eye watched accusingly as I pulled and twisted his ear to an angle which allowed me to peer into it. The sun had already warmed things up and small clouds of steam wafted upward from TT's head and shoulders. The odor wasn't really bad yet, but I was already receiving a stout dose of dead bull smell, enough to hope I would be finished with this part of my job in a hurry. But it still wasn't my lucky day.

TT's ear was so dirty that I saw no sign of an identifying tattoo. I told Tommy, who motioned to one of the fencers. The guy left at a trot, and within 10 minutes, topped the hill coming back. Still trotting, he carried a two-gallon bucket filled with hot water and a pair of clean towels. He also had some soap and a scrub brush. I threw down a towel and knelt on it while dousing the ear generously with water. Then I scrubbed it with soap and the brush, removing a noticeable amount of dirt. Now I could faintly see a tattoo mark here and there but the hair was so thick I was unable to read the characters.

We all agreed that the ear must come off to allow for closer examination and our vets were long gone. Tommy hopped over the fence and walked to the tool box on his Jeep where he extracted a beautiful Bowie knife with an eight-inch blade. He offered it to me, but I never claimed to have a talent for butchering and declined the honor.

Tommy climbed back over and what he did looked ridiculously easy. Wasting no time or motion, he stooped and grabbed TT's left ear, pulling it out straight and tight. Then he laid the blade against the animal's head and stroked downward with one slicing motion of his wrist. With a crisp tearing sound, the ear dropped loose and he shoved it into my hand.

We examined the ear again but still couldn't read it. There was too much hair and dirt for reading. Mr. Byers then suggested we take it up to the shop where it could be further cleaned, and shaved if necessary. Tommy also suggested we remove the other ear while we were at it, thus saving a trip back if we couldn't read all numbers in the first one. I reached across and pulled TT's nose up, rolling his head far enough back so Tommy could reach under and trim off the second ear. Again, with only one deft wrist motion, his sharp Bowie knife performed admirably.

The Mexican crew had watched closely, marveling at this strange Texas activity. Deciding that some sort of celebration was indicated, they all laughed, shouted "Ole" several times and clapped their hands, smiling broadly at each other. I heard them say "Torero" twice but could tell they were a little uncertain about the term because there had been no bullfight. Tommy nodded to them and smiled back. After wiping his knife carefully on the leg of his jeans, he dragged the heavy tarp back to cover TT and weighted its corner with a pair of bricks which had been brought out for that purpose. We climbed out of the pen, hopped into his Jeep and charged uphill once more, leaving Buck to explain to his workers that Old TT had been a famous Toro and was being suitably honored by the Texans.

At the ranch shop building Tommy handed me a pair of small hand clippers. Working carefully, I was able to trim most of the bristly hair out from inside TT's ear. Then, after soaking some pieces of waste batting in gasoline, I scrubbed it hard. After the ear was dried I could read some tattoo marks, especially the year of birth but could not read all the ID numbers. After more discussion, we turned on a 100 watt light bulb and held the ear up to it. The "TT" and the "0" in his number could be read but not the "5". Tommy and I were almost defeated, and admitted it, but Mr. Byers wasn't. Effortlessly exhibiting some of the intelligence that had helped make him a wealthy man, he offered a suggestion.

Take your sharp knife, Tommy," he suggested mildly, "and shave all the hair off the top of this ear. Then, wash it off with gasoline and candle it again." By 'candling', he meant the ear should once more be held up to the open light bulb as grocers and housewives used to do with hen eggs to see if they were spoiled.

Before his boss had stopped talking, Tommy understood what was needed and was already moving. Laying the bottom side of the ear flat on his work table, he tacked a finishing nail into each end to hold it in place, then slowly began to dry-shave all the top hair with his knife. He was finished in less than a minute, and with a piece of waste batting and additional gasoline, he scrubbed off the remainder of TT's built in dirt and grime.

After the ear had dried again, we held it up to the light and our problem was solved! Each of us clearly read the figures "TT-105" and I breathed a sigh of relief. Now, except for reporting everything to the insurance carrier and having my film processed, the investigation was finished.

While packing up, I asked Tommy to keep both of TT's ears because someone else might want to read the numbers. Without saying a word he bent and picked up a folded piece of baling wire someone had dropped on the floor near the work bench. Clipping off two feet of it, he strung it through a nail hole in each of TT's ears. Twisting the wire once or twice near the top of the ears, he turned to a wall stud next to his worktable and fastened the wire head high, around that 2" X 4" board. "They will be right here 'til you tell me to throw them away," he said and his employer nodded agreement.

There was one other matter I needed to explain to the insurance company, and as Mr. Byers and I walked from the shop out to my car, I asked why he had purchased only $50,000 of insurance on his one-fourth interest in the bull when the Oklahoma owner had insured his one-half interest for $400,000, eight times as much. Mr. Byers answered that he had originally spent $100,000 for a half interest in the animal. Afterward he had sold half his interest to a rancher friend in Terrell for exactly what he paid for it, $50,000. All he ever intended was to recover his investment if TT died while he owned him.

"I can't," he finished, "explain why those other gentlemen valued their portions of the animal as they did. In matters of this sort, every man must set his own values and insure them or not insure them in accordance with his own perception of business."

He concluded by saying that the other owners volunteered no information to him regarding their values, and because of that he did not feel it proper to speculate about their reasons. Then he politely thanked me for attending his claim and welcomed me to call on him or Tommy for anything else which "you might require."

This oilman-rancher, I decided, was among the last of a vanishing breed of people who intelligently tended his own business while living in a country that was increasingly addicted to minding not only the affairs of its neighbors, but was encouraging our national leaders to meddle in the affairs of America's friendly allies along with those of dedicated world enemies. I judged that Mr. Byers was a man who paid his bills on time and kept his word when he pledged it. And I wondered why no environmentalist group had been formed to preserve his kind of person as the rarest of all the world's "endangered species." But after thinking further, I decided none of those groups would care.

Early next morning I dictated a detailed narrative report to the voice at Maiden Lane in New York. With luck my secretary would transcribe it by noon. Then it could be edited by my boss and mailed out that afternoon. At the bottom of my report I recommended payment of Mr. Byers' loss and requested a draft be drawn, payable to him in the amount of $50,000 less his $1,000 deductible.

Just as I was sending the report to secretarial, Tommy called. A secretary employed by the complaining Dallas adjuster had telephoned him earlier to advise that her boss could not come to the Byers ranch today as promised but he would fly down next morning, a Wednesday, along with his vet. She specifically requested that TT be preserved until they had examined everything. Tommy was irritated by their way of doing business and wanted to refuse the request, but I advised him to be as patient as possible, managing things as well as he could so that none of the companies would have an excuse to deny a claim. If any company denied, the others would probably follow suit, hoping that some reason they hadn't learned about might pop up to postpone or even deny payment.

My report was mailed that afternoon, and two days afterward, I picked up pictures from the developer and a report from each vet. These were all mailed to the company on the same day and I forgot TT's claim until Tommy called me ten days later. Mr. Byers had asked him to check on their claim.

I told him I had heard nothing from their insurance carrier but felt I would soon receive a settlement draft. Then I asked what he had heard from the Dallas adjuster. Tommy reported that nothing else had been heard from the guy. He also said that buzzards, coyotes and wolves were all trying to scratch Old TT out of his protecting fence. They were becoming a problem, and he wanted to know if they could finally hold TT's funeral. I advised him to be patient as long as he could and placed the file back into our diary system. A week later, I pulled it out again.

Mr. Byers' attorney was calling. He said his client needed to know why we had taken no action on the TT claim. I told this respected Tyler lawyer that a draft had been requested but we had not yet received it or additional instruction from their insurance carrier.

Then he asked why the bull couldn't be buried, and I advised that it should have been as soon as it had been viewed by the Dallas adjusting firm. Those people had never shown up and had sent no further message. The lawyer said he had advised Tommy to bury TT just before calling me. Our conversation was finished on the basis that I would promptly conclude Mr. Byers' claim upon receipt of a loss draft.

One week later I answered my phone and once more listened to the imperative and demanding voice from Maiden Lane. It called at eleven in the morning and talked less than a minute. I was informed that our services were no longer required and I should calculate our bill, which it called a "service invoice," forwarding it for "consideration" along with my final report.

I followed New York's instruction and placed TT's file into closed status, never expecting to see it again, but Tommy called again, one week later. He was hoping to be reassured and frankly admitted he might be looking for a job after next talking with his boss.

Questioning revealed that the Dallas adjuster had shown up at 10:30 that morning, with a vet, and had demanded to see Prince

TT. Tommy told them the bull had been buried and the visitor demanded he dig it up for examination. At this point Tommy said that he had made several bad mistakes during his career and one of his worst had been over-indulging impolite people too often. This morning he had recognized this mistake and decided to remedy it.

Saying nothing more to his visitors he led them out to his Jeep and pointed at it. They got in when he cranked it up and drove down to the tool barn where he left the jeep running and grabbed a pair of shovels, throwing them behind the seats. Climbing back in he drove down to the low flat spot in his pasture where TT's grave had been scooped out with a bulldozer. It was seven feet deep because he wanted to be certain no varmints dug it up.

Shutting off the Jeep, Tommy dismounted and told his passengers that he had last seen TT, seven feet below. He wasn't much to look at that day and "stunk to high heaven. Personally, he continued, he had seen and smelled all the dead bulls he needed to, but he had learned at an early age that there is no accounting for some people's tastes. So, if they wanted to meet TT, they were welcome to grab a shovel, then dig down and visit as long as they felt comfortable about it. "All the innards except the ears," he finished, "are in there with him but the dozer shoved them in first."

Then Tommy threw the shovels down in front of his guests and lectured the Dallas adjuster rather strongly, calling him by at least one uncomplimentary name when he refused to pick up either one. "That guy kicked like a bay mule about being mistreated," Tommy chuckled, "but he didn't offer to dig or fight either. An' his vet looked awful sorry to be down here in East Texas. He never once opened his mouth."

When Tommy said he had other important duties to attend and was leaving, they both elected to take the ride he offered. His last sight of their Cadillac was when it topped the hill headed toward I-20 on its return trip to Dallas.

Tommy also said that the insurance company had offered less than $25,000 in payment of TT's death claim. They insisted he had lived long enough to use up half his usefulness and wanted to depreciate the payment by fifty percent. But their insurance premium had stayed level every year. Mr. Byers didn't argue with them. Instead, he quietly instructed his attorney to file an early lawsuit for recovery of their $50,000, plus interest from date of judgment and costs of suit.

One year later I met Tommy at a golf tournament in Tyler. He seemed glad to see me, and we talked about TT's case for the last time. Everyone was still waiting for their suit to go to trial. The company had increased its offer to thirty five thousand dollars, but his boss wouldn't take it. One trial date had been canceled and another was placed on the judge's docket. And Mr. Byers didn't fire him for running the Dallas adjuster off his ranch. Instead, he laughed heartily when Tommy told him what happened and said he would have done the same.

CHAPTER 42

THE CHRISTMAS PONY—1974

AFTER WE HAD lived in Tyler, Texas for 18 years, the time came for us to sell our horses. The year was 1974 and we were no longer young. I had developed rheumatoid arthritis and was no longer able to ride as I once did. But, more than that, there was no longer a real need for horses in our lives. Our only child, Marlinda, had left home for college. Then, like a normal girl, she had married, and never came home to live again. My wife had never been an avid horse person and my best horse friends had loaded their animals into a trailer and moved away to Lufkin.

Several months of pasture loneliness proved to me that having fun with animals was like having fun at anything else. To be enjoyed, horses needed to be shared and I had no share buddies left. Real estate people had been counseling me for years to sub-divide my pasture. "Make it really produce," they told me. So after thinking about the long winter of night-time feeding which was relentlessly moving toward me, I elected to sell out. Like most decisions involving drastic change, this one plowed up a few surprises.

After deciding to make a sub-division out of my pasture, I hired a development planner and a bull dozer contractor. This meant that my horses had to leave soon because the dozer would arrive in early February. My first problem was that everyone else and his cousin, was also selling a horse. Maybe their kids, like ours, had left home and their wives no longer enjoyed riding. I didn't know the many reasons, but good horses had suddenly gotten dirt cheap and bad ones couldn't be given away. The horse market in Texas had dropped like an elevator and was stuck on the bottom. Average saddle horses were bringing more at a horse butchering plant in Palestine, Texas than anywhere else.

Later that week I heard a wealthy independent oil company owner in the Tyler Petroleum Club tell his associates at lunch that he had finally "gotten out of" the horse business by selling his saddles and giving the horses away. Nobody laughed because he was telling the truth, and people close to him knew that he was not only rich, but was a Texan who loved his animals. That man would have taken them to a back pasture and had them shot before selling them for butchering and shipped to Belgium or turned into dogfood. But as bad as the idea was of butchering good horses, any true horse person would rather do that than sell or give them to ignorant people who wouldn't properly care for them.

My friend solved his problem by giving his animals to real horse people with plenty of money and pasture. My problem was different. I couldn't afford to give mine away. I needed the money they would bring. It looked as if no quick sale was in the making and I would have to postpone development plans until my animals were placed into proper hands. Another long winter of night feeding seemed to be in the cards.

But the problem evened out better than my pessimist horse crowd friends thought it would. My horses were well bred and real horse people knew it. During the next few months, I located a few buyers who knew the difference between a horse and a housecat, and by October only had only two animals left. One was a tall black Stallion, my personal saddle horse and the other was a calendar-beautiful palomino brood mare with a flaxen mane and tail. She had already brought me two gorgeous palomino colts and one orange trimmed sorrel. I was partial to these horses, and so picky about who would own them, that when Thanksgiving arrived, I had started to feed at night again.

That was why I listened politely, two weeks before Christmas, when a friend named Don, called to ask if I knew a place where he could board a pony that Santa Claus was bringing his 11-year-old daughter. Calculating rapidly, I replied that I had no idea where he could board that pony but I did know where he could pasture it for free if it wasn't a filly. He wanted to know why no fillies and I explained that my stud was running loose in the pasture. Don laughed, saying that was no problem because this pony was a gelding. Quickly, he latched onto my offer.

Before closing the lid on this trade I explained that there was one stipulation he might not like. He must buy his pony's grain and take his turn at feeding for two nights each week. Now I knew that Don was as ignorant as a duck about horses, and having never spent a winter at night feeding, he wasn't bothered about this part of the bargain. Without stuttering once, he agreed.

Through lots of intelligence, hard work and some extra-good fortune at leasing mineral rights and drilling oilwells, Don had turned into a prosperous oilman for his age and would probably add a few more millions to the several he already owned. But, like every wildcatter I have seen, he was always short of money. And like everyone else who buys his first horse, he realized way too late that paying for the animal was the cheapest part of going into the horse business.

After getting the horse, he bought his daughter's handsomely decorated saddle, bridle and other tack. Those items cost three times as much as he figured, a lot more than the horse. Then there were stable fees, feed, vet bills, his daughter's horse clothes and other expenses, all of which would keep on keeping on. And there was another factor. His wife had started making noises about buying horses for both of them so that the family could enjoy them together.

Few people become millionaires by spending freely. In fact, one simple trait that greatly aids men to acquire millionaire status is being close with a buck. Don was one of the close ones and my offer of free pasture, a tack room and plenty of hay made a real hit with him and we closed our deal, agreeing that his seller could drop the Christmas pony off at my pasture next Saturday after lunch.

Don had grown up in Quitman, a small farming city 40 miles Northeast of Tyler. From his youngest days, he had dated Debbie who, Quitman folks still said, was the prettiest girl who ever lived there. They were married shortly before leaving home to attend

Texas University and moved to Tyler after graduating. Entering the oil business, Don had worked a small stake into a fair sized one, and by the time of that pony, he and Debbie had a beautiful home, a newly-married older son, and one very pretty 11-year-old daughter.

Most Tyler men watched with envy as Don swept Debbie across the dance floor at Saturday evening dinner dances during the Petroleum Club. And most ladies envied Debbie, and not just because Don was a handsome guy. They really loved her because she was one of those rare women actually as pretty inside as out. And she proved it by avoiding harmful gossip and keeping her hands off their husbands.

Don had worked much harder than he played when growing up and was never exposed to horses. He was vaguely aware that they ate lots of hay and ran faster than the average person. But Debbie was raised in a well-to-do home and had always owned horses until she left for college. Fortunately, she had learned enough to show Don and their pretty daughter much of what they needed to know about a new pony, but there was still a bunch he needed to learn before Christmas.

On Saturday, right after lunch, I went straight to my pasture and saddled up my palomino mare so I could control her when the new pony arrived. This mare had been pasture boss for three years and wasn't above nipping a plug from the newcomer's hide. I wasn't worried about my stallion. He was always polite and never caused a moment's trouble unless a mare cycled into her family mode.

Don arrived shortly afterward and reported that his gelding was on its way. The seller was trailering it over from Athens, in Henderson County, and his rig pulled up twenty minutes later. Within ten minutes the new pony was unloaded and the Athens used horse dealer drove off with a grin on his face big as a wave on one of Don's oilfield slush pits. The reason was, he had just folded and shoved into his shirt pocket four fresh $100 bills Don had given him.

Another reason this country horse trader smiled so big was that he had trimmed down his horse herd. This automatically saved him $150 in hay and winter grain. The final reason for his grin was, after selling the pony, he owned $400 more in fresh money, and all traders love that feeling.

Don's small horse had a shiny black coat and a fist-sized white star above his eyes. He also had two milk-white stockings. He was alert and stylish, weighed about 700 pounds, and tracked out nicely. He looked healthy as a hog and walked confidently on four dainty looking but flint-hard black hooves. I judged he was a three-year-old as the trader had said, but since he wasn't mine, I didn't look in his mouth. He was a friendly animal and might make a good kid horse, so I didn't upset Don by pointing out that the biggest reason why that trader had left grinning like a baboon was that Don had paid $150 more than the little animal was worth.

Instead, I began to teach Don something about horses. He needed to learn fast enough to help his daughter learn how to ride her new pony before spoiling it. If she didn't learn quickly the new pony would be spoiled and he would lose most of his $400 investment because the attractive little animal would have to be traded in on a new model. I started off by showing him how to hold his pony's halter line securely and to be firm but gentle in leading the pony around. A horse, I explained, should be led by suggestion and light tugs, instead of throwing heavy weight against the halter.

After he had learned to lead his pony, I rode my mare over to open the pasture gate so Don could bring the new pony inside. I trailed behind them for two reasons. Allowing the little horse to know that a strange horse was close to his hindquarters would help him decide that following this new owner was a good idea. It also gave my mare a chance to walk near enough to see and smell the newcomer but not so close that she would jump him over Don's head or cause him to rear up or kick back at us, or pitch, or commit any other sort of horse tantrum that could quickly become a bad habit.

That little guy looked better all the time. He stepped out nicely and carried his head well. His deep Arab jaw and short-muscled neck, with his long belly and close-coupled back showed good breeding as well as strength. His bone structure was delicate but solid, and I figured, with a little hard exercise, he would be quick as a cat, tough as a boot and could run like a deer. He would have made an excellent old-time Texas cow pony.

He was also good natured. When my stallion walked over to greet him, each animal pointed his ears forward, interested, rather than irritated. Two hours later, when Don and I left the pasture, they were grazing side by side. I stayed in the saddle, reins close-held, allowing my mare only to watch and smell. I also explained my reason to Don and he nodded his head, listening closely because he had suddenly learned how little he knew about horses and that he had a lot of catch-up ahead of him. Every Texan would like to think that he knows as much about horses as his wife.

In order to show Don where everything was, I had him help me to carry and distribute a bale of my rich Coastal Bermuda hay on a hillside near the lake and what to do with the wire after he had broken a bale open. Then I showed him that small hay blocks should be scattered over the hillside so all the animals could move about, snacking freely, without worrying about attack from the others.

After being unsaddled, my mare decided to exercise her authority. Flattening her ears, she walked up behind the new gelding. Throwing his nose up high so he could look behind, he watched until she shined her teeth and hooked her head toward him before moving in. But there was no fight. Without showing real concern, he surrendered the block he'd been eating and picked one out which was 30 feet away. Then, watching closely, he began to chew again. Ears still flat, she eyed him wickedly and tossed his hay several times with her nose. Then, figuring she'd made her point, she picked a fresh bundle for herself. The first test had been passed. These horses might nip off a spot of hair now and then but the new pony wasn't apt to be seriously injured.

Don told me he'd never been on a horse except to have his picture made. That was when he was five and a traveling photographer leading a Shetland pony which carried a saddle, a pair of boy's chaps and a cowboy hat had visited Quitman. I figured he ought to start learning right then because any ability at all could enable him to avert a world of trouble. We still had an hour and a half of daylight so I brought both my horses up to the tack room. Don watched me bridle the stallion and I watched as he bridled my mare, instructing him closely on ways to slip the bit into her mouth without banging her teeth or bruising her lips.

Next, I carefully smoothed the blanket on my stud's back, feeling for and removing every wrinkle. Don did the same with the mare and watched as I threw on my saddle and cinched it up. I monitored closely while he struggled with the mare's cinch, making three attempts before learning how to tighten and wrap a proper cinch knot.

I stepped onto the stud's back and watched until Don finally worked a leg across the mare's saddle and felt for the off-side stirrup. Then I showed him how to keep from jerking her mouth by leaving the reins loose enough that her head could nod unless he was giving her direction. After explaining that his pony needed to learn about the pasture, I had Don to take off his halter so he could follow us freely.

We walked our mounts for 50 yards before I turned toward the Northern exterior fence line and lifted my stud into a trot, letting Don accustom himself to this rough horse gait. After he had taught himself to stand up in the stirrups and grab the saddle horn to balance himself against the trotting motion, I picked my horse up into a sharp canter, which the mare immediately matched.

Don was frowning while we trotted along and I saw concern quickly cross his face when our speed rose above a trot. But it only took him a few seconds to smile broadly when he realized that riding at a canter is much easier than trotting. In fact, as soon as he relaxed and sat down in the saddle, and was riding comfortably, he had learned the most important horseback lesson which exists. Briefly, it states, "If everything goes right, horseback riding can really be fun." The main object of any sensible horseman is to have everything that possibly can to turn out exactly right. For this to happen, the rider must always be thinking ahead of his horse just as a truck driver looks far down the road ahead of his rig.

We used up an hour loafing around the pasture, changing horse gaits and accustoming Don to horse motion. He had good balance and learned quickly. Back at the barn I had him practice by stripping off both saddles and properly storing them. Following instruction, he quickly removed each animal's bridle and turned them loose at the same time. He asked why and I explained that neither horse enjoyed watching its mate trot away to drink and roll on its back while a hot and sweaty blanket still burned against its own back. Until then he had never realized that horses have opinions on such things and his horse sense began to grow.

As soon as they had finished eating, the horses drank from the lake and rolled on their backs. After that, my pair trotted back for a visit. Don and I took curry combs and brushes, grooming their coats for several minutes. His new pony, after running and pitching a few circles, fully enjoying the size of his new pasture, eased up to Don's side and I was happy to see Don exercise a little more horse sense. Without me saying a word, he reached over to brush the pony's back and curry a few strokes on its mane. That sort of thing always helps to establish good relationships.

While I was storing the combs and brushes, my mare nosed open the stall door nearest to us and trotted impatiently inside. She huffed impatiently and stamped her forefeet, waiting for grain. Don asked me why my stallion still stood patiently at his door, waiting for someone to let him in.

I explained that horses, while looking pretty much the same are very like people, generally very different from each other. Like people, horses can have different emotions, abilities and personalities. Every horse there, I pointed out, was just being the kind of horse he was. The new pony enjoyed running and kicking up his heels because he had been penned up too long in a tight enclosure and was enjoying this new home. He was well fed and didn't care, at the moment, whether he received any grain or not.

My mare, however, was being bossy and trying to run things. She had known how to open stall doors before coming to me and, because I had been involved in helping Don, I had forgotten to chain those doors up. If I didn't keep them chained, she would wear them off their hinges by opening and looking in each stall box anytime a visitor came to the pasture. What she was doing was inducing someone to drop grain into her feed box. And because she was that smart, I had been forced to wire or chain every gate on my place. If I didn't, she broke out whenever she took the notion, leading her pasture mates into lives of sin and trouble.

The stud, I explained, was a patient animal. It never occurred to him that he ought to try opening a stall door or a pasture gate. But the mare, by stomping into her stall, huffing around and moving in and out and banging the doors, was intentionally shoving against the program by creating a fuss. She was also crowding me toward feeding her some grain.

Motioning Don to follow, I entered the barn. Picking up a feed bucket, I scooped a gallon of grain from one of the barrels and poured it into the mare's crib. Nothing else would be heard from her until she had ground and swallowed every grain and had licked her feed box clean. I dumped another gallon in the stud's crib and handed Don a third to give his pony. Back outside, I let my stud into the second stall and locked the mare in hers to keep her from harassing the others after she had finished her measure. Then I waved at Don to put his pony in the third stall.

Uncertainly, he held out his bucket and walked toward his pony. That intelligent little animal had already stopped running and come over to watch and smell. He quickly figured out that my horses were eating grain and, impatient, advanced toward Don, thrusting his nose hard down into the bucket. Don held it up too high and the pony grew impatient. Slinging his head he struck the bucket, knocking it out of Don's hands. Then, pawing the bucket aside he began to snuffle loose feed from the ground.

Angry and uncertain, Don looked at me, knowing that he needed instruction. But speed was also important here, so instead of telling him I demonstrated. His pony was smart, and though he would likely make an excellent horse, it wouldn't take a lot of encouragement for him to outgrow his britches. He had already licked up a lot of his feed and ruined much of the rest. He needed a quick lesson in horse manners. He also needed to be taught that his status was definitely below that of people. A grown horse that doesn't understand this is as worthless as a spoiled child who has entered adulthood without learning self-discipline.

Making certain that Don watched, I walked quietly up to his pony and reached for the bucket. At the same time I swept off my hat and yelled loudly at him. Slapping him hard on the nose with my hat, I made a scary rattlesnake sounding noise down deep in my throat. Wide-eyed and startled, he jumped backward, splay-legged and snorty then watched nervously as I scooped up what feed was left, including a pint of dirt and poured it back in the bucket.

Don watched as I took out a handful and walked over to let the pony smell, then lick from my hand. Then I backed up two or three steps and he followed, licking up more. After three handfuls he was following the bucket easily and licked the fourth handful in his stall after I dropped it into his new feedbox. Then I poured the rest of his bucket in, allowing him to clean up whatever he wanted.

Don's pony, and everyone who worked with him later on, was now much better off. He had learned to follow a feed bucket and also to have a little respect for human beings. Don asked if the dirt would hurt him and I asked if his kids had ever eaten any. He nodded his head "yes" and I said I'd seen a lot of children eat dirt and that while I didn't necessarily recommend it, I never knew it to make any of them sick. Because of that, I saw no reason why a little clean dirt would injure a healthy saddle pony. Don thought about this, then nodded his head up and down.

Before Christmas I met with Don several times at my pasture, allowing him to practice saddling and riding both of my horses so that his entire family could ride together on Christmas Day if the weather was good. On our final trip I saddled and rode his pony, allowing the mare follow along behind. The pony didn't appreciate my heavy weight but minded his manners and didn't complain when I took him away from the other animals for a few minutes during this brief refresher course on doing what people wanted of him. By the time we finished I decided he would do fine as long as Don's girl rode first with one or more other people for a few trips before taking her pony out alone. All this training, of Don and the horses, had been to accomplish this purpose.

On our last ride before Christmas I explained to Don why we had done all these things and told him I thought his family was ready to ride on its own. Riding school was now over except for what they would learn together. That would be a bunch, but now Don knew how to ride and care for my horses as well as his own. As long as his family rode together, they should not experience serious problems.

The main thing Don needed to remember was that horse tasks needed to be performed the same way every time so the horses wouldn't be confused or upset. Also, they needed to ride to different places on every trip, for different lengths of time, so the horses wouldn't memorize each trip and start trying to shortcut or manage the program. I also advised him never to allow the horses to run back toward my barn. All their running should be done away instead of moving out of proper control each time they started home. If they did this, his daughter should be able to enjoy a delightful and permanent Christmas gift.

Christmas Day was bright and dry with only a slight breeze. Our family was out of town for the day but we returned shortly after dark and Don called to thank me thirty minutes after we got home. They had taken their Christmas dinner out to my pasture and eaten it on the ground. Their daughter's first horse ride had been perfect. It was so good in fact that they had fallen in love with my horses and wanted to know if they could buy them, boarding them in my pasture until they could find a pasture of their own.

It took me only 30 seconds to price my horses at $800 for the pair and we made our trade. It wasn't the best horse trade I ever made because I lost money on them but he was paying more money than any other buyer had offered and I had confidence that he would treat my animals kindly. He had also received a bunch of free horse training. Certainly, I had done better than the rich oil producer who had given his horses away. Best of all, I could stop buying expensive horse grain and was no longer forced to spend an hour and a half each night, feeding horses for the rest of that winter. Don offered to pay for the hay in my barn but I had no further use for it and told him to use whatever he needed.

Still there was one more thing I needed to tell him. I had been thinking about the proper time to bring it up and decided that now was as good as any. You see, on Christmas Eve, the day before, I had gone out to feed and noticed some dried blood at the rear of his pony's left flank, halfway down its tail. I thought that the little guy might have gotten a wire cut and, while he was grinding his grain, I eased his tail up to see if he needed any ointment or disinfectant. But there was no injury to be found. When I looked under his stomach for any other sign of an injury or wire cut, I realized that this Christmas pony wasn't a gelding at all. What he was was a healthy little filly, running loose in my pasture and by now, that cute young thing was carrying a new colt that had been sired by my Stud.

Don and his family had just experienced a great Christmas, and I guessed he was probably in as good a mood as I was ever going to find him so now was the time for me to give him the news. I broke it to him in the best way I knew how—real quick. "Don," I said, "you may not know it yet but within a few more months you are going to be a grandpa."

"I know it," he replied irritably, "But who told you? My wife has threatened to kill me if I told anyone our son and his wife are going to have a baby. They are afraid her boss will fire her."

I laughed out loud before answering. "We are on different pages, Don. What has happened is that Santa Claus sort of mixed up your daughter's Christmas present. That gelding you bought isn't a gelding at all. She's a fine young filly and is going to bring you a nice colt in about a year."

Thirty seconds of deep silence followed. When he finally spoke Don's voice was ragged with anger. "That danged horse thief looked me straight in the eye and said his pony was a gelding. He knew I wouldn't have bought a filly."

I kept quiet because I knew he hadn't yet thought everything through. Then, after he did, his voice rose in sudden alarm. "You aren't going to tell people about this are you? I don't want the whole world to know I'm that dumb."

"Why no, Don," I replied, deliberately misunderstanding him. "I'm going to keep your daughter-in-law's secret. Do you think I want her to get fired?"

"That's not what I'm talking about and you know it. I'm talking about me being so stupid that I bought a gelding and that horse trader sold me a filly. I don't want to be laughed out of town."

I paused for a few seconds, taking time to think up my very best answer. After doing so, I let him have both barrels. "I will promise you this, Don. I'm only going to tell one person. That will be the first friend I see next Friday afternoon at the Petroleum Club during happy hour. Anyone else who mentions your filly to me is going to be sent straight to you for the real story."

The name Don called me was neither printable or true but I took no offense. He was under stress at the time, a lot of which was my fault. I finished the conversation by saying, "Don, we both need to rest. You go find Debbie and talk things over with her. Besides, you ought to know that you aren't going to enjoy writing out my $800 check if you're pouty and all swelled up like a horned toad."

THE END

THOSE WHO HELPED

JESSICA BOATWRIGHT is a native Virginian who earned her BA in fine arts from Mary Baldwin College in that state. Spending a large part of her life in Augusta, Georgia, she has reared four children of her own, plus five stepchildren, but still found time to study under eleven noted artists. She has created many murals, drawn many greeting cards and has composed commission work for the Augusta National Golf Club, Georgia Ironworks, Fox Sports and Turner Broadcasting. Her paintings have been exhibited in the Georgia governor's office and the Tour de Bloom in Paris.

PAT CONROY was born in Philadelphia and earned her BA in art at Rosemont college, also in Pennsylvania. After marriage to Joseph Conroy, she lived principally in Westfield, New Jersey where she raised seven children and continued to pursue an art career. She also traveled throughout the world with her husband, always carrying a sketch pad. Now living in Atascocita, Texas, she works mostly with watercolor and pen and ink. Her work is represented in both private and corporate collections as well as the Kingwood art gallery. Pat is an elite signature member of the Houston Watercolor Art Society, a past president of the Kingwood, Texas Art Society and is also active in several other art associations.

RUTH HOLLUB, the editor of two Stevenson books, was born in Sherman, Texas, the youngest of six girls. She was an "army brat," who spent her early life following her dad to military posts throughout the Midwest. At age 27 she returned to Texas. Settling in Kingwood, she provided for her two sons as a stockbroker. After ten years she joined the Administaff Company, helping it to become a publicly traded corporation and is still there. Hobbies are family activities, plus reading and camping. And she adds, "playing trivia with this book's author."

DEVON HELENSCHMIDT is a native of Burkburnett, Texas who now attends Midwestern University in Wichita Fallas, Texas. She is working toward degrees in fine arts and also wishes to teach in public schools as well as to pursue a career in art. Devon has already created many commissioned portraits and has contributed to this book. She is a single person but reports she is also the mother of two. One of her children is a German Short-haired Pointer named Jake. The other is a one-year-old female Labrador called Dixie.

RALPH KELLER, owner of Contractor's Barricade Services, was born in Midland, Texas. He was a member of the high school golf team, and graduated in 1962. Ralph attended Tarleton State College but didn't stay long enough for a degree. He opened an auto and transmission shop in Houston but it didn't live up to his standards so he entered the highway construction business, working with highway construction companies Austin Bridge, T. L. James, and Cecil Ruby. Seeing the need for a better product, he began to design, test, construct, and finally to sell highway crash cushions. His designs had to be acceptable to the Texas Highway Department. After accomplishing this, the field was cleared for him to effect sales to highway contractors performing road work for large cities and the Texas Highway Department.

Now living in Kingwood, Texas, Ralph works hard at his business, which has expanded to world-wide dimension but still finds time to practice his hobby, antique car collecting. He has also found time to offer friendship, assistance, and encouragement to this writer.

HOLLY NOWAK, a hard-working mother of two, is a Houston, Texas native. She began seriously considering art as a career after submitting winning art pieces to the Houston Rodeo Association at an early age. She attended Texas Tech University, studying art and married her childhood sweetheart, Chris, shortly after college. Chris is an artist and a graphic designer. Now living in Kingwood, this couple pursues art as an achieved profession. Holly operates her own mural and convas business and creates murals for both businesses and homes. She is a dedicated mother who has illustrated several children's books as well as contributing to this one.

GARY TUTTLE, is a lifelong resident of Humble, Texas. He was born and raised on "Moonshine Hill," the first home

of Humble Oil Company which was later absorbed by Standard of New Jersey and is now a large part of Exxon Company, USA. An award-winning artist, Gary has been a commercially successful illustrator for 35 years. His most recent award was a Gold Addy from the Houston Advertising Federation for illustrating children's stories.

LISA WEIDNER was born in Wichita Falls and raised in South Texas. A housewife and the mother of four, she creates realistic depictions of life's happenings and says her work is designed to convey expressive "snapshot-type" moments. Lisa currently lives in Conroe, Texas, is a dedicated mother of four and has attended Sam Houston State University. Currently, she is enrolled at Kingwood College.

BRANDI WOOLEY was born in East Houston. She attended C. E. King High School, graduating in 1996. She is married to William Wooley and has a degree in economics from San Jacinto College. Brandi has been employed as office manager at Contractor's Barricade Services since 2000 and has rendered invaluable assistance to this writer. Her hobbies are reading what she calls "good" books and she never stops complaining that this one should have been printed much earlier.